Virtus Romana

STUDIES IN THE HISTORY OF GREECE AND ROME

Robin Osborne, James Rives, and Richard J. A. Talbert, *editors*

Books in this series examine the history and society of Greece and Rome from approximately 1000 B.C. to A.D. 600. The series includes interdisciplinary studies, works that introduce new areas for investigation, and original syntheses and reinterpretations.

CATALINA BALMACEDA

Virtus Romana
Politics and Morality in the Roman Historians

The University of North Carolina Press *Chapel Hill*

© 2017 The University of North Carolina Press
All rights reserved
Set in Arno Pro by Westchester Publishing Services
The University of North Carolina Press has been a member of the
Green Press Initiative since 2003.

Library of Congress Cataloging-in-Publication Data
Names: Balmaceda, Catalina, 1970- author.
Title: Virtus romana : politics and morality in the Roman historians /
    Catalina Balmaceda.
Other titles: Studies in the history of Greece and Rome.
Description: Chapel Hill : University of North Carolina Press, [2017] |
    Series: Studies in the history of Greece and Rome | Includes bibliographical
    references and index.
Identifiers: LCCN 2017007235| ISBN 9781469635125 (cloth : alk. paper) |
    ISBN 9781469668628 (pbk : alk. paper) | ISBN 9781469635132 (ebook)
Subjects: LCSH: Rome—Historiography. | National characteristics, Roman. |
    Rome—Civilization.
Classification: LCC DG205 .B33 2017 | DDC 937/.02—dc23
    LC record available at https://lccn.loc.gov/2017007235

Cover illustration: Reverse side of Roman gold coin featuring Virtus,
wearing tunic and cuirass, standing left, holding Victory on globe in right hand
and parazonium in left. © The Trustees of the British Museum.

Parentibus optimis

Contents

Acknowledgments xi
Abbreviations in the Text xiii

INTRODUCTION
Virtus and Historical Writing 1

   The Setting: Roman Historical Writing
   The Focus: History and *Virtus*
   Outline

CHAPTER ONE
The Concept of *Virtus* 14

   Virtus as Courage
   Virtus as *Arete*
   Stoicism in Rome
   Cicero and *Virtus*
   The Social Expansion of *Virtus*

CHAPTER TWO
Virtus in Sallust 48

   Presenting the Theory and Setting the Tone: The Prologues
   The Presence and Absence of *Virtus*: The Characters in the Monographs
   The Nature and Presentation of Decline: Sallust's Vocabulary of Decay

CHAPTER THREE
Virtus in Livy 83

   The Value of Recording the Past: Livy's Preface
   A Stage for *Virtus*: Rome at War
   An Aim for *Virtus*: The Fight for *Libertas*
   Politics and Partnership: *Virtus* in Women?

CHAPTER FOUR
Virtus in Velleius 129

   Virtus in the *Historiae*
   A Case Study of Roman *Virtus*: The Tiberian Narrative
   Velleius' Conception of History

CHAPTER FIVE
Virtus in Tacitus 157

  The *Agricola* and the *Germania*: Roman *Virtus* beyond the Boundaries?
  The *Histories*: Roman *Virtus* in Imperial Civil War
  The *Annals*: *Virtus* and *Princeps*

CONCLUSION 242

Bibliography 249

Index 285

Illustrations

1 Silver coin with helmeted bust of Virtus 127
2 Silver coin with jugate heads of Honos and Virtus 127
3 Gold coin with Virtus holding Victory 128

Acknowledgments

The completion of this book has taken several years and gives me at last the pleasure of thanking the many friends and scholars who have helped me along the way. First, I would like to thank Michael Comber, whose expert guidance and brilliant teaching opened up new ways of thinking and showed me many unexpected approaches to history; his friendship and patience were constant sources of support at a time when this project was not even conceived. I think he would have liked to see this book. I am also grateful for many inspiring and thought-provoking conversations with Valentina Arena, Rhiannon Ash, Catharine Edwards, Georgy Kantor, John Marincola, Michael Peachin, Chris Pelling, Francisco Pina Polo, Nicholas Purcell, Tobias Reinhardt, Malcolm Schofield, and Felipe Soza: all of them have greatly helped me with their general comments as well as their specific suggestions. Special thanks to Teresa Morgan, who read several draft chapters and gave me relevant feedback by challenging the whole structure of the book, which forced me to look for strategies and ways of presenting my argument more strongly. Miriam Griffin has been extremely generous in helping me throughout and especially on the philosophical aspects of this book: pointing out the weaknesses, and at the same time guiding me in the right direction. I also owe a great debt to Fergus Millar, whose constant support and wise advice have not failed me since my first day in Oxford, many years ago. My friend Henriette van der Blom, who has been involved in this project from the very beginning, has been always willing to share her time talking things over with unfailing reassurance. I am endlessly grateful to Katherine Clarke, who has been key at all stages of my work. Her ever-encouraging and enthusiastic approach to the project, together with her attention to small details and their relation to the broader issues, helped me enormously in the development of this book.

I have been also privileged to have the comments and constructive criticisms from the audiences of different lectures, seminars, and conference papers given at Santiago, Rome, Leicester, Viña del Mar, London, Oxford, and São Paulo.

During the years that I spent writing this book, I benefited from several grants. I was a British Academy Visiting Fellow (2009–10), recipient of the Fondecyt Research Council Award (2010–12) and Wolfson Visiting Scholar

(2013–14). I am grateful for the opportunities these grants gave me to expand my study time and to meet and discuss with important scholars related to my line of research. I am particularly grateful to my home institution, Pontificia Universidad Católica de Chile, which allowed me the time necessary to develop this work and supported me financially and academically at every stage.

I would like to thank the expert hand of Helena Scott, everyone on the editorial team at the University of North Carolina Press, and the anonymous readers for their professional and helpful advice throughout the process.

My family and friends have kept my courage up and contributed greatly to make the ups and downs proper to any research project of this magnitude into a vast majority of "ups," and I am grateful for their patience and generosity, especially for Maureen's constant support and Ana's cheerful friendship. It is to my parents, though, that I owe the greatest debt, and therefore this book is dedicated to them.

Catalina Balmaceda
November 2016

Abbreviations in the Text

References to ancient authors and texts follow the conventions of the *Oxford Classical Dictionary*, 4th edition.

Abbreviations of periodicals follow the conventions of *L'Année Philologique*. In addition, the following abbreviations have been adopted:

ANRW   *Aufstieg und Niedergang der römischen Welt. Geschichte und Kultur Roms im Spiegel der neueren Forschung.* Berlin, 1972–.

CAH^2 *The Cambridge Ancient History*, 2nd edition. Cambridge, 1994.

CIL   *Corpus Inscriptionum Latinarum.* Berlin.

FrHist   *The Fragments of the Roman Historians*, vols. 1–3. Edited by T. Cornell. Oxford, 2013.

ILS   *Inscriptiones Latinae Selectae.* H. Dessau. Berlin, 1892.

ORF^3 *Oratorum Romanorum Fragmenta*, 3rd edition. Edited by E. Malcovati. Turin, 1967.

RIC   *Roman Imperial Coinage.* Vol. 1, *Augustus–Vitellius (31 B.C.–69 A.D.).* C. H. V. Sutherland. London, 1923 (revised 1984).

Unless otherwise indicated, all translations are my own or from the latest Loeb editions, adapted where necessary.

Introduction
Virtus *and Historical Writing*

Virtus ... propria est Romani generis et seminis

Virtus is an inalienable possession of the Roman race and name
—Cic. *Phil*, 4.13

In recent years, it has proved fruitful to approach the history of Roman politics, society, and culture thematically, through the study of key concepts such as *fides, libertas, clementia*, or *pudicitia*. Among such concepts, none was more important to Romans themselves than *virtus*. *Virtus* could be found everywhere and under any circumstance: it was what everybody claimed, an aim for life, a means to achieve *gloria*, a criterion by which to judge people, a spur to action, the courage to undertake brave deeds, the essence of manliness, the moral code of the *maiores* ... For the Romans it was difficult to approach any important topic without referring to *virtus*.

As a moral and political idea, however, *virtus* was present in Roman thinking and acting in many more ways than have been explored hitherto. Past approaches to *virtus* have tended to be word studies. Of particular note is the work of A. N. van Omme, *Virtus, semantiese Studie* (Utrecht, 1946), which was later completed and enriched by the book of W. Eisenhut, *Virtus Romana: Ihre Stellung im römische Wertsystem* (Munich, 1973). Eisenhut's work is an impressive lexicographical exercise; he traces almost every occurrence of *virtus* in classical Latin, but the conclusions are limited and unduly biased toward the view that Greek culture played an essential role in the formation of the concept. Additionally, Eisenhut argues that the different kinds of *virtus* remained fairly stable throughout Roman history.

More recently, other word studies on *virtus* appeared in the same year, yet approaching the theme from different angles. Juhani Sarsila's study *Being a Man: The Roman Virtus as a Contribution to Moral Philosophy* (Frankfurt, 2006) considers and catalogues exhaustively different types of *virtus* in Roman literature from Livius Andronicus to Livy. It is a thorough analysis author by author and concludes that *virtus* must be placed at the very center of the Roman set of values. Unfortunately Sarsila devotes little time to explaining one of the most interesting phenomena, namely, why all these meanings are encapsulated in just one word, and his treatment lacks a final synthesis explaining why the authors used the concept in that particular way or what the characteristics of *virtus* were that made it so flexible and versatile a concept. The other work is that of Myles McDonnell, *Roman Manliness: Virtus and the Roman Republic* (Cambridge, 2006). McDonnell looks for the preclassical (i.e., pre-Ciceronian) meaning of the word *virtus* and bases his argument on a linguistic analysis of *virtus* as manliness. The book deals with an enormous amount of material and is consistent in itself, but in my view it starts from an unsound premise, namely, that native Roman *virtus* was not an ethical quality.[1] In contrast to these previous studies, mine aims to look at *virtus* in action, as represented in the historical narratives of the Roman historians of the late republic and early empire.

At the same time, the role that historians played in Roman society has not always been adequately assessed. Mainly studied as literary artists expressing important ideas of their times, they have seldom been treated as constructors of society in their own right, who, on the grounds of their personal political experience—with the exception of Livy—and knowledge were in a privileged position to evaluate and promote change in political thinking. While aiming to deepen our understanding of a central concept in Roman culture, therefore, this work also seeks to show how a group of Roman historians not only wrote history but also helped to shape it, by endorsing specific values, creating a tradition, constructing identity, and introducing role models.

I shall argue throughout these pages that analyzing and tracing the role of *virtus* in the works of the historians of this period takes us to the very heart of their appraisal of both political change and Roman identity. This examination, therefore, is a study not merely in historiography but also in intellectual history, an investigation into a culture's conceptual categories of self-definition and goodness in action.

The end of the Roman Republic brought a transformation that involved much more than a change in the political system, and therefore this period became a particularly rich one for historical analysis. It is less clear, however, whether or how *virtus*, a key political concept and one intimately related to traditional Roman values, changed with the "revolutionary" (to use Syme's term) transformation from republic to empire. Did this change in regime involve a change in the Roman understanding of what it meant to have *virtus*? Is it possible to trace the evolution of the concept of *virtus* by following the

---

1. Noted also by some reviewers; see Robert Kaster at *BMCR*, February 8, 2007, and Teresa Morgan in *TLS*, January 2, 2008.

narratives of the Roman historians? Was *virtus* adapted to the new political regime, or did the new system have to include traditional forms of *virtus* to make itself acceptable? This work investigates these questions by analyzing the works of Sallust, Livy, Velleius Paterculus, and Tacitus.

In this introduction I briefly address some of the questions that will help explore the relationship of history with both its mode of self-expression and the validation of its subject matter. First, I discuss the nature of historical writing in Rome and its complex relationship with rhetorical and didactic purposes. Second, I deal with the question of whether *virtus* is a valid category for explaining the Roman past, and therefore, whether the analysis of the concept through the narratives of Roman historians is a sound way of approaching Roman historical writing. I also consider the role that political change plays in the (re)definition of the concept of *virtus* and in the development of its expression in practice. I conclude this introductory chapter by giving a short synopsis of the topics treated in the book.

The Setting: Roman Historical Writing

"For who does not know history's first law to be that an author must not dare to tell anything false? And that he must not dare to tell anything but the truth? That there must be no suggestion of partiality anywhere in his writings? Nor of malice? This groundwork [*fundamenta*] of course is familiar to everyone; the completed structure [*exaedificatio*] rests upon the story [*res*] and the diction [*verba*]."[2] Cicero's well-known metaphor of history as a building having foundations and a superstructure has somehow marked the approach to Roman historical writing in a very forceful way. Truth was set as the first law of history and constituted the Ciceronian foundation of the building, and content and form—*res* and *verba*—worked as the building material and the arrangement of the structure. It seemed quite easy to imagine the Roman historian at work, putting the pieces together carefully, with attention to the language and presentation. For centuries, we have continued to analyze, with a greater or lesser degree of awareness, how deep and strong the groundwork should be for the edifice not to collapse, and how the actual arrangement of the material affected the final construction.

---

2. Cic. *De Or*, 2.62–63: *Nam quis nescit primam esse historiae legem, ne quid falsi dicere audeat? Deinde ne quid veri non audeat? Ne quae suspicio gratiae sit in scribendo? Ne quae simultatis? Haec scilicet fundamenta nota sunt omnibus, ipsa autem exaedificatio posita est in rebus et verbis.*

But truth, content, and form have also been at the center of a long and lively debate—sometimes subject to the storms of fashion—on the extent to which classical historiography is more devoted to its dramatic features, as a branch of rhetoric, and whether its moralizing function leads it to be concerned not wholly with the facts and historical truth but also with convincing the reader of a certain interpretation. Peter Wiseman took the view that classical historians employing rhetoric appear to the modern reader to indulge in "unhistorical thinking," with their compositions of speeches, their filling the narrative with plausible—but invented—considerations, and their borrowings from other genres.[3] This analysis necessarily led to the fundamental question about truth and fiction in history, and Anthony Woodman attempted to solve the problem by trying to show that Roman historians even had a different concept of truth, so when in the prefaces of their histories they professed to be telling the truth, what they were denying was bias and not—in our terms—fabrication.[4] In reaction to this, other scholars passionately defended ancient historians' bona fides and reliability up to a certain degree.[5]

It is not the aim of this section to give an account of the phases and positions that this animated discussion has taken, especially when the dichotomy between definite historical evidence on the one hand and literary construct on the other appears to have been overcome and some sort of reasonable middle ground reached, in acknowledging that rhetoric is a necessary condition for history and that while conventions and focus have changed since antiquity, the essence has remained relatively stable.[6] The Roman historian saw himself as giving a true account of the past, and if truth was provisional or only partially attained, at least the orientation toward it made history writing a very particular type of creative literature.[7]

---

3. This particular concept of "unhistorical thinking" is developed in Wiseman, *Clio's Cosmetics*, 41–53.

4. Cf. Woodman, *Rhetoric in Classical Historiography*, chap. 2 on the analysis of Cic. *De Or*, 2.62–64.

5. See, for example, Lendon's fierce critique of Wiseman and Woodman in "Historians without History," 41–62. For others on this position, see Fornara, *Nature of History in Ancient Greece and Rome*; Cornell, "Formation of the Historical Tradition of Early Rome," 67–86; Brunt, "Cicero and Historiography," 181–209; Rhodes, "In Defence of the Greek Historian," 156–71.

6. For summaries of these debates, see, for example, Kraus and Woodman, *Latin Historians*; Marincola, *Greek Historians*; Marincola, "Introduction," 1–9; Nicolai, "Place of History in the Ancient World," 13–26; Balmaceda, "Historia y Retórica," 65–80; Feldherr, "Introduction," 1–8; Balmaceda, "El oficio del historiador romano," 223–31.

7. Cf. Nicolai, "Place of History in the Ancient World," 13–26, and Lendon, "Historians without History," 41–62; Mehl, *Roman Historiography*, passim.

The importance of rhetoric in Roman historiography cannot be overemphasized, and a great amount of scholarship has been devoted to mapping out the relationship between them. To be able to learn something from the past, the facts had to be adequately registered and ordered. In antiquity, this order was given mainly by rhetoric, and that is why Cicero could say that history was a "kind of writing particularly suited to an orator [*opus oratorium maxime*]."[8] The main difficulty with saying that ancient historiography is rhetorical is that rhetoric is commonly seen as an instrument for insincerity.[9] However, this does not necessarily mean that it is an instrument for falsehood; on the contrary, rhetoric can help find the truth because it provides the historian with the appropriate techniques and methods to unfold the narrative and the argument in a clearer way. History benefits from rhetoric in its search for evidence or its alertness to detect bias, because rhetoric offers arguments from probability or imposes a structure on different types of historical materials. History needs rhetoric because it looks for clarity: "facts have to be interpreted, material organised, details selected, events reconstructed, words matched with deeds."[10]

The most problematic aspect related to the acknowledgment that rhetoric played a key role in ancient historiography is, of course, *inventio*. However, *inventio* did not mean a ruthless disregard for truth, but, as its formation from *invenio* (to find) suggests, it meant rather a finding and discovery, searching out by means of reflection, finding a possible explanation by the use of creativity.[11] This is what Badian lucidly called the "expansion of the past,"[12] which rather than mere fiction was a creative reconstruction grounded in the reality of things.[13]

Another feature common to rhetoric and Roman historiography was the importance that both attached to *delectatio*. *Delectare* (to please) and *movere* (to move) were emotions that an orator had to achieve to be considered fully

---

8. Cic. *De Leg*, 1.5, Zetzel's trans., *On the Commonwealth and on the Laws*, 107.

9. One need only think of what is meant by saying, "That is *mere* rhetoric."

10. Comber, "Re-reading the Roman Historians," 54.

11. See Cic. *De Inv*, 1.9: "*Inventio* is the discovery of valid or seemingly valid arguments to render one's cause plausible [*excogitatio rerum verarum aut veri similium quae causam probabilem reddant*]." An important definition and distinction are made by Russell, "Rhetoric and Criticism," 135: "[*Inventio*] is simply the 'discovery' of what requires to be said in a given situation (*ta deonta heurein*), the implied theory being that it is somehow already 'there' though latent, and does not have to be made up as a mere figment of imagination."

12. Badian, "Early Historians," 11.

13. Cf. Morley, *Thucydides and the Idea of History*, 154. See also Rawson, "Cassius and Brutus," 101–19.

successful, and they were legitimate and valid aims for history as well. The Roman historian had to win his audience by telling good stories of the past that would engage the reader in active participation: "We derive pleasure from history, which we are so fond of following up to the remotest detail, turning back to parts we have omitted, and pushing on to the end when we have once begun."[14] This history-reader engagement was attained not only by the way things were told—that is, having recourse to rhetorical models and techniques—but also through the specific content of their narratives that helped to build up a common identity. Roman historians appeared especially keen on projecting a particular image of Rome, and used all the force of their rhetoric to do so. Thus, Roman historical writing was certainly useful for self-definition, and to write about the history of Rome worked somehow as a tool for domestic policy: public life and the development of the *res publica*, the wars for the expansion of the empire, the relations between the ruling elite and the plebs, the leaders and the institutions—everything was there to emphasize their specific role and function in society and to support continuity even in changing circumstances.[15] The topics that history was concerned with also helped to promote the same kind of behavior as had been followed in the past, encouraging fidelity to the *mores maiorum* through *exempla*. The power of exemplarity in Roman culture and society is difficult to assess in all its consequences. It assumes that past actions can be reproduced in the present, as if the possibilities and values of the actors remained the same.[16] History fulfilled a specific and practical part in the community, as Livy said: "what chiefly makes the study of history wholesome and profitable is this, that you behold the lessons of every kind of experience set forth as on a conspicuous monument, from these you may choose for yourself and for your own state what to imitate, from these mark for avoidance what is shameful in the conception and shameful in the result."[17] The Roman historian, then, in a sense acted as a guide to conduct for his contemporaries, by providing good models to imitate and bad ones to avoid.

Thus, a great part of the value of history was perceived in Rome as connected with its educational function, and among the things that one could

---

14. Cic. *De Fin*, 5.19.51.

15. For the topic of identity and role models, see Bell and Hansen, *Role Models in the Roman World*.

16. Cf. Roller, "Exemplary Past in Roman Historiography and Culture," 214–30.

17. Livy, *praef*. 10: *Hoc illud est praecipue in cognitione rerum salubre ac frugiferum, omnis te exempli documenta in industri posita monumento intueri; inde tibi tuaeque rei publicae quod imitere capias, inde foedum inceptu foedum exitu quod vites.*

learn from history, perhaps the central one for Romans was a moral teaching for life: history was *magistra vitae*.[18] Since Roman historical writing had this deep ethical dimension, the historian had to do more than merely tell pleasant stories from the past: he had to pass moral judgment. For Tacitus, for example, this was the *praecipuum munus* or history's highest function: "to ensure that virtue shall not lack its record and to hold before the vicious word and deed the terrors of posterity and infamy."[19] History was a commemoration of virtue, and a deterrent from following bad examples lest one's evil deeds should be recorded for ever. For it was from the study of the past, from the virtues and vices of their ancestors, that the Romans derived their concept of public morality and defined the models to follow. This explicit ethical preoccupation marked Roman historiography so profoundly that it has been regarded—together with rhetoric—as one of its most distinctive characteristics.[20]

But ethical approaches to history have sometimes been viewed with discomfort by the modern reader.[21] In our hyper-rationalistic age, explanations of historical events based on the morals of the individuals have often been thought as naïve, simplistic, or even a distortion of the "real causes" of events in order to point out a moral lesson. Moral explanations are seen as an obstacle to achieving the desired impartiality: "Ancient historiography, despite its claims to objectivity, has a strong moral agenda."[22] But in one way or another, every history has an "agenda," because the historian chooses an orientation and a purpose for his history, a particular way of looking at things. Most of the time, social history has a political agenda and gender history an ideological one. Passing moral judgment, or analyzing human actions by moral standards, need not disqualify the historian's claim to honesty or attempt at accuracy when explaining the past. On the contrary, in Roman historiography that approach is a sign of acuity and sophistication. Just as it is seen as legitimate

---

18. Cf. Cic. *De Or*, 2.36. Polybius had stressed it in similar terms before Cicero's memorable words; cf. Pol. 1.1.2.

19. Tac. *Ann*, 3.65.1: *quod praecipuum munus annalium reor ne virtutes sileantur utque pravis dictis factisque ex posteritate et infamia metus sit*. Cf. Luce, "Tacitus on History's Highest Function," 2914; Woodman, "*Praecipuum Munus Annalium*," 92–93, 103; and Woodman and Martin, *Annals of Tacitus, Book 3*, ad loc.

20. Cf. Auerbach, *Mimesis*, 40. I follow Morgan's view on the distinction between ethics and morality: "There is no general agreement as to when one should use the word 'ethics' and when 'morality.' Some scholars prefer to use 'ethics' of the classical world, feeling that morality has too many modern religious overtones. Others feel the opposite, and others again use both indistinguishably, in keeping with their semantic origins," *Popular Morality*, 2n2. I use them indistinctively.

21. Cf. Dench, "Roman Historians and Twentieth-Century Approaches," 394–406.

22. Braund, *Latin Literature*, 20.

today to discuss history in terms of social, economic, or cultural responses and behaviors, so it was valid for the Romans to attempt to explain change in history through the analysis of moral values. It is important, then, to deal with moral arguments seriously and, as T. Morgan rightly put it, to "treat morality as an aspect of ancient society in its own right, to be assessed on its own terms."[23]

The Focus: History and *Virtus*

The present work is not about moral history or the history of morality in the Roman historians. The questions I am trying to raise are, I think, different in nature and scope. How can the analysis of a specific moral category such as *virtus* be a profitable way of approaching Roman history? Why was this ethical concept relevant to explain the past, and why especially to the historians of the late republic and early empire? One of the aims of this book is to argue that tracing *virtus* in Latin historiography not only tells us something about the meaning and role this concept played in historical writing, but perhaps more importantly, it helps us to understand the Romans' conception of history more deeply.

Virtus is intimately connected to Roman historiography in different ways. At a thematic level, *virtus* as courage appears as an indispensable feature when writing the history of Rome—especially early Rome—since the historical narratives are unfolded primarily through the account of the wars and conquests that the Romans fought against other peoples. *Virtus*, then, being the chief quality of the soldier and general, plays a very important part in the development of these accounts, and its overwhelming presence is not surprising. This is the *virtus* that is to be found abundantly, for example, in the first decade of Livy's *Ab Urbe Condita*, where the author narrates how the city of Rome grew in size and power. In these cases, when the word *virtus* appears in the narratives of the Roman historians, it serves not only to describe people or circumstances but also, to a certain extent, as a specific marker of identity: *virtus* in some way Romanizes the bearer.

However, *virtus* is more than a theme or a topic in Roman historiography. It is not enough for the historians to acknowledge or praise the *virtus* of certain individuals in Roman history; they are expected to give explanations. *Virtus*, then, not only is something to be proud of but also works as

---

23. Cf. Morgan, *Popular Morality*, 3.

an explanatory resource: Romans win and conquer *because* of *virtus*. As they see all changes in moral terms, and important historical issues like causation as a fundamentally moral question, *virtus* plays a key part in the explanation of Rome's past glories. Conversely, the reason why the Romans sometimes do not succeed is the lack of their principal attribute, *virtus*. This is how Sallust, for example, explains the decline of Rome in his monographs or how Velleius Paterculus accounts for the revival of the splendor of the *res publica* under Tiberius' reign. One of the first extant authors to link Roman character to Roman greatness was Ennius. In some way, his *moribus antiquis res stat Romana virisque* ("the Roman state stands strong today, due to its ancient morals and noble men") can be identified as the starting point of a long tradition that was going to be followed faithfully by the historians.[24]

At a third and even deeper level, *virtus* is also part of the very essence of history. Compared with epic, where deities are actively present, Roman historical writing entails a predominantly human point of view: it records the actions of human beings in the past, and it aims to explain the changes and continuities that their choices have brought about. The vital question for the Roman historian is what sort of man did this or that, what type of person is the one who achieved victory or brought failure to the *res publica*. Livy states this unambiguously: "Here are the questions to which I would have every reader give his close attention: what *life* and *morals* were like; through what *men* and by which policies, in peace and in war, the empire was established and enlarged [*ad illa mihi pro se quisque acriter intendat animum, quae vita, qui mores fuerint, per quos viros quibusque artibus domi militiaeque et partum et auctum imperium sit*]."[25] This focusing on individuals, which placed them and their decisions at the very center of causation in Roman history, demanded an understanding of the person's character, with its qualities or vices, and involved reference to *mores*, that is, customs, habits, dispositions, and ways of being. The concept of *mores*, from which the word "morality" is derived, was then essential in illustrating and making sense of the past.

As theme, cause, and core in Roman historical writing, *virtus* is clearly a relevant category by which to explore and examine the development of Roman history at any given time. However, *virtus* not only was a moral concept; it also worked as a key political idea in the complex system of Roman sociocultural values, attitudes, and norms. As such, it constantly needed and received (re)definition and (re)interpretation, commemoration, and restatement. I argue

---

24. Ennius, *Ann.* 5.156.
25. Livy, *praef.* 9 (my highlighting).

that historical writing became an important locus of this process. As *magistra vitae*, history had to teach and provide good examples to be imitated and bad ones to be avoided. Historiography was, therefore, a prime site of negotiation of Roman identity. Roman history was anything but a nostalgic preoccupation with the past: it was a matter of urgent contemporary relevance. The Roman historians, especially in a period when political horizons were constantly being redefined, sought to respond to the present through the evaluation of the past and somehow assumed the responsibility of recording *virtus* as a means to preserve it. Accordingly, their accounts of *virtus* not only contributed to the understanding and explanation of Roman history but helped to shape historical reality by constructing and reconstructing *virtus* in a political culture where exemplarity worked in a particularly powerful way.

Tracing the concept of *virtus* from Sallust onward also leads us to more questions through which to analyze Roman history during the late republic and early principate. When historians sought *virtus*—or vice—as the final explanation of history, were they trying to justify or condemn the system as well as the individual? Could the state as a whole be seen and treated as a moral entity? Did a "monarchical" or individual-dependent system—as opposed to a republican one—make it significantly easier to see the history of the state itself as something that could be analyzed in "moral" or "biographical" terms? Historians of this period had to deal with these questions, and their responses affected their treatment of political changes over time. The step from the republic to the empire necessitated a new interpretation of an old concept: the standards of *virtus* were more necessary than ever to validate the system or to censure it. The historians' different viewpoints on the politics and *virtus* of its players have contributed to enriching and expanding our knowledge of the particular circumstances in which Rome found itself at that time.

In the development of the argument it will appear clearly, I hope, that I have been working with two parallel strands. My analysis is marked inevitably by the problem of the relationship between history and historiography: the time in which the historian writes affects the way he writes about the period he is depicting. The approach of Sallust, who was himself living in times of crisis, is different from that of Livy, writing in a transitional period, or of Tacitus, writing when, for better or for worse, the crisis seemed to have been settled. And their interpretation of history was mirrored and at the same time shaped not only by the political situation of the time when they were writing but also by the complexities of the literary tradition. Roman historical prose meant a step further in the development of cultural history in Rome and henceforward. Sallust, Livy, Tacitus, and even Velleius did not just provide powerful narratives of war, compelling characterizations, or deep political analyses; in some way, they helped to construct the categories by which reality could be measured and expressed—the images and narratives that we experience in life.[26]

Outline

This survey aims to show both the meaning of *virtus* as used by the Roman historians and how the concept evolved in relation to the political changes experienced in Roman society and portrayed by the historians. As will be seen, by "evolving" I mean a relatively neutral term that implies some movement and development but does not automatically signify progression or improvement on the one hand and decline and deterioration on the other.

Before analyzing the works of individual historians, it was necessary to deal with the concept of *virtus* as such, in terms of its etymology and usage, and this is what I do in chapter 1. It does not intend to explain comprehensively the philosophical meaning of the word *virtus* or trace every occurrence, but to give the coordinates through which the chapters on the historians should be read. The section also provides comparisons with its Greek parallels *andreia* and *arete*, and a brief assessment of the influence of Greek philosophy on Roman thought—Stoicism in particular—regarding the term *virtus*. I also propose a classification of the two main meanings of *virtus*, which I have called *virilis-virtus* (courage) and *humana-virtus* (virtue), and show the particular connections between *virtus* and Roman politics. Cicero holds a particularly important place in this chapter, as the creator of a nomenclature and vocabulary that offer an adequate rationalization of the concept of *virtus*.

The chapter on Sallust argues that through his historical works—mainly the two monographs—he emerges both as the advocate of an understanding of *virtus* that expanded the sense he had inherited of what it meant to be a good Roman and as the promoter of the idea of the contestability of *virtus* in the ideological struggles of the late republic. It also gives an assessment of Sallust's profound influence on the moral language of Roman historiography and his analysis of political decline in relation to *virtus*. The section deals with *virtus* in both his prologues and discusses how the thematic variations between the

---

26. Cf. Goldhill, *Invention of Prose*, 44; Cameron, "Postlude," 206–7.

two relate to the different historical narratives. It also explores, through a close analysis of the corruption of *logos* in the text, how Sallust's creation of a "vocabulary of decline" and the devaluation of language illustrate the moving boundaries of the moral and political behavior of the main historical characters.

Moving on to Livy, I discuss how the categories set up in his preface—*vita et mores*—played a key role throughout the narrative of the history of Rome in his *Ab Urbe Condita*. The numerous uses of *virtus* in relation to martial bravery in Livy's accounts of the wars, the link between *virtus* and the history of the gradual acquisition of *libertas* by the Roman people, and the ways in which *virtus* is put at risk are addressed here to explain Livy's interpretation of the concept. Parallels and references to Augustus' *virtus*-language or *virtus*-image are given to place Livy within the broader picture of his time.

The chapter on Velleius shows how through his *Historiae*, he sought to highlight the fact that the principate had come not just to reestablish peace and order, but to restore something very important to the Romans: *virtus*. The examination of men of *virtus* during the republic was used by the author both to emphasize his standpoint of continuity and to prepare the reader for his distinctive interpretation of Roman history. The analysis of the emperor Tiberius in Velleius' work serves as a case study to illustrate his positive interpretation of *virtus*, in which political ideology and Velleius' own version of historical reality blend together.

The analysis of Tacitus' works completes the spectrum of Roman historians treated in this study. I divide his historical writings into three units: (1) the *Agricola* and the *Germania*, (2) the *Histories*, and (3) the *Annals*, not to refer to successive stages in the evolution of his understanding of *virtus*, but to stress the repeated insistence by which he delineates the expressions of *virtus* in three different periods of Roman history. By identifying what was essential to Roman *virtus* and what was superfluous and susceptible to change, Tacitus illustrates how, even though a certain degree of political freedom was lost, there were some Romans who could exercise a more "personal" freedom which led to new manifestations of *virtus*. Tacitus' perception of the nature of political change is one of the main themes used throughout the chapter to plot the barriers that *virtus* had to overcome in the new world of the principate.

The conclusion to this book gives me the opportunity to emphasize again how the historians I discuss throughout the book responded intellectually to one another and established a sort of dialogue among themselves. The investigation of the development of Roman historiography in an integrated manner aims at a more vital and comprehensive approach to Roman cultural and intellectual history.

I FEAR THAT SOMETIMES in the study of historiography we have applied an "unhistorical treatment"—to paraphrase Wiseman—to ethical categories. Somehow we have left aside what we do not consider "proper" history or think of as "unhistorical," and this has only impoverished our approach. We have narrowed down the concept of "moral" so much—almost to one specific standard of behavior—that we run the risk of misunderstanding ancient historiography. As C. Pelling suggested, perhaps we need to accept that "serious moral evaluation was a sign of political sophistication rather than naïveté."[27] In fact, the human being is a moral animal as much as a political or a social one.

Dealing with a concept like *virtus* not only gives us a better comprehension of historians' moral or political appraisal but also opens up new horizons when interpreting Roman history, since *virtus* encompasses politics, values, and historical progress. The analysis of the ways in which the historians account for *virtus* in their narratives sheds new light on the problems and possibilities of historical writing in the late republic and early principate, for it elucidates a crucial moral, philosophical, and political concept that underpinned Roman attitudes to both present and past. Furthermore, the study of *virtus* in historiography leads us toward a reappraisal of the historians and their works as promoters of change or continuity in both Roman political culture and political thought.

27. Pelling, *Literary Texts and the Greek Historian*, 60.

CHAPTER ONE

The Concept of *Virtus*

Appellata est enim ex viro virtus

For it is from the word "man" that the word *virtus* is derived
—Cic. *Tusc. Disp*, 2.18.43

Before we start analyzing what *virtus* meant to the particular historians and the role they assigned to it in their narratives, it will be useful to investigate its original meaning and then try to illustrate the itinerary of this meaning. *Virtus*, as one of the most important ideas that made up the Roman set of values, was a rather dynamic concept. It also aroused emotional responses from different sectors of society: politicians, the Roman people, intellectuals, military men, and others. We shall have to look, then, not for a few brief striking changes whose character is indisputably clear, but for a much longer, more complex, and less easily identified process which was probably one that by its very nature was open to rival interpretation.

It would be rather naïve to aim here at an exhaustive definition or explanation of the essence of *virtus*. The concept can be approached from many different angles; it belongs to moral philosophy, but it also appears as a linguistic phenomenon with political and social implications. The purpose of this book is not only to explore and present a literary debate on a particularly important concept, which can enrich our reading of some ancient texts, but also to consider how the question of the definition and origin of the idea of *virtus* is soon transformed into an issue of wider significance. In searching beyond its literary and historical aspects and conceiving different ways to approach the subject, we start unpacking a piece of intellectual history.

Some of the questions that I will attempt to answer in this chapter are whether *virtus* is a totally Roman concept, what its relationship is with its Greek parallels *andreia* and *arete*, and whether one can translate *virtus* indiscriminately as manliness, courage, or virtue in general. The problem of *virtus* as the attribute of a particular sex, social group, or nation will also be addressed, together with the link to a particular code of moral behavior. Clearly, in the process of responding to these points, many others may arise; value-words such as *virtus* are of a very special kind, and it is difficult to define them because they keep changing, or perhaps they change because they cannot be categorically defined. Both value-words and political words—and *virtus* was both—require interpretation rather than definition.

We find *virtus* working as a complex set of ideas whose meaning and usage varied. The etymology of the word tells us something intrinsically related to its significance, but it falls short when applied to the more general connotations and fails to illuminate what was going to develop later as the common meaning of *virtus*. I will try to show in this section that the supposed contrast between traditional Roman *virtus* and the parallel Greek concepts, although it has been very useful in identifying the differences and particular nuances of the concepts, has also created a misleading dichotomy of the terms. This contrast has been presented by some scholars as the existence of an originally Roman *virtus* meaning courage that later, mainly under the influence of Greek doctrines and especially Stoicism, became a more comprehensive concept specifically related to morality.[1] This is, of course, true in some sense, but it can carry a dangerous presupposition or assumption that the Romans had to wait till Greek culture had become established in Rome to start thinking about their own Roman way of being or the principles of their code of values.

Virtus as Courage

The etymology of *virtus* does not seem to offer problems. All studies agree in going to Cicero's *Tusculan Disputations* for the explanation of the origin of the word: "for it is from the word for 'man' that the word 'virtue' is derived [*appellata est ex enim viro virtus*]."[2] *Virtus*, then, comes from the noun *vir* and the suffix "tus"—which appears to indicate the state or form of existence, in the same way that *senectus* (old age) is the state of being a *senex* (old man) or *iuventus* (youth) of being a *iuvenis* (young man).[3] Its exact Greek parallel would be *andreia* (manliness) from *aner* (man). However, *virtus* seems to have developed more freely than other words with the suffix "tus," and is more commonly used

---

1. One of the latest versions of this view can be found in McDonnell, *Roman Manliness*.
2. Cic. *Tusc. Disp.* 2.43. See Büchner, "Altrömische und Horazische Virtus," 1–22; Pöschl, *Grundwerte römischer Staatsgesinnung in den Geschichtswerken der Sallust*; Haas, "Virtus Tacitea," 163–80; van Omme, *Virtus, semantiese Studie*; Eisenhut, *Virtus Romana: Ihre Stellung im römische Wertsystem*; McDonnell, *Roman Manliness*; Sarsila, *Being a Man*.
3. For an expanded explanation of the formation of the word and its original meaning, see Ernout and Meillet, *Dictionnaire étymologique de la langue latine*, 1305–6; Hellegouarc'h, *Vocabulaire Latin*, 242–46; Eisenhut, *Virtus Romana*, 12–13; and Sarsila, *Being a Man*, 25–30.

not as a state of being man, but as the proper characteristic of a man: what is proper to a *vir* is *virtus*. In giving the origin of the word, Cicero adds a qualification: "And yet, perhaps, though all right-minded states are called virtue, the term is not appropriate to all virtues, but all have got the name from the single virtue which was found to outshine the rest; for it is from the word for 'man' that the word 'virtue' is derived; but man's peculiar virtue is fortitude, of which there are two main functions, namely scorn of death and scorn of pain [*Atqui vide ne, cum omnes rectae animi adfectiones virtutes appellentur, non sit hoc proprium nomen omnium, sed ab ea, quae una ceteris excellebat, omnes nominatae sint. Appellata est enim ex viro virtus; viri autem propria maxime est fortitudo, cuius munera duo sunt maxima mortis dolorisque contemptio*]."[4]

In a highly militaristic society such as Rome, physical prowess and courage—especially shown in war—remained the central elements of manliness throughout the republican period and into the empire. This is why *virtus* is always shown like a warrior (see figure 1). It was the valor of her soldiers that had won Rome the reputation of a fierce and invincible nation. This is found in the early writers, particularly historians; they represented Romans as braver than other people. The concept of courage in Rome worked not only as a self-definition but also as the cause of their success. Claudius Quadrigarius, for example, in his memorable account of the fight between a Gaul and a Roman, located the latter's superiority in his spirit and the courage he showed in challenging a man better armed than himself; thus *virtus* was precisely the reason for his triumph.[5] In Cato this aspect becomes even more evident and explicit; various examples can be summed up in one: the tribune's brave deed to save the state, says Cato, was not exceedingly praised at that time because for a good Roman to serve the *res publica* with valor was not (and should not) be uncommon: "The immortal gods accorded the military tribune good fortune [*fortunam*] to match his courage [*ex virtute*]. This is what happened: although he was wounded many times, his head remained unharmed, and he was recognized among the dead, exhausted by his wounds and loss of blood; they picked him up and he recovered. Often thereafter he gave brave and energetic [*fortem atque strenuam*] service to the state [*rei publicae*]; and by his act in leading off those soldiers, he saved the rest of the army."[6]

This idea was not something exclusive to Roman thought. In Thucydides, for example, we find Pericles proclaiming the willingness of the Athenians to

---

4. Cic. *Tusc. Disp*, 2.43.
5. Cf. Claudius Quadrigarius, *FRHist*, 24.F6 (=Gellius 9.13.6–14).
6. Cf. Cato, *FRHist*, 5.F76 (=Gellius 3.7).

give their lives for the sake of their city.[7] And later, Plato devotes a whole dialogue, the *Laches*, to trying to define what courage is and what the implications are for service to the state.[8] When Cicero says that "brave men do not feel wounds in the line of battle, or feel them but prefer death rather than move a step from the post that honor has appointed,"[9] the meaning he gives to *virtus* is almost identical to the definition that the general Laches gives of *andreia* in the Platonic dialogue: "anyone who is willing to stay at his post and face the enemy, and does not run away, you may be sure, is courageous."[10] Laches defends the traditional view of courage,[11] and both *virtus* and *andreia* are referring here to the manliest characteristic of all: courage. Bravery appears, then, to be semantically related to man and to be the original and basic meaning of *virtus*: manliness, virility, valor. Therefore, it would seem appropriate to distinguish it as *virilis-virtus*.

Courage is not simply a quality of individuals, but a quality necessary to sustain the household or the community. Honor and glory belong to the individual who excels in battle or in a contest as a mark of recognition by his household and his community of the part he played in sustaining public order. To be courageous is to be someone on whom reliance can be placed. Hence courage is an important ingredient in all who have the mission of defending something, like soldiers or politicians. Down through the ages, courage has been seen as a quality that is always usefully and necessarily awarded public recognition and honors; prizes for bravery are still sought after because the courageous are admired, and are objects of gratitude on the part of the community. In this sense, courage had to be always publicly oriented, so Cicero says that "the courage that is prompt to face danger, if it is inspired not by public spirit, but by its own selfish purposes, should have the name of reckless effrontery rather than courage [*verum etiam animus paratus ad periculum, si sua cupiditate, non utilitate communi impellitur, audaciae potius nomen habeat, quam fortitudinis*]."[12] Thus, this *virilis-virtus* appears as a social quality. It is

---

7. Cf. Thuc. 2.39.4. For a more detailed presentation of this idea, see Balot, "Pericles' Anatomy of Democratic Courage," 505–25, and his latest book, *Courage in Democratic Polis*.

8. A thorough exposition and commentary on the main ideas of the *Laches* can be found in Schmid, *On Manly Courage*.

9. Cic. *Tusc. Disp*, 2.24.58: *non sentiunt viri fortes in acie vulnera, vel sentiunt, sed mori malunt quam tantum modo de dignitatis gradu demoveri*.

10. Plato, *Lach*, 190E: εἰ γάρ τις ἐθέλοι ἐν τῇ τάξει μένων ἀμύνεσθαι τοὺς πολεμίους καὶ μὴ φεύγοι, εὖ ἴσθι ὅτι ἀνδρεῖος ἂν εἴη.

11. In opposition to Nicias, who argues for a more "intellectualized" one.

12. Cic. *De Off*, 1.63.

worth pointing out that one of the main features of the Roman ethical system is that moral values are deeply connected with and oriented toward the community: it acts as a reference point morally and at the same time it provides incentives and the social approval needed to support the current sociopolitical arrangements. Courageous behavior is expressed principally in the ability to risk oneself for a reason, namely, valuing somebody else or something else more than your own life or benefit.[13]

Courage, like any other virtue, can be corrupted in two ways, by excess or by deficiency. Thus, the virtue of courage lies between rashness and timidity: "The man who runs away from everything in fear and never endures anything becomes a coward; the man who fears nothing whatsoever but encounters everything becomes rash."[14] It appears, therefore, that it has to be a response to danger according to reason. "Reason possesses an intrinsic element of dignity and grandeur, suited rather to require obedience than to render it, esteeming all the accidents of human fortunes not merely as endurable but also as unimportant; a quality of loftiness and elevation, fearing nothing, submitting to no one, ever unsubdued."[15] Socrates in the *Laches* states that courage is a kind of wisdom: "In my opinion very few people are endowed with courage and forethought, while rashness, boldness, and fearlessness with no prudence to guide it are found in many men, women, children, and animals."[16] Fearlessness and courage are not the same thing. Courage can be regarded, then, as a proper quality only of the human and rational soul.

But perhaps at the beginning, the Romans did not stop to ask themselves whether other qualities such as prudence or reasoning were included in this original and basic idea of *virtus*. It was simply valor, and as such, it had "its precepts and its rules, rules of constraining force, that forbid a man to show womanish weakness in pain," as Cicero would say.[17] Courage had to be

---

13. But this is not to say that somebody cannot genuinely care for others and also be a coward. For courage and other virtues as care and concern of the community, see MacIntyre, *After Virtue*, 179–80.

14. Cf. Arist. *EN* 1104a: ὅ τε γὰρ πάντα φεύγων καὶ φοβούμενος καὶ μηδὲν ὑπομένων δειλὸς γίνεται, ὅ τε μηδὲν ὅλως φοβούμενος ἀλλὰ πρὸς πάντα βαδίζων θρασύς.

15. Cic. *De Fin*, 2.46: *eadem ratio habet in se quiddam amplum atque magnificum, ad imperandum magis quam ad parendum accommodatum, omnia humana non tolerabilia solum, sed etiam levia ducens, altum quiddam et excelsum, nihil timens, nemini cedens, semper invictum.*

16. Plato, *Lach*, 197B: ἐγὼ δὲ ἀνδρείας μὲν καὶ προμηθίας πάνυ τισὶν ὀλίγοις οἶμαι μετεῖναι, θρασύτητος δὲ καὶ τόλμης καὶ τοῦ ἀφόβου μετὰ ἀπρομηθίας πάνυ πολλοῖς καὶ ἀνδρῶν καὶ γυναικῶν καὶ παίδων καὶ θηρίων. ταῦτ' οὖν ἃ σὺ καλεῖς ἀνδρεῖα καὶ οἱ πολλοί, ἐγώ.

17. Cic. *De Fin*, 2.29.94: *Fortitudinis quaedam praecepta sunt ac paene leges, quae effeminari virum vetant in dolore.* There was a tendency to suggest that in general, women were weaker and less

shown in deeds, not in words,[18] especially in a pragmatic society like Rome where a man is what a man does: "the glory of *virtus* is in activity [*virtutis enim laus omnis in actione consistit*]."[19]

Thus, it is difficult to explain why it is that when *virtus* is so clearly "manly courage" by etymology and usage, it also bears a broader ethical meaning, related to the Greek *arete*.

Virtus as *Arete*

As I will try to show, *virtus* as courage or *virilis-virtus* is a much more straightforward concept than *virtus* as *arete*. The way *virtus* came to mean good qualities in general—courage being only one of them—is long and complex, and there are times when it would even seem fruitless to distinguish between the different usages.

The development of the word *virtus* was more complicated than at first meets the eye. The difficulties lie partially in the evidence we have. Most of our earliest sources dealing with *virtus* come from the second century B.C. and thus we have no way to prove whether *virtus* before that meant *only* courage, or more than that. As far as we can trace the concept, we find it meaning something like a quality of men, but in quite general terms.[20] Manliness, militarism, and morality appear inseparable in Roman thought from the beginning, and therefore a term qualifying any of these had to be related to the others. This flexibility and wide range of meanings is found as early as we happen to have written evidence of it. We can take Ennius as an example. His famous *moribus antiquis res stat Romana virisque*[21] offered a complete program of what could be identified as "being Roman."[22] This description of national

---

brave than men, but all the authors I deal with are also generous in attributing "manly courage" to specific women who deserve that praise, and we will see them in due course. For this, see Levick, "Women, Power and Philosophy at Rome and Beyond," 133–56, esp. 139: "Although there was a linguistic difficulty, in that essentially it meant manliness par excellence, women too could possess *virtus*." See also Sarsila, *Being a Man*, 48–49.

18. Plato, *Lach*, 193E.

19. Cic. *De Off*, 1.6.19.

20. Cf. Harris, *War and Imperialism in Republican Rome*, 20. See also Ferguson, *Moral Values in the Ancient World*, 161–62.

21. Ennius, *Ann*, 5.156.

22. Cf. Lind, "Concept, Action and Character," 235–83, who sees in Ennius the initiator of the literary tradition that links Rome's moral and martial greatness, stressing the dependence of the latter upon the former. For Ennius' *Annales* as the invention of Rome's past, see Elliot, *Ennius and the Architecture of the Annales*, esp. 198–232. Cf. Rosenstein, "Aristocratic Values," 365–82.

character and values provided the grounds for self-identification, and even though it did not give an explicit definition of *virtus* as such, it certainly presented the moral atmosphere where *virtus* could arise.[23] In Plautus' comedies one also finds examples of *virtus* meaning not only *virilis-virtus* or military valor but also *humana-virtus* or moral excellence.[24]

Approaching the second half of the second century B.C., Lucilius' work is probably where one can find one of the first definitions of *virtus* as such, and it appears as something remarkably open and general:

> *Virtus*, Albinus, is the ability to pay the true price in whatever business or affairs of life; *virtus* is knowing what there is in every undertaking for a man; *virtus* is knowing what is right and useful and honorable for a man, what is good, bad, useless or shamefully dishonorable; *virtus* is knowing the means and the ends of a pursuit; *virtus* is the ability to pay the price from one's store of wealth; *virtus* is giving to honor that which is in fact due to it, to be an enemy and a hater of bad men and bad habits and, on the other hand, a defender of men of good habits or morals, to make much of these, to wish them well, to live with them as a friend, and beyond these traits, to think first of one's fatherland, then of one's parents, and third and last of one's own interests.[25]

> *Virtus, Albine, est, pretium persolvere verum*
> *Quis in versamur, quis vivimus rebus, potesse;*
> *Virtus est, homini scire id quod quaeque habeat res,*
> *Virtus, scire homini rectum, utile quid sit, honestum*
> *Quae bona, quae mala item, quid inutile, turpe, inhonestum,*
> *Virtus, quaerendae finem re scire modumque,*
> *Virtus, divitiis pretium persolvere posse,*
> *Virtus, id dare quod re ipsa debetur honori*
> *Hostem esse atque inimicum hominum morumque malorum*
> *Contra defensorem hominum morumque bonorum,*
> *Hos magni facere, his bene velle, his vivere amicum;*
> *Commode praeterea patriai prima putare,*
> *Deinde parentum, tertia iam postremaque nostra.*

---

23. For *virtus* in Ennius' fragments, see *Ann*, 6.190–91; 10.333; *Phoen*, 308–11; *Hec. Ly*, 200–201.
24. For example, *Mil. Gl*, 619, 649, 728; *Pseud*, 726; *Truc*, 741. For a detailed account of these occurrences, see Eisenhut, *Virtus Romana*, 24–29; and Sarsila, *Being a Man*, 39–55.
25. Lucilius, 1096–1208. Lind's translation, slightly adapted, in "Concept, Action and Character," 240. He translates *virtus* as manliness, meaning broadly "to be a proper man in all senses"; I have preferred to keep the original word *virtus*.

This definition shows a certain intellectualization of the concept. The repetition of the verb to know (*scire*) makes *virtus* a type of wisdom, just as Nicias had stated in the *Laches*.[26] Even though it has been argued that this fragment owes much to Stoic ideas of *virtus*,[27] it also seems possible that Lucilius' set of maxims worked simply as a code of values for the behavior of aristocratic Roman men. The passage shows some Greek notions of general morality interacting with and blending in specific Roman contexts like the primacy of the love for one's country above parents and the self.[28]

Romans' attitude toward all Greek things, especially Greek culture, involved not only the reception of philosophical ideas from Greece but also the presence of convincing spokesmen to present these doctrines in a way that appealed to a Roman audience. *Imitatio* and *aemulatio* are probably the best words to use in defining in some sense the relationship that Rome developed toward the Greek way of life and knowledge.[29] But imitation and competition were only a part of a very complex liaison between the two cultures, as Horace would try to depict in his verse: *Graecia capta, ferum victorem cepit et artes intulit agresti Latio* (Captive Greece took captive her fierce conqueror, and introduced her arts into rude Latium).[30] The Romans admitted the intellectual superiority of the Greeks—sometimes reluctantly—but they had a tendency to find the Greeks fickle, prone to theorize, and certainly inferior in political, military, and moral practices.[31] Cicero, who devoted a great part of his time to studying and writing about philosophy—which he had learned from Greek masters—also recognizes the dangers of dedicating one's life to intellectual activities detached from the social and ethical values of society. He touches this point emphatically in *De Oratore*, where he argues in favor of the superiority of Rome in matters of morality,[32] natural law,[33] and practical wisdom.[34] In the *Tusculan Disputations*,

---

26. Plato, *Lach*, 194c–d and 199b.

27. Cf. Raschke, "Virtue of Lucilius," 352–69; and McDonnell, *Roman Manliness*, 123–28.

28. For the risk of overvaluing Stoic ideas in Lucilius, see Earl, *Political Thought of Sallust*, 26; and Sarsila, *Being a Man*, 81. For the interpretation of the fragment, see also Görler, "Zum Virtus-Fragment des Lucilius (1326–1338 Marx) und zur Geschichte der stoischen Güterlehre," 445–68.

29. Cf. Cic. *De Fin*, 1.10; *Nat. Deor*, 1.8.

30. Hor. *Ep*, 2.1.156–57.

31. Cf. Cic. *Rep*, 2.1.2; *Tusc. Disp*, 1.1–3. For more on this topic, see Rawson, *Intellectual Life in the Late Roman Republic*, 3–18; and Zetzel, "Plato with Pillows," 119–38.

32. Cf. Cic. *De Or*, 1.47–48.

33. Cf. Cic. *De Or*, 1.193; 1.195; 1.198.

34. Cf. Cic. *De Or*, 1.193; 1.224; 2.18. Cicero expresses his preference also for Roman orators, showing their *auctoritas* in the art of rhetoric as something genuinely and deeply Roman; cf. *De Or*, passim, but esp. 1.23; and *Brut*, 254.

Cicero reiterates the statement that Romans are in some aspects—in fact, the most important ones—superior to the Greeks: "For morality, rules of life, family and household economy are surely maintained by us in a better and more dignified way; and beyond question our ancestors have adopted better regulations and laws than others in directing the policy of government. What shall I say of the art of war? In this sphere our countrymen have proved their superiority by valor as well as in an even greater degree of discipline."[35]

Rome maintained her traditions with pride and taught her children the customs of their ancestors faithfully and even nostalgically, turning a cautious eye on *res novae*,[36] and this was partly the reason for her originality. Romans had a complex relationship with Greek culture, a mixture of admiration and contempt, subjection and domination. The ability to recognize what was superior in Greek culture was combined with the struggle to maintain what was properly Roman in a fight for self-identification that was going to yield rich intellectual fruits. As Velleius Paterculus would later say, "Genius [*ingenia*] is fostered by emulation [*aemulatio*] and it is now envy [*invidia*], now admiration [*admiratio*], which enkindles imitation [*imitationem*], and, in the nature of things, that which is cultivated with the highest zeal [*summo studio*] advances to the highest perfection [*summum in perfecto*]."[37] It was in the process of characterizing themselves and differentiating themselves from others—especially from the powerful, and dominant, Greek culture—that the Romans had to search for appropriate self-definitions that helped them toward a clearer vision of what their mission was. It is here where the concept of *virtus* appears most significant, for, although related to the Greek concepts of *andreia* and *arete*, *virtus* develops a particular history in Roman thought that would make the term crucial to the understanding and evolution of human behavior in Western culture.

Contacts between Greeks and Romans had started a long time ago—"even old Italy was crowded with Pythagoreans, in the days when a part of this land was Great Greece as they called it"[38]—and so the exposure to and intercourse with Greek culture was never totally absent from the formation of Rome.[39] Around the mid-second century B.C., after the eastern wars were finished and

---

35. Cic. *Tusc. Disp*, 1.1.2: *Nam mores et instituta vitae resque domesticas ac familiaris nos profecto et melius tuemur et lautius, rem vero publicam nostri maiores certe melioribus temperaverunt et institutis et legibus. Quid loquar de re militari? in qua cum virtute nostri multum valuerunt, tum plus etiam disciplina.*

36. Meaning at the same time "innovation" and "revolution."

37. Vell. 1.17.7.

38. Cic. *De Or*, 2.154.

39. For the revival of Pythagoreanism in Rome and other philosophical tendencies in the first century B.C., see Schofield, *Aristotle, Plato and the Pythagoreanism.*

Macedonia and Greece were finally conquered, a large influx of Greeks came to Rome in search of better opportunities. The embassy of 155 B.C. brought to Rome the leading philosophers of the day, heads of the three major Athenian schools of philosophy: Carneades (the Academy), Diogenes of Babylon (the Stoa), and Critolaus (Peripatetics).[40] These philosophers were especially attractive to young Romans, including Scipio Aemilianus and his friends, and the effect of their teachings started to spread little by little and became popular. But their influence was not wholly unquestioned, and Rome at this time saw the appearance of the champion of Roman traditional values: Cato the Elder. His attack, as has been said, was not so much on Greek culture as such, but rather on the influence that a misguided or unrestrained training in rhetoric and philosophical education would have on young Romans.[41] He feared, in Plutarch's words, "that the young would rather win a reputation through rhetoric than through deeds and military campaigns."[42] But Cato's warnings were difficult to take into account at a time when Rome seemed to be especially receptive to Greek authority. This was also the period of the influence of the historian Polybius, resident in Rome from 168 to 150 B.C. and the companion of Scipio Aemilianus in Africa and Spain; and of the Stoic philosopher Panaetius.

But philosophy was not the only area of dealings between Greek and Roman culture. The many Greeks who came as captives lived in Rome from the mid-second century onward. They created an almost bilingual atmosphere in the city, and these linguistic interactions became the primary way of exchanging ideas.[43] The presence of a bilingual population was vital for the absorption and development of these new ideas. Apart from the educated Roman elite, who knew Greek perfectly well, and the soldiers who must have picked up some Greek in the wars of conquest, there was a constant stream of Greek slaves or people of servile origin who came to Rome and stayed there. The borrowing of words must have been something relatively common in the streets of Rome around the second century B.C.,[44] and even more so later, when the Romans finally decided that they wanted to write philosophy.

---

40. For a more detailed account of this event, see Wilkerson, "Carneades at Rome," 131–44; Garbarino, *Roma e la filosofia greca dale origini alla fine del II secolo a.C.*; Morford, *Roman Philosophers*, 14–33. For more on Greek philosophy in Rome, see Reinhardt, "Philosophy Comes to Rome," 526–38.

41. Cf. Astin, *Cato the Censor*, 157–81. See also Cic. *De Sen*, 38.

42. Plut. *Cato Maior*, 22.4.

43. Cf. Adams, *Bilingualism and the Latin Language*, 760–62.

44. This is the world portrayed by the comedian Plautus, where most Greek words were spoken mainly by slaves.

In the case of the word *virtus*, it seems to have had an exact Greek parallel in the word *andreia*: both coming from man (*vir—aner*) and related to the manly quality of courage. But *virtus* was also used to translate the word *arete*. Latin's shortage of vocabulary has been given as a possible explanation for this,[45] but the Romans, precisely for that reason, could have borrowed the Greek term for "excellence" as they had done with other Greek words before. It seems probable that the Romans—at least in preclassical Latin—saw little distinction between *arete* and *andreia*. In a highly militaristic society the excellence of a man was manifested primarily in his courage at war. One possible "bridge" between *arete* and *virtus* could be that in fighting one displayed courage and bravery (*andreia*) and thus displayed or possessed excellence as a man (*arete*) according to the nobility's code of behavior. The expansionist wars gave the Romans plenty of opportunity to show their manliness, their courage, and their merit as proper men.

The Greeks understood *arete* as excellence, something that gave a living creature the power to perform its function well. In the Homeric poems *arete* was used for excellence of any kind: a fast runner displayed the *arete* of his feet,[46] and also horses could surpass other horses in *arete*.[47] Thus, the origin of *arete* had no specific connection with ethics.[48] But ethical considerations became more and more popular during the fifth century B.C.: the sophists and Socrates had called into question some of the core moral concepts and brought new aspects of them to light. From this point onward, it is possible to find *arete* used with a more ethical significance, meaning not just excellence, but mainly moral excellence.[49]

When the Greek language became more widespread in Rome—third to second century B.C.—the term *arete* already had a wider range of meaning; thus, the Greek word also influenced the use of *virtus* to denote excellence and in particular moral excellence. To point out the precise moment when *virtus* became predominantly a comprehensive ethical word is hardly possible. It might have been at such an early stage in Roman literature that there

---

45. Cf. McDonnell, *Roman Manliness*, 106–7. Cf. Cic. *De Fin*, 3.2.5.
46. Homer, *Il.* 20.411.
47. Homer, *Il.* 23.276. For this same meaning of "excellence" in *virtus*, see Plautus, *Mil. Gl*, 3.1.131; and more examples in Ferguson, *Moral Values in the Ancient World*, 161–62.
48. Eisenhut, *Virtus Romana*, 16.
49. See, e.g., Thuc., 2.40.4, on Pericles' speech: "In *arete* we stand in sharp contrast to most men [καὶ τὰ ἐς ἀρετὴν ἐνηντιώμεθα τοῖς πολλοῖς]." See also 2.34.5. Cf. Dover, *Greek Popular Morality*.

are no literary sources that retain the exclusive original Roman meaning of *virtus*. Around the third and second century B.C., the *Elogia Scipionum* appeared, with its clear message of *virtus* in the double meaning of courage and moral excellence,[50] and Cato's speeches were delivered, where *virtus* was bravery and virtue in a broader sense.[51] Plautus' and Terence's comedies also had some references to *virtus* in a more general sense than just valor,[52] and we have already seen the meaning that Lucilius assigns to it, so on the whole, it would be unwise to claim that *arete* had an overwhelming influence on *virtus*.[53] Without denying its influence, it seems more plausible that when Romans encountered the Greek terminology for philosophical ideas—and specifically the Stoic and Peripatetic ones—they found that *arete* was the Greek word to translate and signify their own Roman *virtus* in the broader sense, which remained in essence the *virtus* that Ennius and Lucilius had spoken of in their verses and which the early Romans had lauded without explicitly defining it. That would also explain why it was not necessary to borrow a Greek word to express *arete*: they already had a Latin one. Vague, indefinable, and plurisemantic, *virtus* could represent the Greek *andreia* and *arete* simultaneously and without problems, and it was precisely in these features where its power—political, social, moral, and linguistic—lay.

Thus, *virtus* had a different development from its originally Greek parallel *andreia*—we may only speculate upon this process, as language does not always develop as logically as we would like—and came to be identified with virtue in the moral sense in a way that *andreia* never did. *Arete* appears to have influenced *virtus* in the philosophical and rigorous definition we find later, but only later, and it had to wait till Cicero to reach its fullest rational expression in Latin. The very fact that there was only one concept, *virtus*, to signify two different ethical realities, *andreia* and *arete*, makes *virtus* a more complex and multifaceted—and perhaps more relevant—idea in the history of Western values.

---

50. Cf. *CIL*, VI, 1285, 1288, 1289, 1293. Cf. Rosenstein, "Aristocratic Values," 366.

51. Cf. Cato, *ORF*³, fr.146.

52. See, for example, Plautus, *Most*, 139, 144; *Cap*, 690; *Mil. Gl*, 649; and Terence, *Adel*, 257, 442; *Heaut. Tim*, 207.

53. As McDonnell seems to claim, passim. See also Cicero's remark that translating *virtus* as the nonethical Greek *arete* is not appropriate; Cic. *De Leg*, 1.16.45: "we by a misuse of the term talk about the virtue of a tree or of a horse [*nam nec arboris nec equi uirtus quae dicitur (in quo abutimur nomine)*]."

Stoicism in Rome

Stoicism deserves a special place in our account of *virtus* in Rome, since this doctrine placed a noteworthy stress on this particular concept. In this section I will deal with the possible connections of the Stoic philosophical system and the maturity of the Roman concept of *virtus*. Thus, looking at Stoicism can also help us to set *virtus* against its philosophical and intellectual background.

Although Epicureanism had also entered the scene toward the late republic with Lucretius,[54] it was Stoic thought that prevailed in Rome over the other Greek philosophical schools during this period and especially during the early empire.[55] Much has been said about the affinity of Stoic ideas with those of the traditionally hardy and resilient Romans. In fact, we can find a double approach to the relation between Greek Stoicism and traditional Rome. One affirms that the successors of the Greek philosophers, who had come in the embassy of 155 B.C., introduced adaptations to their philosophy that were necessary to make it acceptable to Roman culture.[56] A good example of this could be Panaetius, who seems to have been most appreciated for having adjusted the rigid, dogmatic doctrines of Stoicism to the Roman taste. Cicero comments that "he [Panaetius] fled from the gloom and harshness [of the rigorous Stoics] and did not approve of their thorny arguments. In one branch of philosophy [ethics] he was gentler, in the other [physics and logic] clearer."[57] Another view is that the popularity of Stoicism in Rome lay in its ability to meet the needs of the people of the time. The idea that the world is ruled by Providence or the notion that man's excellence does not depend on success in obtaining external goods was unquestionably appealing in an age of uncertainties.[58]

Although it is hard to calculate the real influence of philosophers on Roman politics, somehow philosophical ideas played a significant role in a society where religion was mainly ritual and practical with little metaphysical and ethical foundation.[59] In his *De Republica*, Cicero mentions that Scipio often

---

54. Cf. Fowler, "Lucretius and Politics," 120–50.

55. Cf. Gill, "School in the Roman Imperial Period," 33–58; Brunt, *Studies on Stoicism*.

56. For this position, see Earl, *Political Thought of Sallust*, passim, but esp. 113. *Contra*: Rawson, *Intellectual Life*, 64.

57. Cic. *De Fin*, 4.79.

58. Cf. Shaw, "Divine Economy," 16–54.

59. Cf. Griffin, "Philosophy, Politics and Politicians," 36; Brunt, "Philosophy and Religion in the Late Republic," 174–98; and Brunt, *Studies on Stoicism*, 5–8.

discussed politics with Panaetius and Polybius, and gives us evidence of their influence in his other writings.[60] Politics and morality were closely connected in Roman life, so much so that moral concepts seem to have been principally social in application as opposed to private, and they concentrated around ideas of public function rather than more individual ethical notions of right and wrong. The modern distinction between ethical concepts and social values was for them, if not nonexistent, at least somewhat blurred.

The ethical scheme of Stoicism presents a consistent set of ideas that work only within the system and the acknowledgment of all its premises and propositions.[61] This involves a certain division between the world of the wise man—as rare as the phoenix—and the everyday world, where the rest of mortals are striving to become like the wise man.[62] The Stoics claim that virtue is the comprehensive goal of the human being; such a goal is set by man's very nature and is indispensable to achieve the *eudaimonia* that all men pursue.[63] Nothing but virtue is necessary for the well-being of men, and therefore any other so-called goods, such as wealth, health, and fame, are only "preferable" to their corresponding contraries: poverty, sickness, and ill-reputation, which are also strictly "indifferent."[64] As far as goodness is concerned, it is of no importance whether one has success in the external world. What counts is having the right mental attitude toward those things. In a strict sense, nothing can be an evil for the sage because he is not damaged by what the eternal plan

---

60. Cf. Cic. *De Rep*, 1.34. Cf. also *De Off*, 2.51, 2.60. See also Vell, 1.13.3; and Gellius, 13.28. The real impact of the so-called Scipionic circle on Roman politics is difficult to measure precisely. For Momigliano, *Alien Wisdom*, 31: "All the contributions to the theory of Roman imperialism which modern scholars have ascribed to Panaetius are of course pure products of the imagination. There is not one fragment of Panaetius dealing with political matters." For a stimulating debate and different opinions, see esp. Astin, *Scipio Aemilianus*, app. 6: "The Scipionic Circle and the Influence of Panaetius," 294–306; and Sommer, "Scipio Aemilianus, Polybius and the Quest for Friendship in the Second Century BC," 307–18. Cf. also Rawson, "Roman Rulers and the Philosophic Adviser," 233–58; Mazza, *Storia e Ideologia in Tito Livio*, 137–49; Eckstein, *Moral Vision in the Histories of Polybius*, 7–9; and Walbank, *Polybius*, 8.

61. Cf. Long, *Hellenistic Philosophy*, 208: "The Stoics offer a complete world picture and in a sense, as they themselves observed, one must swallow the whole thing or none of it." See also Long, "Stoic Eudaimonism," 196, 201.

62. For the wise man, see Brouwer, *Stoic Sage*, esp. 96–134.

63. Cf. Diog. Laert, 7.96. See also 7.53. Describing the fascinating topic of Stoicism in depth would go far beyond the scope of this book, and here I will only give an extremely brief summary of its contents. For good studies on Stoicism published lately, see Inwood, *Cambridge Companion to the Stoics*; Sellars, *Stoicism*; Brunt, *Studies in Stoicism*.

64. Cf. *SVF* 3.119. Stoicism differs on this point from Aristotle's view, in which *eudaimonia* was also achieved by virtue, but which recognized that other possessions may also help in attaining it.

of providence had designed for him and accepts everything, maintaining his soul unalterable even toward great misfortunes. Suffering is ordained by Nature not for its own sake, but for the good of the whole, and men are not always capable of seeing and understanding the deep causes of things. It is not always easy to agree with this optimistic outlook toward natural events no matter how terrible they may seem, and this appears to be one of the difficulties in achieving perfect conformity with Stoicism.[65]

The way to reach perfect happiness is, therefore, to live according to Nature.[66] The human being, with his power of reasoning, is the only creature who can deliberately act harmoniously with Nature, and therefore it is in his power to achieve the final goal of *eudaimonia*. Happiness is not only within the power of all human beings but also what we are made for and equipped to attain. Happiness appears, then, as something objective that is the same for all because it springs from our human nature. To engage with this view is to believe that we are all made with an integral *telos*, a goal for whose sake everything is done, but that is not itself done for the sake of anything: in other words, the *summum bonum*.[67] In general, ancient philosophy started from the supposition that human actions were undertaken for a purpose to fulfill an end: to reach the *summum bonum* of our nature or *eudaimonia*. For the stoics, in fulfilling this end or *telos*—given by nature—our actions must not be based on feelings or utility,[68] but on virtue, the perfection of human nature: what Stoicism tries to teach men is precisely how to behave as proper men.[69] The holistic view of the person made it easier to relate all aspects of life to one purpose: man has a function to accomplish as a human being, as a member of a family, as a citizen, soldier, and so on. Human nature works as a principle that gives unity to the fulfillment of our *telos*: "the end represents reasoning well in the selection and de-selection of things according to nature."[70]

---

65. For determinism, see Frede, "Stoic Determinism," 179–205; and Sharples, *Stoics, Epicureans and Sceptics*, 76–78.

66. Cf. SVF 3.16; Diog. Laert, 7.87–89. Nature, God, and Providence are pretty much the same in Stoic terminology. According to Long, *Hellenistic Philosophy*, 169, Nature is a complex term: "Nature plays a double role in any causal explanation. To say of something that it is natural in Stoicism is to combine description with evaluation. Nature embraces both the way things are and the way they should be." See also Long, "Logical Basis of Stoic Ethics," 134–55.

67. Cf. Arist. *EN*, 1095a16.

68. To name two of the bases of some modern theories.

69. Cf. Diog. Laert, 7.85–86 (SVF 3.178). Long, "Greek Ethics after MacIntyre," 158, says that "the project of ancient moral philosophy is to teach us how to become what we essentially are."

70. Stob, 2.76, 9–15. See also Diog. Laert, 7.88. According to MacIntyre, *After Virtue*, 56, "Moral arguments within the Aristotelian tradition (. . .) involve at least one central functional concept,

Stoicism, then, shared with Plato and Aristotle the doctrine that virtue was necessary to be happy; where the Stoics stood alone was in their claim that happiness consisted *only* in ethical virtue. Of all the Greek schools, Stoicism was perhaps the most ambitious and idealistic one: the sage is a perfect man, and he should resemble the perfection of Nature. Men should develop all the virtues, which is not so difficult, as they are all connected.[71] Understanding one's life as a whole and developing oneself as a unity were very much the purposes of ancient moral ethics; this was, of course, related to the function or mission that one played in society. One's happiness depended on whether one had accomplished the task assigned by nature, and there was no conflict (in theory) between what was good for one as a man and good for those with whom one formed a community.

Making sense of human life as a life with a mission or duty to fulfill toward oneself and others implied that morality was not something that one could choose to ignore; part of being properly human involved living morally.[72] Life and happiness depended heavily on morality, and the attainment of virtues was indispensable for fulfilling one's *telos* as an individual and as a member of a society. This meant that the virtues were on the one hand objective and permanent with regard to nature, and on the other "socially" definable according to one's function.[73] Thus, man appeared to be "answerable" for his actions: he could be questioned as to whether he had or had not fulfilled his task.[74]

We have now arrived at the difficult problem of personal responsibility and freedom. How much are we preconditioned by our personality to act in a particular way? How much are we responsible for developing such a personality? According to Stoicism, it is difficult to change one's own personality, especially once the inner conditions of a person are settled. Moral determinism or necessity has significant consequences when assessing an

---

the concept of man understood as having an essential nature and an essential purpose or function." Long, "Greek Ethics after MacIntyre," argues that Stoicism belongs to this Aristotelian tradition refuting—with abundant evidence—MacIntyre, for whom the Stoic system would be something different and apart from this tradition. See also Long, "Stoic Eudaimonism," 179.

71. Cf. Arist. *EN*, 6. 1144b32–1145a6. For the attainment and progress on virtue, see Roskam, *On the Path to Virtue*, 15–138.

72. Cf. Morgan, *Popular Morality*, 207–10.

73. Cf. Siep, "Virtue, Values and Moral Objectivity," 83–99, esp. 91, and Gill, "In What Sense Are Ancient Ethical Norms Universal?," 15–40.

74. For the complexity of Stoic moral responsibility, see Long and Sedley, *Hellenistic Philosophers*, 392–94, and examples in 386–91. For the same topic not with regard only to Stoicism but in more general terms to ancient ethics, see Adkins, *Merit and Responsibility*.

individual's responsibility for an action; it is necessary to put the emphasis more on the inner condition that is responsible for the act than on the specific action done by the person in a certain situation.[75] This, however, does not exclude the possibility of improvement. Not only can experience affect the internal conditions of an individual, but also society's censures or recompenses may produce long-lasting effects on one's inner nature.[76]

Coming back to the relationship between Stoicism and Rome: how far can we take the claim of finding Stoic influences on Roman writings, on Roman politics, and even on Roman morality? Firstly it is important to distinguish between subscribing to a philosophical creed and being naturally exposed to a certain language and environment. It is difficult to establish connections between particular philosophical doctrines and particular policies, and it could involve simplistic analysis of complex and multilayered realities. Philosophy, rather than giving absolute or unequivocal answers, provided the technical language for intellectuals to analyze and justify their moral and political decisions in a rationalized manner.[77] Thus, the influence of Stoicism on Roman life should not be overvalued; in fact it could be a good exercise just to imagine for a moment what Roman values would have been like had Stoicism not entered the scene at all. Probably not very different, but equipped with fewer philosophical and theoretical arguments for explaining them.

It was in the first century B.C., mainly through Cicero, that there was a formal attempt to define and systematize what has been called *philosophia togata*.[78] He transmitted Greek doctrines on ethics, epistemology, and theology to the Romans in Latin, developing a philosophical vocabulary for which he kept some key Greek words—such as *philosophia* itself—and created new Latin ones. It is to him that we owe the Stoic emphasis on virtue and reason when talking about morality in Rome, even though he regarded himself as a skeptical Academic.

---

75. Cf. Frede, "Stoic Determinism," 196. I shall develop this topic more fully when I deal with Tacitus; see chapter 5 in this book.

76. On Greco-Roman views on character, see, for example, Gill, "Character-Development in Plutarch and Tacitus," 469–87; Gill, "Character-Personality Distinction," 1–31; Halliwell, "Traditional Greek Conceptions of Character," 32–59; and Pelling, "Childhood and Personality in Greek Biography," 213–44. Also Pelling, "Plutarch," 231; and Gill, *Personality in Greek Epic, Tragedy and Philosophy*.

77. Cf. Griffin, "Philosophy, Politics and Politicians at Rome," 34–37. For a similar view, see Brunt, "Stoicism and the Principate," 31 = *Studies in Stoicism*, 304; Wirszubski, *Libertas as a Political Idea at Rome*, 138.

78. Cf. Barnes and Griffin, *Philosophia Togata*.

As stated before, Cicero's aim to define *virtus* and to relate the narrower sense of this term to its origin and to its broader sense seems to have been achieved in the *Tusculan Disputations*: "and yet though perhaps all right-minded states [*rectae animi adfectiones*] are called virtue [*virtutes*], the term is not appropriate for all virtues, but all have got the name from the single virtue that was found to outshine the rest [*una ceteris excellebat*], for it is from the word 'man' that the word 'virtue' is derived [*ex viro virtus*]; but man's peculiar virtue is fortitude [*viri autem propria maxime est fortitudo*], of which there are two main functions, namely, scorn of death and scorn of pain. These, then, we must exercise if we wish to prove possessors of virtue [*si virtutis compotes*], or rather, since the word 'virtue' is borrowed from the word 'man,' if we wish to be men [*si viri volumus esse*]."[79] And later in the same treatise he defines *virtus* as a more generic term: "virtue [*virtus*] is an equable and harmonious disposition of the soul [*adfectio animi constans conveniensque*] making those praiseworthy in whom it is found, and is of its own nature and by itself praiseworthy [*laudabilis*], apart from any question of expediency; there spring from it good inclinations, opinions, actions, and all that makes right reason; though indeed virtue itself can best be summed up as right reason [*ipsa virtus brevissume recta ratio dici potest*]."[80]

We see clearly how there is an overlap in Cicero's definitions. It is not the case that one word serves to identify two completely different realities, as homonyms do, but that even though the two realities expressed by the same word are similar and interconnected, we can still recognize them as two different things. On the one hand we have a particular word to define bravery, and on the other a general term to classify any good qualities, bravery among them.

It might seem a happy development (or it seems to me at least) that the word *virtus* deriving from *vir* came to mean both the excellence of man manifested in actions, and "the natural perfection of a rational being as a rational being."[81] We can say then that while *virilis-virtus* or *virtus*-courage appeared to

---

79. Cic. Tusc. Disp, 2.43: *Atqui vide ne, cum omnes rectae animi adfectiones virtutes appellentur, non sit hoc proprium nomen omnium, sed ab ea quae una ceteris excellebat, omnes nominatae sint. Appellata est enim ex viro virtus; viri autem propria maxime est fortitudo, cuius munera duo sunt maxima, mortis dolorisque contemptio. Utendum est igitur his, si virtutis compotes, vel potius si viri volumus esse, quoniam a viris virtus nomen est mutuata.*

80. Cic. Tusc. Disp, 4.34: *Quando igitur virtus est adfectio animi constans conveniensque, laudabiles efficiens eos, in quibus est, et ipsa per se sua sponte separata etiam utilitate laudabilis, ex ea proficiscuntur honestae voluntates sententiae actiones omnisque recta ratio (quamquam ipsa virtus brevissume recta ratio dici potest).*

81. Diog. Laert, 7.94.

be the attribute proper of a man, "*virtus*-virtue" came to mean what should be the attribute of mankind and it makes sense to call it *humana-virtus*. One might also say that manliness itself had broadened so as to mean the attribute proper to mankind, rather than just men as a sex: now women, slaves, or even barbarians had the chance to develop their excellence as human beings.[82] What was the mark and identification of *virilitas*, that is, courage, evolved to signify the identification of *humanitas* (virtue in general to all mankind).[83] *Virtus*, in the beginning the characteristic of the male sex—*vir*—became an ideal attribute of the human being, an ideal that could actually be achieved: "there is no human being of any race who, if he finds a guide, cannot attain virtue."[84] The semantic expansion of the concept of *virtus* shows the more profound understanding of human nature that philosophy was able to express and the development of the thought from the more physically oriented man to the intellectually oriented human being.

Before I continue with the expansion of the concept of *virtus*, a long and complicated process, I would like to say something about the problem that this overlapping of meanings creates in translating the word *virtus*. The problem actually lies not only in the act of translating *virtus* into other languages—especially in view of the difficulty in translating not just a word but a concept—but also in determining how it was understood by Latin speakers themselves. Some cases are more easily identified than others; one can be almost sure about the meaning of *virtus* in the following passage: *absolveruntque admiratione magis virtutis quam iure causae*: "And they acquitted him, more in admiration of his *virtus* than from the justice of his cause."[85] To contrast virtue with the justice of the law would make no sense at all, and yet there are cases where a courageous action can be placed in opposition to justice; as in this instance, where the war hero Horatius kills his own sister who was crying for her dead betrothed, Horatius' enemy. He is condemned for treason, but his father's appeal manages to save him. The jury absolves him more in admiration of his valor [*virtus*] than from the justice of his cause. This is also the

---

82. For women, see, for example, Livy, 2.13.11 on Cloelia; for slaves, see Tac. *Ann*, 15.57 on the death of Epicharis; and for barbarians, Tac. *Ger*, 29.1 or 35.4.

83. The word *humanitas* has no easy translation; in one sense, it meant humane behavior, but a deeper understanding of the word involved the process of helping a man to develop himself in accordance with his true and proper human nature. For more on *humanitas* and a fuller bibliography, see Lind, "Thought, Life and Literature at Rome," 55–68.

84. Cic. *De Leg*, 1.10.30: *nec est quisquam gentis ullius, qui ducem nactus ad virtutem pervenire non posit*. In this same line are Sallust's prologues.

85. Livy, 1.26.12.

case of Ennius' phrase "justice is better than courage [*melius est virtute ius*]."⁸⁶ We can find many examples of the same situation, or even more clearly, cases where *virilis-virtus* is definitely held by bad men, such as Catiline in Sallust,⁸⁷ for whom bravery was perhaps the only virtue he could claim; or when Caesar decides not to punish some men for their crimes: "overlooking much in consideration of their valor, he postponed the whole matter [*multa virtuti eorum concedens rem totam distulit*]."⁸⁸ The golden shield given to Augustus, mentioned by him in the *Res Gestae*, is another case where *virtus* is clearly used as the particular virtue of courage, where it is listed as one of the four virtues: "a golden shield was placed in the Curia Iulia, whose inscription testified that the Senate and the Roman people gave me this in recognition of my valor, my clemency, my justice, and my piety [*clupeus aureus in curia Iulia positus, quem mihi senatum populumque Romanum dare virtutis clementiaeque et iustitiae et pietatis caussa*]."⁸⁹ If *virtus* in these cases were used as something broader than courage, the text would be meaningless and contradictory.

There are other circumstances where *virtus* is used with its general ethical meaning, referring to a particularly good standard of behavior. When Lucan says that "*virtus* and supreme power do not come together [*virtus et summa potestas non coeunt*],"⁹⁰ it cannot mean anything else but the nonspecific moral virtue, because courage and supreme power is a pair not difficult to find. We also find this general ethical usage of *virtus* in Sallust, especially when he argues that ambition was "a vice nearer to a virtue: *vitium propius virtutem erat.*"⁹¹ And, of course, in the passage from Lucilius quoted earlier.⁹²

However, there are some passages where it is very difficult to discern which kind of *virtus* the author is referring to. See, for example, the translation of Valerius Maximus 2.6.1, *cum aliquanto faciliorem virtutis ad luxuriam quam luxuriae ad virtutem transitum*: "seeing how much easier was the passage of *manliness* into luxury than of luxury into *manliness*."⁹³ We can see that *virtus* here could have been translated also as "virtue," which contrasts nicely with luxury; or even as "courage," as an association is made with *labor, patientia*, and

---

86. Ennius, *Hec. Ly*, 200–201.
87. Cf. Sall. *BC* 57.5; 60.4; 60.7.
88. Caesar, *BC* 3.60.1.
89. *Res Gestae*, 34.2.
90. Lucan 8.494.
91. Sall. *BC*, 11.1, Campbell's trans., 2007. Although Eisenhut thinks that here *virtus* means bravery.
92. 1096–1208.
93. Trans. by Shackleton Bailey, Loeb ed., 2000. My italics.

fortitudo. On the other hand, the oriental customs, to which Valerius Maximus is making reference here, were very much regarded as the pleasures proper to women and therefore opposed to "manliness." Other instances of this are found in Tacitus, for example, when in the *Histories* he says, "Their strength was also corrupted by luxury in contrast to the ancient discipline and maxims of our forefathers, in whose day virtue formed a better foundation for the Roman state than money [*apud quos virtute quam pecunia res Romana melius stetit*]."[94] And also in the *Annals*, when he complains that Germanicus did not have the proper funeral honors: "Where were those usages of the ancients—the image placed at the head of the couch, the set poems to the memory of the departed virtue, the panegyrics [*meditata ad memoriam virtutis carmina et laudationes*], the tears, the imitation (if no more) of sorrow?"[95] We will see more cases of debatable translations of *virtus* because of the ambiguous usage in the text later on when we discuss *virtus* in each particular historian, but now I would like to concentrate on Cicero, as an author in whose works we have more evidence of the two senses of *virtus* being juxtaposed.

Cicero and *Virtus*

It has been said that in his speeches Cicero uses the word *virtus* in the traditionally Roman meaning of bravery or courage, and that in most of his philosophical works he brings forward the "*arete* meaning" of *virtus*.[96] As we shall see, the situation is more complicated than that, but it is true that in his speeches Cicero gives great pre-eminence to *virtus*-courage or *virilis-virtus*, sometimes because it is related to the content of the speeches or the rhetorical points demanded by the political situation. Let us see some passages of the *Pro Murena*: "By serving in the war which was the most important war then being fought by the Roman people, he gave proof of his bravery [*Meruisse vero stipendia in eo bello quod tum populus Romanus non modo maximum sed etiam solum gerebat virtutis*],"[97] or "I cannot think of a more impor-

---

94. Tac. *Hist*, 2.69: *et vires et luxu corrumpebatur, contra veterem disciplinam et instituta maiorum apud quos virtute quam pecunia res Romana melius stetit.*

95. Tac. *Ann*, 3.5: *ubi illa veterum instituta, propositam toro effigiem, meditata ad memoriam virtutis carmina et laudationes et lacrimas vel doloris imitamenta?*

96. Cf. Eisenhut, *Virtus Romana*, 57–76; Sarsila, *Being a Man*, 132; Pöschl, *Grundwerte römischer Staatsgesinnung in den Geschichteswerken der Sallust*, 23; Büchner, "Altrömische und Horazische Virtus," 11; Liebers, *Virtus bei Cicero*, 158.

97. Cic. *Pro Mur*, 12. See also *Pro Mur*, 16; 32; 37.

tant campaign or one conducted with greater skill and valor [*neque maius bellum commemorari possit neque maiore consilio et virtute gestum*]."[98] There is no need for him to say what kind of *virtus* he is emphasizing; here Cicero is clearly talking about Murena's valor; the word does not need a qualifier. The same can be said in the case of the *Pro Milone*, where Cicero attributes *virtus* several times to Milo, and presents him as a brave man who has done many things *pro rei publicae causa*.[99]

For further illustration of this usage of *virtus*, we can give two passages of the *De Provinciis Consularibus*. Here Cicero is again praising Marius' and Caesar's *militaris virtus* and not their moral virtue in general: "The great Gaius Marius himself, whose divine and outstanding bravery was our stay after grievous disasters [*Ipse ille C. Marius, cuius divina atque eximia virtus . . .*]."[100] "Therefore let Gaul remain under the guardianship of him [Caesar] to whose honor, valor, and good fortune it has been entrusted [*Quare sit in eius tutela Gallia, cuius fidei, virtuti, felicitati commendata est*]."[101] And the same meaning is conveyed in several passages of *De Imp. Cn. Pomp*: "Such is the superhuman and unbelievable courage as a commander [*Est haec divina atque incredibilis virtus imperatoris*],"[102] or "the danger . . . was removed by the inspired strategy and extraordinary valor of Cn. Pompeius [*Periculum . . . Cn. Pompei divino consilio ac singulari virtute depulsum est*]."[103]

One possible way of identifying the type of *virtus* is looking at whether it appears in the plural or singular. In the plural, *virtutes* almost always meant virtues or good qualities; one person cannot have "courages" or "braveries," so when the word is written in the plural, the meaning is clearer. This can be seen explicitly, for example, in "not only is this military valor needed which is so peculiarly to be found in Gnaeus Pompeius, but other great and numerous moral qualities/virtues as well [*non solum militaris illa virtus, quae est in Cn. Pompeio singularis, sed aliae quoque virtutes animi magnae et multae requiruntur*]."[104]

When defining the ideal general, Cicero says that he must possess four "attributes [*res*]: knowledge of warfare [*scientiam rei militaris*], ability [*virtutem*],

---

98. Cic. *Pro Mur*, 33.
99. See, e.g., *Pro Mil*, 3; 6; 41; 101. For Cicero's presentation of Milo, see Dyck, "Narrative Obfuscation, Philosophical Topoi," 219–41.
100. Cic. *Prov. Cons*, 13.32.
101. Cic. *Prov. Cons*, 14.35.
102. Cic. *De Imp. Cn. Pomp*, 13.36.
103. Cic. *De Imp. Cn. Pomp*, 4.10.
104. Cic. *De Imp. Cn. Pomp*, 22.64. The difference of the plural and singular is also seen in Cic. *De Imp. Cn. Pomp*, 1.3; 10.27; 11.29; 12.33; 13.36; 23.67; 23.68.

prestige [*auctoritatem*], and luck [*felicitatem*]."[105] Clearly "ability" here should be "courage." What kind of ability, or ability for what, might a general need if he already has *scientia*? What he needs besides prestige, knowledge of military subjects, and luck is valor to undertake brave actions. Although "ability" can be an adequate translation for *virtus* in some cases, in military contexts it is much safer and more fitting to use "courage."

The same could be said about the translation of some passages in the *Pro Murena*, where *militaris virtus*, meaning *fortitudo*, appears in a preeminent position. Cicero praises Murena's exceptional bravery (*egregia virtus*),[106] and greater valor (*maiore virtute*),[107] but then it seems that, quite without reason, the translator has switched to the other meaning: "you spoke with truth and conviction of his exceptional virtue [*praestanti virtute*]."[108] Why not "bravery" again, since it was this bravery to which Cicero was referring to before?[109]

At this point the various possibilities of interpreting *virtus* may seem a little overwhelming. Is there a definitive way of deciding what kind of *virtus* the Roman authors were talking about? To illustrate this difficulty, I will now show some of the mixed results regarding the translation of *virtus* in different editions of Latin texts. Acknowledging the great achievement that these translations represented for the general public, there are some cases in which it is not easy to understand or follow the logic of the choice: in the same paragraph, talking of the same thing, *virtus* is translated as valor and then as good qualities: "the danger . . . was removed by the inspired strategy and extraordinary valor [*virtute*] of Cn. Pompeius; while on the Eastern front the conduct of the campaign by that fine general Lucullus suggests that the great and glorious achievements with which it began were due more to his good qualities [*virtuti*] than to his good luck."[110] Why not use valor again, especially when

---

105. Cic. *De Imp. Cn. Pomp*, 9.28. Trans. Grose Hodge, Loeb ed., 1927, repr. 2000.
106. Cic. *Pro Mur*, 32.
107. Cic. *Pro Mur*, 33.
108. Cic. *Pro Mur*, 66. Transl. C. MacDonald, Loeb ed., 1977, repr. 1996.
109. Of course this problem is not confined to the Loeb editions and it is present in other translations as well. See, for example, how both Eisenhut, *Virtus Romana*, 23, and Sarsila, *Being a Man*, 31, agree that *virtus* in the Twelve Tables (table X) means "excellence": *qui coronam parit ipse pecuniave eius virtutisve ergo arduitur ei* . . . (Cf. Pliny, *NH* 21.7; Cic. *De Leg*, 2.24.60). The Loeb edition (1938, trans. Warmington, repr. 1998) gives "courage" instead. In this case, I agree with the Loeb.
110. Cic. *De Imp. Cn. Pomp*, 4.10: *Sed tamen alterius partis periculum (. . .), Cn. Pompei divino consilio ac singulari virtute depulsum est; in altera parte ita res a L. Lucullo summo viro est administrata, ut initia illa rerum gestarum magna atque praeclara non felicitati eius, sed virtuti, haec autem extrema, quae nuper acciderunt, non culpae, sed fortunae tribuenda esse videantur.*

the same Lucullus a bit later on is praised for his valor?[111] The word is, after all, in the singular and within a military context!

Sometimes Cicero himself is deliberately ambiguous. "In Heaven's name, what has happened to the customs and the *virtus* of our ancestors? [*Pro di immortales! Ubi est ille mos virtusque maiorum?*]."[112] Or: "Gone, gone forever is that *virtus* that used to be found in this republic and caused brave men to suppress a citizen traitor with keener punishment than the most bitter foe [*fuit ista quondam in hac re publica virtus, ut viri fortes acrioribus suppliciis civem perniciosum quam acerbissimum hostem coercerent*]."[113] *Virtus* here implies the old Roman way of life, at whose decline Cicero is hinting in these speeches. Its meaning here is at the same time specific courage and virtue in general. When *virtus* means something rather vague related to the high moral standards of the ancestors and their expression of political freedom in courageously defending the *res publica*, it seems as if *virtus* is being used as a political slogan: *Virtus . . . propria est Romana generis et seminis.*[114]

This political usage of *virtus* was not exclusive to Cicero. We will see how the historians especially seized on this sense of the word, which fitted in very well with their purposes in historical writing. They took advantage of this ambiguity and worked toward presenting a distinct view of Rome and her past. The absence of any better word made *virtus* signify "traditionally free, courageous, morally good, Roman." More difficult to discern is whether this notion was the result of a conscious decision or if it sprang up spontaneously, as an unintentional desire to project an image that could spur the Roman of the present day to action. I am inclined to take the latter view, though at some point they must have realized that they were using an idea and giving it a specific political content; but this did not affect their decision to use it all the more. The claims they were making were at the same time expedient and heartfelt, therefore a valid affirmation to put forward in history as it fulfilled history's two main objectives, being both truthful and useful.

Another serious question about the concept of *virtus* was its purpose. As Cicero said, men did not regard *virtus* as its own reward; they expected a payoff for their display of courage in battle or their virtuous behavior. The prize

---

111. Cic. *De Imp. Cn. Pomp*, 8.20.

112. Cic. *Phil*, 8.23. Shackelton Bailey's trans. 1986, p. 226, says "spirit." The Loeb edition, 1926, repr. 2001, trans. Ker, has "old-world spirit" for *virtus*.

113. Cic. *Cat*, 1.3.

114. Cic. *Phil*, 4.13. For other instances of the same usage, see *Verr*, 4.81: "No man should complain that *virtus* counts for more than anything in Rome, when it is *virtus* that makes Rome the mistress of the world." See also *Pro Mil*, 105; *Verr*, 4.73; *Arch*, 15; *Rosc. Amer*, 27.

for *virtus* was honor and glory: "*virtus* clearly desires honor, and has no other reward [*vult plane virtus honorem, nec est virtutis ulla alia merces*]"[115] (see figure 2); "glory ... follows virtue like a shadow [*gloria ... tamen virtutem tamquam umbra sequitur*]."[116] This is true regarding military *virtus* and any other moral virtue. Cicero is quite insistent in stressing the recompense for *virtus*: "Now the law that prescribes the worship of those of the human race who have been deified, such as Hercules, and the rest, makes it clear that while the souls of all men are immortal, those of brave and good men are divine [*sed fortium bonorumque divinos*]."[117] A special prize is deserved by all those who have shown *virtus* in the service of the state. This is for Cicero the highest calling, and it brings the greatest rewards: "For all who have saved, defended, or increased their fatherland, a special place in the heaven has been assigned, where they may enjoy an eternal life of happiness."[118]

The natural reward and recognition of *virtus* in Rome was glory, which played a particularly important role in the understanding of how the social and political system worked. The social arrangements in republican Rome expressed the idea that the first Romans had achieved glory by performing deeds of *virtus* and thus had become known as nobles. These *nobiles* passed on their glory to their heirs and sons, who felt that this inherited *gloria* imposed a sort of duty on them to perform the same great deeds as their ancestors: there was a certain competition to maintain the high standards of *virtus* set up by their predecessors.[119] Deeds of *virtus* belonged to the Romans in a very special way: "Virtus [...] is the especial possession of the Roman race and seed. Hold on to this, citizens, which your ancestors have left you as an inheritance. All other things are false, uncertain, fleeting, fickle, only *virtus* is planted with deep roots and cannot be shaken by any violence nor moved from its place. By this did your ancestors first conquer the whole of Italy, then destroy Carthage, overthrow Numantia, bring powerful kings and warlike races into subjection to this empire."[120] This passage can be understood as

---

115. Cic. *De Rep*, 3.28.40. See also Cic. *Brut*, 281: *cum honos sit praemium virtutis*. This link between *honos* and *virtus* is explicitly shown on a coin. Cf. Bieber, "Honos and Virtus," 25–34.

116. Cf. Cic. *Tusc. Disp*, 1.45.109.

117. Cic. *De Leg*, 2.11.28.

118. Cic. *De Rep*, 6.13: *Omnibus qui patriam conservaverint, adiuverint, auxerint, certum esse in caelo definitum locum, ubi beati aevo sempiterno fruantur*.

119. For the role of the ancestors, see Flower, *Ancestor Masks and Aristocratic Power*, esp. 185–222.

120. Cic. *Phil*, 4.13: *Virtus ... propia est Romana generis et seminis. Hanc retinete, quaeso, quam vobis tamquam hereditatem maiores vestri relinquerunt. Nam cum alia omnia falsa, incerta sint, caduca, mobilia, virtus est una altissimis defixa radicibus, quae numquam vi ulla labefactari potest,*

Cicero urging his Roman audience to perform acts of *virtus*: they had inherited the glory of *virtus* from their ancestors, but that was not enough: they now had to show that they could win it by themselves.[121]

Cicero addresses the risks of living or relying on the glory of one's predecessor without doing anything to achieve it personally in *De Officiis*. In trying to reunite the *utile* with the *honestum*, Cicero insists that glory—which was certainly something *utile* for the individual—should not be separated from the *honestum*—or virtuous conduct serving the state. This separation, according to Cicero, was one of the main causes of the ruin of the republic.[122] Even if the glory that an aristocrat was trying to achieve was completely *honestum*, it was at the same time very expedient (*utile*) to the competitive lifestyle of the politics of the Roman Republic. To serve the state to achieve *gloria* was all right; in fact, it was a legitimate aspiration for a statesman, but the "passion" for glory was to be avoided: "Beware also the desire for glory, as I have said. For it destroys the liberty for which men of great spirit ought to be in competition."[123] One's desire for glory—if immoderate—could rob others of their freedom.[124] The risk of having a system in which *gloria* was a reward for having served the state by deeds of *virtus* was that the boundaries could become unclear.

Coming back to Cicero's description of courage as one of the cardinal virtues in *De Officiis*—as well as in other philosophical treatises—he seems aware that the translation of *andreia* as *virtus* might create confusion in the readers, and to avoid the seeming tautology of saying something like "*virtus* is a *virtus*...," he chooses the word *fortitudo* for *virtus*-courage or *virilis-virtus*. In *De Republica* he says "this virtue is called bravery which is made up of nobility

---

numquam demoveri loco. Hac virtute maiores vestri primum universam Italiam devicerunt, deinde Karthaginem exciderunt, Numantiam everterunt, potentissimos reges, bellicossisimas gentes in dicionem huius imperii redegerunt.

121. S. Treggiari, "Ancestral Virtues and Vices," 144, says that "*virtus* was the best possible inheritance from one's ancestors. Cicero can claim it for the whole Roman people." I believe that Cicero in *Phil*, 4.13, is referring to this "call to *virtus*" or a certain passion for performing deeds of *virtus* proper to the Romans as what is actually being inherited, but what one inherits is not *virtus* as such—since that is personal—but glory: "the best inheritance that is handed down from fathers to children and one that is better than any patrimony is the glory of *virtus* [*gloria virtutis*] and worthy deeds," Cic. *De Off*, 1.121

122. Cf. also Sall. *BC* 2.9–3.5 for the same idea that decay in morality brought the decline of the republic.

123. Cic. *De Off*, 1.68: *cavenda etiam est gloriae cupiditas ... eripit enim libertatem*. I use the translation of Griffin and Atkins, at p. 28. Cf. Long, "Cicero's Politics in *De Officiis*," 216–17.

124. I shall come back to this important topic of *virtus* and freedom when I deal with Tacitus, in chapter 5.

of spirit and an entire contempt for pain and death."[125] *Fortitudo* was not a common word before Cicero,[126] but he chose to use it so that he could reserve *virtus* to mean "virtue" as both the sum total of all the good qualities and the term to identify any individual good quality.[127] *Virtus* in this general sense also implied strength, which is closely related to fortitude: "There is mighty power in the virtues [*magna vis est in virtutibus*]; rouse them, if maybe they slumber. At once you will have the foremost of all, I mean fortitude [*princeps fortitudo*], which will compel you to assume a spirit [*animo*] that will make you despise and count as nothing all that can fall to the lot of men."[128]

One important aspect of Roman political thought is the doctrine that there is a practical connection between the morality of citizens and their leaders on the one hand and the success of the state on the other.[129] Ennius had said it with his *moribus antiquis res stat Romana virisque*.[130] And Cicero reaffirms that moral excellence must be the foundation of the successful state in several of his philosophical works.[131] Cicero's message can be summarized like this: only if political leaders are men of *virtus* can the republic survive. This is what he says in *De Republica* and also in *De Officiis*, which has often been considered his political testament. Politics for Cicero meant a way of living and acting. The word *officium* was perhaps, then, the best reflection of his main idea: the appropriate action, function, duty, obligation. They all point to acting in a fitting way. A society like this, oriented to action, conceives types of excellence or virtues as those qualities that enable an individual to *do* what his role requires. Because the whole glory of virtue is in activity,[132] it was not enough to learn it or possess it as if it were some sort of knowledge

---

125. Cic. *De Rep*, 5.7.9: *quae virtus fortitudo vocatur, in qua est magnitudo animi, mortis dolorisque magna contemptio*.

126. Although *fortis* was used as the adjective of someone possessing *virtus*. For this, see Hellegouarc'h, *Vocabulaire Latin*, 247–48; and Moore, *Artistry and Ideology*, 14–15.

127. Cf. Sarsila, *Being a Man*, 139–40.

128. Cic. *Tusc. Disp*, 3.17.36: *Magna vis est in virtutibus: eas excita, si forte dormiunt. Iam tibi aderit princeps fortitudo, quae te animo tanto esse coget, ut omnia quae possint homini evenire contemnas et pro nihilo putes*. For the didactic purpose of the *Tusculan Disputations*, a "drama on Roman education," see the excellent analysis by Gildenhard, "Paideia Romana," esp. chap. 2.

129. An idea that will become even more important for the principate; see chapters 4 and 5 in this book.

130. Ennius, *Ann*, 5.156.

131. See *De Leg*, 1.62; and *Tusc. Disp*, 1.1.2.

132. Cic. *De Off*, 1.19.

only; *virtus* is to be put into practice by deeds not words, and the noblest use was the government of the state.[133]

The practice of *virtus*—in the twofold sense of *virilis-virtus* and *humana-virtus*—is therefore very much a social ideal. There is something public in the definition and interpretation of it. A person has courage for something, to defend or protect the weak, other men, or his country. Good standards of behavior implied behaving well toward the community. The individual had a social and public role to fulfill; it was not enough to be "privately good" or "privately brave," at least for the Roman aristocrats. They were the ones who had a mission toward the state, of supporting, maintaining, and enlarging it, while others had a mission toward the aristocrats. The idea of *telos* appears in this Roman identification of the function of men. It becomes *telos* as such only when one makes the link with Greek philosophy, but that does not mean that it did not shape the Roman collective imagination before in a prephilosophical manner.[134]

Cicero's contribution to philosophical debate in Rome is difficult to estimate with justice. He not only showed the Romans a method of doing philosophy—the Platonic dialogue—but also provided them with the right precepts according to Roman standards. Regarding *virtus*, his novelty was not the identification of this concept with that of *arete*, but the conscientious and systematic way he dealt with both. By using well-known conventional concepts and examples based on Roman traditions[135] together with philosophical arguments, he was informing ethical and political decision-making in a very forceful way. What he looked for in philosophy was not realistic compromises—he had enough of those in real life—but inspiring ideals that could move people to act courageously. He wrote philosophy to encourage himself and others to be brave.[136] He showed that philosophy was not only speculation but also an

---

133. Cic. *De Rep*, 1.2.1: *Nec vero habere virtutem satis est quasi artem aliquam, nisi utare . . . usus autem eius est maximus civitatis gubernatio et earum ipsarum rerum quas isti in angulis personant, reapse non oratione perfectio.*

134. Cicero is reluctant to attribute too much importance to Greek philosophy in defining what he considers Roman tradition; see, e.g., *De Amic*, 6.20–21: "There are those who place the chief good in *virtus* and that is really a noble view. (. . .) To proceed then, let us interpret the word *virtus* by the familiar usage of our everyday life and speech, and not in pompous phrase apply to it the precise standards that certain philosophers use."

135. For *exempla* in Cicero, see van der Blom, *Cicero's Role Models*.

136. In "The Composition of the *Academica*," esp. 2–14, Griffin deals with Cicero's reasons for writing philosophy under three headings: intellectual, personal, and political. Although this scheme accounts for the specific case of the *Academica*, it can also help us to understand Cicero's motives for his philosophical writings more broadly.

arena for displaying courage. When writing about *virtus* in philosophical terms, Cicero was displaying his own *virtus* in the Roman way.

The Social Expansion of *Virtus*

For the Roman *nobilitas*, *virtus* was a term primarily and originally concerned with them.[137] They were who, at the formation of the republic, had performed acts of *virtus* in the service of the state and, precisely for that reason, had become *nobiles*. Thus, the republican *nobilitas* expressed its ideal in the concept of *virtus*: the Roman aristocrat was expected to show courage and wisdom—*virtus* and *ingenium*—which were seen and accepted as the most needed and important qualities for a general or a magistrate. War and public office were the two main ways—in fact the only ways for an aristocrat—to serve the republic. They were also the only ways for achieving true *gloria*. Glory and honor were the rewards of *virtus* shown in the public service of the state. In its strict application for the nobility, *virtus* was a performative concept because it put the emphasis on actions (*facta*) and at the same time an exclusive one, because it was only the service of the *res publica* that was regarded as the proper field for the exercise of the noble's ability.

But this aristocratic ideal of *virtus* that involved the whole *gens*—past generations as well as future ones—started gradually to shift its emphasis. Even by the time of M. Porcius Cato at the beginning of the second century B.C., the nobility was being seriously attacked for the abandonment of the standards of public and private morality, for feminine luxury, and for the decay of religious observation. More and more the stress was laid on the fact that true honor and glory did not come with birth or blood but through good deeds and *virtus*, which started to seem independent or disconnected from the *nobilitas*. The glory of the ancestors was now a weak support for the claim of possessing *virtus*. What really mattered were the individual's achievements and his personal moral standards.

Cato, Marius, and Cicero—all *novi*—in their speeches and writings appeared to have introduced the idea that *virtus* was the particular quality of the new men. *Virtus*, that vital energy proper to a man, seemed to them the distinguishing mark of the *homo novus*, just as noble birth was the mark of the aristocrat. In his *Pro Sestio*, Cicero states, "You, young Romans who are noble by birth, I will rouse to imitate the example of your ancestors; and you, who

---

137. Cf. Earl, *Political Thought of Sallust*, 18–27; Badian, *Roman Imperialism in the Late Republic*, 13; Harris, *War and Imperialism*, 20; Alston, "Arms and the Man," 205–23.

can win nobility by your talents and virtue, I will exhort you to follow that career in which many new men have covered themselves with honor and glory [*vosque, adulescentes, et qui nobiles estis, ad maiorum vestrorum imitationem excitabo, et qui ingenio ac virtute nobilitatem potestis consequi, ad eam rationem in qua multi homines novi et honore et gloria floruerunt cohortabor*]."[138] Talking to youths in this speech, Cicero distinguishes between two kinds of *nobilitas*: that obtained by birth and that acquired by *virtus*.

According to Cicero, *virtus*, then, could also be attained by other men and was not the exclusive attribute of the aristocrats; on the contrary, acts of *virtus* made a *nobilis*. He summarized this idea by his phrase *moribus non maioribus*.[139] A noble like Catiline, then, might be a complete scoundrel and inferior to the best *homines novi*: "Regal powers and military commands, nobility of birth and political office, wealth and influence, and their opposites, depend upon chance and are therefore controlled by circumstances. But what role we ourselves may choose to sustain is decided by our own free choice [*nam regna, imperia, nobilitatem, honores, divitiae, opes eaque, quae sunt his contraria, in casu sita temporibus gubernantur; ipsi autem gerere quam personam velimus, a nostra voluntate proficiscitur*]."[140] Being virtuous depended for the *novus* only on oneself; it was related to personal freedom and choices, it was not something given by the gods or inherited. That is why it becomes the main characteristic of the *homo novus*, the self-made man, who does not owe his qualities to the gods, or noble birth to his parents like the aristocrats: "but virtue no one ever imputed to a god's bounty [*virtutem autem nemo umquam acceptam deo rettulit*]. And doubtless with good reason, for our virtue is just grounds for others' praise and a right reason for our own pride, and this would not be so if the gift of virtue came to us from a god and not from ourselves [*Nimirum recte; propter virtutem enim iure laudamur et in virtute recte gloriamur; quod non contingeret, si id donum a deo, non a nobis haberemus*] ... Did anyone ever render thanks to the gods because he was a good man? No, but because he was rich [*dives*], honored [*honoratus*], secure [*incolumis*]."[141] This is not to say that there was a strict polarity of claims: the *novi* claiming *virtus* and the *nobiles* claiming *genus*. Rather, there was an interconnection of the two claims: the new men

---

138. Cic. *Pro Sest*, 136.

139. Cic. *Pis*, 1: "When I was elected quaestor among the first, aedile ahead, praetor first, by all the votes of the Roman People, they gave the office to the man, not the family, to my character, not my ancestors [*moribus non maioribus*], to the *virtus* which they perceived, not to a nobility of which they had heard."

140. Cic. *De Off*. 1.115.

141. Cic. *Nat. Deor*, 3.86–87.

maintained that because of their *virtus*, they should be considered *nobiles*,[142] and the nobles, even if most of the evidence concentrates on status and the glory their ancestors had won, claimed that they also had *virtus* and were morally superior; the term belonged to them because they were the *boni*.[143]

The perfect pair of qualities that could define the *homines novi* was *virtus* and *industria*.[144] "Because, although you were [only] the son of a Roman knight, by your valor and energy you made good your claim to the highest distinction [*quod virtute industriaque perfecisti ut, cum equitis Romani esses filius, summa tamen amplitudine dignus putarere*]."[145] And this we find not only in Latin defense speeches, used as a kind of political slogan, but also in some of Cicero's politico-philosophical works. In his *De Republica*, immediately after he has dealt with the republican heroes Metellus, Fabius Maximus, and Marcellus, who had freed the republic from the terror of Carthage, Cicero starts talking about Cato the Elder and how he should be the prototype for the Roman of his day: "Marcus Cato, an unknown man of no pedigree [*homini ignoto et novo*]—a man who serves as a model of industry and virtue [*exemplari ad industriam virtutemque*] to all of us who share his goals."[146] These were the qualities to be sought by the ordinary man. It was obvious that not everybody belonged to the *nobilitas*, but this was not a prerequisite for being a man of *virtus* and *industria*.

With the *novi* also aspiring to and achieving *virtus*, it could be said that the concept underwent a social expansion. *Virtus* belonged to whoever was committed enough to practice it. And *virtus* started to be displayed not only in military undertakings, but in any sphere of social life, precisely because there were many other ways—besides war—of serving the state, for example, writing history.[147] As the *homines novi* were gaining more and more prestige and offices, it seemed appropriate that they should want to justify their

---

142. This is the new *nobilitas* which Sallust puts in Marius' mouth in *BJ*, 85. For an expanded explanation of this, see chapter 2 in this book.

143. Cf. Earl, *Moral and Political Tradition in Rome*, 47–51; and Woodman, *Velleius Paterculus*, 257.

144. We will see many examples of this when dealing with the historians individually. Of course, the one who makes this theory his own is Sallust, even though he says that even the *homines novi* have been corrupted and adopted the vices of the *nobilitas*. Cf. Sall. *BJ* 63; 76.1.

145. Cic. *Pro Mur*, 16. For the same claim cf. Cato, *ORF*³, 51.

146. Cic. *De Rep*, 1.1.1, Zetzel's trans. in *Cicero: On the Commonwealth and on the Laws*, 2.

147. Cf. Rawson, *Intellectual Life*, "Historiography had long been seen almost as an extension of public life," 91. For the expansion of the activities with which men could gain glory through *virtus*, see Sall. *BC* 3.1. and *BJ* 4.1.

position—as the aristocrats had done—by saying that because they had *virtus*, they also deserved an important role in society and the public sphere.

John Dugan's study on Cicero is precisely concerned with this point.[148] Cicero in his speeches presents himself—and the other *novi*—as the possessor of true *virtus*, gained by his own merits and *industria* as opposed to the nobility, "on whom [even] when they are asleep all the honors of the Roman people are showered [*quibus omnia populi Romani beneficia dormientibus deferentur*]."[149] The new man attains his successes on account of his own *virtus* and does not hide himself behind the reputation of his predecessors, those smoked waxed *imagines*, but shows his well-deserved *imagines* with pride: in Cicero's case, his writings.[150] He wants to present himself as a new man, not only because he is the first one to have achieved the consulate but also because he represents a real "new man" who by his cultural development and his intellectual work does good to the state in a way similar to that of the *maiores*. For Dugan, Cicero challenges the traditional Roman suspicions of intellectual activity and constructs a real "new man": a politician whose power rested mainly on his intellectual and literary achievements.[151] This statement, being true in some sense, needs to be moderated a little; otherwise there would be no point in Cicero being so insistent in presenting himself also as a preeminent political figure, savior of the republic and model of a good provincial governor.

The presence of the overlapping meanings of *virtus*, as described in Cicero, showed the real complexity of the term within the Roman tradition and at the same time expressed an "intellectualization" of the concept of manliness. Words—especially political words—are not fixed realities,[152] but on the contrary, usage determines meaning, and the continuous development of a concept was expressed in its redefinition and reinterpretation. The imprecision of Roman political terminology, which does not help us to find one consistent translation, demonstrates that we are dealing with a piece of "evolving vocabulary."[153] Roman political life was in constant expansion and transformation, and language—being a sign of reality—portrayed this phenomenon in a very powerful way. With all their emphasis on tradition and the *mores*

---

148. Dugan, *Making a New Man*.
149. Cic. *Verr*, 2.5.180.
150. In Marius' case, his wounds received in battle.
151. Dugan, *Making a New Man*, 20.
152. See, for example, the case of the words "democracy," "freedom," and so on.
153. Hellegouarc'h, *Vocabulaire Latin*, 569, talks about "un vocabulaire en pleine gestation."

maiorum, the Romans were incessantly adapting the old to the new. This, together with the process of cultural Hellenization that Rome was undergoing during the mid-republic, brought to real political life a kind of conflict by which the divergent meanings of *virtus* were publicly contested. There were two parallel processes going on more or less at the same time: on the one hand the semantic broadening of the word *virtus*, and on the other, the social expansion of it. These phenomena were publicly seen in the political arena; furthermore, the struggle played an ideological role in the crisis of the late republic, which is evident in the literature of the period.[154]

IN THE COURSE of our journey through the "ethico-political" understanding of the concept of *virtus* in the historians of the late republic and early empire, we will see several cases in which these competing ideals of *virtus* are expressed in opposing political figures, but more often we will witness that there were men in whom several kinds of *virtus* dwelt at the same time.[155] On the other hand, I am conscious that the very classification of matters in "ethico-political" pigeon-holes belongs to us, and it is anachronistic; morality as something distinct from politics did not yet exist. The Romans thought of their lives, especially their political life, in terms of *virtus* in a way that we can perhaps imagine but would not dare to express.

Virtus had been related to the republic in a very forceful way. Their national heroes had been known for their *virtus*, and the tradition—like every tradition in Rome—had to be kept and encouraged. This was the task of the historians. As we approach the final collapse of the republican system and the establishment of the imperial order, we register that the Romans became more and more aware that they needed to justify and define what they thought was the essence of being Roman and its main quality: *virtus*. Philosophy came up with some help by providing the necessary background and terminology with which to explain these concepts; it helped them to reflect in a deeper way on something very meaningful to every Roman.

Virilis-virtus was specific and restricted, *humana-virtus* was general and open, but both formed part of *virtus Romana*. *Virilis-virtus* worked as the quality that enabled Romans to carry out their social role and helped them in the achievement of *humana-virtus*, which equipped individuals to move toward the realization of the specifically human *telos*. *Virtus* had to do with *telos*

---

154. Perhaps the best example is Sallust, but we also find interesting traces in Lucan's *Bellum Civile*.

155. As will be seen in the cases of Tiberius in Velleius or Agricola in Tacitus.

before the Greeks said it explicitly; it was the end and function of the aristocracy to defend their state courageously. *Telos* and social purpose were identified when Rome was an aristocratic and militaristic society and also later, when it ceased to be. Roman *virtus* in its cooperative side, then, was related to the social function of men, mainly to serve the community or the state. At the same time, Roman *virtus* was also competitive, not only in the challenge to outdo other men in excellence but also in measuring up to one's own nature. Together, they contributed to the comprehension of what men do and are.

The aim of this chapter has been to show that *virtus*, in its narrower and broader meaning, was a Roman ethical concept. *Virtus*, in its origin the quality related to *vir*, came to mean courage, and as such, was from the beginning an ethical quality. *Virtus* developed and expanded to include the other good qualities because, whereas it had meant the "ideal man" in a primarily militaristic society, later it became the idealization of what a man should be in any society. *Virtus*, interpreted as virtue in general, owes to *arete* not so much its meaning as its rationalization. *Virtus*—Roman *virtus*—will appear clearly as the constant protagonist, with an overwhelming presence, throughout the narratives of the Roman historians. It will be up to them now to show how and why they made *virtus* play that leading role in history.

CHAPTER TWO

Virtus in Sallust

Postquam divitiae honori esse coepere et eas gloria,
imperium, potentia sequebatur, hebescere virtus

After riches began to be held in honor and led to the acquisition of glory, positions of authority, and political influence, then *virtus* began to lose its edge
—Sall. *BC* 12.1.

Sallust's works seem the natural starting point when one approaches the topic of *virtus* in Latin historiography. His insistent and almost obsessive treatment of a concept that was so central not only to historical writing but also to the very self-definition of being Roman was bound to lead him into a serious analysis of the causes of political decline. His study of crisis intended to help the reader understand what a complex concept *virtus* was, and what the dangers of these complexities were. It is not contradictory to begin our survey of *virtus* in the Roman historians with an author who denounces the lack of *virtus*, the debasement of the concept, and the need for a reinterpretation of it; sometimes it is precisely in these contrasts that one can find the most illuminating nuances for the comprehension of a term. And, as will be seen, Sallust is especially attracted to contrasts. His monographs are, in fact, investigations in which different and contrasting kinds of *virtus*—corrupted and pure, old and new, true and false—are put to the test as they interact and serve to explain political change.

The *Bellum Catilinae* (*BC*) and *Bellum Jugurthinum* (*BJ*) offer us different levels of analysis. The first one is, of course, the topics themselves. The choices of the Catilinarian conspiracy and the war against Jugurtha are both important and irrelevant to Sallust's goal. At the end of the two prologues, Sallust explicitly tells his audience why these chosen moments in Roman history are important: Catiline's conspiracy was extraordinary for its nature and danger;[1] the war against Jugurtha had been long and cruel, and had given the people the opportunity to confront the arrogance of the nobles.[2] On the other hand, one may wonder whether, had Sallust chosen other instances of political

---

1. Sall. *BC* 4.4.
2. Sall. *BJ* 5.1. For the translation of the *BJ*, I have used Comber and Balmaceda, *Sallust*.

turmoil in Rome—such as the crisis of the Gracchi or the civil war between Marius and Sulla, for example—the outcome of his investigations would have been very different from the one we now have.

A second level of analysis can be found in Sallust's determination to illustrate decay. By an apposite choice of words and phrases, he will not only achieve a powerful exposition of the nature and spread of political decline but also highlight the connection between the unwholesome condition of the state and the *mores* of its citizens. Syme called Sallust "the historian of the decline and fall,"[3] and the reference to Gibbon is certainly justified, because Sallust's focal subject is political corruption. Sallust seems interested in making his readership aware of the disconcerting impossibility of drawing a fine line between *virtus* and *vitium*, and in finding out whether the latter was a product of decline or, on the contrary, its origin.

On an even deeper level, one can see the ultimate meaning of writing history for Sallust: if *virtus*, as he shows, had become contaminated and polluted, it was necessary to find an alternative formulation to prevent its total disintegration. Sallust's unspoken purpose when writing his monographs appears to be to provide his audience with a more comprehensive concept of Roman *virtus*. This is going to be clearly shown in the *BC* and the *BJ* in many ways: in the philosophical discussions of the prologues, throughout the narratives, and especially in the speeches. The broader comprehension that Sallust proposed of a key concept in Roman politics and morality such as *virtus* needed careful interpretation to carry conviction, and he could not change the accepted meaning of the word in a merely superficial way. Sallust was interested in both causation and decline but also in human nature, moral conduct, and Roman politics. What I will argue here is that through his historical works, Sallust emerges both as the advocate of an understanding of *virtus* that expanded the sense he inherited of what it meant to be a good Roman, and as the promoter of the idea of the different types of *virtus* in the ideological struggles of the late republic.

I will show in this chapter how these three levels of analysis interact with one another and how Sallust broadens the concept of *virtus* by moving it away from a particular, closed social group—the *nobilitas*—to a more open one: the *homines novi*; and also how with his new appraisal, the traditional, aristocratic notion of *virtus* becomes a common "ideal" for all Romans. Paradoxically

---

3. Syme, *Sallust*, 56.

(and impressively), he will reinforce the need for this missing *virtus* by developing a "language of decline and *vitium*."

Presenting the Theory and Setting the Tone: The Prologues

The prologues of the *BC* and *BJ* have been the subject of a long discussion that started in antiquity with Quintilian: "In the *Jugurtha* and the *Catiline* Sallust begins with proems that have nothing to do with history [or the history] [*C. Sallustius in bello Iugurthino et Catilinae nihil ad historiam pertinentibus principiis orsus est*]."[4] It is agreed that Quintilian may have meant one of two things here: on the one hand, that the prologues had nothing to do with the genre of historiography but were more appropriate to the manner of epideictic oratory, or on the other hand, that they had nothing to do with the historical themes chosen by Sallust, that is, with the subsequent narrative of the events.[5]

The debate has been summed up by Syme, who asks, "Are the prologues necessary and relevant?"[6] One may certainly wonder what the discussion of the superiority of the mind over the body has to add to the particular cases of Jugurtha or Catiline, especially since such thoughts seem more appropriate to philosophy or ethical treatises.[7] But they actually do add something: they provide weight and evidence to Sallust's main point when writing history. With these general reflections on human nature, Sallust is taking for granted—and what is more important, he is making the reader take for granted too—that all men are equal and equipped with the same means: *ingenium* and *animus* to achieve *gloria*. *Nobiles* such as Metellus, Catiline, or Sulla; *novi* like Marius or Cicero; and even foreigners like Jugurtha—who in a sense is a *novus* as well—are presented as equals regarding their actions and their consequences. All of

---

4. Quint. *Inst.*, 3.8.9.

5. Cf. Earl, *Political Thought of Sallust*, 5–17. But see also Paul, *Historical Commentary on Sallust's Bellum Jugurthinum*, 9–11, who argues that Quintilian must be referring to irrelevance. For a more complete version of this debate, see Tiffou, *Essai sur la Pensée Morale de Salluste à la Lumière de ses Prologues*, chap. 1. There is an enormous amount of material on the prologues of Sallust; see, for example, Egerman, *Die Prooemien zu den Werken des Sallust*; Leeman, "Sallusts Prologe und seine Auffassung von der Historiographie," 323–39; La Penna, "Il significato dei proemi Sallustiani," 23–43 and 89–119; Büchner, *Sallust*, 93–130; Feeney, "Beginning Sallust's Catiline," 139–46; Grethlein, "Nam Quid Ea Memorem," 135–48; Ramsey, *Sallust's Bellum Catilinae*, 55–68; Krebs, "Imagery of 'The Way,'" 581–94; Comber and Balmaceda, *Sallust*, 188–92.

6. Syme, *Sallust*, 240.

7. Cf. Earl, "Prologue-Form in Ancient Historiography." Sallust's proems show borrowings from Plato's *Seventh Letter* and several parallels with the works of Seneca the Younger.

them show their *virtus* at some point, all of them fall into different vices as well, and they are responsible for both. These considerations make us keep the prologues in our mind constantly, and we are unconsciously referring to them in our comprehension of the narrative. The prologues, therefore, shadow forth the specifically Roman themes that provide the moral-political underpinning of the whole work.

It is probable that most of Sallust's readers would have agreed with the ideas expressed in the prologues; he was not saying anything particularly novel, and the influence of Plato, Aristotle, Posidonius, and the Stoics has been recognized in these claims.[8] But being unoriginal and using beliefs that were commonly accepted at the time does not automatically imply that what he was saying was not important or that those ideas were not applicable to the contemporary situation. The relevance of the prologues is precisely that although they convey ideas common to philosophers and rhetoricians, they were also useful for a historian to express *his own* ideas and give them the twist he wanted to prove his theory. It could be said that Sallust was more anxious to put across what he says in his prologues than in his narrative.

Both proems start with similar topics and deal with them in a fairly similar way: the supremacy of the mind over the body, the advantages of leading a life ruled by *virtus*, and the disasters that come from being carried away by bodily passions. They both acknowledge that the human soul is immortal and that men are able to control *fortuna* if they want. *Virtus* appears here as a socially comprehensive term, not exclusive to a particular sector of society. The remarkably general terms—*omnis homines* and *genus humanum*[9]—are placed in the opening sentences to set the tone of his considerations; Sallust is talking to and about all mankind: "We employ the mind to rule, the body rather to serve; the one we have in common with the gods, the other with beasts."[10] Therefore, any man can take the *via virtutis*.[11] The "meritocratic system" in which everybody starts from the same basis and can achieve equal results when striving for the main goal of human endeavors—in the Roman case, *gloria*—is, according to Sallust, open to all. In thinking so, he was clearly shifting the emphasis away from social status and locating it in something more personal, although its manifestations were still very public and crucial to the well-being of the state.

---

8. For a detailed account of this influence, see Perrochat, *Les Modèles Grecs de Salluste*.
9. Sall. *BC* 1.1 and *BJ* 1.1, respectively.
10. Sall. *BC* 1.2.
11. Sall. *BJ* 1.3.

Traditionally, the nobles had attached *virtus* to their public discourse. They claimed that they were the ones who had displayed *virtus* in the service of the state—war or public office—and through that they had achieved *gloria* and became *nobiles*. It concerned not only the individual but the whole family, and insistence on this point was sometimes extreme.[12] Thus, the nobles became more and more self-conscious of their status and prerogatives, and as a consequence, their claims to *virtus* came to be almost a complement of good birth. It was this tradition that Sallust wanted to break with, and to present *virtus* instead as a general *ideal* open to everybody who wanted to take up the challenge of achieving great deeds by the exercise of their natural abilities and good qualities.[13] The notion of this *virtus* based on *ingenium*, nature or inborn talent, will consequently lack the exclusiveness of the aristocratic idea, which was restricted to the *nobiles*.[14] Although Sallust was trying to give a new conceptual meaning to a familiar word, he was not aiming at changing its very Roman core.[15] *Virtus* was and would always be a very Roman idea, and thus its attributes of being public and active were still present in this more intellectual presentation of it. This practical idea of *virtus* had few of the theoretical characteristics of Platonic *virtus* and a lot of the *sapientia maiorum*.

Another common thread in both proems—which sprang precisely from the inclusiveness of everybody's "call to *virtus*"—touches on a theme particularly dear to Sallust, where he talks about another way of attaining *virtus* apart from war or politics, namely, by writing history. Sallust's reflection on his own occupation provides us with one of the earliest references to the glory and fame that belong to the historian, which are based mainly on surmounting the difficulties attached to writing about the past.[16] When justifying his change from politics to historiography, Sallust's tone in both monographs is somewhat defensive; his *apologia pro vita sua* appears valid, but perhaps not wholly convincing: "although I am aware that by no means equal repute attends the narrator and the doer of deeds, yet I regard the writing of history as one of the most difficult tasks."[17] But what is of most interest here is the

---

12. See, for example, the *Elogia Scipionum, CIL* VI.1: 1284–94.
13. Cf. Earl, *Political Thought of Sallust*.
14. For a different view, see Sarsila, *Being a Man*, 117–26.
15. Cf. Tiffou, *Essai sur la Pensée Morale de Salluste à la Lumière de ses Prologues*, 137; and Syme, *Sallust*, 242.
16. For the difficulties of writing history as an ancient historian, see Marincola, *Authority and Tradition in Ancient Historiography*, 148–58.
17. Sall. *BC* 3.2.

connection that Sallust makes between writing history and *virtus*: "as many others have spoken of its *virtus* [i.e., of recording the past], I see no need to add anything more [*Quoius de virtute quia multi dixere, praetereundum puto*]."[18] It is quite significant that Sallust uses the word *virtus* to speak about the value, merit, or worth of writing history. The choice is conscious and full of meaning. The *virtus* that Sallust is referring to here implies at least two things: on the one hand, strenuous *labor et industria* on the part of the historian when recording past deeds because the style and diction must be equal to the deeds recorded (*facta dictis exaequanda*), and on the other, definite courage, necessary to overcome and put up with malicious reproaches "because such criticisms as you make of others' shortcomings are thought by most men to be due to malice and envy. Furthermore when you commemorate the distinguished virtue and fame of good men [*ubi de magna virtute atque gloria bonorum memores*], while everyone is quite ready to believe you when you tell of things that he thinks he could easily do himself, everything beyond that he regards as fictitious, if not false."[19] By this explicit association of *virtus* with historiography, Sallust is, in a novel way, presenting himself as a man of *virtus*, a *virtus* that he did not show in military campaigns or public office—although he was involved in both—but mainly in the *memoria rerum gestarum*.

In the proem to the *BJ*, Sallust adds an idea that will strengthen his own claim to *virtus* even more. The traditional wax images of the ancestors that inspired and inflamed younger generations of nobles with a burning desire to pursue *virtus* are compared explicitly with the *memoria rerum gestarum*. Both "products" or material representations of history fulfilled a similar aim: on the one hand, they publicized the *virtus* of the past, and on the other, they aroused emulation for the present. This perception of the past influenced and, in a certain way, shaped history in the present. Again, one can see Sallust broadening the narrow aristocratic tradition of ancestor masks to a wider panorama open to all: the memory of the past.[20] As a promoter of *virtus*, Sallust also looked to reflect his own.

It is important to bear in mind, however, that although Sallust gave this example of multifaceted *virtus* in the prologue, in his narrative he only portrays the typical personification of men of *virtus*, that is, men who held public

---

18. Sall. *BJ* 4.1.
19. Sall. *BC* 3.2.
20. For the dialectical relation between history and memory, see Grethlein, "Nam Quid Ea Memorem." For the role of the wax images of the ancestors, see Flower, *Ancestor Masks and Aristocratic Power in Roman Culture*.

office or were brave in war. This could be another way for him of contrasting the theory of *virtus* and its practice at a particular time in Rome.

Coming back to Quintilian's remark about *nihil ad historiam pertinentibus*, it is possible to say that there is a certain amount of truth in what he says, but on the other hand, Sallust seems to force us to approach what history is all about from a broader perspective. The prologues of the *BC* and *BJ* can be seen as forming an indivisible union with the narrative that follows, perhaps not so much in the content of the topics as in the intention and purpose of the author: the prologues explain Sallust's main concern, and the narrative—in a quite distinctive way—will support his thesis.

The Presence and Absence of *Virtus*: The Characters in the Monographs

As seen in the preceding section one aspect of the traditional aristocratic Roman idea of *virtus* was the winning of *gloria* by serving the state. This service to the *res publica* worked harmoniously in times of *concordia*,[21] a quality that for Sallust was particularly important: people fought for freedom, and the state grew stronger because of *libertas* and *disciplina*: *virtus omnia domuerat* (*virtus* had conquered all).[22] This is, of course, Sallust's idealization, but it is put there—and even exaggerated—to present a real contrast with the times of decline that he aims to portray.

Following a certain tradition, Sallust claims that it had all started with the fall of Carthage.[23] The end of *metus hostilis* had such pernicious consequences for Rome that she would never be able to recover. It is striking that Sallust, who took Cato the Elder as his model not only in style but also in ideology, could disagree with him about such an important matter.[24] The respective themes of *metus hostilis* and *delenda est Carthago* seem quite irreconcilable approaches to one's enemies. Although in the end Cato had won the

---

21. Cf. Sall. *BC* 9.1. For the importance of *concordia* in Sallust, see Kapust, *Republicanism, Rhetoric, and Roman Political Thought*, 42–50.

22. Cf. Sall. *BC* 6.5–7.6.

23. Cf. Sall. *BC* 10.1 and *BJ* 41.2. Sallust seems to have borrowed this idea from Posidonius. Cf. Wiedemann, "Reflections of Roman Political Thought," 527; on the other hand, it was also a *topos* in ancient thought; cf. Xen. *Cyr*, 3.1.26; Plato, *Laws* 3.698b ff; Arist. *Pol*, 7.1334a–b; Polyb. 6.18. On the significance of the fall of Carthage, see Purcell, "On the Sacking of Carthage and Corinth," 133–48.

24. For the influence of Cato on Sallust, see Levene, "Sallust's 'Catiline' and Cato the Censor," 179–91, esp. 176–80.

debate against Scipio Nasica and Carthage had been finally destroyed, Sallust shows in the monographs that perhaps this was not the right decision. Once fear of the enemy had disappeared, Rome had little incentive to keep her discipline and her *virtus*, and according to the historian, everything was left to the mercy of fortune.[25] He sums up the state of the city in a way that would become paradigmatic of his approach: "Hence a craving first for money, then for power increased [*igitur primo pecuniae, deinde imperi cupido crevit*]; these were the root of all evils. For greed [*avaritia*] subverted trustworthiness [*fidem*], integrity [*probitatem*], and other virtuous practices; in the place of these it taught insolence [*superbiam*], cruelty [*crudelitatem*], to neglect the gods [*deos neglegere*], to set a price on everything [*omnia venalia*]."[26] Glory was still the goal, but now it was won not through *bonae artes* (good qualities), but *dolis atque fallaciis* (by fraud and deceits).[27] The ambition for *imperium* and *honores* had become so violent that the way they were obtained no longer seemed to matter.

Sallust's theory of presenting *virtus* as an ideal, and more specifically as an ideal that brought *nobilitas* to the *homo novus*,[28] seems to collapse with the realization of the presence of *ambitio* at all levels of society. Nobody escaped from this poison, nobles and "even the new men, who formerly always used to outstrip the nobility by their virtue [*virtus*] alone, now force their way into commands and distinctions by underhand intrigue and open robbery, instead of by honorable means [*bonis artibus*]."[29] In a calculated move, Sallust deliberately undermines or contradicts what he had said in the prologue. The more he has emphasized the universality of this call to *virtus*, the more dramatic and desperate the situation seems to be when everybody is failing at it. Sallust chose the monograph format for his history as being the best way to produce a strong impact on his audience. He offers drama, surprise, and suspense, change of fortune of outstanding individuals, and the theme of high politics.[30] He will use all these elements to wake people up, providing joy and distress, hope and fear to stir them to react.

---

25. Cf. Sall. *BC* 10.2.
26. Sall. *BC* 10.3–4.
27. Sall. *BC* 11.2.
28. It was, however, a *nova nobilitas* (*BJ* 85.25) as opposed to the *vetus nobilitas* of the *nobiles* (*BJ* 85.4). I will come back to this point when I deal with Marius' speech.
29. Sall. *BJ* 4.7.
30. Although it is difficult to prove an explicit connection between the two authors on this point, Cicero had recommended precisely all these elements for the writing of a successful monograph in his letter to Lucceius; cf. Cic. *Ad Fam*, 5.12.6. For the use of Cicero's letter to Lucceius

I shall not analyze every character in Sallust's works, but will only look at the ones who played a special role in the developing of his theory of *virtus*. Sallust was exceptionally good at illustrating character, and he did so in such a way that sometimes these descriptions worked as the narrative of events. This has been considered by some as a literary mastery, but on occasions has been seen as damaging his historical rigor.[31] Regarding Sallust as a literary artist, however, should not undermine him as a historian. On the contrary, style, psychological insight, and ethical approach to human nature may enhance the narrative and provide the reader with a richer analysis; it does not necessarily mean obliterating historical truth.

One last general observation that I would like to make before moving onto the actual narratives is Sallust's peculiar usage of the word *virtus*, always in the singular. That the word never appears in the plural, *virtutes*, is of course a conscious choice. *Virtus* in Sallust is difficult to translate; it is not easy to render it as meaning simply courage or valor in some instances, or virtue in general in others, and the context does not always help in arriving at a clear-cut identification. It would have been easier for us to identify the type of *virtus* he was talking about if he had used it in the plural on some occasions. When he talks about good qualities, for example, which Cicero calls *virtutes*, namely, *fides, probitas, industria*, and others, Sallust uses the word *bonae artes*, so that he can always use *virtus* in the singular alone. It seems as if he is looking for a way of keeping *virtus* separate from everything, as a clean and unchanging concept, for the sake of his main purpose: to present *virtus* not just as another virtue, but as *the* ideal to which every Roman could and should aspire. Every time he writes the word *virtus* in his works, it appears as a solid, compact, almost monolithic notion, which will, in fact, contradict the view that he develops in the narratives. In almost every instance, one can say that *virtus* in Sallust deliberately means at the same time both *virilis-virtus* and *humana-virtus*.

Sallust's prose-writer contemporaries used the word *virtutes* to refer to good qualities. Cicero has already been mentioned; similarly, Nepos, Varro, and Caesar do not seem to have any problem about using *virtus* in the plural. Caesar, for example, in his historical works, *Bellum Gallicum* and *Bellum Civile*, often uses the word *virtus*.[32] It is not surprising that the meaning of the

---

by historians, see Woodman, *Rhetoric in Classical Historiography*, 125–26; and Moles, "Livy's Preface," 141–68.

31. Cf. Goodyear, "Sallust," passim, but esp. 106; and Usher, *Historians of Greece and Rome*, esp. 148–60.

32. For Caesar's *virtus*, its occurrences, meaning, and purpose, see Grillo, *Art of Caesar's Bellum Civile*, chap. 2.

word is valor or bravery in the overwhelming majority of the occurrences, but it is also possible to find a more general meaning of virtue and even the plural *virtutes* a number of times. Keeping *virtus* always in the singular was a particular feature of Sallust's writings, and in this sense, his use of *virtus* is, in fact, different from that of all the other historians analyzed in this book.

Virtus *in the* BC

Sallust's *Bellum Catilinae* is very quick-paced, somehow mirroring the speed with which the events of 63 B.C. might have been perceived by the Romans themselves. I will try to show in this section how Sallust's haste, his *immortalis velocitas*,[33] is related to the fragmented way in which he chose to develop not only the narrative but also his theory of *virtus* in his first work. Different, sometimes even unconnected, bits of information are provided, and this gives a real sense of the disorder and corruption that ruled Rome at the time. He does not present a simple, neat account of the struggle between good and evil; the situation is much more complicated and not completely under control: the ones who are supposed to behave like heroes show signs of weaknesses and even vices; the criminals, on the other hand, display noble virtues on several occasions.[34]

Catiline, for example, is described as the personification of wickedness and the worst possible influence on young men: "his body could endure hunger, cold, and want of sleep to an incredible degree; his mind was reckless, cunning, treacherous, capable of any form of pretense and concealment. Covetous of others' possessions, he was prodigal with his own; he was violent in his passions. He possessed a certain amount of eloquence, but little discretion. His disordered mind ever craved the monstrous, incredible, gigantic [*Corpus patiens inediae, algoris, vigiliae supra quam cuiquam credibile est. Animus audax, subdolos, varius, cuius rei lubet simulator ac dissimulator, alieni appetens, sui profusus, ardens in cupiditatibus; satis eloquentiae, sapientiae parum. Vastus animus immoderata, incredibilia, nimis alta semper cupiebat*]."[35] But, at the same time, he is so brave that Sallust cannot but admire his courage.[36] He

---

33. Quint. *Inst*, 10.1.102.

34. For interpretations of the *BC*, see, for example, Batstone, "Intellectual Conflict and Mimesis in Sallust's Bellum Catilinae," 112–32; Gunderson, "History of the Mind and the Philosophy of History in Sallust's *Bellum Catilinae*"; Feldherr, "Translation of Catiline," 285–90.

35. Cf. Sall. *BC* 5.1–5. See also 16.1–3. Sallust's description of Catiline would mark literature henceforward in a very forceful way; see, for example, Livy's description of Hannibal (21.4) and Tacitus' Sejanus (*Ann*, 4.1).

36. Cf. Sall. *BC* 57.5; 60.4; 60.7.

possesses the finest martial qualities of the republic, and his army exhibits the *virtus* proper of old times (*prisca virtus*) There are several paradoxes in this character: he is an aristocrat, and as such he had the mission of contributing to the republic's welfare, yet he plans to destroy it by overthrowing the government;[37] he had many of the qualities belonging to proper *virtus*, such as strength and vigor of both mind and body (*magna vi et animi et corporis*), but they were perverted by his evil and deprived nature (*ingenio malo pravoque*).[38] He was greedy and extravagant, but he was also able to die in the most valiant way and as a true noble Roman.[39] The complex picture of Catiline—studied by many[40]—his ambiguous position between heroism and villainy, exemplifies Sallust's view of the shifting grounds of the configurations in which people embody good or evil. In some sense, Catiline is what "old *virtus*" must have been like in the nobility, but now it appears corrupted and is used toward the wrong end. The personal story of Catiline reveals a sad diagnosis for the Roman republic: *ambitio*, *avaritia*, and *luxuria* had spread like a deadly plague.[41] The physicality in which the decline is described—one can almost see the muddy wave of corruption invading society—is a striking feature of the *Bellum Catilinae* that somehow serves to match *verba et facta* (words and deeds), and establishes a close match between the individual body and the social body,[42] and also between individual *virtus* and social *virtus*. I will come back to this point later in this chapter.

Decline of *virtus* brought the degeneration of the aristocracy and its role in politics. But Sallust shows that the corruption of public morals at Rome extends far beyond the conspirators, and it would be shallowly optimistic to make the conspirators unredeemably black since, if the rot consisted of only a handful of men, then the state could be easily purged.[43] Sallust shows that the conspiracy was both a product and a cause of decline, and Catiline is at the same time a natural result of a diseased state, and the very origin of its disease.

---

37. Cf. Sall. *BC* 16.4.
38. Sall. *BC* 5.1.
39. Sall. *BC* 60.7.
40. See, for example, Wilkins, *Villain or Hero*; Levene, "Sallust's 'Catiline' and Cato the Censor"; Ramsey, *Sallust's Bellum Catilinae*; Krebs, "Catiline's Ravaged Mind"; Vasaly, "Characterization and Complexity"; Batstone, "Catiline's Speeches in Sallust's Bellum Catilinae."
41. Sall. *BC* 36.5.
42. Expressed almost brutally in the ablative nouns at 14.2. Cf. McGushin, *Sallust: Bellum Catilinae* and Malcovati, *Sallustio*, ad loc.
43. I owe this idea to Michael Comber.

Also ambivalent is the recognition of the vanquished by the victors, a remarkable note on which to end. This expired community tells us not only of the pass to which Rome has come but also of the indelible links there are between those who are branded as the carriers of decline, from whom society would henceforth be free, and those who remain within the pale. That Sallust should refrain from heaping execration on Catiline and his fellows is a mark of his humanity.

Sallust's extremely demanding view of *virtus* made him count only a pair of individuals as deserving to be credited with the quality in its fullness: Caesar and Cato.[44] He presents them as equals in birth, years, and eloquence, but with different personalities.[45] He deeply admires them both, although their *virtus* was quite dissimilar: Caesar was praised for his generosity and benefactions (*munificentia ac beneficiis*), Cato for the uprightness of his life (*integritate vitae*); one was gentle and compassionate; the other possessed a dignified severity. The easygoing nature of Caesar was contrasted with Cato's steadfastness. The former wanted to show his *virtus* in a new war and longed for great power; the latter, on the contrary, cultivated self-control, propriety, and above all austerity.[46] The final conclusion of the comparison of these two men of enormous *virtus* (*ingens virtus*)has been another field for debate.[47] But trying to find Sallust's "number one" or forcing him to take sides does not appear expedient; moreover, Sallust's portrayals are influenced by intervening events. In 63 B.C. (the date of the conspiracy), Cato did not yet enjoy the generalized reputation of being a "republican hero," and Caesar had not yet had opportunities to show his *clementia* as victor. Writing after their deaths, Sallust was freer to color and embellish their portraits and qualities.

Caesar's and Cato's speeches in the *BC* are presented by Sallust as matching one another. Caesar's speech against putting the conspirators to death relies mainly on historical *exempla* and jurisprudence, precisely where one might expect Cato to ground his argument. Caesar acknowledges the pressing situation that the consul and the Senate were facing at that moment, but pleads for moderation. Caesar maintains his legal argument, and while acknowledging a long chain of Roman innovations, he insists on following the

---

44. Sall. *BC* 53.6.
45. This claim does not seem in fact entirely true: Caesar was an aristocrat and at least five years older than Cato, who belonged to a plebeian family, though the eminence of Cato the Censor had conferred a certain dignity on it.
46. Cf. Sall. *BC* 54.
47. Kraus and Woodman, *Latin Historians*, 19: "for every reader who believes that he ranks Caesar over Cato there is another one who believes exactly the opposite."

exemplum of the *maiores* who had already refused on different occasions to apply the extreme penalty. In the end he proposes exile and not death. Cato's speech instead very dramatically favors capital punishment, and gives the reason for so harsh a penalty: "our very freedom and lives are at stake [*libertas et anima nostra in dubio est*]."[48] Answering Caesar, he claims that a truthful exegesis of the *maiores* would only give evidence of the need for more *severitas*.[49] In the end, Cato's advice prevails and the conspirators are put to death. Cato the Younger seems to be following Cato the Elder's *exemplum* in his approach toward the enemy: total annihilation. It is quite significant that Sallust listed so many of the consequences of the destruction of Carthage at the beginning of the monograph, because it accentuates the link between the two Catos and the failure of their policies in the long term. In this case, Cato's *virtus*—carefully detailed in the syncrisis—proved to be totally ineffectual for the well-being of the *res publica*.

It might seem, then, that Sallust is suggesting that these two men of *virtus* together were going to provide the republic with a solution to the crisis, as if the *virtus* of one could work in a complementary way to that of the other and save the situation.[50] But for Sallust the crisis of *virtus* involves an unsettling element, a nontraditional opposition. In fact, Sallust frustrates the expectations that the reader might have placed on Caesar and Cato; *virtus* is certainly there, but in a fragmented way.[51] *Virtus* in the *BC* is shown in broken pieces as it were: little bits of *virtus* in Caesar and little bits in Cato (there are bits of *virtus* even in Catiline). But that was not enough to amend Rome's calamitous state. Apart from fragmented *virtus*, Sallust described another serious problem with *virtus* at that time, namely, its dangerous closeness to vice: *vitium propius virtutem erat*.[52] *Virtus* no longer worked as a straightforward antidote against evil: too much self-interest and ambition appeared in Caesar constantly giving away *beneficia*; a principle of cruelty might be seen in Cato's strict *severitas*; Caesar's *munificentia* could be explained by his desire to excel

---

48. Sall. *BC* 52.6.

49. Showing that to a certain extent the recourse to the *maiores* could be used either way depending on where one placed the emphasis.

50. For this view, see Syme, *Sallust*, 120; Usher, *Historians of Greece and Rome*, 149; von Albrecht, *History of Roman Literature*, 452; Wiedemann, "Sallust's Jugurtha," 48–57; and Wiedemann, "Reflections of Roman Political Thought in Latin Historical Writing," 527–28.

51. For this view, see esp. the illuminating article of Batstone, "Antithesis of Virtue." A similar position is held by R. Sklenár, "La République des Signes"; D. Levene, "Sallust's 'Catiline' and Cato the Censor"; Kapust, *Republicanism, Rhetoric, and Roman Political Thought*, 75.

52. Sall. *BC* 11.1.

over others and Cato's *constantia* proved self-destructive in Utica.⁵³ In fact, in the final syncrisis it looks as if Sallust is opposing *virtus* to *virtus*; a disjointed *virtus* turns against itself. This is the dark panorama of the historian's time: if *virtus* can be so subdivided, and even contradict itself, is it in fact worthy? Disjunction and fragmentation were not going to rescue the republic and Sallust protests: *virtus* in pieces was all that was left in Rome after the fall of Carthage.

Virtus *in the* BJ

Virtus in the *BJ* seems to evolve more obviously than in the *BC*. Sallust presents a progression or development—mainly for the worse—of the characters of Jugurtha, Metellus, Marius, and even Sulla. This opposes in some way the more fixed characters of Cato or Catiline as portrayed in the *BC*. There is a succession of protagonists in the narrative: first Jugurtha, second Metellus, then Marius, and third Sulla. There is almost a sense of replacement, as the next takes over from the previous one in action, virtue, and hopes, until vices start to make their way in and another character has to make his entrance.⁵⁴ It is in this successive replacement that *virtus* in the *BJ* appears most striking.

The villain of Sallust's second monograph is a cunning foreigner who divided the opinions of senators and nobles at Rome. The description of Jugurtha at the beginning of the work portrays a splendid young man: great physical appearance, superior intellect (*ingenio validus*), and universally liked. The character sketch of the young Jugurtha is highly favorable: his early career is free from the vices of luxury and idleness mentioned in the proem, and he emerges as following the Numidian version of Roman *virtus*—hunting, for example—and excelling all in glory.⁵⁵ In contrast to the positive side of Jugurtha's character, which is described directly, the other side of the coin is presented through a vivid reconstruction of King Micipsa's fears and anxieties. On the one hand, Micipsa was anxious that Jugurtha's *virtus* should contribute to the glory of his kingdom, but on the other, he feared the natural disposition of human nature that moves from *virtus* to glory and from glory to being greedy for power, so he sent Jugurtha to the war in Numantia with the hope that he would die in battle while displaying his valor.⁵⁶

---

53. Cf. Sall. *BC* 54.2–5.
54. Cf. Kraus, "Jugurthine Disorder." For more on the development of the war itself, see Gsell, *Histoire Ancienne de l'Afrique du Nord*; Holroyd, "Jugurthine War"; Berthier, Juillet, and Charlier, *Le "Bellum Jugurthinum" de Salluste et le problème de Cirta*; Oost, "Fetial Law"; Brescia, *La Scalata del Ligure*; Morstein-Marx, "Alleged 'Massacre' at Cirta."
55. Cf. Sall. *BJ* 6.1.
56. Cf. Sall. *BJ* 6.2–7.2.

However, the results of the king's plan were totally unexpected. Jugurtha, besides his generous nature and ready wit, displayed bravery in war and wisdom in counsel, and won the intimate friendship of many Romans.[57] Sallust ascribes these traditional Roman qualities, along with hard work, to a foreign enemy. It is important to have this detailed account of young Jugurtha's character because, to a certain extent, Sallust hints that what happens next is paradoxical. In some way, Jugurtha is not absolutely responsible for his ambition. The venal Romans put into his head the idea of gaining supreme power illegally: he himself stood first in *virtus*,[58] while in Rome "everything was for sale."[59] Rome, which should have been the home of *virtus*, appears as an influence for its destruction. It is also interesting to note that Jugurtha's character was not corrupted from the beginning, as Catiline's had been. The idea, common in antiquity, of attributing a fixed character to individuals from birth is missing here,[60] perhaps to emphasize once again the way corruption and vice are not completely separate from *virtus*, but on the contrary alarmingly near; especially ambition, which is the vice closest to virtue because it can lure upright men with the promise of achieving even more.[61]

Things started to go wrong for Jugurtha after the murder of Hiempsal. Sallust tells us that he began to be afraid of the Roman people and to believe that his only hope of escaping their anger lay in buying up the avaricious Roman nobles with his own riches. This is another of the many parallels between Jugurtha and Marius, both being concerned with popular approbation as *novi*. In any case, this assessment of Jugurtha was very pertinent to Sallust's theory of nobles in decline: the opinion of the Roman people mattered more to Jugurtha because the nobles could be disposed of through their greed.[62] Jugurtha's character is an important example of the Sallustian concept of *virtus* and its decline, but so are the nobles' characters; Jugurtha's *ambitio* finds a free channel in the nobility's *avaritia*. Sallust seems keen to emphasize that there was not one side of justice and righteousness fighting against another of injustice and corruption; there was not only one person guilty for the outbreak of this war.

One can recognize a somewhat tragic element in Sallust's villains. Just as Catiline—an incarnation of wickedness—had attracted Sallust's and our ad-

---

57. Cf. Sall. *BJ* 7.7.
58. Sall. *BJ* 8.1: *in ipso maxumam virtutem*.
59. Sall. *BJ* 8.1.
60. Cf. Sall. *BC* 5.1–2; Plut. *Cato minor*, 1.2.
61. Cf. Sall. *BC* 11.1.
62. Sall. *BJ* 13.5. Cf. von Fritz, "Sallust and the Attitude of the Roman Nobility." For Jugurtha's influence on the Senate, see Allen, "Source of Jugurtha's Influence."

miration for his courage and masterly command of his troops, Jugurtha's noble personality moves us to sympathize with him, all the more when it appears that he has been seduced by the greedy Romans to behave as he does. Although Catiline and Jugurtha are put forward as undoubtedly "bad," they are not completely repulsive. Moreover, Sallust himself chooses to speak out through this illegitimate and criminal Numidian king. It is interesting to see how Sallust uses a non-Roman as the mouthpiece for moral judgment: "The Romans," said Jugurtha, "were without justice, of insatiable greed, the common enemies of all mankind. They had the same motive for a war with Bocchus as they had for a war with Jugurtha himself and other nations, namely, their lust for empire [*lubidinem imperitandi*] which made them hostile to all monarchies."[63] Sallust seems to be following a long tradition of using outsiders to promote thought about one's own customs,[64] and in this case in particular it raises questions over how culturally constructed *virtus* is.

The war becomes long and tiresome; the continuous and frustrating efforts made by the Romans to catch Jugurtha produced nothing but annoyance and disappointment. In Sallust's portrayal Jugurtha manages to combine postponement and swiftness, all wrapped up with shrewd dissimulation, to throw the Roman offensive into confusion. Neither Metellus' nor Marius' strategies or *virtus* were able to put an end to it, but only Sulla's bargain with Bocchus. It is striking that the Romans, who possessed good generals, soldiers, and weapons, were able to win the war only through treachery. In fact, they win by using the same deceitful techniques as the Numidian king had used before. The only difference was that the Romans used these skills—mainly deception and bribery—more effectively.[65] Although it is actually Bocchus who in the end decides to hand over Jugurtha to the Romans, the latter's negotiations throughout the war have been marked by the same dishonesty and duplicity. For Sallust this was not, by any means, a virtuous triumph, nor could it be counted as a fair victory over the enemy. But the sense of confusion and corruption that "had invaded" (*invaserat*) everything made it more difficult to distinguish honorable behavior. This verb, *invado*, as we will see later, is prominent in Sallust's narrative.[66] It shows the way corruption, decline, moral disease, and military decay spread through

---

63. Sall. *BJ* 81.1.
64. See, for example, Hdt. 3.38 or Aesch. *Persae* 230 ff.
65. For reasons of the prominence of bribery in Sallust's narrative, see Paul, *Historical Commentary on Sallust's Bellum Jugurthinum*, app. 1.
66. For more instances of the word in the *BJ*, see 32.4; 84.3; 89.6.

society like a deadly plague. The ones who are supposed to show *virtus* employ evil practices instead, and what is worse, they win the war.

Jugurtha fades into the background to make way for Metellus, who will now hold center stage until Marius takes over. The presence of the noble Quintus Caecilius Metellus in the *BJ* gives a wider overview of the Numidian war. He is placed neither on the side of Jugurtha nor on that of Marius, whom he disregards for his *novitas*. Sallust's description is very enthusiastic; he is introduced with the same epithet as that used of Jugurtha: a man of action (*acer*),[67] and of consistent and unblemished reputation (*fama aequabili et inviolata*) who showed himself a great and prudent man (*magnum et sapientem*), mainly by balancing popularity-seeking and excessive harshness.[68] A large portion of the narrative in the *BJ* is devoted to Metellus' achievements in the war against the Numidian.[69] Victories and successes came steadily, and although the war was difficult and strenuous, Metellus did not seem to make a single mistake in his advance toward the enemy, and his fame increased nonstop. Metellus behaved like a good general of old times, restoring the discipline in the army according to the *mos maiorum* and showing his *virtus* in battle.[70]

Catiline had been a corrupt aristocrat, who perfectly matched Sallust's picture of nobles in decay, although he too could be seen as an example of ruined *virtus*, and all the more dangerous for it. But Metellus is a more complex character. He does not exactly decline in the course of the *BJ*: he reappears in full popularity in Rome later on, and Sallust certainly gives him his due.[71] But he does have the aristocratic vice of arrogance, which has seriously damaging consequences.[72] He is a man of *virtus*, but not true *virtus*, for he had a dominant trait within himself that worked self-destructively: his *superbia*.

This *superbia* was destined to spoil his brilliant career. The unmanly behavior that Metellus displayed when he heard the news that the province of Numidia had fallen to Marius—also attested in Plutarch[73]—was condemned not only by Sallust but also by the people of Rome.[74] Metellus' *superbia*, which gave him a real dislike for Marius, finally led him to compromise the conduct of the war, showing once again the decline of *virtus* toward *vitium*.

---

67. Cf. Sall. *BJ* 20.2.
68. Sall. *BJ* 43.1; 45.1.
69. Cf. Sall. *BJ* 43–83.
70. Sall. *BJ* 55.1.
71. Cf. Sall. *BJ* 88.1.
72. Cf. Sall. *BJ* 64.1.
73. Cf. Plut. *Marius* 10.
74. Sall. *BJ* 82.3–4. Cf. also 73.4.

Sallust gives the details of the feelings of Metellus—who repressed neither his tears nor his tongue—precisely to emphasize the depth of the lack of *concordia* and sometimes even hatred between parties, which seemed to correspond exactly with what he had said in the excursus on party strife.[75] Metellus seemed to have had many advantages over Marius, but in these times of confusion what was previously considered a privilege ceased to be so, and the order of things was turned upside down: "the general's noble birth, until then a badge of distinction, now became a source of unpopularity, whereas the other's [Marius] humble origin won him all the more favor. In both cases, however, it was party spirit [*studia partium*] that was the guiding influence rather than the good or bad qualities of the men themselves."[76]

Metellus' character and performance are subtly contrasted with those of another nobleman: Sulla. The whole description of this successful aristocrat is tainted with ambiguity: he was learned, eloquent, and hardworking; friendly and generous but too ambitious, pleasure seeking, and a simulator.[77] Sallust's portrayal of Sulla is not only ambiguous but also enigmatic. He describes his qualities but not his actions; he does not tell us what Sulla did in his *otio luxurioso*, why his behavior could have been *honestius* with his wife, or what the purposes he wanted to disguise were. He omits Sulla's actions, precisely the field where *virtus* should have shone. Sallust does not provide his audience with an explicit final opinion about Sulla's personality (*incertum habeo*);[78] he had some good qualities but was not Sallust's hero.[79] Sulla's *luxuria* hints that this vice was preventing him from achieving true *virtus*. This *luxuria*—like Metellus' *superbia*—was one of the common defects of the nobility.[80]

It was Sulla, however, who brought the war to an end. The shrewdness he displayed in the speech convincing king Bocchus that he should cooperate in Jugurtha's capture,[81] together with his characteristic good luck,[82] seemed to have worked favorably toward the successful completion of the war. "Before his victory in the Civil War," Sallust adds, "he had enjoyed unparalleled good fortune, but it was never greater than his energy warranted, and many have

---

75. For this, see Comber and Balmaceda, *Sallust*, 216–22.
76. Sall. *BJ* 73.4.
77. Sall. *BJ* 95.3–4. For Sulla, see Zecchini, "Sylla selon Salluste"; Keaveney, *Sulla*.
78. Sall. *BJ* 95.4.
79. In fact, nobody fits this category in Sallust's narrative.
80. As it is shown in Sall. *BC* 5.8 and 25.1–5.
81. Cf. Sall. *BJ* 102.5–10.
82. Sulla adopted the name of Felix, "the Fortunate," in late 82 B.C. out of a belief of his good luck. For Sulla's cognomen, see Baldson, "Sulla Felix," 1–10.

wondered whether he was braver or just luckier [*Atque illi felicissimo omnium ante civilem victoriam numquam super industriam fortuna fuit, multique dubitavere, fortior an felicior esset*]."[83] Some may have wondered, but not Sallust. He deliberately never speaks about Sulla's *virtus*, but rather his *industria*, and when he refers to his courage he talks of *fortitudo*. Sulla's career in the *BJ* is untarnished, but the decline into which he was to fall beyond the strict scope of the monograph would surely have been a matter of common knowledge and would have highlighted the contrast. This is another example, like Jugurtha, of the development of a character, though it is not shown explicitly in the text, but hinted at by future events.

With the entrance of Gaius Marius on the scene, Sallust appears to have reached the summit of the exposition of his theory of *virtus*. In his idealized description of Marius' character, he confers on him all the qualities he would have liked the *homo novus* to have: energy (*industria*), integrity (*probitas*), great military skill (*militiae magna scientia*), an indomitable spirit in war (*animus belli ingens*), modesty in peace (*domi modicus*), superiority to passions and riches (*lubidinis et divitiarum victor*) greed only for glory (*tantum modo gloriae avidus*).[84] Marius displayed no Grecian eloquence, no elegance of the city, things that were signs of corrupted *mores*. Marius' *virtus* seems like the old Roman *virtus* proclaimed by Cato the Elder, made of toil, endurance of hardships, military valor, moderation, and frugality. In short, "no new man was so famous or so illustrious for his deeds."[85] Though it is worth noting that Sallust himself never says that Marius was a man of *virtus*, this assumption is either implicit or mentioned by Marius himself or his supporters.

Talking about Marius' *virtus*, M. McDonnell devotes a long section of his *Roman Manliness* to distinguishing how two versions of Sallustian *virtus* were opposed: Marius' *virtus*, which for McDonnell was Roman and martial, versus Metellus' *virtus*, which was Hellenized and ethical.[86] This seems to me too neat an exposition, an excessively coherent analysis: once again, the warrior Roman against the learned Greek. Sallust's Marius, certainly, shows no interest at all in Greek instruction: *neque litteras Graecas didici; parum placebat eas discere;*[87] but his insistence on his morally upright behavior through-

---

83. Sall. *BJ* 95.4.
84. Sall. *BJ* 63.2. For Marius, see Passerini, "Caio Mario come uomo politico"; Carney, *Biography of Caius Marius*; Evans, *Gaius Marius*.
85. Sall. *BJ* 63.7.
86. McDonnell, *Roman Manliness*, 265–92; and also 368–78.
87. Sall. *BJ* 85.32.

out his life makes his *virtus* hardly nonethical. He relies on himself: his *virtus* and his *innocentia*.[88] Similarly, Metellus, the exponent of the Hellenized ethical *virtus* according to McDonnell, relies also on his courage. He treated his army in the fashion of old (*more maiorum*) and won the battles by his valor (*virtus*).[89] Contrasting one type of *virtus* that is ethical, private, and Greek with another that is Roman, public, and "courageous" does not help much toward the comprehensive understanding of the concept of *virtus* in Sallust or in any other Roman historian, and one may fail to engage with the complexities that the word conveyed as a whole. The old generals of the republic described in the histories—Camillus, Marcellus, Fabius Maximus, and others—were brave *and* honest; they displayed courage in battle *and* other virtues necessary to be regarded as men of *virtus*. The intended dichotomy appears, then, somewhat artificial. More than dualism in *virtus*, one finds that its various elements intermingle.[90]

Marius' greatest achievement was undoubtedly to have won the consular election. He had succeeded despite Metellus' humiliating comment, partly because of his own merits, partly because his *ingenium*, inflamed by ambition and resentment, moved him in that direction. He had been elected with the ardent support of the commons, and once in power he began to attack the aristocrats, making remarks to glorify himself and exasperate them.[91] The antagonism between the aristocracy and the *populus* became more and more heated. Both parties, as Sallust had mentioned earlier in the narrative, were exercising the same corrupt practices; nobles, *novi*, and people alike had abandoned the path of *virtus*.[92] Thus, fortune or luck was responsible for success, rather than *virtus*. People exaggerated Marius' merits, and every ill-advised action of his was taken as a proof of his *virtus*, which won him glory instead of blame.[93] On the one hand, Sallust emphasizes the uniqueness of Marius, but at the same time he is making it clear that his *virtus* too was tainted. All of Marius' good qualities start to wither because this excessive desire of acquiring glory led him into ambition: "later on ambition brought about his downfall [*nam postea*

---

88. Cf. Sall. *BJ* 85.4. See also 85.7; 85.10; 85.14; 85.34; 85.47.
89. Sall. *BJ* 55.1.
90. McDonnell, *Roman Manliness*, 382–84, applies the same opposition to Cato's and Caesar's *virtus*, the former being more ethical and Hellenized and the latter more martial and Roman.
91. Sall. *BJ* 84.1.
92. Cf. Sall. *BJ* 41–42.
93. Sall. *BJ* 92.2–94.6.

ambitione praeceps datus est]."[94] Again, we see *virtus* shading and mingling with vice because of *ambitio*.

To encourage men to enroll and go to fight in Numidia, Marius delivered a speech full of fire, in which he presented himself as a man worthy to be followed and obeyed, not sparing self-praise and contrasting his own good qualities with the arrogance of the nobles.[95] Although there are some parallels with Plutarch's speech in his *Marius*,[96] it looks as if it is Sallust's own way of dramatically presenting the personality of Marius: he is the combative new man, bitterly and self-righteously resentful of the traditional aristocracy. Sallust, through Marius, stressed some of the ideas he had put across in the prologue: that all men share the same nature; the importance of actions not words;[97] that nobility springs from virtue,[98] and therefore it cannot be inherited.[99]

One particular expression of *virtus* was to overcome hardship and danger (*labor et periculum*). These actions had been carried out by the nobility to justify their position; they had won their *virtus* by facing adversities and perils. These would now become something particularly linked to the *novi*. This revision of political concepts involved the "appropriation" of aristocratic ideas with the consequent "adaptation" to the *homines novi*, made by Cicero and Sallust in their works. Marius says, "I have lived a life that is no stranger to every kind of hardship and danger [*labores et pericula*],"[100] equating himself to the first Roman nobles in *virtus*. He can claim *virtus* with the *nobiles*' terminology, because he has actually performed in the *nobiles*' way. This fact could also be used to undermine Marius' speech: he fails notoriously to adopt any new terminology, because of his own anxiety to win the traditional approval and good opinion of the *populus*. This failure, of course, raises questions about how much had really changed or how new his *nova nobilitas* really was.

---

94. Sall. *BJ* 63.3.

95. For discussions on Marius' speech, see von Carolsfeld, *Über die Reden und Briefe bei Sallust*, 52–55; Ullmann, *La technique des discours dans Salluste, Tite-Live et Tacite*, 37 (on chapter 31); Skaard, "Marius' Speech in Sallust, Jug. Chap. 85"; Vretska, *Studien zu Sallust*; Carney, "Once again Marius' Speech after Election in 108 B.C."; Büchner, *Sallust*, 182, 196; Syme, *Sallust*, 168–69. Raimondi, "Discorsi di Caio Mario," 95–100. See also Paul, *Historical Commentary on Sallust's Bellum Jugurthinum*; and Comber and Balmaceda, *Sallust*, comm. ad loc.

96. Plut. *Marius* 9.

97. Sall. *BJ* 85.14. Sallust implies that deeds are greater than words (as he had said plainly in *BC* 3.2 and 8.5) but attempts to prove in his writings that they can at least be equal.

98. Sall. *BJ* 85.17.

99. Sall. *BJ* 85.38.

100. Sall. *BJ* 85.7 and also 85.30.

But the presentation of Marius as a man of *virtus* was not just a Sallustian device to expound his theory of the *homo novus* and this new nobility. In fact, the historical Marius did consider himself a true representative of *virtus*, and this is best illustrated in his dedication of a temple to *Honos et Virtus* with the spoils of the campaign against the Cimbri and Teutones in 102–1 B.C. With this temple, which was the only monumental building of Marius' political career, he was possibly emulating Fabius Maximus and Scipio Aemilianus, who had done the same in 234 and 133 B.C., respectively, but perhaps, in Marius' case, with more emphasis on the *industria* characteristic of the new men.[101]

Nobilitas and *novitas* are key ideas to both Sallust and Marius, but the terms are elusive and difficult to grasp. They seem best dealt with by simultaneous approaches: philological, political, and social. As said in chapter 1, the term *nobilis* appears to be related to the verb "to know," *noscere*, and means in essence "notable." A *nobilis* was *notus*, or rather, because one was *notus*, one could be counted as a *nobilis*. This notability, expressed in *gloria*, had been acquired by serving the state with great deeds, or showing exceptional courage in its defense or enlargement. These achievements, then, had been performed by the *virtus* of certain individuals. *Virtus* had made these individuals famous and glorious: *nobilitas* sprang from *virtus*, and not the other way around.[102] This notability was transferred to the family, and it manifested its most beneficial effects at the elections of magistrates. They were the descendants of the "great doers," they were known as such, and consequently they seemed better equipped for holding office. *Nobilitas*, then, was a semitechnical term, not to be wholly identified with aristocracy, and at the same time a concept with political and social implications. This had significant repercussions in terms of those who could aspire to the quality and those to whom it was debarred. The same vagueness can be found in the definition of *homo novus*. It may be used in general of those who were the first of their families to reach the Senate and in a more special sense to those among this latter group who were the first to achieve the consulship. The *homines novi* are better understood as individuals who rose politically. Even though they did not form a party, they did, nevertheless, represent the aspiration of a social group that

---

101. Cf. Vitruvius, 3.2.5; Val. Max. 1.7.5. For more details and the location of this temple, see *Lexicon Topographicum Urbis Romae*, III, 33–35; Platner and Ashby, *Topographical Dictionary of Ancient Rome*, 259–60; Coarelli, *Il Foro Romano*, 101–2; Richardson, "Honos et Virtus and the Sacra Via," 240–46; and Richardson, *New Topographical Dictionary of Ancient Rome*, 190.

102. Cf. Tiffou, *Essai sur la Pensée Morale de Salluste à la Lumière de ses Prologues*.

wanted to establish a proper place in society and politics that matched its social and economic importance.[103]

Considering that there is no exact Roman definition of *nobilis* or *homo novus* it is difficult to construct strict categories for them; rather, it seems likely that these terms were determined more by usage. What is relevant for our understanding of Sallust's standpoint is that in his judgments and attitudes he seems to distinguish between political groups and individuals. Thus, he treats the *nobilitas* as a whole with severity[104] but does not withhold praise when a *nobilis* deserves it, as is the case with Metellus, Sulla, or Caesar. However, toward "the few" or *pauci*, which is not a social category but a political one, Sallust is never positive. It was the oligarchy that incarnated all vices. *Nobilitas* does not identify per se with the *pauci*, but the *pauci* belonged to the *nobilitas*, of whom they constituted a very politically active part, expressed in their actual power: the *potentia paucorum*.[105] Sallust's opinion regarding the *homines novi* appears similar to—though not exactly the same as—his opinion of the nobles as an entity. He expresses disappointment at the bitter reality that "even new men, who formerly always used to outstrip the nobility by their *virtus* alone, now force their way into commands and distinctions by underhand intrigue and open robbery, instead of by honorable means [*etiam homines novi, qui antea per virtutem soliti erant nobilitatem antevenire, furtim et per latrocinia potius quam bonis artibus ad imperia et honores nituntur*]."[106] But he is also eager to praise their individual virtues and qualities.

Coming back to Marius' speech and the *virtus* of the *homo novus*, it is possible to see some interesting parallels with Cicero's thought as shown in chapter 1. They may well be Sallust's adaptation for the propaganda of the *homines novi*. Cicero had developed a more complex form of the new man's ideology, which he defined as its moral sense and the central role of *virtus* in it. This, as previously said, was summarized as *moribus non maioribus*,[107] meaning that what counted more was not the ancestors but the actual character of the per-

---

103. For the discussion of *nobiles* and *novi*, and the different views held by modern scholars, see mainly Gelzer, *Roman Nobility*; Wiseman, *New Men in the Roman Senate*; Dondin-Payre, "*Homo novus*, un slogan de Caton à Cesar?"; Brunt, "Nobilitas et Novitas"; Shackleton Bailey, "*Nobiles* and *novi* Reconsidered." For a thorough exposition of the *status quaestionis*, see van der Blom, *Cicero's Role Models*, 35–59.
104. Cf. Sall. *BJ* 64.1: *contemptor animus et superbia, commune nobilitatis malum*.
105. Cf. Sall. *BJ* 3.3; *BC*, 20.7; 39.1; 58.11.
106. Sall. *BJ* 4.7.
107. Cic. *Pis*, 1.

son. "Nobility is nothing but recognized virtue," says Cicero later on,[108] and in his speech Marius put forward the same idea in very similar words. Both *novi*—Marius and Cicero—try to legitimize a new nobility. And even if there is no certainty as to Marius' actual words, one can assume that a *novus* would have attempted to validate his claim to *nobilitas* in this way: "I cannot, to inspire confidence, display the portraits, triumphs, or consulships of my ancestors, but, if the occasion demands, I can show spears, a banner, trappings, and other military honors, not to mention scars on the front of my body. These are my family portraits [*hae sunt meae imagines*], these are my nobility [*haec nobilitas*], not bequeathed to me in an inheritance, as theirs were to them, but won by dint of countless toils and perils on my part (. . .) is plain enough in itself [*ipsa se virtus satis ostendit*]."[109] The core of Marius' argument here is that the first Roman *nobiles* had once been *novi homines* like himself, without ancestral *imagines*, and that they had achieved their *nobilitas* by showing their *virtus*. Marius seems to denounce as inconceivable the claim that nobility can be self-justified. But if *virtus* was the *nobiles*' justification, then the *novi*, champions of *virtus*, could also reach *nobilitas*. Marius' reinterpretation of a key social and political word allows him to reinterpret the Roman past as well, and in doing so he will show a particular keenness for a more inclusive and open society: anybody could be noble if he had *virtus*, in the same way even the *capite censi* (those counted by head) could join the army if they were willing.[110] In thus stressing the accessibility of *virtus*, Sallust was probably portraying his own world rather than that of Marius, but the beginnings of this "openness" may have started with Marius. All this *virtus*-ideology was greatly advertised by the two distinguished *novi* from Arpinum, Marius and Cicero; and Sallust was assembling what must have been a fairly common thought in the forties and thirties B.C.

In spite of what has been said, one should not identify Marius as Sallust's hero. He is led by *ambitio* in the same way as the nobility had been, and does not always use the *bonae artes* of his *ingenium* to achieve greater glory. The unmanly way Marius denigrates his commander, Metellus, and the unjustified risks he later runs in order to emulate him tarnish his original *virtus* and

---

108. Cic. *Ad Fam*, fragments VI.3 (Shackleton Bailey): *cum enim nobilitas nihil aliud sit quam cognita virtus*.

109. Sall. *BJ* 85.29–31. For the importance of the *imagines* in political elections, see Flower, *Ancestor Masks*, 60–90.

110. Cf. Sall. *BJ*, 86.2. For Marius' military reform, see Harmand, *L'armée et le soldat à Rome de 107 à 50 avant notre ère*; Brunt, *Italian Manpower*, 406–8; Keppie, *Making of the Roman Army*, 57–79.

upset the tentative division we had made between the decayed *nobiles* and the sound new men. Sallust's final evaluation of Marius is a combination of admiration for the man who opposed the arrogance of the *nobiles* and a somewhat less enthusiastic awareness of the responsibility Marius was to bear for the civil wars.

Was there any safe solution for Rome? Could, for example, Metellus' *virtus* together with that of Marius have done a better job if they had worked in *concordia* and cooperatively?[111] As in the *BC*, there is the temptation to think that there might be two types of *virtus* that would complement each other. But if corruption had made it impossible to trust the nobility, there was not much hope coming from the *novi* either. The *mos partium et factionum* (the way of parties and factions) meant that there could be no unity, only disintegration.

In his monographs Sallust gives us an uneven treatment of the episodes of the *bella*, chronological and geographical mistakes, and a biased view of the motives of the nobility in the war, because he is too focused on his own scheme.[112] He seems anxious to prove that after the destruction of Carthage, *virtus* abandoned Rome and decline made its entrance through *ambitio, avaritia et luxuria*. Sallust seems actually more concerned with *virtus* and its decline than with the narrative itself, and he will push the narrative a little to fit his theory better.

The odd, open endings of the two monographs suggest that this decline is still present in Sallust's own society. At the time Sallust was writing, probably under the second triumvirate (and its proscriptions), the end of the *BC* was still very much in front of their eyes: "Many too who had gone from the camp to visit the field or to pillage, on turning over the bodies of the rebels found now a friend, now a guest or a kinsman; some also recognized their personal enemies. Thus the whole army was variously affected with sorrow and grief, rejoicing and lamentation."[113] Romans in Sallust's times were still in the same position: feeling happy that their enemies had fallen, and sad for their fallen friends. And above all, Rome's future was still in the hands of one man—whoever won the civil wars between Octavian and Antony—as is seen in the

---

111. The digression on the Philaeni brothers (Sall. *BJ*, 79–80) could suggest that cooperation within the community would bring success.

112. For these inaccuracies, see Paul, *Historical Commentary on Sallust's Bellum Jugurthinum*, esp. 1–8; Earl, *Political Thought of Sallust*; and Syme, *Sallust*. For Sallust's bias, see Calevo, *Il problema della tendenziosità di Sallustio*; and Parker, "*Roma omnia venalia esse.*" For the *BJ* as being part of a larger work, see Levene, "Sallust's Jugurtha," 53–70.

113. Sall. *BC* 61.9.

ending of the *BJ*: "Marius was made consul in his absence and the province of Gaul was assigned to him. On the calends of January, amid great pomp and as consul, he celebrated a triumph. At that time all the hopes and resources of the state were in his hands."[114] It is difficult not to think of the rivalry of the triumvirs. For Sallust, not much had changed since Jugurtha, very little since Catiline. The republic continued its race downhill. There seemed to be no boundaries to corruption: Rome "by gradual changes has ceased to be the noblest and best [*pulcherrima atque optuma*], and has become the worst and most vicious [*pessuma ac flagitiosissuma*]."[115]

The sense of the unfinished, which keeps the reader hovering between retrospection and anticipation, makes the monographs highly effective pieces for Sallust's purpose.[116] Our attention is at the same time on the present moment and on the future. Sallust planned it that way. His prologues make perfect sense if one detaches them from the following narrative: the supremacy of mind over the body, the reign of *virtus* (public and active) over chance, and the natural human goal placed in *gloria* serving the *res publica*. But when one arrives at the end of the stories, the final conclusion seems to be that it does not actually work like that, and one is left with a question mark.

The Nature and Presentation of Decline: Sallust's Vocabulary of Decay

One final point I would like to touch on in this chapter concerns the importance that Sallust gives to the nature of decline and the way it spreads. I will show in this section how he achieves a sophisticated presentation of political decline that, with careful diction, elaborates, develops, and at the same time contradicts the picture that he had portrayed in the prologues. It is arguable that in the narratives of his monographs Sallust presents a disquieting interconnection between decline and *virtus*, and through careful choice of words and constructions, this interrelation attains such rhetorical power that the form of his arrangement becomes at the same time part of the content.

One way in which Sallust explains political decline is through the devaluation of language: the use and abuse of important, traditional political words to signify new ideas or behaviors. This was not a new topic for historians, and Thucydides' influence on Sallust regarding this point has been duly

---

114. Sall. *BJ* 114.3–4.
115. Sall. *BC* 5.9.
116. Cf. Scanlon, *Spes Frustrata*; Grethlein, *Experience and Teleology in Ancient Historiography*.

emphasized by scholars.[117] The passage on stasis at Corcyra is a classic example of Thucydides showing that civil war and devaluation of language mutually reinforced one another: "they exchanged their usual evaluations of deeds for new ones, in the light of what they now thought justified."[118] Subversion of political vocabulary was something that Thucydides had denounced as an inevitable feature of internal political struggle, and it was something that Sallust would pick up in his presentation of decline.

For Thucydides it was civil war, the *biaios disdaskalos*,[119] that was responsible for this devaluation; for Sallust the debasement of language as a sign of decline had a different origin. For him, decline in Rome stemmed mainly from the absence of foreign threat. The end of *metus hostilis* had brought all bad things: leisure, wealth, and desire for money and power, and it had a direct impact on the use of words: "the terms good [*boni*] and bad [*mali*] were applied to citizens, not on the yardstick of services rendered to (or injuries inflicted on) the state [*non ob merita in rempublicam*], since all were equally corrupt [*omnibus pariter corruptis*]; any individual of outstanding wealth and irresistible in his lawlessness was considered good because he was the preserver of the existing conditions."[120] The meaningful word *boni* was now susceptible to willful misunderstanding; it was applied mainly to the defenders of the *status quo*, and it worked as a false cover to their deeds.[121] Sallust also warns his audience against the use of fine words such as "tranquility" (*otium*) for what in reality is "slavery" (*servitium*).[122] He even attacks the misuse of *dignitas* and *libertas* to cover selfish passions.[123] And he has Cato sinisterly proclaiming that all the honors reserved for *virtus* are now claimed by *ambitio*.[124] Thus, the language of *virtus* of the beginning of the monographs is at some point replaced by the language of decline, with its particular vocabulary of *vitium*, till it reaches a stage where it is used with frightening interchangeability.

---

117. For Thucydides' influence on Sallust, see Scanlon, *Influence of Thucydides on Sallust*. See also Perrochat, *Les Modèles Grecs de Salluste*, and contrast with Grethlein, "Unthucydidean Voice of Sallust."

118. Thuc. 3.82.4 with Wilson's translation, "The customary meaning of words were changed," 18–20. Cf. Swain, "Thucydides 1.22.1 and 3.82.4."

119. Thuc. 3.82.2.

120. Sall. *Hist*, 1.12.

121. For more on *boni*, see McGushin, *Sallust: The Histories*, ad loc. For a comprehensive study of Sallus's political concepts, see Paananen, *Sallust's Politico-Social Terminology*.

122. Cf. Sall. *Hist*, 3.13.

123. Cf. Sall. *BJ* 41.5.

124. Cf. Sall. *BC* 52.22: *omnia virtutis praemia ambitio possidet*. This idea is developed further in the *Histories* 1.12.

Cato's speech in the *BC* explicitly touches on the theme of the debasement of language with all its dramatic implications: "in very truth we have long since lost the true names for things [*iam pridem equidem nos vera vocabula rerum amisimus*]."[125] For Cato, it is because giving away the property of others is now called "generosity"; or destructive temerity, "bravery" that the republic is reduced to dire straits. It is quite striking how Sallust gives the subversion of some words as the direct cause of decadence. Change of language affects everybody at all levels of society. Words and language are the means that sustain communication in society; if the word becomes corrupted, social life will not remain unaffected. If man reshapes the evaluation of what he considers generosity or courage, he will unconsciously start changing the grounds on which he operates and, in the end, his conduct. The idea behind Sallust's phrase is that meanings can move the boundaries of behavior.

The very word *amisimus*—"we have lost"—in Cato's speech suggests that in some way men were not totally aware of these changes, but that it was the force of the decadent state of affairs in Rome that had drawn them to these new evaluations. On the other hand, the Romans themselves were responsible for this decadence: they "had fallen" into *ambitio*, *avaritia*, and *luxuria* as a result of the wealth and peace after the fall of Carthage, and nobody seemed ashamed of working for their own benefit instead of the state's.[126] "After riches began to be held in honor and led to the acquisition of glory, positions of authority, and political influence, then virtue began to lose its edge, poverty to be considered a disgrace, innocence to be regarded as wickedness [*Postquam divitiae honori esse coepere et eas gloria, imperium, potentia sequebatur, hebescere virtus, paupertas probro haberi, innocentia pro malevolentia duci coepit*]."[127] *Hebescere virtus* seemed to have been the main problem that came with wealth, hence the violent introduction (*invasere*) of vices: "to rob, to squander, to set little value on their property, to covet the goods of others, to scorn modesty, chastity, things human and divine, to have no scruples and no moderation [*rapere, consumere, sua parvi pendere, aliena cupere, pudorem, pudicitiam, divina atque humana promiscua, nihil pensi neque moderati habere*]."[128] The insistent use of *coepere*, *coepit*, and infinitives here suggests an ongoing

---

125. Cf. Sall. *BC* 52.11. For the role of *vocabulum*, see Haynes, "Tacitus' Dangerous Word," 33–61.
126. And even more, they were corrupting others, e.g., Jugurtha.
127. Sall. *BC*, 12.1. For *hebescere virtus*, see Krebs, "Hebescere Virtus."
128. Sall. *BC* 12.1 (my highlighting).

process, and Sallust is emphasizing when those things started to happen, and that they have not yet come to an end.[129]

One of the dangers was that ambition *vitium propius virtutem erat*.[130] Both *virtus* and *ambitio* longed for glory, honor, and power; the first achieved them through good practices (*bonae artes*), the latter through treachery and deception (*dolis atque fallaciis*).[131] Sallust acknowledges the disturbing proximity of *vitium* and *virtus* as a distinctive feature of political decline.

There are so many instances in which Sallust denounces the corrupted state of the city that to give all references would be repetitive and tiresome.[132] The idea of disorder and disruption was omnipresent and, in some way, also overwhelming: it had started gradually (*paulatim*), but then, quickly and destructively it had spread like deadly plague. The word "spread" is a poor reflection of the original *invasit*. Sallust's insistence on using this particular verb is related to one notable aspect of his obsession with corruption and decline, namely, the manner of its spreading.

Both military and disease imagery runs through Sallust's language of *vitium*. When, in keeping with this train of images, Sallust wishes to depict an access of violent emotion, he uses the same verb, *invado*: "after the tyranny of Sulla, Catiline *had been assailed* by the greatest passion for seizing control of the government [*hunc* (Catilina) *post dominationem L. Sullae lubido maxuma invaserat rei publicae capiundae*],"[133] or "*therefore as a result of riches, youths were suddenly consumed* with luxury and greed together with insolence [*igitur ex divitiis iuventutem luxuria atque avaritia cum superbia invasere*],"[134] and "a disease of such great intensity, and just like a plague, *had infected* the minds of great many of our countrymen [*tanta vis morbi aeque uti tabes plerosque civium invaserat*]."[135] The verb "to invade" can be used of an army invading a terri-

---

129. For other uses of the historical infinitive, see von Albrecht, *Masters of Roman Prose*, 71–72; and Hessen, *Der Historische Infinitiv im Wandel der Darstellungstechnik Sallusts*.
130. Sall. *BC* 11.1.
131. Sall. *BC* 11.2.
132. See, for example, *BC* 5.8; 5.9; 10.4; 10.6; 11–12; 38.4; *BJ* 8.1; 20.1; 35.10; 41; *Hist*, 1.13.
133. Sall. *BC* 5.6.
134. Sall. *BC* 12.2.
135. Sall. *BC* 36.5. For more *invadere* in the *BC*, see 2.5; 10.6; 31.1. The presence of the verb *invadere* is equally well attested in the *BJ*; see, for example, 24.2: *tanta lubido extinguendi me invasit (Iugurtha)*; 32.4: *tanta vis avaritiae animos eorum veluti tabes* invaserat; 41.9: *ita cum potentia avaritia sine modo modestiaque invadere . . .* ; 84.3: *tanta libido cum Mario eundi plerosque invaserat*; 89.6: *Eius potiendi Marium maxima cupido invaserat*; 106.6: *tum vero ingens metus nostros invadit*.

tory or of an infection invading the body.[136] Both represent aggressiveness, inevitability, and a certain speed. There is also a touch of unpreparedness that relates to losing control and the sense of being overcome with little or no possibility of escape. This is the way in which *vitium* takes over *virtus*, and examples of this phenomenon occur in both monographs and among the masses and individual characters representing the personal and the political bodies: Roman soldiers are invaded by *avaritia*,[137] the youth by *superbia*,[138] Marius by the *cupido potiundi*,[139] and Catiline by his *lubido rei publicae capiundae*.[140]

The equivalent of *invado* in the language of *virtus* is the verb *incedo*. *Incedere* is similar to *invadere*, but it also differs from it in several ways: firstly in its pace; *incedere* means to advance, to approach, or to march forward (almost in a stately manner), and therefore the pace is slower. Secondly it is less violent and does not necessarily imply aggressiveness; and lastly, there is no sense of being totally overcome by it; there is more control. Sallust uses *incedo* when speaking of the summit of *virtus* in early times, when Romans with *virtus* competed with one another for *gloria*: *tanta cupido gloriae* incesserat (such a craving for glory had grown forth).[141] Later on in the narrative, one can see that something is going seriously wrong when Sallust chooses the same verb *incedo* to announce the depths of corruption: "but there had arisen an equally strong passion for lewdness, gluttony, and other accompaniments of luxury [*sed lubido stupri, ganeae ceterique cultus non minor* incesserat]";[142] or in the *BJ*: "the regular companions of prosperity, license and arrogance appeared [*ea quae res secundae amant, lascivia atque superbia* incessere]."[143] The verb that had previously described *virtus* is now illustrating *vitium*. Although much has been said of the devaluation of language in Sallust and its connection with Thucydidean stasis,[144] it is also possible to say that the real corruption of language lies not so much in the change of meaning of words, but especially in

---

136. See also Thucydides' use of *epepese* in 3.82.2: together with the military meaning of "falling upon an enemy," there is the other meaning of "falling down," being ruined. This is what the plague and the stasis produced in Corcyra.

137. Cf. Sall. *BJ* 32.5.

138. Cf. Sall. *BC* 12.2.

139. Cf. Sall. *BJ* 89.6.

140. Sall. *BC* 5.6.

141. Sall. *BC* 7.3.

142. Sall. *BC* 13.3.

143. Sall. *BJ* 41.3.

144. For a different view, see Batstone, "Word at War," where he claims that duplicity and verbal warfare are not special linguistic features of stasis.

the disturbing way words that usually refer to *virtus* are now used to refer to *vitium*, and the proximity of meanings that, for Sallust, is even more dangerous. In this sense, for example, the problem is not that when Catiline gives his speech to his soldiers and talks of *virtus* he is debasing the meaning of the concept by perversion or demagoguery so that it is a false *virtus*.[145] On the contrary, the serious difficulty for Sallust is that Catiline is actually talking about true *virtus*, and encouraging his soldiers to be genuinely brave in the fight to free themselves from the *potentia paucorum*. And this is precisely what his soldiers are going to do.

Another instance of this disconcerting proximity between the languages of *virtus* and *vitium* is Sallust's praise of his ideal republic of the past and its young men well trained for toil and hardship: "Accordingly, to such distinguished men, no task was unfamiliar, not any place too rough or steep, no armed stranger too formidable [*igitur talibus viris non labor insolitus, non locus ullus asper aut arduus erat, non armatus hostis formidulosus*]."[146] These hardy republicans are perhaps too close to the all-enduring Catiline: "His body could endure hunger, cold, and sleeplessness to an incredible degree [*corpus patiens inediae, algoris, vigiliae supra quam cuiquam credibile est*]."[147] Sallust does not present a simple transition from virtue to vice; he also insists on the impossibility of circumscribing corruption, and on the permeability of its boundaries.[148]

Sallust's description of Sempronia is also valuable in showing important aspects of Sallust's thinking about the nature and pervasiveness of political decline.[149] I quote the passage in full:

> This woman in birth and appearance, in her husband and children too, was quite favored by fortune; she was well versed in Greek and Latin literature, at playing the lyre, at dancing more skillfully than a virtuous woman needed to, and in many other accomplishments which are instru-

---

145. Cf. Sall. *BC* 20 and 58 with Vretska, *Studien zu Sallust*; McGushin, *Sallust: Bellum Catilinae*; and Ramsey, *Sallust's Bellum Catilinae*, comm. ad loc. For a more recent and comprehensive analysis of Catiline's speech, see Batstone, "Catiline's Speeches in Sallust's *Bellum Catilinae*."

146. Sall. *BC* 7.5. Campbell's trans., 2007.

147. Sall. *BC* 5.3. Campbell's trans., 2007. Another example of this proximity in meaning is 7.4 and 17.6, where the restlessness of Catiline's men is somewhat akin to the strenuous martial vigor of early Rome.

148. For altered and disordered boundaries in the *BJ*, see Kraus, "Jugurthine Disorder," 217–47, esp. 221.

149. For Sempronia playing an important part in the narrative of the *BC*, see Boyd, "Virtus Effeminata and Sallust's Sempronia." Contra Syme, *Sallust*, 68.

ments of wantonness. But there was nothing that she held so cheap as modesty and chastity; you could not easily decide whether she was less sparing of her money or her reputation; her lust was so heated that she pursued men more often than she was pursued. Even before the time of the conspiracy she had often broken her word, repudiated a debt, been an accessory to murder, rushed headlong to ruin as a result of extravagance and lack of means. Nevertheless, her intellect was by no means contemptible; she could compose verses, raise a laugh, use language that was modest, or tender, or wanton; in short, she possessed much wit and much charm.

Haec mulier genere atque forma, praeterea viro atque liberis satis fortunata fuit; litteris Graecis et Latinis docta, psallere et saltare elegantius quam necesse est probae, multa alia, quae instrumenta luxuriae sunt. Sed ei cariora semper omnia quam decus atque pudicitia fuit; pecuniae an famae minus parceret, haud facile discerneres; lubido sic accensa, ut saepius peteret viros quam peteretur. Sed ea saepe antehac fidem prodiderat, creditum abiuraverat, caedis conscia fuerat; luxuria atque inopia praeceps abierat. Verum ingenium eius haud absurdum: posse versus facere, iocum movere, sermone uti vel modesto vel molli vel procaci; prorsus multae facetiae multusque lepos inerat.[150]

Here we have much more than a straightforward, prolonged attempt to criticize Sempronia's conduct. In Sallust's portrait, her good qualities are as prominent as her depravity. But this does not seem mere evenhandedness: Sallust is not trying to make his account of Sempronia's vices more convincing by giving a few incidental and lightweight virtues, nor is he attempting to deepen indignation into outrage by making vice stand out all the more sharply for being offset by virtue. The virtue and vice in the passage do not just exist side by side: the passage is concerned to demonstrate their interconnection, to show how virtues decay into vices, and to illustrate an easy symbiosis of the two that tells us much of what we need to know about the liabilities and susceptibilities of any society and any person.

The *BJ* makes a similar point about the interrelation of virtue and vice: "Jugurtha also had a generous nature and a shrewd wit, qualities that had won him a number of close friends among the Romans [*Huc accedebat munificentia animi et ingeni sollertia, quis rebus sibi multos ex Romanis familiari amicitia coniunxerat*]."[151] This is offered as the climax of Jugurtha's achievements

150. Sall. *BC* 25.
151. Sall. *BJ* 7.7.

among the Romans and of his *cursus virtutis*; but, at the same time, it is precisely these contacts that facilitate his *largitio* and confirm him in corruption.[152] The difference between *munificentia* (munificence) and *largitio* (bribery) is shown as only a matter of degree.

This carefully engineered promiscuity of diction is disturbing (as well as impressive) because through it Sallust suggests the ease of transition from zenith to decline. Proximity has something to do with it: "But, at first, great ambition, rather than greed, occupied the minds of men, which was, nevertheless, a vice nearer to a virtue [*Sed primo magis ambitio quam avaritia animos hominum exercebat, quod tamen vitium propius virtutem erat*]."[153] Virtue and vice are not poles apart. The problem for Sallust is—and here one can confidently say that he is aligning himself with Cato—that no distinction can be made between good and bad men.[154] As said above, Jugurtha and Metellus bribed to achieve what they wanted; Bocchus and Sulla used deceit for their goals; Jugurtha and Catiline had displayed courage: *inter bonos et malos discrimen nullum* . . .

Sallust himself had defined a successful historical style as one in which there was a measure of closeness between words and deeds: *facta dictis exaequanda*. And one can see that he achieved what he had called in his prologue the arduous labor of history, and he satisfied his own criterion: shocking facts were presented with shocking words, and this vocabulary of decay became so powerful that it would mark literature henceforward. Matching words and deeds involved mimesis; it tackled the difficult task of conforming actions and actors by means of style. To do this, Sallust had to create his own style: contorted, abrupt, even harsh, to be able to reproduce his view of the world, to mirror the conflicts and paradoxes of late republican Rome. It has been said that in Sallust, "style reflects ideology,"[155] and one could add that, in some way, also his vocabulary becomes narrative, as his choice of words is part of the content enabling them to do the work of the narration.

IT SEEMS QUITE STRIKING that at the same time Sallust was so concerned to denounce and condemn the change in the meanings of some significant words, this is precisely what he sets out to do himself with the concept of

---

152. Sall. *BJ* 8.2.
153. Sall. *BC* 11.1. Campbell's trans., 2007.
154. Sall. *BC* 52.22.
155. Kraus and Woodman, *Latin Historians*, 12. See also O'Gorman, "Politics of Sallustian Style."

virtus. He had attacked the *devaluation* of some traditional good Roman qualities and had given this as the cause of the decline in moral behavior, and then he daringly proposed a new *reevaluation* of *virtus*, precisely because he wanted to move people to act and behave differently and thus, perhaps, save the republic from its dreadful state.

Sallust's redefinition of *virtus* is a fine balance between reinforcing the concept's core and changing it: an old value is dressed in a new sensibility. The imprecise limits of the concept of *virtus* had put the term at risk of weakening, but this same imprecision was going to save it and make it much richer. *Virtus* as a political idea—and political meant moral in Rome—had become in the late republic a notion traditionally attached to a certain sector of society; a mental image thought of as a quality or attribute possessed by the *nobilitas*. In his monographs, Sallust was going to challenge this conception. *Virtus* as a political "ideal" was presented as a model at its highest perfection, a standard or principle to aim at, a value to be achieved. This ideal, meant for everyone, involved having to "strive" for it, and this struggle for *virtus* carried out through *bonae artes* made one gain *gloria*. Hence the importance of the general remarks in the prologues.

The *nobiles* had certainly been the group that had traditionally identified most closely with the functioning of the *res publica*; they had won their prestige and glory by serving it. When this tradition started fading away, when ambition and avarice took over from service after the fall of Carthage, the republic for Sallust was destroyed not by external forces, not by some abstract process of economic or historical development, but *primo pecuniae, deinde imperi cupido* (the lust for money first, then for power) of its very citizens.[156]

In the end, for Sallust, the discussion of political decline came down to a discussion of persons. Political decline does not happen automatically, but results from conscious decisions made by individuals: and the hopeful corollary of this firm judgment is that decline can be halted and reversed by the resolute efforts of individuals. The moral responsibility for the health of a nation rests with its citizens. Sallust will not allow us the escape of shifting the blame for decline away from ourselves and onto our circumstances or the course of history. It is this comfortable self-deceit that is rebuked in the opening chapter of the *BJ* 1.4: *falso queritur* ... In Sallust's view, power itself does not necessarily instigate decline, and men cannot shift their responsibilities onto any general cause.

---

156. Sall. *BC* 10.3.4.

It looks as if Sallust stresses personal and individual *virtus* not because of a Stoic or Hellenizing foreign influence, but because at the time he was writing the sense of serving the republic had been lost; political interest was confused with individual interest and, if the needs of the individual had always been subordinated to those of the state, now, even among the *homines novi*, this hierarchy seemed upside down. Sallust spoke a language that his contemporaries understood, claiming at the same time tradition and novelty. Placing all the responsibility on the individual's *virtus* and *industria* entailed above all an active conception of *virtus* that matched the demands of Roman thought.

What about the validity of approaching history as he did? For Sallust, explaining history through moral standards was unquestionably valid. The analysis of the connection between the collapse of the republic and the failure of *virtus* is certainly illuminating: the apparent moral commonplaces disguised the political reality by which personal power and position were sought not to serve the state, but at its expense. It seems reasonable to analyze the breakdown of the republic with regard to the distortion and corruption of its ideal. Moral questions, like social, political, or economic ones, are indeed valid in history, although their answers may be harder to find.

Sallust does not seem to solve the problem of the decadence of the republic, nor does he provide his readers with an answer, because he does not have one himself. The old *virtus* had gone downhill; he proclaims the need for a new type: Marius? Caesar? Cato? The theory that *virtus* was something personal that brought nobility to its owner was perfectly consistent and logical, but it was doomed to failure. In the dark panorama of the late republic, where decline had invaded the very basis of politics, Sallust's appropriation of the language that had traditionally belonged to the corrupted nobles did not work as a means of escape. But in one sense Sallust was right, that *virtus* would stay alive and would bring nobility to some: he, at least, did what he could with his work of *facta dictis exaequare*, and he served the state by writing history.

CHAPTER THREE

Virtus in Livy

Nominis Romani ac virtutis partum vestraeque memores vertite

Call to mind the Roman name, and your fathers' *virtus* and your own

—Livy, 4.33.5

Not many years after Sallust's monographs, Livy's *Ab Urbe Condita* (AUC) showed his contemporaries that the annalistic tradition still had a role to play in Roman historical writing and, at the same time, that the development of this tradition had matured in such a way that it almost meant an altogether different approach to history. The choice of Livy as my second step of *virtus* in Roman historiography is intended to show not only how change and continuity interact at the "real-historical" level but also how this interaction is mirrored in the writing of history itself. Livy's awareness of change contrasts with his presentation of persistent continuity.

I will argue in this chapter that in recording deeds of past *virtus*, Livy was constructing—and to some extent also fixing—Rome's memory so as to protect and safeguard her true identity in an age of changes. More than any other writer, perhaps, Livy was able to give a persuasive illustration of what it had meant to be Roman, in such a way that it became canonical for posterity. The author's intention was—as he explicitly says in the preface—to provide "lessons of every kind of experience set forth as on a conspicuous monument,"[1] and from those lessons to choose what to imitate and what to avoid. By giving lessons through examples first and foremost, he makes his readers identify themselves with the Romans of past times. *Exempla* can be perceived as such only if there is something in common, if—to some extent—the situation, the circumstance, or the actors appear familiar.[2] Only by recognizing what is presented as truly Roman will the Romans of Livy's times be able to draw the continuous line that links the Romans of the past with themselves.

---

1. Livy, *praef.* 10.
2. For exemplarity in Livy, see Chaplin, *Livy's Exemplary History* and "Livy's Use of Exempla," 102–112. For more general approaches to *exempla*, see Roller, "Exemplarity in Roman Culture," 1–56, esp. 1–10; Walter, *Memoria und res publica*, 42–83; Bell, "Introduction," 1–39; Roller, "Exemplary Past in Roman Historiography and Culture," 214–30; van der Blom, *Cicero's Role Models*, 12–17; Langlands, "Roman *exempla* and Situation Ethics," 100–122, esp. 100–103.

Livy's use of *exempla* can also be seen as the historian somehow engaging with his predecessor, Sallust. It is precisely the view of Roman history as a blend of change and continuity that drives Livy to select an earlier subject matter than that preferred by Sallust: *if* there has been change and decline as Sallust claims, and *if* history is to provide *exempla*, as Sallust also states, then the logical step is to seek those *exempla* in the period before decline started. But the search for *exempla*—clearly shown in Livy's narrative, as will be seen—is not the only link between the two historians. I will try to show how in some way Livy responded to the concerns Sallust developed in his monographs.

Questions about whether or not Livy is an Augustan author, whether he subscribes to the Stoic concept of determinism or whether he is to be considered a tragic historian, have, of course, been valid to analyze and interpret Livy's work, but the answers have not given us a full understanding of his conception of Roman history or of the *AUC* as a record of the past. What would perhaps be more helpful in achieving this is the analysis and comprehension of Livy's concept of the role of memory as a means to attain identity. I will show in this chapter that Livy presents Roman identity as being closely connected first with the concept of *virtus* and then also with the concept of *libertas*. *AUC* is, on the whole, the history of the gradual acquisition of *libertas* for the Roman people through acts of *virtus*: first, with the consulate, the Romans achieve an aristocratic *libertas* and then, with the tribunes of the plebs and the right to be elected for all the other magistracies, a plebeian *libertas*. At the same time they gain liberty from a foreign master. We could expand the title of Livy's work without losing its original meaning: *Historia libertatis populi Romani ab urbe condita*. By recording deeds of *prisca virtus* of Romans of former times bravely defending *libertas*, Livy can be seen as encouraging the Romans to preserve their freedom—perhaps under threat in his own times—in the same way.[3]

---

3. It does not seem necessary to deal here with two topics that have been important in Livian scholarship in the past, namely, source criticism on the one hand and the influence of Hellenistic historiography on the other, as they do not provide an explanation for Livy's motivation in writing his history or why he wrote it in that particular way, and because they are far removed from my specific interest in *virtus*. An enormous amount of material has been dedicated to *Quellenforschung* and the "tragic history" of Livy; see, for instance, Burck, *Die Erzählungskunst des T. Livius*; Klotz, *Livius und seine Vorgänger*; Walsh, *Livy*; Burck, *Wege zu Livius*; Ogilvie, "Livy," 162–70. This approach has led some critics to consider Livy as a gifted storyteller, but a second-class historian, who appeared to have chosen his sources more or less randomly and then followed them without any critical sense; see Walsh, "Livy," 137. From the work of T. J. Luce onward, much Livian scholarship appears to have developed in a different direction. For a summary of these views, see especially Luce, *Livy*, xv–xxvii; and Miles, *Livy*, 1–7.

In my approach to Livy's work in this chapter, I would like to move away from pigeonholing the individual passages, trying instead to find some of the threads that make the *AUC* a coherent and intelligible historical narrative, and then see how the narrative as a whole works toward the author's main aim. I am, of course, aware that I will be unable to treat every aspect of so vast a text in one chapter, but, within the topic that is relevant to my task of analyzing *virtus*, I will focus on different overarching themes that will show how and why *virtus* occupied an essential role in Livy's historical narrative.

The Value of Recording the Past: Livy's Preface

In this section I will approach Livy's concept of history as a record of change within a framework of continuity. Like other Roman historians, Livy wrote his *AUC* to encourage action, and he stressed it even more by choosing to address his audience using the second person singular: there could be no mistake that he was telling "me" to "do" something: "What chiefly makes the study of history wholesome and profitable is this, that *you behold* the lessons of every kind of experience set forth as on a conspicuous monument; from these *you may choose* for *yourself* and for *your* own state what to *imitate*, from these mark for avoidance what is shameful in the conception and shameful in the result [*Hoc illud est praecipue in cognitione rerum salubre ac frugiferum, omnis* te *exempli documenta in inlustri posita monumento* intueri; *inde* tibi tuae*que rei publicae quod* imitere capias, *inde foedum inceptu, foedum exitu, quod* vites]."[4]

It was precisely Livy's awareness of change that made him write his history in the way he did. He was able to see and appreciate the transformation and reordering of his own country; how much had been reshaped from the republican past, and the problems and effects this reshaping was having in his own generation. To look at the past, to see how their predecessors had reacted to change and draw *exempla* from them, thus became an especially valuable task to help the Romans decide on their behavior and forge their identity in moving toward the uncertain future. As Kraus and Woodman put it, Livy's work was not "the past preserved in amber," but a record of deeds to imitate or avoid, because history was effective only when it was brought to the present.[5]

It is, I think, to this process, namely, signaling clearly to his audience how to get involved with Rome's past, that Livy is referring at the beginning

---

4. Livy, *praef.* 10 (my highlighting). Cf. Chaplin, "Livy's Use of Exempla," 111.
5. Kraus and Woodman, *Latin Historians*, 55–56.

of the preface. "Whether I am likely to accomplish anything worthy of the labor, if I record the achievements of the Roman people from the foundation of the city, I do not really know [*Facturusne operae pretium sim si a primordio urbis res populi Romani perscripserim nec satis scio*]."[6] The first sentence of *Ab Urbe Condita* could, of course, be interpreted just as the conventional words to win over the empathy of the reader to approach the work with *benignitas*—just as nowadays eminent authors ask for forgiveness if after many corrections mistakes remain.[7] Despite the fact that he did not have the background of a retired politician who wrote history as the noblest occupation to which he could dedicate the rest of his life, Livy managed to produce, by his own skill, an exceptional work in which we come to ignore or somehow disregard his lack of previous experience and credentials as a traditional Roman historian.[8] However, it can be said that the doubt that the author expressed in the first sentence of this monumental work was above all concerned with the impact the work would have on his contemporaries, and the service it would render to the present. And this, of course, Livy could not know.

In projecting an idea of Rome, Livy chose *virtus* and *vitium* as the key to understanding what life and morals were like (*quae vita, qui mores fuerint*),[9] putting the stress especially on the *virtutes* of the past rather than the *vitia* of the present. This emphasis has generated an equivocal understanding of Livy's approach to Roman history. His patriotism has been seen as the mark of his naïveté and the creation of an immovable image of Rome.[10] One of the initiators of this "Livian prejudice" was probably R. Collingwood, who, in 1946 in his *Idea of History*, declared that in the *AUC* "Rome is the heroine of his narrative. Rome is the agent whose actions he is describing. Therefore Rome is a substance, changeless and eternal. From the beginning of the narrative Rome is ready-made and complete."[11] Collingwood's remark left a profound mark on the appreciation of Livy, and was afterward followed by others whose main criticism of Livy was the static nature of his history; he was considered a writer with indisputable literary skills, but who was unable to appreci-

---

6. Livy, *praef.* 1.
7. Livy's *captatio benevolentiae* has not, however, worked well with all his readers; see Syme, *Tacitus*, 148: "Gracious and engaging though the modesty may be with which he excuses his undertaking, it is a feeble exordium when a historian in his first sentence conveys not facts or confidence but a doubt."
8. Cf. Marincola, *Authority and Tradition in Ancient Historiography*, 140.
9. Livy, *praef.* 9.
10. See especially Walsh, *Livy*, 66; but also Ogilvie, *Commentary on Livy, Books 1–5*, passim.
11. Collingwood, *Idea of History*, 43.

ate change.[12] Denying the development in the process of creation of Rome's identity, however, shows some sort of misreading of Livy's preface, where after saying that the life and morals of the Romans will be the topic of the work, he adds, "with the gradual relaxation of discipline, morals *first* gave way, as it were, *then* sank lower and lower, and *finally* began the downward plunge which has brought us to the *present time*, when we can endure neither our vices nor their cure [*labente* deinde paulatim *disciplina velut desidentes* primo *mores sequatur animo,* deinde *ut magis magisque lapsi sint,* tum *ire coeperint praecipites,* donec *ad haec tempora quibus nec vitia nostra nec remedia pati possumus perventum est*]."[13] *Deinde, paulatim, primo, tum,* and *donec* are put in the preface precisely to reinforce the evolution of Rome through time.

Livy's preface is, then, about change and continuity. He had to maintain a fine balance between what he was recording as Rome's individuality and the transformations she had undergone specifically to acquire and defend this identity. Livy not only praises Rome but also shows where she went astray, in order to save his own times.[14] For on the whole, Livy's prologue does not seem to give a warm welcome to the new order of things. The intriguing phrase "the present time when we can endure neither our vices nor their cure [*ad haec tempora quibus nec vitia nostra nec remedia pati possumus*]"[15] has been the object of much discussion,[16] and somewhat narrow-mindedly this statement has been traditionally understood in the light of his moralizing concept of history.[17] But these *vitia* and their *remedia* were cleverly kept implicit. Thus, he could not be accused of anything, but he left it open to the reader to answer these questions: those vices have sometimes been seen probably related to immorality; their cure, on the other hand, was heavy and difficult to bear because it was apparent to everyone that Augustus' moral legislation—if there was such a thing at all—had not been welcomed and was, in the long term, doomed to

---

12. See esp. Walsh, "Livy and the Aims of *Historia,*" 1069. For a more developed account of this idea and its limitations, see Luce, *Livy,* introduction and 232–49; Miles, *Livy,* chap. 1: "History and Memory"; and Chaplin, *Livy's Exemplary History,* chap. 5: "Precedents and Change," with n68, where she gives Walsh and Ogilvie as the primary exponents of this view of Livy in English scholarship. Mazza, in *Storia e Ideologia in Tito Livio,* was one of the first scholars to react against this "Livian prejudice."
13. Livy, *praef.* 9 (my highlighting).
14. Kraus, *Ab Urbe Condita VI,* 18.
15. Livy, *praef.* 9.
16. See especially Moles, "Livy's Preface," 141–68; Walsh, "Livy's Preface and the Distortion of History," 369–83, and "Livy and the Aims of *Historia,*" 1058–74.
17. Leeman, *Orationis Ratio,* 194.

fail.[18] But those vices could also be related to civil war. Civil war in itself was a vice; *virtus* could not flourish in it.[19] Could autocracy, then, be considered the burdensome and oppressive cure? It was safer for Livy to leave these questions unanswered. This enigmatic sentence may show that the historian was neither wholly opposed to the Augustan regime nor uncritical of it. In fact, he emerges as being exceedingly sensitive to the main concern that Augustan Rome was facing at that time, namely, the ratification of the new order and the exchange of *libertas* for *pax*.

If it was risky for Livy to enter into that discussion, it was on the other hand a wholesome and profitable (*salubre ac frugiferum*) exercise to draw lessons from the past, which worked not only by providing *exempla* to imitate or avoid (adapting them to one's own situation), but mainly by giving his audience the possibility of reinterpreting and scrutinizing the past in a new way so as to understand and make more sense of the present. Exemplarity was something familiar and dear to the Romans, but it was something particularly attractive to Livy's own times when the *exempla* helped to build the much-needed political stability; and it worked, reassuringly, as a tool to remind Romans that the interpretation of that complex past could lead to a safer time in the near future.[20]

Livy's approach to Roman history is, therefore, more optimistic than that of his predecessor, Sallust. In a sense, Livy's work constitutes a response to Sallust's monographs.[21] Both historians presented slightly different interpretations of the history of Rome, but based on similar principles: Rome had been a field where *virtus* had shone, but the present time, together with political turmoil, was hostile to it. For Sallust, corruption had started after the destruction of Carthage, when the lack of a powerful enemy had made Rome grow greedy and ambitious of dominion until "everything was for sale [*omnia venalia esse*]."[22] For Livy, instead, vices such as ambition and avarice had crept into the city slowly and late, until not only these *vitia* but also their re-

---

18. For discussion on this passage, see lately Mineo, "Livy's Historical Philosophy," 139–40; and Vasaly, *Livy's Political Philosophy*, n.1. On what has been termed Augustan moral legislation, see, for example, Frank, "Augustus' Legislation on Marriage and Children," 41–52; Bouvrie, "Augustus' Legislation on Morals," 93–113; Badian, "Phantom Marriage Law," 82–98; Galinsky, *Augustan Culture*, passim, but esp. 128–40.

19. Cf. Lucan 1.667–68; 1.366; 1.682; 2.3.

20. Cf. Chaplin, *Livy's Exemplary History*, passim.

21. Cf. Ducos, "Les passions, les hommes et l'histoire dans l'oeuvre de Tite Live," though for him Livy refutes the main ideas postulated by Sallust.

22. Sall. *BC* 10.4; *BJ* 8.1.

media were too heavy burdens for the shoulders of the Romans. In some sense, Livy completes and nuances what had been so harshly stated by Sallust. In his preface, the Paduan historian engages with Sallust almost explicitly: "I myself, on the contrary, shall seek in this an additional reward for my toil, that I may avert my gaze from the troubles that our age has been witnessing for so many years, so long at least as I am absorbed in the recollection of the brave days of old, free from every care, which even if it could not divert the historian's mind from the truth, might nevertheless cause it anxiety [*ego contra hoc quoque laboris praemium petam, ut me a conspectu malorum quae nostra tot per annos vidit aetas, tantisper certe dum prisca (tota) illa mente repeto, avertam, omnis expers curae quae scribentis animum, etsi non flectere a vero, sollicitum tamen efficere posset*]."[23] Livy would have certainly read Sallust, and he consciously decided to move away from his predecessor's fierce content and style, so that—without denying the flaws of his country—he may give some hope of restoration, both political and moral, to his own generation. Although Livy may have written chronologically after Sallust, one can understand Sallust better after reading Livy.

Besides responding to Sallust in the preface, Livy can also be read as engaging with Augustus' ideology and has even been considered as part of what has been called "Augustan culture." In his writings, one can see how Livy seems to share with Augustus some religious, social, and above all moral standards, although labeling him as an "Augustan historian" may not help us all that much. A long debate—not wholly conclusive—has taken place on the subject, and it appears mainly to be related to the charged meaning of the word "Augustan."[24] Opinions will differ, of course, depending on the meaning they attribute to the adjective. For Syme, Livy emerges as the last of the republican writers because he "seems comparatively untouched by the era of tribulation. The Ciceronian features of his style make him something of a stranger in his own generation. His mind was formed before the battle of Actium, his history begun before *pax et princeps* was firmly established."[25] Walsh

23. Livy, *praef.* 1.
24. For the discussion of Livy as an Augustan author, apart from the references given in the text, see, for example, Peterson, "Livy and Augustus," 440–52; Mette, "Livius und Augustus," 269–85; Deininger, "Livius und der Prinzipat," 265–72; Burck, "Livius und Augustus," 269–81; Badian, "Livy and Augustus," 9–38; Burton, "Last Republican Historian," 429–46; Vasaly, "Livy's First Pentad and the Augustan Poetry Book," 275–90; Oakley, *Commentary on Livy Books 6 to 10*, vol. 1, 379; Gaertner, "Livy's Camillus and the Political Discourse of the Late Republic," 51–52; Cataudella, "Livio storico augusteo?," 175–95.
25. Syme, "Livy and Augustus," 57.

describes him as "not an Augustan in any significantly political sense."[26] And for Woodman, who thinks that Livy started writing as early as before the battle of Actium,[27] he "cannot have had Augustus in mind when he wrote his early books. He was simply putting forward a series of ideals with which Augustus later came to identify himself."[28] Is Livy "Augustan" in style, then? It has been argued that he must have written in a style that would be acceptable under the canons of Augustan refinement.[29] The issue of Livy as an Augustan author can, of course, be developed much more extensively, but that would take me beyond the boundaries of my research on *virtus*. I do, however, place the historian within the Augustan literary tradition; not only does he have much in common with other "Augustan authors," but he also appears aware of the new sensibilities of the era that promote a specific set of themes and topics in what is called the "Augustan age."[30]

The question, then, is not so much whether Livy with his writings supported Augustus in his comprehensive program or not, but how nearly they coincide in their appreciation of the needs of their times. Perhaps what gives Livy and Augustus a similar approach toward the present Rome is their common discernment of the need for change, without breaking with traditional values. They both put forward—one with his history, the other with his government—a combination of the new and the old: novelty within tradition. According to Galinsky, what makes Livy an Augustan author is not so much a strict ideology, but the reformulation of the central ideas of his times: a decided preoccupation with moral decline, the need for patriotism and peace, and the consideration that the interpretation of the past was effective for transforming the present.[31] Livy and Augustus believed in the exemplary value of history, and both of them used all the means they could to give the "right" examples: Livy with his historical narrative and Augustus with his *forum* provided Romans with a gallery of *viri illustri* to be imitated.[32] Both of them appeared trying to promote the same traditional standards and were concerned with maintaining the Roman identity in spite of the evident change. We can compare two important specimens of Augustus' values with Livy's *Ab*

---

26. Walsh, *Livy*, 287. But he does consider Livy an Augustan author in terms of style; cf. 58.
27. This too is the subject of an interminable debate.
28. Woodman, *Rhetoric in Classical Historiography*, 137.
29. McDonald, "Style of Livy," 171.
30. It is interesting to note that Livy writes his history of Roman virtue at a time when virtue is being promoted officially especially through legislation or the *Ludi Saeculares*.
31. Cf. Galinsky, *Augustan Culture*, 283.
32. On the relationship of both, see Luce, "Livy, Augustus, and the Forum Romanum," 123–38.

Urbe Condita: the *clypeus aureus* and the *Res Gestae*. Both are memorials—*monumenta*—where the epigraphic information is meant to suggest Augustus' own *virtus*-image in a similar way to Livy's *virtus*-language.

The golden shield (*clypeus aureus*) was given to Octavian by the Senate and the Roman people in 27 B.C., the same year that he received the name of "Augustus."[33] It was an acknowledgment of the virtues displayed in his fight to free the *res publica* from its oppressors, mainly Antony and Cleopatra. The inscription engraved on the shield and registered in the *Res Gestae* reads, "A golden shield was placed in the Curia Julia whose inscription testified that the Senate and the Roman people gave me this in recognition of my valor, my clemency, my justice, and my piety [CLVPEVS AVREVS IN CVRIA IVLIA POSITVS, QVEM MIHI SENATVM POPVLVMQVE ROMANVM DARE VIRTVTIS CLEMENTIAE IVSTITIAE PIETATIS CAVSA]."[34] The first virtue mentioned here is *virtus*, meaning bravery or courage. The choice of these particular four virtues must have been something carefully pondered and approved by Augustus, always jealous of the image he projected to Roman society.[35] An interesting aspect to point out about the selected virtues is the combination of traditional values—*virtus* and *pietas*—with new—*clementia*—which appears more forcefully with Julius Caesar and is clearly something of a two-edged virtue.[36]

The *Res Gestae* as a whole can also be read in parallel with Livy's historical narrative. Both works constitute large monuments—one because of its sheer size, the other because of its length—to commemorate the achievements (*rerum gestarum memoriae*)[37] of Roman individuals. The *Ab Urbe Condita* was *res gestae* too; if not *divi Augusti*, at least *Populi Romani*. Though totally different in style, both works commemorate heroic feats and seemed very much in tune with each other. But one cannot necessarily infer from this that Livy was a faithful loudspeaker of Augustus' values; instead, it can show the real need of the times for explicit exemplarity.

Livy's choice of a central thread for developing and explaining Roman history is made clear from the preface of his monumental work. As he is interested in the *mores* of the people who forged the great empire, his methodology—in

---

33. For the coin depicting the *clypeus virtutis*, see *RIC* I 42a.
34. *Res Gestae*, 34. See Cooley, *Res Gestae Divi Augusti*, comm. ad loc.
35. Zanker, *Power of Images in the Age of Augustus*, passim.
36. For more on the *clypeus*, see Weinstock, *Divus Julius*, 227–59; and Galinsky, *Augustan Culture*, 83–90. For a more detailed treatment of *clementia*, see Konstan, "Clemency as a Virtue," 337–46; and chapter 5 in this book.
37. Livy, *praef.* 3.

keeping with the Roman tradition and suited to his own turbulent times—required examples of *virtus*. Livy will show that *virtus* gave continuity to Roman history and, at the same time, explained when, why, and how change occurred. With his preface, Livy presents to his audience, with uncommon clarity, his purpose in writing history.

A Stage for *Virtus*: Rome at War

Without doubt it was through the wars waged by Rome that Livy chose to unfold his historical narrative. There are also other important topics that the author will deal with, but it is through wars and battles that he explains how Rome became a large and powerful empire, now tottering under its own grandeur. It was in wars that the occasion for *virtus* to shine came forth; it was through wars that humans' highest heroism and basest degradation could be seen.[38] It was the attitude of soldiers, generals, politicians, and people toward wars—though not exclusively—that helped to shape their ideal, modeled society, and created a collective identity.

Even though it seems hardly necessary to justify dealing with the topic of war when talking about Livy and *virtus*, it is important not to take things for granted: just because Livy was talking of the past did not mean to say that all wars would be heroic and therefore *virtus* would always play a prominent role.[39] On the contrary, we will see that each war poses different challenges to *virtus* and Livy's treatment is consequently diverse.

Let us start with the quantitative evidence that, in this case, is so overwhelming that it speaks for itself. Livy uses the word *virtus* almost 300 times in the extant books, and in more than three-quarters of these occurrences, *virtus* is used in the most basic traditional Roman meaning of bravery or valor.[40] *Virtus* is by far the most common word of praise in Livy; it is possessed by armies as a whole or by individual soldiers, generals, and political leaders.[41] *Virtus* in Livy is, above all, courage, determination, and energy in

---

38. For the opposite scenario or *otium* being bad for *virtus*, see Frank, "Dangers of Peace," 1–7.

39. There is also a lot of unnecessary violence acknowledged; cf. Johner, *La Violence chez Tite-Live, mythographie et historiographie*.

40. Moore, *Artistry and Ideology*, 5, has a little less dramatic proportion (two-thirds), and I suppose the difference is due to varying interpretation in translating the word. For an altogether contrasting opinion, see Eisenhut, *Virtus Romana*, 126, who argues that Livy uses *virtus* in a non-Roman way, following instead the more Greek meaning of it, *arete*.

41. For the exact location of all the occurrences of *virtus* and other virtues, see Moore, *Artistry and Ideology*, app. 2.

fighting obstacles and enduring adversity mainly in performing military duties. *Virtus* is what leads to success in battle, and war is omnipresent in Roman history. But *virtus* is also used for success in internal politics, where the individual with *virtus* always has the welfare of the state as a priority in his actions. Other virtues, such as *pietas, magnitudo animi, constantia, moderatio,* and *fortitudo* are also spread throughout Livy's work, and they all convey an emotionally charged meaning when describing a Roman, but it is *virtus* that appears to be quintessentially Roman. Even when at times other ideals seem more prominent, such as *libertas* or *res publica, virtus* is always intimately connected with them: "by courage they had got back their liberty [*virtute libertatem reciperatam esse*],"[42] or "Praised be your courage, C. Servilius, you have delivered the commonwealth! [*Macte virtute, C. Servili, esto liberata re publica*]."[43]

It is striking that Livy seems to take for granted that the Romans excelled in courage or *virilis-virtus*. In the *AUC*, he places bravery at the center of Roman character, and as the main reason for the greatness of the empire, but does not provide a proper explanation to account for this. He talks of the gods in Book 1: Mars, the warrior-god, was the father of the twins Romulus and Remus,[44] and later on it was Jupiter himself who commanded the Romans to fight against the Sabines,[45] but deities do not appear granting courage to the Roman people, nor the Romans asking them for valor in battle.[46] On the contrary, quite early in the narrative Livy has king Tullus—also a warrior king—giving thanks for their victory against the Albans, a success for which they should give thanks to the gods (*dis immortalibus*) *and* to their own valor (*ipsorum virtute*),[47] meaning that the gods had helped them in the struggle, but the Romans had been courageous by themselves. They acknowledge that success and a great name are reached by the aid of the gods and by their own courage: "those which are aided by their own *virtus* and by the

---

42. Livy, 3.58.4. See also 5.42.7; 8.4.6; 34.59.5.
43. Livy, 4.14.7.
44. Cf. Livy, 1.4.2.
45. Cf. Livy, 1.12.7: *Romani, Iuppiter optimus maximus resistere atque iterare pugnam iubet*. For Livy's representation of the period of the monarchy and early Rome, see, for example, Miles, *Livy*; Fox, *Roman Historical Myths*, 96–141; Forsythe, *Livy and Early Rome*; and Vasaly, *Livy's Political Philosophy*.
46. For Livy, the gods, and religion, see, for example, Kajanto, *God and Fate in Livy*; Liebeschuetz, "Religious Position of Livy's History," 45–55 with addendum in Chaplin and Kraus, *Livy*, 377–79; Levene, *Religion in Livy*, passim, but esp. 126–47; Linderski, "Roman Religion in Livy," 53–70; and Davies, *Rome's Religious History*, 86–142, esp. 87–88; 105.
47. Livy, 1.28.4 (my highlighting).

favor of Heaven achieve great power and renown [*quas sua virtus ac di iuvent magnas opes sibi magnumque nomen facere*]."[48]

Livy was not the first one taking courage for granted, as if it were something peculiar to the Romans, or their special feature. Polybius, for example, had not offered an explanation either as to why courage was so important to the Romans, but had just stated it: "courage, nearly the most essential of virtues in all states and *especially* so in Rome [τὴν ἀνδρείαν μέρους καὶ κυριωτάτου σχεδὸν ἐν πάσῃ μὲν πολιτείᾳ μάλιστα δ' ἐν τῇ Ῥώμῃ]."[49] Cornelius Nepos had given a similar declaration: "If it be true, *as no one doubts*, that the Roman people have surpassed all other nations in valor ... [*Si verum est, quod nemo dubitat, ut populus Romanus omnes gentes virtute superarit* ...]."[50] There are no reasons given to explain why courage played such a key role *especially* in Roman life and why this was so *evident* to all. Livy, then, perhaps following this tradition, simply affirms that "the Roman surpassed in courage [*virtute Romanus superat*]."[51] Romans acquired a reputation and their name was linked and paralleled to courage: "Call to mind the Roman name, and your fathers' valor and your own [*nominis Romani ac virtutis patrum vestraeque memores vertite*]," and also "It is due to the valor of your soldiers, it is due to the Roman name [*Haec virtute militum vestrorum, haec Romano nomine sunt digna*]."[52] With a particular choice of words and expressions, Livy constructs a Roman ideal and sanctions the manner by which the Romans aspired to be regarded by other peoples. The "Roman way" (*Romanis artibus*) of winning wars was through courage, toils, and arms (*virtute, opere, armis*).[53]

As said before, Livy attributes *virtus* to whole armies and individuals, and although he also assigns *virtus* to Rome's enemies (both armies and individuals), *virtus Romana* is overwhelmingly more frequent.[54] As it would be tire-

---

48. Livy, 1.9.3.
49. Polyb. 31.29.1 (my highlighting).
50. Nepos, *Hannibal*, 1.1 (my highlighting).
51. Livy, 9.32.7. See also Livy, 1.12.10: *res Romana erat superior*. But from the fact that Livy does not give a proper rational explanation about the warlike nature of the Romans, it does not necessarily follow that this had to be explained almost in biological terms; cf. Harris, *War and Imperialism in Republican Rome 327–70 B.C.*, 9–53. For a different position, see North, "Development of Roman Imperialism," 1–9.
52. Livy, 4.33.5 and 5.6.6.
53. This is what Camillus said about the conquest of the Faliscans: *ego Romanis artibus, virtute opere armis, sicut Veios vincam*, Livy, 5.27.8.
54. The proportion is 79 percent for Roman *virtus* to 21 percent for foreign *virtus*, which becomes still more marked if one considers that frequently, when foreign *virtus* is mentioned, it accompanies an implicit reference to Roman *virtus*.

some to show all the instances where Livy used the word *virtus*, I will summarize and group together the similar situations where the historian pointed out specifically the valor of Romans at war. A first group consists of Livy's praise of the *virtus* of the Roman army or the soldiery in general. There is a vast amount of evidence that shows Livy attributing courage to whole military units, not only individuals, and so the successes were due to the courage and good fighting of all. In the early books Livy persistently presents an army whose courage, combined with military discipline and fortune, made Rome the winner of almost all the battles and wars against the neighboring peoples. *Virtus militum*, the bravery of the Roman soldiers, appeared to be greater than that of the many enemies they had to fight: the Sabines, the Albans, the Latins, the Etruscans, the Volsci, and others.[55] Roman generals fostered the *virtus* of their soldiers by praising it loudly and inspired them with *exempla* to be followed.[56] The conflicts that early Rome had to face appear in Livy to have been mainly battles for survival and independence, and although he is not blinded by patriotism and acknowledges misbehavior when he sees it,[57] almost all the wars in the first decade are presented in a context of honor, freedom, and legitimate dominion.

The second Punic war at the end of the third century B.C., of course, also provided countless situations where the Roman army could show its *virtus*.[58] But it is striking to see that in these books Livy is slightly less inclined to attribute *virtus* to the soldiery in general as he had previously done, but more often has the Romans themselves boasting of or corroborating their own *virtus*. Expressions such as "our own strength and courage [*nostra vis virtusque*]"[59] or "your valor [*vestra virtus*]"[60] are mainly addressed by the generals to the soldiers, and it is not Livy who assigns *virtus* to them directly. The many times that *virtus* appears linked with the Roman army not through Livy's own voice

---

55. For examples of the army's courage [*virtus militum*] in the first decade, see Livy, 1.25.2; 2.63.5; 2.65.3; 3.63.2; 5.40.1; 5.43.6; 6.30.6; 7.23.8; 9.14.10; 9.32.7–8.

56. Livy, 2.12.14–15; 3.61.7; 3.62.2–5; 4.33.5; 4.40.8–9; 5.6.6; 5.54.6; 7.30.8; 7.35.3–4.

57. Army indiscipline: 2.44.10.

58. For a more recent and detailed examination of Livy's third decade, see Levene, *Livy on the Hannibalic War*. For the outbreak of the second Punic war, see Händl-Sawage, *Der Beginn des 2. Punischen Krieges*; for the second Punic war in general, see Cornell, Rankov, and Sabin, *Second Punic War*; Le Bohec, *Histoires Militaires des Guerres Puniques*, 129–54; Hoyos, *Companion to the Punic Wars*, 223–392. Still good for a short account is Lazenby, *Hannibal's War*. Important thematic studies are Kukofka, *Süditalien im zweiten punischen Krieg*; Daly, *Cannae*.

59. Livy, 21.40.17; another *vi ac virtute*: 22.4.2. See also *nostra virtus* at 21.43.6 and 27.49.9.

60. Livy, 24.38.2. See also 21.43.13; *vestra virtus* in *oratio obliqua* 24.15.6; 25.38.10; 26.41.6; 26.48.4; 26.48.13; 28.8.12; 28.25.6.

but through the generals' direct or reported speeches perhaps suggests that Livy is keen to tell us how the Romans saw themselves when fighting the Punic wars. By the time Livy was writing, in the final quarter of the first century, the war against the Carthaginians was seen as something distant and heroic that was also used by orators and politicians to revive the spirit of Roman courage.[61]

The last fifteen books (31–45) of the *AUC* are grouped as a unit narrating the Macedonian wars. A very remarkable feature of this section is that here Livy attests the *virtus* of the Roman soldiers and denounces their *vitia* in equal measure. He acknowledges the soldiers' courage less frequently than he had previously done, and furthermore, he reports in detail how the enemy must have seen the Romans.[62] Focalizing from the enemies' point of view for a large part of the narrative of the Macedonian wars, Livy leaves the reader with an unmistakably sweet-and-sour aftertaste. The Romans were accused of being inconsistent in their behavior,[63] and of a long chain of vices: stubbornness (*pertinacia*),[64] pride (*superbia*),[65] avarice (*avaritia*),[66] cruelty (*crudelitas*),[67] and insubordination (*licentia*).[68] Most of these faults can, of course, be identified as the *topos* of an imperialist army,[69] but the combination of their presence with the lower frequency of the word *virtus*, and Livy himself criticizing the Roman army in his own authorial voice,[70] gives a particularly somber tone to the account of the Macedonian wars.

A second group of references to *virtus* at war in the *AUC* is that regarding leaders. Among them, Camillus, Fabius Maximus, Marcellus, Scipio Africanus, and Aemilius Paullus stand out particularly because they commanded the army for a longer period of time and, therefore, presented the opportunity for fuller description than is afforded by just one episode.[71] Among the characters that appeared only briefly in Livy's work, though, there are some

---

61. See, for example, Cic. *Cat*, 4.21.
62. Livy, 32.9.1; 35.6.9; 37.30.2; 37.30.6; 40.40.9.
63. Livy, 35.16.2.
64. Livy, 42.62.7; 42.62.13.
65. Livy, 42.62.7; 43.2.1; 43.7.8.
66. Livy, 43.2.1; 43.7.8; 45.36.8.
67. Livy, 43.7.8.
68. Livy, 31.29.4; 45.36.8.
69. Livy has also recorded some of these vices appearing in previous wars: 8.33.13; 24.32.1.
70. Livy, 39.1.3–4; 39.6.6–7.
71. For an analysis on different angles of the characters of Fabius, Marcellus, Scipio Africanus, see Levene, *Livy on the Hannibalic War*, chap. 3, "Persons and Peoples," 164–260; Bernard, *Le portrait chez Tite-Live*.

very important individuals whose courage in defending the state Livy also shows, and we are not suggesting by any means that their role in the narrative is less relevant to Livy's goal. Horatius Cocles defending the bridge against Porsenna's army,[72] Mucius Scaevola bravely burning his right hand,[73] and Cincinnatus' exemplary dictatorship[74] are placed in the early books in preparation for the later heroes. They all provide an impressive example of courage, placing the welfare of their city before their own. This self-sacrifice for the good of the commonwealth was going to constitute the very core of Livy's real men of *virtus*.

Among the early wars, perhaps the predominant figure is that of Camillus.[75] In the capture of Veii or the war against the Volsci, for example, he is the main individual figure who is praised for his *virtus*: "Camillus distinguishing himself for his skill and courage in the Volscian war ... [*Camillus, consilio et virtute in Volsco bello ... insignis*]."[76] And some years later, in 390 B.C., when the Gauls destroyed the city and burned it, it was Camillus, *maximum imperatorum omnium*,[77] who reversed the situation: he would not suffer the Romans' paying a ransom.[78] He delivered a speech with which he lit the flame of Roman courage: "they must win their country back with iron instead of gold."[79] To fight and not to pay was the Roman way of dealing with their enemies. After the victory, Camillus was praised as another Romulus, Father of the Country and second Founder of the City.[80] The similarities with Augustus' titles are too striking to be overlooked.[81] The title of *Pater Patriae*, officially given to Augustus, had connotations with that conferred on Camillus,[82]

---

72. Livy, 2.10: *Grata erga tantam virtutem civitas fuit.*

73. Livy, 2.12–13.5. Livy uses four times the word *virtus* narrating this episode.

74. Livy, 3.19.3: *virtute sua* and 4.13.13: *non consilii modo, sed etiam virtutis.*

75. For Camillus, see Hellegouarc'h, "Le Principat de Camille," 112–32; Stevenson, "*Parens Patriae* and Livy's Camillus," 27–48; Bruun, "M. Furius Camillus," 41–68; Coudry, "Camille," 47–81; Mineo, "Camille, dux fatalis," 159–75; Gaertner, "Livy's Camillus," 27–52; Takacs, "Image of Camillus in Livy's Book 5 and 6," 205–11: values, history, politics; Gowing, "Roman *exempla* Tradition in Imperial Greek Historiography," 332–47.

76. Livy, 6.27.1. For more instances of Camillus' *virtus*, see Livy, 5.26.8; 5.26.10; 5.27.8.

77. Livy, 5.23.1.

78. Cf. Livy, 5.48.9.

79. Livy, 5.49.3.

80. Cf. Livy, 5.49.7. For the differences with his contemporary Manlius Capitolinus, see Jaeger, "Custodia Fidelis Memoriae," 350–63.

81. These have been duly noted by scholars; see lately Mineo, "Livy's Historical Philosophy," 146–48.

82. *Res Gestae*, 35: *senatus, et equester ordo populusque Romanus universus appellavit me patrem patriae*. Cf. Cooley, *Res Gestae Divi Augusti*, ad loc.

and the notion of a new founder was particularly linked with the idea of renewal in all aspects—Camillus and Augustus both embarked on large projects of reconstruction and restoration of the city—especially turning the clock back on decline and starting anew.[83]

The third century B.C. saw the Fabian family shining for their consulships and their courage in war. Among the later Fabii, Q. Fabius Maximus Cunctator is the one who stands out, and it is precisely because his display of courage and leadership is presented by Livy as something a little unconventional. Fabius' strategy of delaying actual fighting with Hannibal was misunderstood by many at the time,[84] and the general had to bear from his master of the horses what was perhaps the strongest reproach for a Roman general: to be cowardly (*timidus*).[85] Fabius' subordinate, Minucius, is an example of indiscipline and disrespectful conduct toward the dictator; he sarcastically calls Fabius a "new Camillus,"[86] and urges the troop to fight "the Roman way," by daring and action (*audendo atque agendo*).[87] Through Fabius' example, Livy shows that *virtus*, as real courage, is much more than acting recklessly or temerariously; bravery as a virtue is the mean between foolish rashness and weak pusillanimity. In this instance, Fabius shows more courage by putting up with the criticisms from the Romans than by facing Hannibal in battle. It required a special type of valor to be held in contempt by everyone and keep one's resolutions firm. In the end, Fabius' steadfastness and magnanimity,[88] though unpopular, proved efficacious.[89] Through Fabius Cunctator, Livy showed that there was more than one way of displaying *virtus* in war.

Livy, having the advantage of hindsight of Fabius' success, acknowledges his prudence and opportune action on several occasions—he talks about Fabius' skilled deferral (*sollers cunctatio*)[90]—and he has Hannibal not only

---

83. For the significance of the reconstruction of Rome, see Kraus, "No Second Troy," 267–89.

84. Fabius had to deal with the accusation of wanting to prolong his consulship to keep the command of the war; cf. Livy, 24.9.1.

85. Livy, 22.12.12: *pro cunctatore segnem, pro cauto timidum, adfingens vicina virtutibus vitia*. Also, 22.14.4. The general Varro would later on use the same words to describe Fabius: *timidus* and *segnis* in 22.43.5.

86. Livy, 22.14.9.

87. Livy, 22.14.14.

88. For Fabius' *magnitudo animi*, see Livy, 24.9.11. Other manifestations of this magnanimity according to Livy were that he served his country as lieutenant of his own son (24.44.10), and sold his farm for the benefit of the state (22.23.8). Cf. Plut. *Fab*, 1.3.

89. Livy, 22.15–23.

90. Livy, 22.23.1. See also 24.14.1; 24.19.2; 24.20.7; 24.45.4–10.

recognizing Fabius' *prudentia* and *constantia*[91] but even imitating his own strategy of inaction and delay (*artibus Fabi sedendo et cunctando*).[92] In this way, Fabius became an *exemplum* not only to Romans but also to his very enemies.

Fabius' colleague in the consulship in 214 B.C. was M. Claudius Marcellus, another of Livy's heroes of the second Punic war.[93] Marcellus—this being his third consulship—had already gained a reputation as an energetic and brave man when in 222 B.C. he had not only beaten the Gauls in the battle of Clastidium but also killed their leader Viridomarus in single combat, thus winning for himself the highest military honor in Rome.[94] Although Marcellus' greatest feat—winning the *spolia opima*—is not told to us by Livy, but by Plutarch,[95] it is clear that for Livy, Marcellus was an exceptional man. Marcellus' achievements as praetor and proconsul are narrated in Book 23, and when he finally joins Fabius Maximus as colleague in 214 B.C., Livy presents both consuls as being complementary: "for many years there had been no such pair of consuls [*multis enim annis tale consulum par non fuerat*]."[96] Like Sallust comparing Cato and Caesar—the two men of *virtus* in the *Bellum Catilinae*—Livy compares the two generals with their different but both highly effective strategies against the Carthaginians throughout Book 24. This comparison was going to be neatly summarized by another author saying that "Fabius was known as the shield of Rome, and Marcellus as its sword."[97]

Marcellus is best portrayed by Livy in the capture of Syracuse. His *auctoritas*,[98] his vigor and valor (*praeterquam vi ac virtute ducis*),[99] his tenacity of action in taking the city,[100] is blended in the narrative with his tears foreseeing the end of it,[101] the leniency through which he attempts to save the

---

91. Livy, 22.12.6. See also 22.23.3. Attested also in Plut. *Fab*, 5.2–3.
92. Livy, 22.24.10. Another instance of the Fabian way [*Fabianis artes*] is 22.34.7. For the origin of the cognomen "Cunctator," see Stanton, "*Cunctando Restituit Rem,*" 49–56.
93. For more on Marcellus, see Carawan, "Tragic History of Marcellus and Livy's Characterization," 131–41; Rives, "Marcellus and the Syracusans," 32–35; Rossi, "Tears of Marcellus," 56–66; Jaeger, "Livy and the Fall of Syracuse," 213–34.
94. Plut. *Marc*, 8. Cf. Livy, *per*. 20. See Flower, "Tradition of the Spolia Opima," 34–64.
95. Plut. *Marc*, 7–8.
96. Livy, 24.9.7.
97. Reported as being said by Posidonius in Plut. *Marc*, 9.4 and *Fab*, 19.3.
98. Livy, 25.6.5.
99. Livy, 25.23.1.
100. Livy, 25.24.7.
101. Livy, 25.24.11.

Syracusans by asking for their voluntary surrender,[102] and his regrets for Archimedes' slaughter.[103] But Marcellus' conduct is not praised indiscriminately by the historian; although matters in Syracuse had been settled with honesty and integrity (*fides ac integritas*) that added to Marcellus' own *gloria* and also to the *dignitas* of the Roman people, the legitimate spoils of war—magnificent works of Greek art—that were carried to Rome had the disastrous effect of license (*licentia*) and bad *exemplum* for later plunder.[104]

Livy mentions another interesting connection of Claudius Marcellus with *virtus*: a temple dedicated to this deity.[105] It was, indeed, after the capture of Syracuse in 211 B.C. that Marcellus renewed his vow to dedicate a temple to *Honos* and *Virtus* which he had promised to build after the battle of Clastidium in 222 B.C. In the end the vow was fulfilled not by building a new temple, but by adding an image of *Virtus* to the temple of *Honos* dedicated by Fabius Maximus in 234 B.C. This temple, however, splendidly decorated with Marcellus' spoils from Sicily, could not be properly dedicated in his own time because Marcellus, following the orders of the *pontifex maximus*, had to build another vault to the second deity, transforming the temple into a double shrine. By the time this was finished, Marcellus had died and his son had to dedicate it in 205 B.C.[106] This is considered to be the first record that we have of a temple dedicated to *Virtus* in republican times.[107] The fact is quite significant because *virtus*, a term very much associated with the Roman nobility, was in this case promoted by the plebeian Marcellus.[108]

After his victory at Syracuse, Marcellus was denied the triumph by the Senate and was granted only an ovation in Rome.[109] Like his colleague Fabius, he also had political enemies whose acts were motivated by envy.[110] Livy narrates Marcellus' final days with certain ambiguity, as a combination of courageous behavior fighting against Hannibal and a little cruelty (*saevitia*) that had not appeared before when dealing with the vanquished, or even with

---

102. Livy, 25.24.15.
103. Livy, 25.31.9.
104. Livy, 25.40.2.
105. Livy, 27.25.7–9. See also 25.40.3; 26.32.4. For the implications of this temple, see Clark, *Divine Qualities*, 112–13.
106. Livy, 29.11.13.
107. For more details of this temple, see Balmaceda, "*Virtus* en la Ciudad de Roma," 159–80.
108. See chapter 1 in this book. The second temple to *Virtus* was dedicated by the *homo novus* Marius after the battle against the Cimbri and Teutoni in 102–101 B.C., as reported in chapter 2.
109. Livy, 26.21.6.
110. Livy, 26.29.5: *invidia Marcelli*. See also 26.26.5.

his own soldiers.[111] Marcellus would also be compared with Fabius in the way he handled the spoils of war and booty; Fabius had shown more magnanimity in restraining from plunder.[112] Marcellus would finally encounter hostility in Rome: he was criticized for his prolonged command and his obsession in keeping on fighting with Hannibal until he finally died in battle.[113] He is, however, certainly one of Livy's men of *virtus*.

P. Cornelius Scipio Africanus will be our last case of *virtus* in Roman generals of the second Punic war. Livy's account of his life and deeds during the second Hannibalic war, matched with magnificent speeches, shows that Africanus was one of the author's favorite Roman commanders and, in his view, one of the greatest.

Scipio Africanus was described by Livy as a brave man since his youth. One of the first acts of courage recorded by Livy might have been saving his own father's life in the battle of Ticinus.[114] Later on, he was the only brave man who volunteered to be sent to Spain, when all others considered it a death sentence, and was unanimously voted proconsul at the age of twenty-four.[115] Scipio would also be praised by Livy both for his reasoning and planning—he calls him cautious and foresighted (*cautus et providens*)[116]— and because he fought in the most dangerous place in battle, leading, exhorting, and encouraging his men.[117] He appears at the center of military action, never just giving orders, but fighting along with his soldiers at great risk.[118] Besides his own courage, Scipio in Livy is shown to be generous in praising and rewarding the *virtus* of his soldiers (*militum deinde virtutem conlaudavit*), a fact that undoubtedly fostered more new acts of *virtus*.[119] In his addresses to the army, with extraordinary eloquence, the general called for the Roman ideals to come to the fore: the safety of the *res publica* should be defended with the *virtus* of the Roman people and was to be placed before any personal

---

111. Livy, 27.13.1.
112. Livy, 27.16.8.
113. For Marcellus' death, see Bernard, "*Historia magistra mortis*," 30–39. Cf. also Flower, "Memories of Marcellus," 39–52.
114. Livy, 21.46.7.
115. Livy, 26.18.7. Polybius (10.6.7) says that he was twenty-seven, in any case younger than he should have been for that office.
116. Livy, 25.34.7.
117. Livy, 25.34.11.
118. Livy, 28.19.17.
119. Livy, 26.48.4. See also Livy, 26.48.13–14: *Digitium pariter in murum escendisse, seque eos ambos virtutis causa coronis muralibus donare. Tum reliquos prout cuiusque meritum virtusque erat donavit.*

interests.[120] Scipio is presented as a worthy guardian (*custodius*) of the Roman people who places their protection in his hands.[121]

But the historian also assigns other admirable virtues (*mirabilis virtutibus*) to Scipio.[122] The use of the plural *virtutes* is not common in Livy, and this may suggest either that he chose to name individual virtues that stood out in people or that for him there were not many cases of individuals in whom several virtues might be recognized at the same time.[123] Some of these virtues are not explicitly connected with courage, but are nonetheless very important to a commander in accomplishing his goal—in this case, to win the war against Hannibal—and also in providing an example of fair behavior during and in the aftermath of the war. Scipio showed *fides*,[124] *clementia*,[125] *benignitas*,[126] *consilium*,[127] and *magnitudo animi*,[128] and was constantly giving *beneficia*.[129] This humanitarian conduct toward prisoners and hostages, obtaining more cooperation through favors and kindness in Hispania, helped in portraying the Romans as liberators as opposed to conquerors.[130]

Looking at Scipio from another angle, Livy's stories about his protection of women are also quite remarkable. Though I will deal with women in more detail in a separate section, I would like to point out now that when Scipio delivers the beautiful young Spaniard to her betrothed, he pronounces a speech in which he talks, once again, of his personal option to serve the state as his first and foremost choice in life, which has left him no time for dedicating himself to other noble pursuits. This proof of his self-control and generosity—he restores the woman untouched and with a considerable sum of gold—wins him favor with the people in Spain, who will later on reward Scipio with 1,400 cavalrymen.[131] It is interesting to note that the most important virtues that

---

120. Cf. Livy, 26.41, for Scipio's speech in *oratio recta*, where he uses the word *virtus* four times. For more on Scipio's speeches, see, for example, Douglas Botha, *Speeches of Scipio Africanus*; Tedeschi, *Lo Storico in Parola, Livio, Scipione l'Africano e le tecniche dell'argumentazione*, 41–133.

121. Livy, 22.53.10–13.

122. Livy, 26.19.3.

123. Only eighteen times in his whole extant work. For more on the plural of *virtus* in Livy, see Moore, *Artistry and Ideology*, 8; and Eisenhut, *Virtus Romana*, 124–45.

124. Livy, 28.32.1.

125. Livy, 28.34.3.

126. Livy, 26.50.13.

127. Livy, 30.28.11.

128. Livy, 28.17.2.

129. Livy, 26.50.13; 27.20.5; 28.34.8; 30.17.10.

130. Livy, 26.49.8.

131. Livy, 26.50.

Scipio himself acknowledges in his own persona, according to Livy, are self-restraint and continence (*temperantia et continentia*).[132] These virtues are also in some way related to the martial sphere of life. Temperance, no doubt, required a tough internal battle to be achieved, and the language used by Scipio to attain self-control has an explicit belligerent flavor: "conquer yourself! [*vince animum*]."[133] The way to acquire other virtues was also a type of war; it was a fight of another kind, but one that required courage too. This aspect of *virtus* would become increasingly important when approaching the principate, especially in Tacitus' works.

In Rome, Scipio's fame grew more and more on account of his never-ending successes.[134] Moreover, the effect of Scipio's presence was wondrous on allies and enemies alike. Not only the remembrance of his military exploits, but also his cleverness (*ingenium*) and courtesy (*comitas*) produced great admiration in enemies.[135] Even Hannibal is said to have acknowledged Scipio's courage and piety (*virtus pietasque*).[136]

In spite of all these qualities, or perhaps precisely because of all the fame and glory that these qualities brought to Scipio, he was not free from powerful political enemies in his own country: "the greater his fame, the more it was exposed to jealousy."[137] Other leading citizens of Rome grew envious of their general, especially for the novelty of the duration of his command, which meant an extension not for a fixed period, but till the end of the war.[138] Later, the rumors that he was being extravagant and indulgent with the discipline of the army,[139] together with the final accusation of accepting bribes from King Antiochus,[140] somewhat spoiled Scipio's end in Livy's narrative. The historian's account of Scipio's death in voluntary exile in Liternum, and the fact that nothing was known of his funeral or of the existence of a *laudatio funebris*, is given as a sad contrast to Livy's own closing remark on this exceptional man: "nevertheless, since he brought to an end the Punic war, than which there was waged none greater nor more dangerous by the Romans, he

---

132. Livy, 30.14.5–6.
133. Livy, 30.14.11. Scipio tells Massinissa after his rash and passionate marriage to Sophonisba.
134. Livy, 27.20.9.
135. See, for example, the cases of Hasdrubal, 28.18.6–7; and Indibilis, 29.1.19.
136. Livy, 30.30.13.
137. Livy, 35.10.5: *maior gloria Scipionis et quo maior eo propior invidiam.* Cf. Livy, 29.19.
138. Livy, 30.1.10.
139. Livy, 29.21.13.
140. Livy, 38.51.1–2.

has secured a singular pre-eminence of fame."[141] A subtle tone of complaint appears in that "nevertheless" (*tamen*) as if Livy were bemoaning the unfairness of Africanus' end, as if it had been Scipio's insatiable desire for bravery (*inexplebilis virtus*)[142] that had brought about the end of the Romans' predilection for their greatest war hero. This fact also seems to prefigure the "dangers of *virtus*" that will appear more openly in an autocratic government.

None of these three Roman generals in the second Punic war—Fabius Maximus, Claudius Marcellus, and Scipio Africanus—are presented as flawless by Livy; in fact, there is some criticism—sometimes more open, sometimes less—of all three of them. Nonetheless the final overview regarding their *virtus* is positive: they faced the dangers they encountered by exercising their *virtus* in different ways. Livy connected their names and actions not only with courage (*virilis-virtus*) but with moral excellence (*humana-virtus*) as well, and they were men who appeared always to have placed their country before any personal gain.

The third set of wars, by contrast, the Macedonian wars, do not appear to have had such great heroes as the Punic ones according to Livy. The Romans had indeed better generals and armies than their enemies, but there were also other factors that gave the Macedonian wars the somewhat darker touch that was mentioned before.

Undoubtedly, Flamininus was an excellent commander; he not only defeated King Philip V of Macedon in the battle of Cynoscephalae in 197 B.C. but also made the stiff Macedonian phalanx useless and obsolete compared with the flexible Roman legion.[143] However, there are no explicit references to Flamininus' courage, or to any other virtue, in Livy's account of the second Macedonian war. Flamininus is presented by the historian mainly as the consul who fulfilled his duty and was successful.

A different case is that of L. Aemilius Paullus in the third Macedonian war, a man who is said to have behaved with dignity and according to the majesty of Rome.[144] Livy introduces Paullus as one who would not fight without spirit (*non segniter*), but as a warlike man (*vir militaris*).[145] Even if these attributes do not appear as positive *virtus*, they do tell us something of the Roman

---

141. Livy, 38.53.11.

142. Livy, 28.17.2–3.

143. Livy, 44.41.7. Cf. Balsdon, "T. Quinctius Flamininus," 177–90; Walsh, "Flamininus and the Propaganda of Liberation," 344–63.

144. Livy, 45.40.4. For more, see Reiter, *Aemilius Paullus, Conqueror of Greece*; Eigler, "Aemilius Paullus," 250–67.

145. Livy, 44.18.1.

general's disposition toward waging war. But Paullus' achievements—like Flamininus'—will be recounted by Livy in a slightly more matter-of-fact way than that used for the Punic wars: instead of a vivid account of the fight between the two leaders, he has a magistrate announcing that Aemilius Paullus fought a pitched battle with King Perseus and defeated him.[146] The mere announcement of a victory sounds rather flat compared with the descriptions of successful battles we saw in the earlier books. Furthermore, later on he simply states that Paullus kept the old-fashioned discipline (*antiqua disciplina*) of the army with severity, adding no comment or personal opinion indicative of praise.[147] There are fewer speeches by commanders encouraging soldiers before battles, less enthusiasm in Livy's narrative, and certainly less *virtus* too. It is very telling that, in fact, the word *virtus* does not appear at all in Books 43 and 44, a complete novelty for Livy, and that when he narrates the end of the third Macedonian war and the final conquest of Greece in Book 45, he uses the word *virtus* only once, and then through the mouth of a Rhodian, failing again to provide authorial endorsement.[148]

The Macedonian wars were fought with good generals and powerful armies, but at the same time, Livy records that diplomacy and money were seen as playing a more significant role among the Romans. The provincials' complaint before the Senate about the greed and arrogance of Roman officials,[149] together with Roman public men showing pride, greed, and cruelty,[150] and even Roman soldiers behaving with license and greediness,[151] shows a change of circumstances, which brings also a change in the vocabulary.[152] The frequency with which Livy reports deeds with the words *crudelitas* and *avaritia* toward the end of his extant work is very meaningful. Moreover, it is not just cruelty and avarice, it is intensified: *crudelius et avarius*.[153] This has little to do with the language of honor and virtue of the early books, and is closer to the Sallustian language of decline. The word *clementia* also starts appearing more often, perhaps because there are more possibilities of being

---

146. Livy, 45.1.8–9. For the importance of battle description in Livy, see Koon, *Infantry Combat in Livy's Battle Narratives*, esp. 26–28.

147. Livy, 45.35.6. For Aemilius Paullus' triumph, see Pelikan, *Livy's Contested Triumphs*, 246–74.

148. Livy, 45.23.1.

149. Livy, 43.2.1: *avaritia superbiaeque* . . .

150. Cf. Livy, 43.7.8: *praetor Romanus superbe, auare, crudeliter fecisset* . . .

151. Livy, 45.36.8: *licentiae atque avaritia* . . .

152. For the change of vocabulary, though in more stylistic terms, see Adams, "Vocabulary of the Later Decades of Livy," 54–62, esp. 57 in reference to *luxuria*. For immorality in wars, see Gilliver, "Roman Army and Morality in War," 219–38.

153. Livy, 43.4.5.

cruel,[154] and thus, it appears more important to promote mercy as a virtue of the victor.[155] Besides, a sort of servility toward the grandeur of the Romans is now recognizable in the speeches of the vanquished and the allies.[156] Even the Greeks were rather overwhelmed with Roman ceremonies and pageantry.[157]

The victorious Romans gave independence to the Macedonians and Illyrians and reduced the taxes that they had been accustomed to pay their kings. Livy adds that "it should be clear to all nations that the forces of the Roman people brought, not slavery to free peoples, but on the contrary, freedom to the enslaved. The Senate wished nations that were free to consider that their freedom was assured and lasting under the protection of the Roman people, and that those who lived under kings should feel for the time being that their rulers were milder and more just under the eye of the Roman people, and, if at any time their kings should make war on the Roman people, that the outcome of the war would bring victory to the Romans, but freedom to themselves."[158] The quotation is long, but worth giving in full, as it reflects the interestingly twisted argument that to be associated with the "free republic," even as a subject, somehow made one free. The previous wars that Rome had fought had been to secure Roman freedom and safety in which *virtus* had played an important role; these latter wars allegedly brought liberty to other nations, but to the Romans only more power and wealth and, therefore, *virtus* is noticeably less present. It would have been very interesting to see how Livy dealt with the wars of the late Roman Republic: language, style, description of commanders, and even enemies were changing rapidly throughout the *Ab Urbe Condita*.

A last note can be added regarding the enemies of the Macedonian wars compared with the previous ones. Livy appears generous in attributing *virtus* to foreigners when they deserve it, and many leaders of the opponents are described in his work: the Etruscan Porsenna, Brennus and Ambigatus, kings

---

154. Livy, 42.38.4; 43.1.1; 44.9.1; 44.31.1; 45.4.7; 45.8.5; 45.17.7; 45.22.4.

155. Recall *clementia* in Augustus' golden shield. Seneca in his *De Clementia* (1.21.2) gives a clear explanation of the political consequences of exercising clemency toward one's enemies: "for that man has lost his life who owes it to another, and whosoever, having been cast down from high estate at his enemy's feet, has awaited the verdict of another upon his life and throne, *lives on to the glory of his preserver*, and by being saved confers more upon the other's name than if he had been removed from the eyes of men. For he is a *lasting spectacle of another's prowess*; in a triumph he would have passed quickly out of sight" (my italics). *Clementia* appears as a very two-edged virtue, as it can also be the gift of a tyrant.

156. Livy, 45.3.6; 45.22.5.

157. Livy, 45.29.2–3.

158. Livy, 45.18.1–2.

of the Gauls,[159] Massinissa,[160] Attalus,[161] and others. But the first and foremost is, of course, Hannibal.[162] The war against the Carthaginians had produced great soldiers and great generals partly because the enemy had been great. Hannibal's courage was such that even a Roman general felt quite overpowered by it: "Though made equal to Fabius in authority, he finds Hannibal his superior, both in courage and in fortune [*Fabio aequatus imperio Hannibalem et virtute et fortuna superiorem videt*]."[163] This looks very different from the later descriptions of Rome's enemies like King Philip V, a lustful man,[164] unfaithful to treaties and a joker,[165] or Perseus' treachery and cruelty.[166]

It looks as if *virtus* was not something to be taken for granted in the wars that Livy recounts. The stage for *virtus* was prepared, but not only good fighting was necessary to show the ideal image of courageous behavior. An interesting pattern or design that could be followed in the analysis of the presence or absence of *virtus* in the wars recounted by Livy may depend on these four elements: firstly, to see what the main goal of the war waged was; whether the Romans fought for self-defense, freedom, imperialism, power, or dominion.[167] Secondly, it is also important to consider the character of the Roman general leading the war, as has been shown earlier in this chapter with the cases of Camillus, Fabius Maximus, Claudius Marcellus, or Scipio Africanus, because the leader would be key to the behavior of his men. Thirdly, it was worth taking into account, too, the type of enemy against whom the war was waged. Bravery was not something exclusive to the Roman people; the difference was that they said they had it to a far higher degree, and expressed it far more often, than their enemies. Characterizing a foreign enemy as possessor of *virtus* played an important part in the creation of the historical tradition of a "worthy enemy." The fourth and last element to consider when analyzing Roman *virtus* at war in Livy is the relation between the actual battles fought and the aftermath of the war, that is, the behavior of generals and armies once the war was concluded: whether the war respected the *ius*

---

159. Cf. Livy, 5.34.2.
160. Cf. Livy, 29.31.3.
161. Cf. Livy, 38.23.11.
162. Cf. Livy, 22.58.3; 23.42.4; 23.43.10; 30.35.10; 31.1.6; 35.43.1.
163. Livy, 22.29.2. For an interesting comparison between Hannibal and Scipio, see Rossi, "Parallel Lives," 359–81. See also Harris, "Can Enemies Too Be Brave?," 465–72.
164. Livy, 27.31.
165. Livy, 32.33.10 and 32.34.3, respectively.
166. Livy, 40.56.1 and 40.58.8, respectively.
167. For one possible interpretation of the causes of each war waged by Rome, cf. Harris, *War and Imperialism in Republican Rome 327–70 B.C.*, 163–254.

gentium, the moderation (or lack of it) with which they dealt with plunder and spoils, and the terms and conditions of peace imposed on enemies.

These elements may help to discern what type of war Livy is dealing with, and to gain a rough idea of the presence of *virtus* one will probably encounter in the narrative. For example, after having analyzed Livy's wars by applying these four categories, it is not surprising to see the noticeable decrease of the use of the word *virtus* as the narrative progresses along the extant books. Put into numbers this comes to seventy-three instances in the first pentad and only fifteen in the last one (with two books with no occurrence of *virtus* at all). Having in mind how much of Livy's work is lost, one has to be cautious in assigning too much relevance to this information, but taken at face value it tells us that something has changed either in the nature of the wars that Rome is fighting or in the people fighting them.

Wars in Livy appear as the natural stage and backdrop for *virtus*. The generals, the soldiers, and the enemies were all potential candidates to incarnate it. But Livy shows that *virtus* needed certain conditions to flourish properly; otherwise it would not be real *virtus*—linked to *humana-virtus*—but only rash temerity.

An Aim for *Virtus:* The Fight for *Libertas*

Just as the wars with foreign enemies had been a stage for *virtus*, the development of internal affairs in the city of Rome gave opportunities for *virtus* to shine, and these were related to *libertas*.[168] As I said at the beginning of this chapter, one can distinguish a history or a sequence of events that worked toward the acquisition of *libertas*, firstly a patrician *libertas*—the freedom from *regnum*—and secondly a long and strenuous struggle for the plebeian *libertas*, which implied the liberation of the plebeians from the exercise of privileges by the nobles, and thirdly, the fight for freedom from an external threat, namely, a foreign master, and self-sovereignty. All these freedoms resulted in the creation of the *libera res publica*, one of the greatest Roman achievements.

In Livy's view, after the founding of the city, the monarchy had been a necessity to establish Rome as an ordered city, with limits and laws; without the monarchs, says the historian, the nation would have disintegrated in endless

---

168. The study of *libertas* in Rome has lately seen a comprehensive analysis in a very well-documented book by Valentina Arena, where she reconstructs not only Roman political thinking about liberty but also its political practice during the late republic: *Libertas and the Practice of Politics in the Late Roman Republic*. Also of interest is Cogitore's book *Le doux nom de liberté*.

conflicts before it had matured.¹⁶⁹ But this had been the solution only because they did not know any better; the Romans had not yet tasted the sweetness of freedom (*libertatis dulcedine nondum experta*).¹⁷⁰ A striking feature of Livy's account of the end of the monarchy is the meaningful view of this process as "liberation," and the immediate identification of the new political regime with "freedom." Livy's theme from the second book onward, as he would himself declare it, was the deeds of war and peace of the free Roman people (*res pace belloque gestas liberi Populi Romani*),¹⁷¹ and in the first two chapters of Book 2 alone, he uses the word *libertas* eleven times. It is also interesting to note that this liberty—according to Livy—had nothing to do with the diminution of the consuls' powers compared with those that the kings had exercised, but only with the collegiality and the limitation of their authority to a year,¹⁷² and that the rest of the offices were set and defined according to the needs and having liberty as their chief concern (*prima cura*).¹⁷³ The logical consequence for the patricians, having employed such efforts and energy (*ops*) to acquire and establish freedom, was that monarchy would soon become synonymous with slavery.¹⁷⁴

But at the same time, the threat of foreign domination was always present. The kings had fought to set up the people of Rome as a free nation, and the new *res publica* would, therefore, need to be doubly engaged—*domi militiaeque*—in the defense of liberty. In the previous section, we dealt with some of the men, of high or less high status, who fought for Rome's liberty from foreign perils, and they deserved Livy's highest praise. It was clear that the struggle for the freedom of one's own country was the utmost manifestation of *virtus*; in fact, it appears that for Livy the whole meaning of having *virtus* was to use it to defend and preserve the *libertas* of the fatherland. But was it the same with the fight of a group to attain *libertas* understood as civil rights?

For Livy, the history of the early republican Rome at home—*domi*—was going to be centered on the gradual acquisition of freedom for the plebeians.

---

169. Cf. Livy, 2.1.6.

170. Livy, 1.17.3. Rule by one man as a prerequisite for order was very much an Augustan theme also; cf. Tac. *Hist*, 1.1: "But after the battle of Actium, when the interests of peace required that all power should be concentrated in the hands of one man." See also Strabo 6.4.2: "but it was a difficult thing to administer so great a dominion otherwise than by turning it over to one man, as to a father." For a similar view, see Dio, 53.17.1.

171. Livy, 2.1.1.

172. Cf. Livy, 2.1.7.

173. Cf. Livy, 2.2.2.

174. Livy, 2.15.3: *Non in regno populum Romanum sed in libertate esse*.

This freedom meant, above all, that they could hold the same magistracies as the nobles held, and little by little abolish their hereditary privileges. These internal "battles," better known as the "struggle of the orders," gave the history of the Roman Republic a particular hue of civil discord—which had started right at the beginning with Romulus and Remus—which was overcome only temporarily when Rome had to unite and fight an external war and had no time for dissension at home.[175]

To give an account of the relationships between *virtus* and political *libertas* in Livy's work, I will need to provide at least a short, somewhat sketchy description of some of the events of this struggle in order to be able, later on, to read them through the lens of *virtus*.[176]

Conflicts between the Senate and the plebeians did not take long to arise in the newly founded republic.[177] In 495 B.C. the trigger of the quarrel was slavery for debt. Livy reports the injustice done to those plebeians who, after being abroad at war, had come back to Rome and were forced into slavery because they had lost their land and got into debt. The dispute is presented by the historian as a matter of freedom: men were fighting in foreign lands for the liberty of Rome, but had been enslaved and oppressed at home by fellow citizens. The complaint seemed fair enough: "the freedom of the plebeians was more secure in war than in peace, among enemies than among citizens [*tutioremque in bello quam in pace et inter hostes quam inter cives libertatem plebis esse*]."[178] The end of the conflict came when the commons put the consuls under threat and said that they would not fight unless liberty was granted.[179] Divisions and quarrels continued until the dramatic secession of the plebeians to the Aventine. In 493 B.C., it was finally decided that the plebeians were to have magistrates of their own, who should be inviolable, and who should possess the right to aid the people against the consuls, nor should any senator be per-

---

175. For the struggle of the orders in general, see Raaflaub, *Social Struggles in Archaic Rome*, esp. the chapter "From Protection and Defense to Offense and Participation," 198–243; and Mitchell, *Patricians and Plebeians*. See also Cornell, *Beginnings of Rome*, 242–71; Smith, *Roman Clan*, 275–80. For Rome's "tradition" in civil wars, see Breed, Damon, and Rossi, *Citizens of Discord*.

176. Many comments on historical points could be brought into consideration here, but I will restrict myself to drawing attention only to some. For a more detailed account on Rome's early history, see, for example, CAH^2, vol. 7, pt. 2: "The Rise of Rome to 220 B.C."; Cornell, *Beginnings of Rome*; Forsythe, *Critical History of Early Rome*.

177. Although for Cornell, *Beginnings of Rome*, 244, there was no conflict of orders as such until the fourth century B.C.

178. Livy, 2.23.2.

179. Cf. Livy, 2.28.2.

mitted to take this magistracy.[180] Certainly, the creation of the tribunate of the plebs is presented by Livy as an achievement that brought protection from the possible abuses of the nobles and as an important step forward to the acquisition of political rights and plebeian *libertas*. In spite of the positive light with which the historian narrates this episode, he also shows the tribunes themselves most of the time as being the cause and instigators of the dissensions and madness [*furia*] of the plebs against the Senate and the nobles.[181] With their "usual poison [*suo veneno*],"[182] the tribunes sowed subversive ideas among the plebs against the consuls and the authorities. These ideas revolved mainly around land laws and the levy of soldiers: the commons demanded agrarian reforms, while the patricians needed men to defend Rome from foreign threats.[183] Livy reveals the tension between the tribunes of the plebs preventing the levy and the Senate blocking the laws as an endless struggle of one group to prevail over the other. Some of these disputes escalated into a race of violence, which sometimes ended in the death of the tribune—violating his *sacrosanctitas*[184]—or bloodshed among the citizens.[185]

Later on, during the time of the decemvirs, the plebeians saw a large step backward for their civil rights as their tribunician power was suspended. Livy reports this period as having unmistakable signs of tyranny in the city and shows that the general feeling of the people was hopeless and forlorn: "they mourned for liberty as forever lost [*deploratur in perpetuum libertas*]."[186] Livy, who up to now had presented his authorial voice as somewhat neutral, sided with the plebeians this time, showing that the arrogance of the decemvirs had gone too far. The several attempts to recover freedom are narrated in detail, as are also the other consecutive acquisitions of plebeian rights: the right to appeal,[187] mixed marriage,[188] and later on, even the consulate.[189]

As the struggle of the orders is present throughout several of the books of the *AUC*, it might be helpful to identify certain patterns in the narrative that will aid us in the interpretation of *virtus* in the struggle for *libertas*. First of all,

---

180. Cf. Livy, 2.33.2. See also Bruno, "Libertas Plebis in Tito Livio," 107–30.
181. Livy, 5.3.2. See also 2.54.2; 3.25.9; 5.2.2; 5.10.6; 5.25.12; 7.18.8; 10.6.11.
182. Livy, 2.52.2. Also *suo more*, 3.25.9.
183. Cf. Livy, 2.41.3; 2.42.6; 2.54.2; 2.63.2; 3.1.2; 3.25.9. For the political implications of agrarian redistribution, see Arena, *Libertas and the Practice of Politics*, 220–43.
184. Cf. Livy, 2.54.9.
185. Cf. Livy, 2.60.4.
186. Livy, 3.38.2.
187. Livy, 3.45.8.
188. Livy, 4.1–6.
189. Livy, 6.42.9.

the association of the word *virtus* with the fight for plebeian freedom does not appear as something straightforward in Livy precisely because of the nature of the conflict itself. Fighting for one's own political freedom was, in general, done in a considerably less heroic way than waging wars against powerful foreign enemies; the struggle seemed to have a touch of self-interest or self-advantage that was not present when the war had as its main goal the freedom and welfare of the *res publica* from an external threat. This, for Livy, definitely tainted the fight for freedom. He will complain out loud that it should be so: "So difficult it is to be moderate in the defense of liberty, since everyone, while pretending to seek fair play, so raises himself as to press another down [*Adeo moderatio tuendae libertatis, dum aequari velle simulando ita se quisque extollit ut deprimat alium, in difficili est*]."[190] The historian shows regularly that both sides were more often lacking in certain virtues—such as moderation, justice, or magnanimity—than exercising real courage (*virtus*) as it had been seen in foreign wars. The nobles were accused especially of greed and arrogance,[191] reproached for their jealous, narrow-minded defense of their privileges and their incapacity to seek the common good for the whole *res publica*, as though any measure to protect the liberty of the plebs meant a reduction of their own power: "the patricians were as angry as though they had not merely shared their offices with the plebs but had lost them."[192] The tribunes of the plebs, on the other hand, are presented as rebellious and stubborn by Livy, and he is constantly reminding the reader of their untrustworthiness and deliberate manipulation to achieve their aims: "This was in itself a serious grievance, but it was made to appear more so by the seditious harangues of the tribunes of the plebs [*Haec per se gravia indigniora ut viderentur tribuni plebis seditiosis contionibus faciebant*]."[193] Besides, they were never contented with the measures suggested by the patricians: "the tribunes of the plebs were the only persons who did not partake in the general joy and good feelings of both orders. They said that the measure would be neither so agreeable nor so favorable to the whole body of the citizens as the latter believed [*Tribuni plebis, communis ordinum laetitiae concordiaeque soli expertes, negare, tam id laetum patribus civibus universis nec prosperum fore quam ipsi crederent*]."[194]

---

190. Livy, 3.65.11. See also 4.6.11–12; 4.54.6.
191. See esp. the case of Appius Claudius, 9.33–34.
192. Livy, 4.54.6. Cf. also 3.37.8; 3.55.2; 10.8.5.
193. Livy, 5.10.6.
194. Livy, 4.60.3. See also 2.54.2: *agrariae legis tribuniciis plebs furebat*.

However, having said this, there are occasions when traditional *virtus* does shine forth in the struggle between patricians and plebeians. The cases are not very many, but they are quite significant because they provide light to the understanding of the concept of *virtus* itself. *Virtus* is not present in Livy's history when the defender of liberty acts as a *factio*. Overcoming *dissentio* or disagreement in a jealously divided community did not merit the behavior where *virtus Romana* as we have hitherto described it may play an important part. There was something petty and unworthy about it; it did not seem right to fight with the same animosity and courage against their common foreign enemy and against their own fellow countrymen.[195] Livy—following Sallust's criticism of *mos partium et factionum*[196]—acknowledges that "party spirit and consideration for private interests [are] things that have been always hurtful to public deliberation and always will be [*factione respectuque rerum privatarum (...) semper offecere officientque publicis consiliis*]."[197] *Virtus*, as we have seen, needs to be exercised for the benefit of the people of Rome, for the commonwealth, not just to bring advantage to a group. Thus, *virtus* does appear explicitly when the struggle of the orders transforms itself into a fight to defend the freedom of the commonwealth as a whole against an internal threat. This is shown in several occasions, and some of the most conspicuous cases are those of the end of the decemvirate in Book 3, Maelius' threat in Book 4, and the attainment of consulship for the plebeians in Book 6.

Lucius Icilius appears in the context of the decemvirate, around 449 B.C., defending not only his fiancé from the lust of the patrician Appius Claudius but also the whole of the Roman people against the injustice and tyranny of the decemvirs.[198] Lucius Icilius is highly praised by Livy as an "active man of proven courage in the cause of the plebeians [*viro acri et pro causa plebis expertae virtutis*]."[199] For the historian, this situation was grave and had the same consequences of Lucretia's crime, the change of political system: "the same end befell the decemvirs as had befallen the kings, and the same cause deprived them of their power."[200] The case presented by Livy at first sight seemed private, but in reality affected the whole community, and champions of liberty arise to defend the weak side. The plebs saw in Icilius' courage and

---

195. See Livy, 3.61.3: *Turpe esse contra cives plus animi habuisse quam contra hostes et domi quam foris servitutem magis timuisse*. See also Livy, 3.66.
196. Sal. *BJ* 41.1.
197. Livy, 2.30.2.
198. For an interpretation of Appius' conduct, see Vasaly, *Livy's Political Philosophy*, 65–73.
199. Livy, 3.44.3.
200. Livy, 3.44.1. For Lucretia's case, see next section.

determination to fight Appius the hope of recovering their freedom from the abuses of the decemvirs,[201] and therefore, a personal matter was transformed into a state matter. It is the citizenship that flooded the forum in expectation,[202] and it is they that go again to the Aventine in secession.[203] The plebeians finally recover the tribunician magistracy and with it, their freedom: *fundata deinde et potestate tribunicia et plebis libertate*.[204] They had obtained a common good for all through fighting with courage and facing up front the arrogance of a faction, and moreover it is a patrician who acknowledges it: "By courage they had got back their liberty [*Virtute libertatem reciperatam esse*]."[205] The relationship could not be clearer: through *virtus* they achieved *libertas*.

Maelius' case, on the other hand, was very different; he was a plebeian eques who wanted to win the plebs over by distributing free grain. This conduct and other actions gave the indication that Maelius was seeking kingly powers in the city and that he was truly plotting against the state.[206] He was summoned by the dictator Cincinnatus to face his charge, but as he did not want to obey, Servilius Ahala, the dictator's master of the horses, killed Maelius. The threat of becoming a king was something dangerous not only for the patricians but for all Romans; Maelius had divided the Roman people, and therefore Servilius is applauded by Cincinnatus for his *virtus* in saving the republic as a whole: "Praised be your courage, C. Servilius, you have delivered the commonwealth [*Macte virtute, C. Servili, esto liberata re publica*]."[207] Again it was *virtus* that had preserved *libertas* to all.

Later on, in a similar way, Livy narrates how gaining the consulship meant the final acquisition of plebeian *libertas*: "This was the citadel of liberty, this was its pillar. If they attained to this, then would the Roman people hold that the kings had really been driven from the city and their freedom firmly based [*eam esse arcem libertatis, id columen. Si eo perventum sit, tum populum Romanum vere exactos ex urbe reges et stabilem libertatem suam existimaturum*]."[208] Once again Livy shows a direct link between the exercise of *virtus* and the attainment of *libertas*; in this case it was the *virtus* or valor of G. Licinius and

---

201. Livy, 3.49.1: *multitudo (...) spe per occasionem repetendae libertatis.*
202. Cf. Livy, 3.47.1.
203. Cf. Livy, 3.52.
204. Livy, 3.56.1.
205. Livy, 3.58.4.
206. Cf. Livy, 4.13–14.
207. Livy, 4.14.17.
208. Livy, 6.37.10.

L. Sextius (*duorum hominum virtute, L.Sexti ac C. Licini*...),[209] fighting for fairer laws that had procured the consulship for the plebeians, the paramount bastion of their liberty.[210]

It is possible to say, then, that *virtus* does not appear playing a prominent role when the orders are fighting with greed or seeking personal advantage. Livy does not use the word *virtus* in his account simply when the powerful are fighting the weak, or when the lower group is merely rebelling against the higher one. *Virtus* is present only when a major benefit for the state is at stake: magistracies that imply freedom, equality of rights that mean fairer opportunities to both orders. *Libertas* can be an aim for *virtus* in civil struggles when there is unjust oppression of the whole citizenship from a faction of individuals.

One last point that deserves attention in relation with the struggle of the orders and the fight for *libertas* is the question of *novitas*. Livy's account of the gradual attainment of *libertas* by the people in Rome appears to have similarities to the views on *novitas* developed and articulated by Cicero and Sallust.[211] The plebeians' access to the consulship is certainly reported by Livy as an achievement, and although he is not too explicit, the language shows both a tone of satisfaction and, at the same time, a subtle reproach to the nobles for having denied this magistracy to the commons for so long and granted it so reluctantly.[212] Equality of rights meant that all men—nobles or not—were free to access the same honors through merit, not blood. And this is where *virtus* came to the fore in relation to liberty. It had been through courage (*virtus*) that they had achieved their liberty represented in the consulship, and it was through courage that they should maintain it. When Livy recounts the history of Rome in Book 4 through Canuleius' words, he asserts that some kings had been elected for their *virtus* and merit, not for their birth or ancestry which they lacked: Lucius Tarquinius, for example, was not even from Italian stock. Tanaquil, Tarquinius' wife, when persuading her husband to fight for kingship, referred to the Romans as a *novus populus* and points out that Rome was likely to have a place for him because "where all nobility was sudden and founded on *virtus* there would be room for a brave and vigorous man [*ubi omnis repentina atque ex virtute nobilitas sit, futurum locum forti ac strenuo viro*]."[213] Tarquinius' speech before he is elected king mirrors that of

---

209. Livy, 7.18.5.
210. For the consequences of these laws, see Develin, "Integration of the Plebeians," 293–311.
211. For a fuller account of Cicero's and Sallust's theory of the *homo novus*, see chapter 1 and chapter 2, respectively. And specifically in Livy, see Miles, *Livy*, 150–51.
212. Livy, 6.41–42; 7.1.1.
213. Livy, 1.34.6.

Marius in Sallust's *BJ*, though it is shorter and less dramatic than Marius'; the claims of both "new men" to be elected to the highest office appeared to be identical: the merits of their deeds.

And Tarquinius had not been the only *novus* being king: Servius Tullius was the son of a captive woman and Titus Tatius was a Sabine, and despite this, Rome had increased and become great through their *virtus*.[214] As Miles put it, "the characterization of Rome's 'best kings' as *homines novi*, then, provides the strongest kind of sanction for the new men's arguments."[215]

In the same way, before the battle with the Samnites, consul Valerius delivers a speech that powerfully recalls that of Marius in Sallust's *BJ*. Although Valerius is a noble, he recognizes that he can be an example to the plebeians too, who can look at him for his deeds, because the consulship is now open to anyone who has *virtus* and it is no longer a reward for birth: "But now the consulship lies open on equal terms to us, the patricians, and to you plebeians, nor is it any longer a reward of birth, but of *virtus*."[216] Similar in gist is the speech of Publius Decius, placing *virtus* at the center of honors: "native *virtus* had of its own strength won the right to be recognized in any class of men."[217] Livy's view of the *homo novus* being empowered in the Roman Republic through *virtus* could be a consequence of years of exposure to such rhetoric, which may have become a relatively common *topos* by Livy's times, mainly through Cicero's speeches, and the monographs of Sallust.[218] Livy, then, proposed a sort of pattern in the struggle of the orders: every new institution or office was rejected at first by the nobles, but later approved by consensus, and thus new men had been thrown into the political arena. But Livy's acceptance of new men in Roman politics could also have been influenced by what he was seeing as a political strategy in his own time, with Au-

---

214. Livy, 4.3.12–13: *L. deinde Tarquinium, non Romanae modo sed ne Italicae quidem gentis, Demarati Corinthii filium, incolam ab Tarquiniis, vivis liberis Anci, regem factum? Ser. Tullium post hunc, captiva Corniculana natum, patre nullo, matre serva, ingenio,* virtute *regnum tenuisse? Quid enim de T. Tatio Sabino dicam, quem ipse Romulus, parens urbis, in societatem regni accepit? Ergo dum nullum fastiditur genus in quo eniteret* virtus*, crevit imperium Romanum. Paeniteat nunc vos plebeii consulis, cum maiores nostri advenas reges non fastidierint, et ne regibus quidem exactis clausa urbs fuerit peregrinae* virtuti*?* [my highlighting].

215. Miles, *Livy*, 151. See also 4.3.17: *optimis regum, novis hominibus*. For the same idea, see Syme, *Tacitus*, 350, and "Livy and Augustus," 55.

216. Cf. Livy, 7.32, esp. 7.32.14: *nunc iam nobis patribus vobisque plebei promiscuus consulatus patet nec generis, ut ante, sed virtutis est praemium.* Cf. Raimondi, "I discorsi," 95–100.

217. Livy, 10.24.8: *quoad potuerint, patres adnisos ne plebeiis aditus ad magnos honores esset; postquam ipsa uirtus perviceirt ne in ullo genere hominum inhonorata esset...*

218. See chapters 1 and 2 in this book.

gustus giving important posts to new men, such as M. Agrippa or Statilius Taurus.[219]

In Livy's narrative of internal affairs at Rome, *virtus* appears related with the fight for freedom or *libertas* when the common good is put at risk; there is no *virtus* when a powerful group is struggling against another just to achieve more power. There can be *virtus* in both sides when the welfare of the state as a whole, *tota res publica*, is saved from the danger of a faction, and as a result *concordia ordinum*, the harmony of the orders, is achieved. If discord and internal disunity weakened Rome and made her vulnerable, Livy is keen to highlight the periods when harmony between the orders was enjoyed by all as the greatest good for the *res publica*: "by courage they had got back their liberty, by showing mercy they had it in their power to establish harmony between the orders [*virtute libertatem reciperatam esse, clementia concordiam ordinum stabiliri posse*]."[220] Livy acknowledges the presence of *virtus* when fighting for *libertas* at home in a much more restricted way than he had done when the same aim was sought fighting against a foreign enemy. There has to be a real benefit for the entire community, because *virtus* was not just an individual quality, but mainly and primarily a quality to sustain the whole community.

Politics and Partnership: *Virtus* in Women?

Another overarching theme throughout Livy's history is the presence of women and the role they play in the narrative, especially in the early books. In this section, I will argue that Livy's women appear in his account of Roman history not simply as the life-companions of important political or military men, or as merely passive spectators of what happened in the city, but on the contrary, Livy shows them actively displaying different virtues, mainly standing out for their chastity and bravery but also for their prudence and generosity in actions that have political consequences for the republic.

In general, one can say that when women appear in Livy's narrative, they are portrayed as individuals, usually with their proper names—except when Livy refers to them in general as "matrons"—and having a distinct personality and character. This is a feature particularly present in the narration of the times of the kings in Rome. Monarchy appears as an appropriate setting for individual women to act: Lavinia, Tanaquil, Tullia, and Lucretia are all

---

219. Cf. Vell. 2.127.
220. Livy, 3.58.4. For more on *concordia ordinum*, see also Livy, 3.69.4; 5.7.10; 6.42.12. Also called *concordia patrum ac plebis*, 3.57.7.

women of the royal period whose actions are politically relevant.[221] It is tempting to see a connection between Livy's account of women's actions in politics in his *AUC* and important women acting in Livy's own times: Fulvia with her three marriages, the last one being to Mark Antony, the dynast; Augustus' sister, Octavia; his wife Livia; and his daughter Julia. All of them, to a certain extent, can be seen as performing analogous roles in government to the aristocratic women in Livy.[222] Although the actual passages with descriptions of women in his narrative are relatively few considering the scale of Livy's work, on the whole they are very rich in content and meaning, and almost always the author treats them as men's equals.[223] Moreover, Livy confers a variety of good qualities on women, which will show us different models of feminine virtue put into action.

Regarding the main virtues that Livy acknowledged in women, chastity appears at the top of the list and as the highest praise that the historian can bestow on a Roman woman. Chastity (*castitas*) and modesty (*pudicitia*) are recognized in many women, and are related to *virtus* in a very special way. The explicit connection is shown most clearly in Book 10, around 295 B.C., with the erection of the temple to Plebeian Modesty.[224] The circumstances were as follows: a patrician woman who by marrying a plebeian had been denied entrance to the temple of Patrician Modesty decided to set up a temple so that modest women among the plebeians could also participate in the ceremonies. During the dedication of the temple, she urged plebeian matrons to compete in modesty in the same way as their men competed in courage: "As the men of our state contend for the rewards of valor, so the matrons may vie for that of modesty [*quod certamen virtutis viros in hac civitate tenet, hoc pudicitiae inter matronas sit*]."[225] *Pudicitia* appears here as a womanly virtue worthy of competition with other women, analogous to the competition that Roman men exercised over *virtus*. The idea conveyed in this short speech, powerfully expressed in *oratio recta*, does not leave room for doubt: among men, courage is the quality that appears to be most valued and for that reason merited ri-

---

221. Cf. Stevenson, "Women of Early Rome as Exempla in Livy," 175–89.

222. Cf. Purcell, "Livia and the Womanhood of Rome," 78–105, esp. 81. For the topic of Augustan women, see, for example, Treggiari, "Women in the Time of Augustus," 130–48; Hallett, "Women in Augustan Rome," 372–84.

223. There are some cases when Livy allows sexist comments with a pejorative touch, but these are very few and may respond to the prejudices of his time. For these, see 6.34.7; 34.7.7; 38.57.7.

224. For the cult of Pudicitia, see Langlands, *Sexual Morality in Ancient Rome*, 44–49.

225. Livy, 10.23.7.

valry; among women, on the other hand, modesty fills that place. It is interesting to note that the woman delivering the speech is acknowledging that this competition happens in Rome: *in hac civitate*, therefore, presenting it as something peculiar to Romans. This may just be part of a rhetorical resource, but it is important to see that this is not said in general, or as part of human nature, but on the contrary, it is presented here as a distinctively male Roman feature. The comparison allows that the same can be said of *pudicitia*, then, being also presented as a particularly feminine Roman quality. Besides, the fact that a temple for plebeian women is being dedicated shows that in the same way that any man can compete for *virtus*—noble or not—the contest for *pudicitia* is open to all women as well.

The most paradigmatic individual case of feminine modesty is, no doubt, that of Lucretia.[226] The story, cleverly situated at the end of Book 1, works also as a kind of encouragement for the reader to continue with the history of the brave Roman people. The vividness with which the scene is set helps us to get into the atmosphere with a formidable touch of reality: the time at night, the way in which Tarquinius held Lucretia down, her fear, his lust, her tears, his joy, and so on. The whole scene is presented as Lucretia—the heroine—might have seen and lived it, and by having her as the focalizer, Livy makes his audience sympathize with her feelings rather than with those of Tarquinius. In the end, it does not matter if her husband, father, and faithful friends tried to comfort her; for her there is no consolation and only one solution: death. Lucretia, killing herself out of shame, is presented by Livy as performing a heroic act, a situation where the innocent person does not escape punishment, but accepts it, in this case for the sake of *exemplum*. One can measure the significance that Livy gives to this episode when the historian chooses to finish off the first book of his monumental work of the history of the Roman people with a case for admiration of *Romana pudicitia*.

The story of Lucretia has all the characteristics of a good tragedy, and the heroine's end could not have been more tragic.[227] But there is something more:

---

226. Livy, 1.57.7–58.

227. Cf. Ogilvie, *Commentary on Livy*, 186, who regarded this episode as Livy "writing his own tragedy," opposing the views of Wright, *Recovery of a Lost Roman Tragedy*, and Michels, "Drama of the Tarquins," for whom Livy must have had the plots of one or more tragedies in mind. For historical theatrical performances and the idea of Roman historical tradition created by dramatic performances, see Wiseman's "trilogy": *Historiography and Imagination*; *Remus*; and *Roman Drama and Roman History*. For tragic history, see Walbank, "History and Tragedy," 216–34; Marincola, "Beyond Pity and Fear," 285–315.

Lucretia, possessor of Roman womanly virtues such as *castitas* and *pudicitia*,[228] together with her being busily engaged working with wool, is representing here as feminine Romanness incarnate;[229] thus the rape by Tarquinius can be seen to symbolize the assault of the tyrant upon Rome herself, and that is why the consequences of the act are not only personal but also political.[230]

In promising revenge for the crime committed against Lucretia—which is personal—Brutus is at the same time promising the liberation from tyranny to the whole of the Roman citizenship.[231] Lucretia here represents not only all women, but the Roman people. The woman's devotion for the virtue of chastity and Brutus' love for his country are emphasized equally in this example. Of course the greatest consequence of Brutus' deed in routing Tarquinus and his family is not the avenging of Lucretia, but the deep and groundbreaking political change: the creation of the *libera res publica* or, as Livy puts it, *res liberi populi Romani*.[232] After the foundation of the city, this is given by the historian as undoubtedly the most important achievement of early Rome, and its origin can be traced back to the offense against a Roman woman.

Another case where the defense of a woman's chastity is given as the cause of a serious change in Roman political practice is that of Verginia.[233] The period of the decemvirs ended in a very similar way to that of the monarchy. Appius' story is given to strengthen once again the idea of how people suffer when they are under the oppression of one man.[234] Nothing is safe; not only political rights but also the citizens' welfare is at risk: justice for the plebs, chastity for women—everything goes according to the tyrant's will. The whole affair is presented by Livy as a violation of liberty, an assault upon "republican rights." It is Verginia's betrothed Icilius, who is described by Livy as

---

228. For Lucretia's chastity, see Livy, 1.57.10: *spectata castitas*, and for her modesty, 1.58.5: *obstinatam pudicitiam*, 1.58.7: *amissa pudicitia*.

229. As attested by numerous epitaphs for women that routinely praise these skills and qualities, cf. Lattimore, *Themes in Greek and Latin Epitaphs*. For more on this, see Ogilvie, *Commentary on Livy, Books 1–5*, ad loc.

230. A theme amply discussed. See, for example, Bruno, "Crimen, regni e superbia in Tito Livio," 236–5; Feldherr, "Livy's Revolution," 6–57; Joplin, "Ritual Work on Human Flesh," 51–70; Joshel, "Body Female and the Body Politic," 112–30; Arieti, "Rape and Livy's View of Roman History," 209–29. For the role of women in Livy in general, see Haberman, "*Nefas an libidine ortum*," 8–11; Hallet, "Women as Same and Other," 59–78; Moore, "Morality, History and Livy's Wronged Women," 38–73; Claassen, "Familiar Other," 71–103.

231. Livy, 1.59.1.

232. Livy, 2.1.1.

233. For an interpretation of Lucretia's and Verginia's stories in Livy within the context of Roman sexual morality in general, see Langlands, *Sexual Morality in Ancient Rome*, 85–109.

234. Cf. Livy, 3.36.

a man of proven courage (*expertae virtutis*),[235] who defended her, though to no avail. The final result of the struggle—after long debates and deliberations—was the end of the decemvirate and the reestablishment of tribunes of the plebs. The right to appeal, seen by the people as one of the foundations of liberty, was also restored.[236]

In order to give an account of two major political changes in early Rome, Livy designedly uses examples of women being attacked by the highest authorities with *imperium*. The use of women here is not coincidental, but planned. The women, one a chaste and faithful wife, the other a pure young girl, portray different aspects of the Roman political body: both the state and women needed protectors so as to maintain their status; women and the state appear vulnerable and defenseless against the attacks of the powerful. *Pudicitia* and *castitas* are presented by Livy as fulfilling a similar role to women as that of *libertas* to the *res publica*: something to safeguard, be proud of, and defend with courage.

The care of the virtue of chastity is also linked with politics in the cases of Vestal virgins being condemned for *impudicitia*.[237] By their improper conduct—the violation of their Vestal vows was seen as *nefas*, similar to an act of pollution—they had put the state at risk.[238] Livy gives these cases to provide *exempla* to the internal audience, that is, to other Vestals in his narrative, as well as to the external one, namely, women in Augustan Rome.[239] Again, it is difficult to assess with certainty whether the fact that chastity is given so prominent a position in Livy's narrative with reference to women is directly related with Augustus' so-called moral legislation and the banishment of the two Julias for adultery.[240] But, no doubt, the exile of Augustus' own daughter and granddaughter must have been something much talked about at that time.

So far, the examples that I have given about chastity and its relationship to politics and *virtus* have been more of a passive type. Men or women have

---

235. Livy, 3.44.3.

236. Cf. Livy, 3.56.6 and 3.56.8. For the right of *provocatio*, see Arena, *Libertas and the Practice of Politics* chap. 2, "The Citizens' Political Liberty," esp. 48–51 and 70–71.

237. For cases of Vestal virgins condemned to death for unchastity, see 2.42.11; 4.44.11; 8.15.7; 22.57.2; *Per*. 14; 20; 63.

238. Livy, 22.57.4.

239. For different types of audiences, see Chaplin, *Livy's Exemplary History*, passim, but esp. 4; 50–53; 103.

240. Julia the Elder, exiled on 2 B.C. to Pandateria; Julia the Younger, exiled on A.D. 8 to Trimerus.

defended women's modesty, and as a result something has changed in the management of the state. But Livy is also keen to show that women too have been actively doing things in favor of the republic.

From the very beginning of Livy's work, women also appear actively engaged for the benefit of the state, sometimes audaciously risking their lives in the attempt. The story of the Sabines, known to us mainly through Livy and Plutarch,[241] marks the express decision of the Roman historian to present women having an almost equally important role to fulfill within the family and the state as men had. They are the ones who manage the reconciliation between their Roman husbands and Sabine fathers: they "dared to go among the flying missiles, and rushing in from the side, to part the hostile forces and disarm them of their anger, beseeching their fathers on this side, on that their husbands, that fathers-in-law and sons-in-law should not stain themselves with impious bloodshed, nor pollute with parricide the suppliants' children, grandsons to one party, sons to the other."[242] These "pre-Roman" women do not get the praise of having *virtus*, but only of being *ausae*, a term more morally neutral than *virtus*. The Sabine women are described by Livy as being daring and bold, although they do set a real precedent for later Roman women defending the state.

The episode of the Sabine women is relevant also because it is possible to see how Romulus explains to them what marriage means to the Romans: "they should be wedded and become co-partners in all the possessions of the Romans, in their citizenship and dearest privilege of all to the human race, in their children [*illas tamen in matrimonio, in societate fortunarum omnium civitatisque et quo nihil carius humano generi sit, liberum fore*]."[243] Romulus' speech, reported in *oratio obliqua*, is probably a very good example of cultural anachronism, as it is hard to believe that Romans had that socio-juridical sense of *matrimonium* at such an early stage, but it allows us perhaps to see Livy's own contemporary thinking, and it certainly sets the tone with which Livy will deal with women throughout his work.[244]

---

241. Livy, 1.9–13; Plut. *Romulus*, 15; 19.

242. Livy, 1.13.1–2: *ausae se inter tela volantia inferre, ex transverso impetu facto dirimere infestas acies, dirimere iras, hinc patres, hinc viros orantes, ne sanguine se nefando soceri generique respergerent, ne parricidio macularent partus suos, nepotum illi, hi liberum progeniem.*

243. Livy, 1.9.14. For more on the episode of the Sabines, see Miles, *Livy*, chap. 5: "The First Roman Marriage and the Theft of the Sabine Women," 179–219.

244. For the specific concept of *matrimonium*, see Gardner, *Women in Roman Law and Society*, 31–65; Treggiari, *Roman Marriage*, 3–80.

On several occasions Livy relates that women have been as effective as men in defending the city. In this sense they are presented as actively fulfilling their political duty toward the *res publica* in a feminine manner. The matrons' way is not through fighting, but by prayers and tears: their wailings and supplications to the gods are a sign that maintaining the *pax deorum* is not only men's duty, but that of all the members of society.[245] There are quite a few instances when the swords of men were incapable of defending Rome, or pestilence and disease had taken many Roman lives, and it had been the matrons' supplication that had brought relief to the state: "the wailings of women were heard not only from private houses, but from every direction matrons pouring into the streets ran about among the shrines of the gods, sweeping the altars with their disheveled hair, kneeling, holding up their palms to heaven and the gods, and praying them to rescue the city of Rome from the hands of the enemy and to keep Roman mothers and little children unharmed (*ploratus mulierum non ex priuatis solum domibus exaudiebatur, sed undique matronae in publicum effusae circa deum delubra discurrunt crinibus passis aras verrentes, nixae genibus, supinas manus ad caelum ac deos tendentes orantesque ut urbem Romanam e manibus hostium eriperent matresque Romanas et liberos parvos inviolatos servarent*)."[246] Other times, it had been the matrons' generosity (*munificentia*) that had stood out, supplying the treasury with all the gold of their adornments for public use.[247] Livy recognizes the real help that women have provided to the *res publica* and he is liberal in bestowing honors on them.

Among these matrons Livy highlights the conduct of Veturia, Coriolanus' mother; and Volumnia, his wife. They appear in the narrative as defending the city against the attack of the Volsci and play a double role: on the one hand, they have a personal mission to accomplish, that is, to go and face Coriolanus in the hope of recovering their son and husband, and on the other, a public and political one: to ask him to withdraw his forces from Rome. They are successful in both missions and so they achieve *gloria*, the greatest manly honor reserved for those who accomplish something for the good of the *res publica*.[248]

Many of these examples certainly qualify to apply the word *virtus* to them, as the deeds of these women are undoubtedly brave and courageous, but Livy avoids using *virtus*—so much the quality of a *vir*—and gives other synonyms.

---

245. Cf. Livy, 2.40.1.
246. Livy, 26.9.7–8. See also 3.7.8 and 27.50.5.
247. Cf. Livy, 5.25.9; 34.5.9.
248. Livy, 2.40.12.

It is only in Cloelia's case where the term *virtus* is used to describe the action of a woman for the benefit of the state.[249]

The specific context in which Livy places the story of Cloelia is significant, as he has just been narrating about the courage of Horatius Cocles and Mucius fighting against the Etruscan king Porsenna. Cloelia's feat is reported as the third example of Roman *virtus* in this same war.[250] The view of the hostage girl swimming the river under a rain of hostile darts shows a readiness to put her life at risk for the safety of the Roman people in a different way from that of other women or Roman matrons. They had performed brave acts in defense of the republic, but the deeds themselves had been proper to women's resources: crying, wailing, imploring to the gods, giving up their jewelry, even going amid soldiers to prevent battle between fathers and husbands can be seen as something proper to women and feminine in its melodramatic manner. Those are means that, up to a certain extent, can be expected from women anyway. But Cloelia does something unpredictably masculine, something that requires not only valor but also great physical endurance, and moreover she does something parallel to what has just been praised on Horatius. Livy, therefore, cannot but honor the girl for her "manly courage" attributing *virtus* to her: *novam in femina virtutem*.[251] This brave act obtains mercy from Porsenna, who promises to send her safely back to her friends. In fact, Cloelia's *virtus* awakes so much admiration on her enemies that her deed has public consequences as well as personal ones: on the one hand, "she is restored inviolate to her people [*intactam inviolatamque ad suos remissurum*],"[252] and on the other, "peace was reestablished [*pace redintegrata*]."[253] It is something new to have a woman performing acts of manly courage. Before Cloelia, and also after her, women had shown bravery in a feminine way: they had been audacious, daring, bold, and intrepid, but this was different, and Livy makes it clear that it was so: "the Romans rewarded this new valor with a new kind of honor, an equestrian statue, which was set up on the summit of the Sacred Way, and represented the maiden seated on a horse."[254] A brave manly action—leading a group of female prisoners swimming in the river to escape—done for the

---

249. For an interpretation on Cloelia's case, see Walker, *Hostages in Republican Rome*, 263–70.
250. For the war against Porsenna, see Livy, 2.9–15, of which 2.10 refers to Horatius and 2.12–13 to Mucius.
251. Livy, 2.13.11.
252. Livy, 2.13.8.
253. Livy, 2.13.11.
254. Livy, 2.13.11: *Romani novam in femina virtutem novo genere honoris, statua equestri, donavere; in summa Sacra via fuit posita virgo insidens equo*. Similar versions of this episode are re-

benefit of the state—she was allowed to recover male hostages and the war was finally ended—merited this new reward. *Virtus*, the specific attribute of a *vir*, is now bestowed on a woman, and this is something new in Rome and a novelty in Livy too.

Women in Livy present several characteristics that allow us to see how the author appreciates feminine presence throughout the history of Rome. Following traditional Roman values, Livy's highest quality in women seems to be chastity (*castitas*) or modesty (*pudicitia*) as it is shown often in the narrative and to which manly *virtus* or courage is especially related and compared to. But the historian also allows us to see and ponder how women participate through their feminine resources in politics and the activity of the government, either monarchy or republic. Their actions—or the actions done to them—matter and bring about changes for good or evil. Many times they show their bravery in defending the state or their family, though the word *virtus* does not appear often. Coming from *vir*, *virtus* is still a very masculine quality which Livy seems reluctant to bestow on women, especially when the actions they perform seem conventionally feminine. On the contrary, *virtus* is acknowledged in a woman when her brave action appears almost as a masculine achievement and therefore, it is proper to confer the quality of a *vir*.

THROUGH THE RECORDS of this exemplary history, Livy provides material for creating the collective memory that will shape the Roman identity and character. He achieves the goal set in his Preface of giving the characterization of the people—*quae vita qui mores*—who took part in the events of Roman political history. For Livy, it was men and women that counted; institutions had for him a much lesser role to play. Furthermore, institutions bore the character of the people who composed them.

Within these *exempla*, Roman *virtus* appears as a prominent and programmatic feature in the narrative. *Virtus* is for Livy action performed for the benefit of the community; it means overcoming natural inertia and risking one's own comfort for the good of the *res publica*. But above all, *virtus* for Livy represents the thread he follows in unfolding the narrative and explaining historical change. He reflects on present reality in the light of the past, seeking the roots of what is happening in his time, so as to offer his contemporaries, both the individual and the nation, an opportunity to arrive through memory at a keener awareness of their identity. Thus, the historian presents *virtus*

---

corded in Val. Max. 3.2.2; Dion. Hal. 5.35; and Pliny, *NH* 24.28–29, among others; cf. Ogilvie, *Commentary on Livy, Books 1–5*, ad loc.

both as a demanding model of the past to follow in the present and as an aspirational ideal for Roman society of his time. The account of acts of *virtus* keeps the fight for it alive. The value of recording *virtus* is that it maintains it in existence.

Livy's *exempla* involved the application of the past to the present and the present to the future, creating the links that were necessary to define identity. Thus, *exempla virtutis* unify the history of Rome; they show change and continuity—in Livy's work and in Roman history.

FIGURE 1. Q. Fufius Calenus, P. Mucius Scaevola. Silver, 71 B.C. (*obverse*) Helmeted bust of Virtus. (*reverse*) Warrior, holding shield in left hand and raising up fallen figure with right hand. © The Trustees of the British Museum.

FIGURE 2. Mn. Aquillius. Silver, 70 B.C. (*obverse*) Jugate heads of Honos and Virtus. (*reverse*) Italia on left and Roma on right, clasping hands; between clasped hands, cornucopia; behind Italia, caduceus. Roma wears diadem, holds fasces in left hand, and places right foot on globe. © The Trustees of the British Museum.

FIGURE 3. Galba. Gold. A.D. 68–69. (*obverse*) Head of Galba, laureate, right; globe at point of neck. (*reverse*) Virtus, wearing tunic and cuirass, standing left, holding Victory on globe in right hand and parazonium in left. © The Trustees of the British Museum.

CHAPTER FOUR

Virtus in Velleius

Eadem virtus et fortuna subsequenti tempore ingressi Germaniam imperatoris Tiberii fuit

Tiberius showed the same *virtus* and was attended by the same fortune when he entered Germany on his later campaign

—Vell. 2.121.1

For some scholars, the panegyrical tone in which the historian Velleius Paterculus refers to Augustus and especially Tiberius has seemed to permeate the whole work, destroying every possibility of getting anything good or interesting from it. His style appeared to them the supreme example of servility toward power and acquiescence in the lack of freedom of speech—the worst kind of vices in one aiming to write "proper" history.[1] For these reasons, the two-book summary history of Velleius, the *Historiae*, has been a work often relegated to "the problem drawer."[2] In the 1970s, Anthony Woodman started a sort of "rehabilitation" of Velleius, writing a commentary on what he called *The Tiberian Narrative*,[3] and by now it is more or less agreed among scholars that Velleius as a historian can be analyzed through different lenses with very interesting results, as the recent book *Velleius Paterculus: Making History*, edited by E. Cowan, shows.[4]

In this chapter I will not embark on another *apologia pro Velleio*, but will try to show how by condemning him, some modern historians have failed to see the importance of the change that occurred in historiography with the advent of the principate. By insisting on looking for the same characteristics that dominated historical writing during the republic in an era where not only the

---

1. See, for example, Syme, Velleius' most powerful enemy: "Mendacious as well as misleading," in "Marcus Vinicius (cos. 19 B.C.)," 147n3; "fraudulent," in *Roman Revolution*, 393n1.; "an uneasy amalgam of adulation and mendacity," in "Livy and Augustus," 69; "adulatory and dishonest," in *Ten Studies in Tacitus*, 47. Also Leeman, *Orationis Ratio*, 248: "*miles sapiens* turned into a *historicus insipiens*"; and Paladini, "Studi su Velleio Patercolo," 71: "Velleio è un storico di non troppi scrupoli e di nessuna profondità."

2. Marincola, "Genre, Convention and Innovation in Greco-Roman Historiography," 317.

3. Woodman, *Velleius Paterculus*. The commentary covers chaps. 2.94–131.

4. It is odd, though, that this collection does not include a specific paper dealing with the emperor Tiberius, who is acknowledged as the principal figure of Velleius' whole work.

main actors but also the rules of the political game had changed, historians applied to Velleius standards that were not his. Kraus and Woodman have rightly summarized this somewhat shortsighted view of early imperial historiography when they say that Velleius' history is no more partial than Dio's, Suetonius' or Tacitus'; the difference lies in the particular aspects of the times that they analyze.[5] It is, in fact, to our advantage when reconstructing the history of the early empire to have a text like Velleius'; otherwise we would be left only with the equally biased account of Tacitus to re-create Tiberius' reign. However much inclined we might feel to identify with one or the other version, there is no need to choose between Tacitus and Velleius: neither of them is—or rather, can be—wholly impartial.

Velleius' *Historiae* constitutes a particularly interesting opportunity to study *virtus* in historiography, since he represents a twofold phenomenon during the early years of the principate. On the one hand, he incarnates the spirit of his time: a man of action, a soldier, and one who was then rewarded for his years of service with political posts in Rome.[6] Velleius feels free not to conceal his recent origin; he, like many other *homines novi*, is aware of the possibility of climbing to the highest levels of Roman society of the time. He does not idealize the past; he appears fully satisfied with the new regime, which he sees as the dawning of a much better era.[7] Disciplined, courageous, and proud of the empire that he has contributed to make great, Velleius highlights in some of his contemporaries the qualities and virtues that have been placed at the service of the political system of the moment, which he considers the fairest and most appropriate one possible. On the other hand, Velleius represents a change in historical writing, and he functions as a "historiographical hinge." In spite of being part of the Roman historiographical tradition, which links him with Sallust or Livy in their shared view of the central place Rome played in universal history, and their conviction that the morals and character of men were the main cause of events, Velleius is able to express the new attitudes toward history in a very original way. Writing about the events of 27 B.C. and after brought new challenges to historians, as Cassius Dio recognizes: "The events occurring after this time cannot be recorded in the same manner as those of previous times."[8] Velleius displays the naturally skewed per-

---

5. Cf. Kraus and Woodman, *Latin Historians*, 83.

6. For Velleius' career, see Sumner, "Truth about Velleius Paterculus," 265–79; Millar, "Ovid and the Domus Augusta," 5–6; Levick, "Velleius Paterculus as Senator," 1–16.

7. Cf. Noè, *Storiografia imperiale pretacitiana*, 95.

8. Dio, 53.19.2.

spective of someone who is too near to judge or give an unbiased account of the events, and he assigns the emperor Tiberius a leading role as the individual figure who embodies not only the virtues but also the increasing power of Rome. In view of this, to say that "the traditional environment of Roman historiography was long lost," and that "it would be almost another century before Tacitus would reconcile in a skillful way the problems that the new age presented for Roman historiography,"[9] can be misleading. Roman historians did produce new answers to the new challenges of historical writing, and this response, even if it does not coincide with our modern taste, was a valid one.

Velleius offered one answer to the question of how to write history under the principate. He would write universal history, cultural history, and contemporary history, all wrapped up in a style that was going to develop as the imperial rhetoric.[10] But what is perhaps his main achievement is the realization and consequent implementation of the idea that the history of the principate and the life of its head were one thing, not two. In the years after A.D. 14, it was not easy to separate the life and the personality of the ruler from the development of the state and the processes of government.[11] And if the characters of individuals had always appeared to be the causes of historical events,[12] it was all the more necessary for the historian now to provide a full illustration of such characters in order to make sense of those events.

There is, I think, something refreshing in Velleius' *Histories*. Even if one does not agree with his point of view or does not like his much-criticized style, there is an element of freshness in his work, perhaps related to his distinct optimism. The remembrances of a soldier, developed, embellished, but also meditated and pondered upon, are a valid testimony of his time that can provide not only useful information unavailable elsewhere but also, and most importantly, the feelings and emotions experienced by a large number of people during the period.[13]

Velleius emphasizes that the principate had come not just to reestablish peace and order, but to bring back something very important to the Romans: *virtus*. Velleius is hopeful and positive. The confidence and optimism of his approach appear all the more valid and justified for him since this era

---

9. Toher, "Augustus and the Evolution of Roman Historiography," 153.
10. For a recent analysis of Velleius' historical work, see Rich, "Velleius' History," 73–92.
11. Cf. Syme, "History or Biography," 481. See also Woodman, *Velleius Paterculus*, 28–56.
12. As Cicero had suggested in *De Or*, 2.63.
13. Here I aligned myself with Schmitzer, "Roman Values in Velleius," 199. See also Balmaceda, "Tiberio, *optimus princeps* en Veleyo Patérculo," 309–19; and Lobur, *Consensus, Concordia, and the Formation of Roman Imperial Ideology*, 115.

belonged to people like Velleius himself. The *princeps* and the *novi* are the main actors in the principate. For the author of the *Historiae*, it is the *virtus* and *virtutes* of the *princeps* and the *novi* that would save the empire from falling and would be able to "reestablish" the morals of the republic. According to him, the principate's aim was to restore *virtus*, lost since the fall of Carthage, to its original place in Roman life,[14] and this is what Augustus does and Tiberius helps to consolidate: *prisca illa et antiquae rei publicae forma revocata* (the old and traditional form of the republic was restored).[15] Following and using Augustus' language of restoration, Velleius is able to create the necessary link between republicanism and empire.

The reader will perhaps wonder why I devote to a summary history of Rome as much space as, say, the works of other more important historians, but in terms of my question about the transformation of *virtus* and its role in the explanation of history, they all appear equally interesting.

Virtus in the *Historiae*

In this section I plan to show how Velleius uses the concept of *virtus* as the mortar to build this bridge between republic and empire. Many things had changed in Roman history, but Velleius' narrative from the very beginning—it is important to remember that he starts his work with the fall of Troy—till Tiberius' government is a catalogue and a display of men of *virtus* that show a continuum in the history of the Roman people.

It is significant to note that the word *virtus*—with its plural, *virtutes*—is used sixty-three times in Velleius' narrative.[16] This is a large number considering the shortness of his work. Velleius' use of *virtus* presents some characteristics that are peculiar both to the type of history he was writing—that is, related to the more formal aspects of this compendium of Roman history—and in terms of content and even ideology. For instance, Velleius differs noticeably from Sallust in the usage of *virtus* in his historical narrative, especially in that he uses the plural *virtutes* quite frequently, something that Sallust never does. This is part of the form of his work—it is certainly a recurrent feature when he describes individuals—and it is also a programmatic trend of a historian who is writing a

---

14. Vell. 2.1.1: *quippe remoto Carthaginis metu sublataque imperii aemula non gradu, sed praecipiti cursu a virtute descitum, ad vitia transcursum.*

15. Vell. 2.89.3.

16. For the difference in meanings of *virtus* and *virtutes*, see, for example, Eisenhut, *Virtus Romana*; McDonnell, *Roman Manliness*; Sarsila, *Being a Man*; Balmaceda, "Virtus Romana en el siglo I a.C.," 285–303.

brief account of Roman history, and who might have been aiming at the ideal of *brevitas*.[17] By using the plural of *virtus* in a general way, Velleius was probably saving time and space in his abridged version of the history of Rome by describing a good man as having several virtues or *virtutes*—*virtus*-courage being only one among them—at the same time. I point out this difference of treatment of the word *virtus* between Sallust and Velleius precisely because in other aspects, Velleius turns specifically to Sallust for help not only in expressing some key ideas—such as the *metus hostilis*,[18] or his thoughts about the theory of history[19]—but also for the expression of some sentences that are markedly Sallustian in style.[20] And *brevitas* is indeed one trait that does appear in both authors. Brevity consisted of the ability to say everything that was required in as few words as possible, rather than leaving some events out in order to cut down one's narrative. For this purpose, Velleius acquired the habit of narrating an event in a single unit—sometimes even in a single sentence.[21] The technique responds to the need of the historian to cover as much as possible within the smallest possible space, and it is probably related to the Romans' keenness for concise, self-contained *exempla*.[22] Thus, Velleius used the word *virtutes* as a convenient summary of good qualities when describing Romans. This can be seen, for example, in the descriptions of important politicians and military men such as Scipio Aemilianus,[23] Scipio Nasica,[24] Q. Catulus,[25] Marcellus[26], Drusus,[27] or Marcus Lepidus.[28] There may be another reason

---

17. Speed was advised by Lucian when the information and data were too extensive in *De Hist. Conscr*, 56: "Rapidity is everywhere useful, especially if there is no lack of material." See also Dion. Hal. *De Thuc*, 24 and 53; Quint. *Inst*. 10.1.2 and 4.2.45. Cf. Woodman, "Questions of Date, Genre and Style in Velleius," 272–305.

18. Cf. Vell. 2.1.1 = Sall. *Hist*, 1.12.

19. Cf. Vell. 2.92.5 = Sall. *BC* 3.2.

20. E.g., Vell. 2.4.4: *fugaret ac funderet* = Sall. *BJ* 21, 2: *fugant funduntque*; 2.112.7: *dignum furore suo habuit exitum* = Sall. *BC* 55.6: *dignum moribus factisque suis exitum*.

21. See, for example, 2.89.3; 2.126.2.

22. Cf. Starr, "Velleius' Literary Techniques," 295.

23. Cf. Vell. 1.12.3: *Scipio Aemilianus, vir avitis P. Africani paternisque L. Pauli virtutibus simillimus* . . .

24. Cf. Vell. 2.3.2: *Tum P. Scipio Nasica* (. . .) *ob eas* virtutes *primus omnium absens pontifex maximus factus est*.

25. Cf. Vell. 2.22.3: *Q. Catulus, et aliarum* virtutum *et belli Cunbrici gloria, quae illi eum Mario communis fuerat celeberrimus*.

26. Cf. Vell. 2.93.1: (. . .) *iuvenis, sane, ut aiunt, ingenuarum* virtutum *laetusque animi et ingenii fortunaeque, in quam alebatur, capax*.

27. Cf. Vell. 2.97.2: *Druso Claudio, fratri Neronis, adulescenti tot tantarumque* virtutum, *quot et quantas natura mortalis recipit vel industria perficit*.

28. Cf. Vell. 2.125.5: *M. Lepidus, de cuius* virtutibus *celeberrimaque in Illyrico militia praediximus* . . .

for Velleius' frequent use of the plural *virtutes* in his narrative. By the time he was writing, around A.D. 30, Ciceronian terminology had become more and more widespread, and words that had previously had a specific philosophical connotation were now part of the common vocabulary.[29] This was the case of *virtutes* when referring to good men in general.

In contrast to Livy, on the other hand, Velleius avoids using the word *virtus* ascribed to groups of people, armies, or the soldiery in general.[30] He talks only once about the courage of the Roman soldier in general: "But in this crisis the valor of the Roman soldier claimed for itself a greater share of glory than it left to the generals [*Sed Romani virtus militis plus eo tempore vindicavit gloriae quam ducibus reliquit*]."[31] As Livy was dealing with the history of Rome from the foundation of the city, it seemed more appropriate to stress the growth of the empire as a collective effort of the Roman people throughout the centuries. Velleius, instead, writing under the principate, was more inclined to structure his history somewhat "biographically,"[32] relating the events through the lives of the individuals concerned in a long succession of men whose characters were always presented through the lens of their *virtus* or lack of it. This, of course, becomes more evident as we approach the sections of Roman history in which Velleius deals with the heads of government in Rome who lasted the longest, as seen in what have been called the Caesarian, Augustan, and Tiberian narratives.[33]

Another characteristic of Velleius' use of *virtus* in his historical narrative is the mixing of meanings between *virilis-virtus* or *virtus*-courage and *humana-virtus* or *virtus*-virtue. There are cases in which the sense of *virtus* is clearly courage, for instance, in the reference to Pompey: "Syria and Pontus are monuments to the valor of Gn. Pompeius [*Syria Pontusque Cn. Pompei virtutis monumenta sunt*],"[34] or to Germanicus: "In the Dalmatian war Germanicus, who had been dispatched in advance of the commander to regions both wild and difficult, gave great proof of his valor [*Magna in bello Delmatico experimenta*

---

29. See, for example, the use of *virtutes* in *De Finibus* and *De Officiis*, passim. Cf. Reinhardt, "Philosophy Comes to Rome," 526–39.
30. See chapter 3, section 2, in this book.
31. Vell. 2.112.5.
32. For the biographical approach to history under the principate, cf. Woodman, *Velleius Paterculus*, esp. "History, biography or panegyric?" and for the concept of "biostructure," see Pelling, "Biographical History?," 117–44; and more recently his "Velleius and Biography," 157–76.
33. This terminology is Woodman's.
34. Vell. 2.38.6.

virtutis in incultos ac difficilis locos praemissus Germanicus dedit]."[35] *Virtus* is used here within a military context of war and conquest; therefore, bravery seems the natural description of the actions involved.[36] On the whole, one can say that Velleius uses the word *virtus* meaning *virilis-virtus* more often than meaning *humana-virtus*, but not very many more times.[37] More difficult to assess, however, are some cases in which either sense of the word—courage or virtue—can be used to describe a particular action. This is the case, for example, of Cicero in handling Catiline's conspiracy, where the consul, according to Velleius, proved both his courage and righteousness at the same time: "At this time the conspiracy of Sergius Catiline, Lentulus, Cethegus, and other men of both the equestrian and senatorial orders was detected by the extraordinary *courage/virtue*, firmness, and careful vigilance of the consul Marcus Cicero, a man who owed his elevation wholly to himself, who had ennobled his lowly birth, who was as distinguished in his life as he was great in genius, and who saved us from being vanquished in intellectual accomplishments by those whom we had vanquished in arms."[38] It is also the case of Cato Uticensis, who is praised for his virtuous conduct in general,[39] and shows his bravery by leading his legions to face Caesar's army in spite of the great difficulties,[40] and whom Velleius calls a "man who resembled *virtue/valor* itself [*homo virtuti simillimus*]."[41] In both instances we can see Velleius playing with the meanings of *virtus* to suit his descriptions best, and he may have been consciously ambiguous with the connotations of the concept because both senses were appropriate to Cicero and Cato in Velleius' eyes.

Moving away a little from the way Velleius used *virtus* as an evaluative word for people in general, it would also be interesting to see precisely which characters in his narrative he described as possessing *virtus*. It has been argued that the praises of men of *virtus* in Velleius' *Histories* have an "ideological" element. For I. Lana, for example, the exaltation of the *homines novi* was

---

35. Vell. 2.116.1.
36. For more instances of *virtus* as courage, see, for example, 1.11.2; 1.12.5; 2.4.2; 2.18.1 (*virtus* of the Roman enemy Mithridates); 2.74.4; 2.78.1; 2.98.2.
37. Thirty-six times *virtus* as courage, and twenty-seven as virtue.
38. Vell. 2.34.3: *Per haec tempora M. Cicero qui omnia incrementa sua sibi debuit, vir novitatis nobilissimae et ut vita clarus, ita ingenio maximus, quique effecit, ne quorum arma viceramus, eorum ingenio vinceremur, consul Sergii Catilinae Lentulique et Cethegi et aliorum utriusque ordinis virorum coniurationem singulari* virtute, *constantia, vigilia curaque aperuit* (my highlighting).
39. Vell. 2.35.1.
40. Vell. 2.54.3.
41. Vell. 2.35.2. For more examples of *virtus* having both meanings, see 2.83.2; 2.126.4; 2.129.1.

the main feature of Velleius' work.[42] According to Lana, Velleius praised "virtuous" new men in order to validate and support Tiberius' chief policy, and especially to demonstrate that the regime was respectful of the *res publica* while being very far removed from the former debased version of it.[43] Certainly, Velleius devotes a great part of his energy to trying to describe the role the *homines novi* played in the Roman expansion and the consolidation of the new political system, and moreover, the significance of the important responsibility that Velleius attributes to the *novi* can be explained as being part of his own political understanding of the mission of the principate. As noted earlier, Velleius stood nearer to the *novi* than to the *nobiles*, both in social position and in political ideas. For the *homines novi*, the main issue did not center on the republican crisis and the decline of the Senate, but on the positive aspects implied by the birth of a new order. The imperial regime brought them new opportunities and did not imply the loss of anything. Velleius' perspective, that of an army officer unconditionally supporting the system, resulted in a rather skillful idealization.[44] His work aimed at the defense not so much of Tiberius the man, but of Tiberius the prince, in the eyes of his contemporaries. This was probably due to the fact that there was still a need to reinforce the concept of the principate as the natural evolution of the republican phase, which was overtly opposed by the sectors of the longest-standing aristocracy in the Senate.

The frequent praise for the *homines novi* in Velleius' narrative could be seen as support for the imperial policies of Augustus and Tiberius but also because Velleius himself, being a *homo novus*, was more aware of the great men who came from within his own group and were elevated to high position because of their merits. In his general tribute to these *homines novi*, Velleius strongly affirms that the real nobles are the best people, and this had nothing to do with birth: "the Senate and the Roman people regard as most noble that which is best."[45] This idea had already been expressed in similar terms by Cicero and Sallust. Cicero explicitly linked *novitas* with *virtus* in reference to Cato the Elder: "believing that his *virtus*, not his birth was gaining him his

---

42. Cf. Lana, *Velleio Patercolo o della Propaganda*, esp. chap. 2, "Tiberio favorisce gli uomini nuovi," and chap. 4, "Velleio esalta gli uomini nuovi."

43. Cf. also De Vivo, "Luxuria et mos maiorum. Indirizzi programmatici della storiografia velleiana," 260.

44. Cf. Vell. 2.126.

45. Vell. 2.128.1: *senatus populusque Romani est putandi, quod optimum sit, esse nobilissimum.* Cf. Woodman, *Velleius Paterculus*, ad loc.

countrymen's approval,"⁴⁶ and later on, in his *Pro Sestio*, he gave a more general remark encouraging the young *novi* to win nobility through *virtus* because it is by merit that it could be acquired and not only by birth.⁴⁷ In Sallust's case, the whole of Marius' speech is a tribute to the *virtus* of the *homo novus*: "my hopes are all vested in myself and must be maintained by my own *virtus* and integrity, for all other supports are weak."⁴⁸ Some decades later, Velleius follows this tradition; for him *virtus* was seen and acknowledged as something personal, not a prerogative or an attribute of a social class.

The examples of prominent and distinguished *homines novi* are given in a long list: Tiberius Coruncarius, Spurius Carvilius, Cato the Censor, Mummius, Gaius Marius, Cicero, Asinius Pollio.⁴⁹ All of these *novi* possessed *virtus—in cuiuscumque animo virtus inesset—*and Velleius is probably meaning *virtus* as a broad idea that involved several virtues, courage being one of them. A special place is held for the *novi* who were eminent helpers of important politicians like Laelius for Scipio, and Agrippa or Statilius Taurus for Augustus.⁵⁰ Among these men, a particularly striking example in Velleius' narrative is the case of Sejanus, the prefect of the praetorian cohorts under Tiberius.⁵¹ Velleius appears to follow his programmatic scheme of attributing virtues to the prefect as he had done to other *novi*, but the final portrayal is not really straightforward praise: "he [Sejanus] combined a great capacity for labor with loyalty to his master, and possessed a well-knit body to match the energy of his mind (...) stern but yet jovial, cheerful but yet strict; busy, yet always seeming to be at leisure (...) calm in expression and in his life, though his mind is sleeplessly alert."⁵²

---

46. Cf. Cic. *Verr*, 5.180: *qui cum se virtute, non genere, populo Romano commendari putaret*. And again at 5.181: *novorum hominum virtus et industria*.

47. Cic. *Pro Sest*, 136: *et qui ingenio ac virtute nobilitate potestis consequi, ad eam rationem, in qua multi homines novi et honore et gloria floruerunt, cohortabor*.

48. Sall. *BJ* 85.4: *mihi spes omnes in memet sitae, quas necesse est virtute et innocentia tutari; nam alia infirma sunt*. See also 85.9; 85.17; 85.21; 85.31–33; 85.38.

49. Cf. Vell. 2.128.1–4.

50. Vell. 2.127.1.

51. Velleius' presentation of Sejanus has been used to demonstrate the historian's servility toward the emperor and his *adiutor*; see esp. Syme, *Tacitus*, 368. Hellegouarc'h, "L' Éloge de Séjan dans L'*Histoire Romaine* de Velleius Paterculus," 152, instead, rejects the use of terms like "panegyric" or "eulogy" because for him, "c'est Tibère, et lui seul, qui est loué; l'éloge de Séjan se rattache au discours que tiennent depuis longtemps déjà les *homines novi* pour assurer leur promotion." For further discussion on this point, see Sumner, "Truth about Velleius Paterculus," 295–96.

52. Vell. 2.127.3–4: *ipsum vero laboris ac fidei capacissimum, sufficiente etiam vigori animi compage corporis (...) virum severitatis laetissimae, hilaritatis priscae, actu otiosis simillimum ... vultu vitaque tranquillum, animo exsomnem*.

It is worth pointing out that some of these characteristics given by Velleius to Sejanus are also found in Tacitus. Of course the attitude of the two authors toward this *homo novus* is very different, but the reference in both to his vigorous, untiring mind[53] and the sharp allusion to his dissimulation show that the two descriptions coincide in their main ideas.[54] The man's tirelessness also finds parallels in Livy's portrait of Hannibal and Sallust's Catiline.[55] If one looks carefully at this description, one can read between the lines a certain ambiguity in the compliments the historian makes. Sejanus is a complex man, and so we have a complex portrait of him. The contrasts and antitheses of his personality can be taken as a warning against the man himself and his projects. Velleius could not have written something openly attacking the man who was climbing up so swiftly and whose power and influence could do anything to defeat his enemies, but his tone is somewhat ambivalent.[56] And it becomes even more intriguing when one relates the Sejanus passage with the final prayer of Velleius' work, which has a plea for caution particularly concerning succession: "Grant him [Tiberius] successors until the latest time, but successors whose shoulders may be as capable of sustaining bravely the empire of the world as we have found his to be: foster the pious plans of all good citizens and crush the impious designs of the wicked."[57] These words could be interpreted as a clear and direct hint about Sejanus' intentions, or Velleius' fears for the system of inherited power, but this would be no more than speculation. What one can say with a certain degree of confidence is that Velleius shows some inconsistency in his portrayal of Sejanus. There is no other ambiguous or uncertain characterization in his narrative. In all other descriptions we find a clear moral judgment: *virtus* or its absence was the clear parameters. But Sejanus' depiction makes one hesitate: on the one hand, where is the virtue of a man who seems to be something that he is not? Even if the qualities he is hiding are good ones, real virtue has nothing to do with concealment. On the other hand, Velleius does attribute virtues to him: "In

---

53. Cf. Vell. 2.127.3–4: *vigori animi . . . animo exsomnem* = Tac. *Ann*, 4.1: *animus audax . . . saepius vigilans*.

54. Cf. Martin and Woodman, *Tacitus*, ad loc.

55. Cf. Livy, 21.4 and Sall. *BC* 5.1–5. Some of the features of these men are certainly good qualities, but on the other hand, they can very easily become a perverted version of *virtus*. For more on this, see McGushin, *Sallust: Bellum Catilinae*, 57–62; and Ramsey, *Sallust's Bellum Catilinae*, 68–70. On Hannibal, see Levene, *Livy on the Hannibalic War*, esp. 86–125, 164–213.

56. Woodman, *Velleius Paterculus*, 247–48, and Sumner, "Truth about Velleius Paterculus," 294–96, agree that Velleius would have felt little attraction toward Sejanus, and demonstrate that Velleius was not just Sejanus' flatterer.

57. Vell. 2.131.2.

the value of his virtues the judgment of the state had long vied with that of the emperor [*In huius virtutum aestimatione iam pridem iudicia civitatis cum iudiciis principis certant*]."[58] He could not have said something unsympathetic about the second man of the empire; he had to say that he possessed virtue—that was the "rule" if he wanted to praise somebody—but the results are atypical: too much justification of the emperor's decision to promote Sejanus, too many contradictory terms to describe the man. Although Velleius places Sejanus' description in sequence with that of other *novi*, it looks as if he was more interested in justifying Tiberius' treatment of the prefect within a traditional pattern than in praising him specifically as a *homo novus*.

The antithesis between *nobiles* and *homines novi* will become evident when this new emergent group is the one that displays the fidelity to Roman values and the *mos maiorum* that the *nobiles* had traditionally claimed their own, and on which the principate had built its ideological foundation. Here, then, Velleius appears to be very much in line with the combination of traditionalism and innovation that characterizes the principate.

But his praise for the *homines novi* should not be understood in complete and absolute opposition to his view of the *nobilitas*. In fact, compliments for the aristocrats are numerous, either as families—such as the Domitii and the Caecilii[59]—or as individuals, such as L. Aemilius Paullus,[60] Metellus,[61] or Scipio Nasica.[62] Velleius is interested in merits, and these men are praised for their good qualities, especially *virtus*; their nobility or high birth is given as an extra reference. Members of the *nobilitas* such as Perpenna, Clodius, Curio, or Lollius are criticized not because Velleius only wanted to praise *homines novi*, but for their actual lack of *virtus*. Thus, Perpenna was "more distinguished for his birth than for his character,"[63] and Clodius was described as a "man of noble birth, eloquent and reckless, who recognized no limits either in speech or in act except his own caprice, energetic in the execution of his wicked projects, of ill-repute as the debaucher of his own sister, and accused of adulterous profanation of the most sacred rites of the Roman people."[64] Curio, on

---

58. Vell. 2.128.1.
59. Vell. 2.10.2 and 2.11.3, respectively.
60. Vell. 1.9.3.
61. Vell. 1.11.2.
62. Vell. 2.3.2.
63. Vell. 2.30.1: *gentis clarioris quam animi*.
64. Vell. 2.45.1: *P. Clodius, homo nobilis, disertus, audax, quique neque dicendi neque faciendi ullum nisi quem vellet nosset modum, malorum propositorum executor acerrimus, infamis etiam sororis stupro et actus incesti reus ob initum inter religiosissima populi Romani sacra adulterium.*

the other hand, was blamed for his *luxuria* and *ambitio*: "no wealth and no pleasures sufficed to satiate his appetites,"⁶⁵ and M. Lollius was a man of many vicious habits, according to Velleius.⁶⁶

A somewhat striking point in Velleius' illustration of characters is his presentation of Julius Caesar and the absence in it of the word *virtus*. In all the long description he gives, it seems as if Velleius is consciously avoiding the use of this word; other qualities are mentioned, such as *vigor animi, munificentia, fides, celeritas,* or *patientia*,⁶⁷ and yet we find the word *virtus* only once and not related to martial bravery explicitly, but mentioning Caesar's *virtus* in civil posts: "his praetorship and quaestorship passed in Spain, in which he showed wonderful energy and *virtus* [*et praetura quaesturaque mirabili virtute atque industria obita in Hispania*]."⁶⁸ Even when he talks about his courage, a Caesarian quality indeed, Velleius does not mention the word *virtus* and prefers *animus*. The Velleian dialogue with Sallust on *virtus* that I have suggested earlier in this chapter makes Caesar's characterization all the more significant in that for Sallust, Caesar did have *ingentem virtutem*.⁶⁹ The name of Caesar is in Velleius more associated with *fortuna* than with *virtus*.⁷⁰ On several occasions the author points out his *fortuna*, and he also stresses the main quality of it: *sua*.⁷¹ It was Caesar's habitual good luck that aroused envy and jealousy in his enemies, and it was also by *sua fortuna* that he triumphed against Pompey in the civil war, and Pompey's son in the battle of Munda.⁷² The reluctance to bestow *virtus* on Julius Caesar shows that Velleius did not attribute this quality to all the important characters of his work unrestrictedly or by default, but that it was something pondered upon and given conscientiously.

To sum up this section on *virtus* on the *Historiae* in general, it is possible to say that the characters throughout Velleius' history are evaluated mainly according their *virtus* or *vitium* and not with regard to their social class or to

---

65. Vell. 2.48.3: *neque opes ullae neque cupiditates sufficere possent*. It is striking the way Velleius describes Clodius and Curio, using the same words for both. Clodius: *homo nobilis, disertus, audax*, and Curio: *vir nobilis, eloquens, audax*.

66. Vell. 2.97.1: *inter summa vitiorum dissimulationem vitiosissimo*.

67. Vell. 2.41.1.

68. Vell. 2.43.4.

69. Sall. *BC* 53.6.

70. This reminds us of Sallust and his use of *fortuna* rather than *virtus* to characterize Marius. As I have mentioned in chapter 2 in this book, Sallust himself never attributes *virtus* to Marius, but always through others.

71. Cf. 2.51.2; 2.55.1; 2.60.1.

72. Cf. Vell. 2.55.1 and 2.55.3.

their political position. Velleius' use of the words *virtus* and *virtutes* is paramount in his narrative especially as a way of describing in few words an honest conduct in any given situation—military and civil—and by anybody: nobles and *novi*. If *virtus* were the property only of a certain group in society, there would be little point in recording its achievements. *Virtus* is contagious, that is, the whole reason of giving all these examples. *Exempla virtutis* create a sense of tradition of vital importance for the Romans of the first century A.D.; it was one way of connecting the imperial present with the republican past, and this is precisely one of Velleius' aims, especially as we approach Tiberius' time in power.

A Case Study of Roman *Virtus*: The Tiberian Narrative

In this section, I will illustrate how the virtues attributed to Tiberius by Velleius—the center of so many discussions[73]—fulfill multiple functions within his *Historiae*. I will argue that the *virtus* and the other *virtutes* ascribed to Tiberius have a programmatic mission within Velleius' historical narrative in a unique way, different from that of previous historians. I shall not give an exhaustive catalogue of Tiberius' *virtutes*, but show the most important ones and the different roles they played in Velleius' historiographical scheme. By placing the account of the *princeps*' qualities at the center of the narrative, Velleius assigns them the force of historical facts, and a political-ideological purpose, key to the understanding of his work, especially in the time he was writing. These elements work in parallel with Velleius' purpose in writing, which derives from his conception of history, and which makes his *Historiae* appear as a happy progression toward the triumph of good over evil. The "Tiberian narrative" will work, therefore, as a case study to show how *virtus*, mainly a moral concept, can serve both as a channel for political analysis and as a tool for historical explanation.

Velleius was a soldier serving under Tiberius before the latter became emperor of Rome. His perception of Tiberius was totally different from that of the court. Neither was he an aristocrat nor had he been harmed by the arrival of the imperial regime—unlike most of the aristocrats and senators. Whatever

---

73. For a more detailed account of Tiberius' virtues, see, for example, Rogers, *Studies in the Reign of Tiberius*, 3–88; Seager, *Tiberius*; Levick, *Tiberius the Politician*; Woodman, *Velleius Paterculus*; Hellegouarc'h, "La figure de Tibère chez Tacite et Velleius Paterculus," 168–83; Kuntze, *Zur Darstellung des Kaisers Tiberius und seiner Zeit bei Velleius Paterculus*; Christ, "Velleius und Tiberius," 180–92; Gowing, "Imperial Republic of Velleius Paterculus," 411–18; Balmaceda, "Virtues of Tiberius in Velleius' *Histories*," 340–63.

he had become, he had Tiberius to be grateful for: military tribune in Thracia and Macedonia; *praefectus equitum* in Tiberius' army in Germany in A.D. 4; *quaestor* in A.D. 6; legate of Tiberius (who was his leader in the wars of Dalmatia and Pannonia and in the successive Rhine campaigns); and *praetor*, together with his brother, in A.D. 15.[74]

Velleius' motives and his interest in highlighting Tiberius' figure in this way are therefore clear to see. He has been a soldier under his orders, he has witnessed the general's concern for the soldiers, he has been a victor alongside him, and a close bond of affection, a combination of comradeship and admiration, has been formed. And there is more. They share a vision, a political idea: their faith in the principate and its head, the emperor. By means of his writings, Velleius seems to be defending the emperor and, through him, the institution of the principate, from every possible attack by those who accuse the prince of having repressed freedom and suppressed any authentically republican form. The regime created by Augustus and continued by Tiberius had a repairing mission: it guaranteed *pax* abroad and *pax* at home: "Credit has been restored in the forum, strife has been banished from the forum, canvassing for office from the Campus Martius, discord from the Senate house; justice, equity and industry, long buried in oblivion, have been restored to the state; the magistrates have regained their authority, the Senate its majesty, the courts their dignity [*Revocata in forum fides, summota e foro seditio, ambitio campo, discordia curia, sepultaeque ac situ obsitae iustitia, aequitas, industria civitate redditae; accessit magistratibus auctoritas, senatui maiestas, iudicii gravitas*]."[75]

With no desire to justify the partiality of Velleius' view, it should be pointed out that in his work he refers only to the first part of Tiberius' reign. In other words, he restricts himself to the period that, in general, has been considered as enjoying good government, even by Tiberius' detractors.[76] It is only around A.D. 26 when there were signs that indicated a change: Tiberius retired to Capri and the domination of Sejanus became evident. Between that moment and the beginning of A.D. 30, the time at which Velleius had stopped writing, there were unmistakable manifestations of anxiety that Velleius allows himself to express in the final and fervent prayer to ask the gods to guard

---

74. Cf. Vell. 2.124.
75. Vell. 2.126.
76. Dio, 57.18.11: "Up to this time, as we have seen, Tiberius had done a great many excellent things and had made but few errors, but now when he no longer had a rival biding his chance, he changed to precisely the reverse of his previous conduct, which had included much that was good." See also Tac. *Ann*, 1.72; 4.6; Suet. *Tib*, 26; and Sen. *Clem*, 1.1.6.

the state of Rome and Tiberius, Rome's *optimus princeps*: "Let me end this volume with a prayer (...) guard, preserve, protect the present state of things, the peace which we enjoy, the present emperor [*Voto finiendum volumen est (...) custodite, servate, protegite hunc statum, hanc pacem, hunc principem*]."[77]

For Velleius, Tiberius gave assurance of the security and continuity of the political system that was started by Augustus because he embodied all the characteristics of a *princeps* even before becoming one. A new political culture was developing quickly; the importance and qualities of the successor were going to be intimately related to the functioning of the government; "princes were seen to incarnate the future stability of the regime."[78] There is a passage that is of great significance for the main idea conveyed in Velleius' Tiberian narrative: "made equal to Augustus [*aequatus Augusto*] by sharing with him the tribunician power; the most eminent of all Roman citizens save one—and this because he wished it so; the greatest of generals [*ducum maximus*], attended alike by fame and fortune; veritably the second luminary and the second head of the state [*vere alterum rei publicae lumen et caput*]."[79] Here Velleius is attempting to bestow on Tiberius an *auctoritas* similar to that of Augustus.[80] What the author tries to make clear is that before Tiberius took over the government of Rome as *princeps*, and even before his adoption by Augustus, he had already built up a prestige that could not be compared with that of any other citizen, and this prestige had been earned by his personal merits.

In the brief synopsis of Tiberius' reign quoted above, Velleius lists the various good qualities that Tiberius has restored: *fides, iustitia, aequitas, industria, gravitas*... [81] The key word here is *revocata*.[82] The continuity of the restoration is for Velleius the main achievement of Tiberius as it had been his predecessor's. The almost identical statement given some chapters before confirms that Tiberius was being faithful to the wishes of his political father: "[*revocata pax*...] peace was restored (...) validity was restored to the laws, authority to the courts and dignity to the Senate; the power of the magistrates was reduced to its former limits (...) the old traditional form of the Republic was restored [*restituta vis legibus, iudiciis auctoritas, senatui maiestas, imperium magistratuum*

---

77. Vell. 2.131.
78. Rowe, *Princes and Political Cultures*, 2.
79. Vell. 2.99.1.
80. Cf. Schmitzer, *Velleius Paterculus und das Interesse an der Geschichte im Zeitalter des Tiberius*, 230–31.
81. Cf. Vell. 2.126.
82. Cf. Woodman, *Velleius Paterculus*, 234.

ad pristinum redactum modum... Prisca illa et antiqua rei publicae forma revocata]."[83]

It seemed quite reasonable for Velleius to praise Tiberius for his "continuation policy." For him, Augustus' reign had been a model of peace and prosperity, and there was nothing else that the Roman people could desire but a prolongation of it. Moreover, one cannot really say that Velleius was making things up in his compliments to the emperor: strife had truly been banished from the forum and the Senate, and the magistrates had regained their authority and the courts their dignity after years of instability, civil wars, and anomalous leadership with the triumvirs. Tacitus too acknowledged as much.[84] After Augustus' death, Rome could have gone back to all this; instead, peace and normality were the inheritance of the *princeps'* reign.[85] According to Velleius, Tiberius with his *auctoritas* calmed the anxieties and dissolved the threats.

Velleius gave an account of Tiberius' merits and qualities not only because he pursued a didactic purpose, promoting a model and encouraging confidence toward the emperor, but because what he had seen gave him some reason to believe that Tiberius' *virtutes*—which he took care to describe in full—were something real and tangible that linked the *princeps* with the Roman republican past, so much so that he made them the substance of his narrative about restoration: *revocata in foro fides*...

The image of Tiberius conveyed by Velleius' *Historiae* is perfectly defined in his description of *optimus princeps*:[86] "for the best of emperors teaches his

---

83. Vell. 2.89. For the idea of the principate as a restoration of the republic, see Eder, "Augustus and the Power of Tradition," 73; Kuntze, *Zur Darstellung des Kaisers Tiberius und seiner Zeit bei Velleius Paterculus*, 155–68; Gowing, *Empire and Memory*, 34–35.

84. His summary of Tiberius' government at the beginning of Book 4 is very telling: "public business and the most important private matters were managed by the Senate: the leading men were allowed freedom of discussion, and when they stooped to flattery, the emperor himself checked them. He bestowed honors with regard to noble ancestry, military renown, or brilliant accomplishments as a civilian, letting it be clearly seen that there were no better men to choose. The consul and the praetor retained their prestige; inferior magistrates exercised their authority; the laws too, with the single exception of cases of treason, were properly enforced."

85. Gabba, "Historians and Augustus," 82, believes that "at the cost of contradicting Sir Ronald Syme, Velleius gives us a better idea than Tacitus of the atmosphere in Rome at the moment of the death of Augustus; it was a moment of fear and confusion. It was the *maiestas* of Tiberius, admitted even by Tacitus (*Ann*, 1.46.2; 1.47.2), which calmed men's fears and evaporated the dangers."

86. And so it was for Valerius Maximus, cf. 2 *praef*. For a comparison with Velleius, see Bloomer, *Valerius Maximus and the Rhetoric of the New Nobility*, 192–93; Millar, "Ovid and the Domus Augusta," 4–5; Jacquemin, "Valère Maxime et Velleius Paterculus," 147–56. The edict of Strabo Libuscidianus expresses something similar, claiming that Tiberius is both *optimus princeps* and *maximus principum* (lines 14 and 4, respectively); cf. Mitchell, "Requisitioned Transport in the Roman Empire," 106–31.

citizens to do right by doing it and though he is greatest among us in authority, he is still greater in the example that he sets [*nam facere recte civis suos princeps optimus faciendo docet, cumque sit imperio maximus, exemplo maior est*]."[87] From the very beginning Velleius insists on presenting Tiberius as a prince, both as regards physical aspects and in his successful performance of tasks, in which he displays all the virtues: *praecipuis omnium virtutum*.[88]

There are, however, some aspects that stand out among others, which Velleius uses to show his prince to advantage and to give him an outstanding place in the empire because of his qualities even before taking over power as a *princeps*. In fact, the majority of the text refers to Tiberius before he became an emperor and gives a full account of the deeds of young Tiberius, specifically, from the year 22 B.C. The period of his reign is touched upon very cursorily by Velleius, and he refers only to the first sixteen years of Tiberius' government in very general terms,[89] and overlooks a series of rather complex events such as Germanicus' death and Sejanus' promotion.

As noted earlier in this chapter, Tiberius' virtues have received enough attention from those studying the virtues as such, but this section, rather than listing them, is concerned with the role they play in Velleius' narrative. I have divided them into two groups: first, the qualities that are specifically and only found in Velleius, and second, the virtues about which even the "anti-Tiberian sources" agree with him.

Within the first cluster of virtues, Tiberius' central merits, according to Velleius' account, have to do with his military accomplishments which, at the same time, provided fertile ground for the development of a series of other virtues. It is also worth mentioning that Velleius pays little or no attention to the political posts held by Tiberius. His military capability and his being widely acknowledged by Roman society as a good general at the time are the aspects that are most stressed in his work. Thus *virilis-virtus*, or *virtus* with the specific meaning of courage, appears as the first and foremost quality of the *princeps* from the very beginning of the Tiberian narrative: "he carried on [the war] with his customary valor and good fortune [*quod is sua et virtute et fortuna administravit*]."[90] Great proof of courage is also shown by Tiberius during the Dalmatian war: *Magna in bello Delmatico experimenta virtutis*,[91] and in all of

---

87. Vell. 2.126.4. For the same idea of exemplarity, see the *Senatus Consultum de Cn. Pisone Patre* (*SCPP*), lines 90–93.
88. Cf. Vell. 2.94.4.
89. From the year A.D. 14 to the year A.D. 30.
90. Vell. 2.97.4. In Germania, years 12–9 B.C.
91. Cf. Vell. 2.116.1. In the year A.D. 9.

his incursions in Germany: *eadem virtus et fortuna subsequenti tempore ingressi Germaniam imperatoris Tiberii fuit* (Tiberius showed the same *virtus* and was attended by the same fortune when he entered Germany on his later campaign).[92] Later on, during the Gallic insurrection of Sacrovir and Florus Iulius, it is his bravery together with his swiftness (*celeritate ac virtute*) that will be praised.[93]

For Velleius, the principal commander in the battlefield was unquestionably Tiberius. After Agrippa's death, Tiberius was the empire's leading general.[94] Tiberius' victories came one after the other in endless succession: he beat the Raeti and the Vindelici,[95] the Pannonians,[96] and the Germans.[97] It was vital for Velleius' purpose to present Tiberius as a brave and successful general if he sought to link him with the history of the republic. Through his military achievements Tiberius acquired not only the all-important *gloria* but also the necessary political weight to become the head of state. The Romans acknowledged Tiberius' military competence: they trusted him and thought that his prestige as a good general was well deserved. Besides, from Velleius' point of view, in terms of actual fighting, he was the kind of general who joined his soldiers and fought in the battlefield. He did not restrict himself to giving the relevant orders from the protection of his tent, without exposing himself to the same danger as his soldiers: "they were pacified not under the mere generalship, but by the armed prowess of Caesar himself [*sed manibus atque armis ipsius Caesaris*]."[98] Velleius also pointed out that Tiberius was not only brave in battle but also kind to the soldiers in the camp, where he displayed a *singularis humanitas*: he looked after the sick and shared his vehicles, physicians, kitchen, and bathing equipment, as is described in chapter 114.[99] Velleius appreciates this attitude of equality on the part of a superior officer toward his subordinates, and this generates in the soldiers a deep affection for their commander.[100] There was something of the old-fashioned generals of the republic

---

92. Cf. Vell. 2.121.1. In the years A.D. 10–12.
93. Cf. Vell. 2.129.3. In the year A.D. 21.
94. Cf. R. Seager, *Tiberius*, 25. Cf. also Tac. *Ann*, 1.4 and Suet. *Tib*, 8–9; 16.
95. In 22 B.C., cf. 2.95.
96. In 19 B.C., cf. 2.96.
97. In A.D. 5, cf. 2.106. For Tiberius' military exploits, see Christ, "Velleius und Tiberius," esp. 182–89.
98. Vell. 2.115.
99. For Tiberius' *humanitas*, see also *SCPP*, line 100.
100. As shown in his soldiers' behavior: "the tears that sprang to their eyes in their joy at the sight of him, their eagerness, their strange transports in saluting him, their longing to touch his hand, and their inability to restrain such cries as 'Is it really you that we see, commander?,' 'Have

in Tiberius' way of conducting wars, something that people had seen in Livy's Marcellus or Fabius and that they had liked. Of course these military qualities were part of the good-general *topos*[101]—but that precisely was one of Velleius' purposes: to include Tiberius in this republican tradition.[102]

Apart from his *virilis-virtus* and military merits, Velleius attributes to his general and emperor a character that combines keeping a certain distance from power and not shirking public service; being unwilling to receive honors and staying above such manifestations, yet ready to show himself available to do whatever might be needed, that is, putting the *res publica* first and above his personal advantage. His divorce from Vipsania and his marriage to Julia after Agrippa's death and his voluntary exile to Rhodes in order not to overshadow the young princes Gaius and Lucius are given by Velleius as concrete examples of Tiberius placing the well-being of the state before his own. The manner in which Tiberius acts, according to Velleius, is precisely what an *optimus princeps* should do for his countrymen. We will come back to this point later in this section.

Another characteristic that Velleius attributes to the new *princeps* is his remarkable political loyalty to Augustus, which in Tiberius' case goes even further, since it not only represents an unbreakable loyalty in matters political and military but also can be likened to the typical *pietas* of a good son toward his father, a concept that acquired much strength in the times of Augustus.[103] The historian presents both of them as an example of the father-son relationship. In several passages he insists on Tiberius' filial relationship with Augustus, whom he describes as a happy man on the day that he adopted Tiberius: "The rejoicing of that day, the concourse of the citizens, their vows as they stretched their hands almost to the very heavens, and the hopes that they entertained for the perpetual security and the eternal existence of the Roman empire, I shall hardly be able to describe to the full."[104] For Velleius, the question of Augustus' succession was the natural consequence of Tiberius' merits. The choice had already been made: Augustus should be succeeded by whoever had the most

---

we received you safely back among us?' [*At vero militum conspectu eius elicitae gaudio lacrimae alacritasque et salutationis nova quaedam exultatio et contingendi manum cupiditas non continentium protinus quin adiicerent, 'Videmus te, imperator?' 'Salvum recepimus?'*]," in Vell. 2.104. See also 2.114.1–3.

101. For more on this *topos*, see Woodman, *Velleius Paterculus*, 174–76.

102. Cf. Marincola, "Explanation in Velleius," 135.

103. Cf. Augustus' *clypeus aureus*. For *pietas* in Tiberius, see 2.99.2; 2.105.3; 2.126.1. For Tiberius' *pietas* in the *SCPP*, see line 119.

104. Vell. 2.103.4.

merits, which according to Velleius undoubtedly pointed to Tiberius: "Caesar Augustus did not long hesitate, for he had no need to search for one to choose as his successor, but merely to choose the one who towered above the others."[105] Such assertions appear misleading because, even for Tiberius himself, his adoption marked the beginning of a difficult and traumatic relationship with power, and Augustus and Rome were fully aware of this.[106] The historian could not have been ignorant of the doubts that Augustus had had before adopting Tiberius. He had to wait several years before Augustus publicly recognized the power he possessed as a successful general, and the *princeps* had had other choices before turning to Tiberius: Marcellus, Gaius, and Lucius; and in the year A.D. 4, he had adopted Agrippa Postumus at the same time as he adopted Tiberius, whom in turn he forced to adopt Germanicus. Tiberius, perhaps because of envy—if we are to believe Tacitus—or because of an exacerbated susceptibility, had undergone moments in which his relations with Augustus had been somewhat strained; his retirement to Rhodes can be seen as an example, and their friendship would be mended later mainly through the death of all the other possible successors.[107] But Velleius portrays Tiberius as a faithful son and general who acted just as the emperor himself would have done. There are numerous passages that demonstrate this, not only or mainly on the battlefields but also in civil action.[108] This is the political faithfulness that a ruler should observe in a hereditary regime with respect to his predecessor and his projects. However, according to Tacitus, events unfolded very differently, as the first deed of the new principate was the murder of Agrippa Postumus.[109] Velleius does not or cannot see things in the same way as Tacitus. For him, the new *princeps* follows in the steps of his predecessor as closely as he can and is moved "by some admirable, incredible, and inexpressible feeling of piety toward Augustus [*mira quadam et incredibili atque inenarrabili pietate*]."[110]

Apart from *virtus*, *humanitas*, and *pietas*, there is a second group of virtues that Velleius attributes to the emperor Tiberius that are also attested in the anti-Tiberian sources. These qualities play an important part in the historian's

---

105. Vell. 2.103.
106. For Tiberius' adoption and relationship with Augustus, see Levick, *Tiberius the Politician*, 31–67; Seager, *Tiberius*, 14–47; Marsh, *Reign of Tiberius*, 39–41; Birch, "Settlement of 26[th]th June AD 4," 443–50. For a different account of the adoption, see Tac. *Ann*, 1.3; Suet. *Tib*, 17 and 21.
107. Cf. Suet. *Tib*. 10–11. See Levick, "Tiberius' Retirement to Rhodes in 6 B.C.," 779–813.
108. See, for example, Vell. 2.124.
109. Cf. Tac. *Ann*, 1.6.
110. Vell. 2.99.2.

development of the explanation of his narrative. They are fulfilling not only a descriptive function but above all a methodological one: Velleius uses them as a way or the means to show us much of Tiberius' governmental policies.

The first of these virtues is *prudentia* or *pro-videntia*, as manifested in his behavior as a military chief.[111] A prudent general is one who foresees situations and can thus find a solution; a prudent and judicious man is one who does not let himself be carried away by the passions of the moment. Tiberius' *prudentia* became evident especially in his military campaigns, which showed his careful planning: "What opportunities did we avail ourselves through the foresight of the general ... with what judgment did he place our winter camps [*Quantis prudentia ducis opportunitatibus furentes ... qua prudentia hiberna disposita sunt*]"[112]; "the plans of the commander were never governed by the opinion of the army, but rather the army by the providence of its leader [*necumquam consilia ducis iudicio exercitus, sed exercitus providentia ducis rectus est*]"[113]; "with what prudence did he draw Rhascupolis to Rome! [*qua ille prudentia Rhascupolim ... Romam evocavit!*]."[114] Evidence for his prudence is given by Velleius throughout the Tiberian narrative,[115] but, as the greatest mission of the principate was to maintain peace and order after the chaos of the civil wars, Tiberius' *prudentia* has its supreme expression in the fact that he kept a peaceful empire: *pax augusta omnis terrarum orbis angulos ... servat* (the *pax augusta*, ... preserves every corner of the world safe).[116]

Another virtue displayed by Tiberius is *munificentia*, which toward the end of his work, Velleius qualifies as *pia*, and which also takes the shape of *liberalitas*. This virtue was particularly suited to the politician,[117] and the author gives numerous examples of it: "the munificence of the emperor claims for its province the losses inflicted by fortune not merely on private citizens, but on whole cities! [*fortuita non civium tantummodo, sed urbium damna principis*

---

111. For *providentia* as being part of the virtue of *prudentia*, cf. Cic. *De Inv*, 2.160.
112. Vell. 2.111.4.
113. Vell. 2.115.5.
114. Vell. 2.129.1.
115. See also Vell. 2.110.3; 2.120.1–2; 2.120.4; 2.130.2.
116. Vell. 2.126.3. See also *SCPP*, lines 13–14: *tranquillitatem praesentis status rei publicae, quo melior optari non pote et quo beneficio principis nostri frui contigit*("the present tranquil condition of the commonwealth, than which no better could be desired and which the beneficence of our Princeps has made it possible to enjoy", Griffin's transl. "The Senate's Story," 250). For Tiberius' *providentia/prudentia* in other literary sources, see Dio, 56.14; 56.24; 57.14.8; Suet. *Tib*, 18–19; Tac. *Ann*, 3.69; 4.6.4–6; 4.38.
117. Cf. Hellegouarc'h, *Vocabulaire Latin*, 217–21.

munificentia vindicat]";[118] "How often did he honor the people with largesse, and how gladly whenever he could do so with the Senate's sanction, did he raise to the required rating the fortunes of senators ... [*quotiens populum congiariis honoravit senatorumque censum, cum id senatu auctore facere potuit, quam libenter explevit...*]";[119] "With what pious munificence, exceeding human belief, does he now rear the temple to his father! [*quam pia munificentia superque humanam evecta fidem templum patri molitur!*]".[120] *Liberalitas* occurs frequently in the literary sources, and perhaps if Tiberius' enemies were forced to name one of his virtues, they would point to his generosity.[121] Tacitus expresses this with a pungent remark: "he was eager to spend money for honorable purposes—a virtue that he long retained, even when he abandoned all others."[122] Dio tells us that he restored buildings that had been damaged, completed the ones that Augustus had begun but not finished, and ornamented public works.[123] This *munificentia*, far from luxury or sumptuousness, took the form of generosity with respect to others and splendor as regards whatever might contribute to the aggrandizement of the state.

Tacitus, Suetonius, Dio, and Velleius are notably in agreement about a virtue that all four of them consider as remaining constant from the start of Tiberius' career to his being promoted prince, and which they think his prevailing quality: *moderatio*.[124] From the very beginning of his reign, Tiberius had opportunities to exercise this virtue. Immediately after his accession, he had to deal with senatorial flattery toward Livia, but he rejected all the honors and titles proposed for her.[125] Such sobriety and moderation characterized Tiberius in terms of his governmental actions: over Asinius Gallus' proposal about elections,[126] over provincial taxation,[127] regarding the funerals of the imperial family,[128] and in the application of the *lex maiestatis*.[129] And also *moderatio*

---

118. Vell. 2.126.4.
119. Vell. 2.129.3.
120. Vell. 2.130.1. Also Vell. 2.114.2–3.
121. Cf. Tac. *Ann*, 1.8.3; 2.42.1; 3.29.3; 4.4.1; Suet. *Tib*, 48.2; 54.1; 76; Dio, 55.10.1; 57.10.4; 58.18.2; 59.2.1–2.
122. Tac. *Ann*, 1.75.
123. Cf. Dio, 57.10.
124. For Tiberius' *moderatio* in anti-Tiberian sources, see Dio, 56.13.2–4; 57.8; 57.10.1–3; 57.11; 57.13.3; 57.15.2; Suet. *Tib*, 18; 26–27; Tac. *Ann*, 1.8.3; 1.14.1–3; 3.6; 3.56.1; 3.59.2; 3.69; 4.6; 4.37–38.
125. Cf. Tac. *Ann*, 1.14; and Suet. *Tib*, 50.
126. Cf. Tac. *Ann*, 2.36.
127. Cf. Suet. *Tib*, 32.2; Dio, 57.10.5; Tac. *Ann*, 1.76.4; 2.42.7; 2.56.4; 4.6.7.
128. Cf. Tac. *Ann*, 1.8.6; 3.5; 3.6.1; 4.8.2; 4.13.1; 5.1.6; 5.2.1; Suet. *Tib*, 52.1; Dio, 57.14.6; 57.22.3; 58.2.1.
129. Cf. Suet. *Tib*, 28; Tac. *Ann*, 3.25.1; 3.28.6; 3.56.1.

with the honors that the Senate wanted to confer upon him or when people called him *dominus* and spoke of his *sacrae* or *divinae* occupations, he replied, "I am *dominus* to my slaves, *imperator* to my soldiers, and first citizen to the rest,"[130] and suggested that his activities were rather laborious than divine.[131] For Velleius, the virtue of moderation in Tiberius was manifested in a certain kind of modesty that went beyond simple self-control, as shown when, having justly earned seven triumphs, he celebrated only three: "Among the other acts of Tiberius Caesar, wherein his remarkable moderation [*singularis moderatio*] shines forth conspicuously, who does not wonder at this also, that, although he unquestionably earned seven triumphs, he was satisfied with three?,"[132] and especially when he refused the principate for some time when it was offered to him: "He is the only man to whose lot it has fallen to refuse the principate for a longer time, almost, than others had fought to secure it."[133]

Probably one of the most striking manifestations of Tiberius' *moderatio* was his hatred of flattery. Suetonius dedicates the whole of chapter 27 to exemplifying it, and Tacitus has a sharp comment about it: "speech was constricted and risky under an emperor who feared freedom and hated flattery."[134] More than once Tiberius complained about the servility of the senators, and he used to exclaim in Greek after leaving the curia, *O homines ad servitutem paratos.*[135] For Velleius, Tiberius' dislike of flattery is shown in that the emperor was, in general, reluctant to accept more honors than was needed: "But in the case of this man, one does not know which to admire the more, that in courting toils and danger he went beyond all bounds or that in accepting honors he kept within them."[136]

The qualities that we have been looking at, *virtus* (as courage), *pietas*, *humanitas*, *providentia*, *munificentia*, and *moderatio*, are Tiberius' virtues, and we can find some of them not only in Velleius but also in coins and inscriptions

---

130. Dio, 57.8.2.
131. Cf. Suet. *Tib*, 27.
132. Vell. 2.122: *Quis non inter reliqua, quibus singularis moderatio Ti. Caesaris elucet atque eminet, hoc quoque miretur, quod cum sine ulla dubitatione septem triumphos meruerit, tribus contentus fuit?* Also Vell. 2.94.3; 2.111.4; 2.125.3.
133. Vell. 2.124.2: *solique huic contigit paene diutius recusare principatum, quam, ut occuparent eum, alii pugnaverant.*
134. Tac. *Ann*, 2.87.2.
135. Tac. *Ann*, 3.65.
136. Vell. 2.122.2: *Nam in hoc viro nescias utrum magis mireris quod laborum periculorumque semper excessit modum an quod honorum temperavit.*

of the period,[137] as well as in the anti-Tiberian literary sources, as has been shown. For Velleius, for whom unquestionably Tiberius' appellation as *optimus princeps* was fully deserved, these virtues, apart from describing the *princeps* himself, also fulfill another important mission within his work: they are the means by which the author narrates the events that happened during Tiberius' time and they unify the narrative. We know that there was a fire in the Caelian hill through Tiberius' *liberalitas* in helping the needy;[138] we know that he waged war in A.D. 21 against Florus and Sacrovir in Gaul because of his *celeritas* and *virtus* in repressing it.[139] It is Tiberius' *gravitas* that tells us that Drusus Libo was put on trial before the emperor,[140] and his *prudentia* that made Rome's dangerous enemy, Rhascupolis, go back to Rome.[141] Through the account of his *moderatio* we learn that Tiberius actually earned seven triumphs although he did not celebrate them.[142] Examples of this sort are the substance of the Tiberian narrative.

In Velleius' account of Tiberius' reign, virtues and historical facts seem to work methodologically together as a way to describe and analyze not only the *princeps* but also the period. Imperial history is starting to be written through the emperor's virtues just as we saw republican history being written by Livy through the virtues of the Roman people and by Sallust through their vices.

Velleius' Conception of History

Everything that Velleius has seen and lived through provides him with more than enough evidence to state that the principate is and shall be the best possible form of government that Rome could have. His view of Roman history is positive and has even been described as "triumphal."[143] In arriving at this conclusion, Velleius has undeniably been influenced by his own political ideas and his personal experience which have led to his promotion from plain *homo novus* to high administrative and military positions.

---

137. Such as the dupondius (a brass coin) with MODERATIONE SC inscribed on it and the SCPP.
138. Cf. Vell. 2.130.1.
139. Cf. Vell. 2.129.3.
140. Cf. Vell. 2.129.2.
141. Cf. Vell. 2.129.1.
142. Cf. Vell. 2.122.1.
143. Cf. Millar, "Ovid and the Domus Augusta," 2–6; de Monte, "Velleius Paterculus and 'Triumphal' History," 121–35.

This perspective can also account for his praise of Tiberius. The second emperor of Rome had provided examples of all the civil and military virtues that had given him the necessary prestige and an *auctoritas* of his own to govern and become a true *princeps* who, according to Velleius, was not only accepted but also most wanted and needed. Augustus' government had been a miracle of order and peace,[144] and it passed to a successor who opted for proving that this way of governing was not a transient remedy for the ills of the moment—the return of order after decades of violence—but a permanent political need.

Velleius has given an account of Roman *virtus* throughout his history of the Roman Republic, and he needs to continue this trend in describing the principate if it is really going to be presented as a restoration of the *mores maiorum* and a remedy against corruption;[145] hence the stress on the key word *revocata*. According to him, Tiberius had the *virtus* and all the *virtutes* before being adopted by Augustus. Among these, there were some that shone out especially: courage, loyalty toward his political father, moderation, providence, largesse, and mercy.[146] These qualities are presented not only as the continuation of Roman history but also as its culmination.[147]

The Tiberian narrative definitely appears different from the rest of the *Historiae*, but at the same time, it fits in perfectly well with the work as a whole. The fact of beginning with the remotest past—the fall of Troy—has an important function in this account; the tensions that Velleius illustrates make it necessary to start with the deeds of the first Romans. The Tiberian section is not a simple eulogy or panegyric of the emperor. It plays a key role in the work: Tiberius represents not only the summit of Roman history but also the epitome of Roman *virtus*. However, it would have been impossible to reach this pinnacle if there were not a past full of *exempla* to follow, if *virilis-virtus* and *humana-virtus* had not been the eternal companions of men. Velleius is stressing the continuity in Roman history by every possible means. With the same forcefulness with which Tacitus highlights the break with the republic, Velleius underlines the steady course of the Roman people toward moral and social progress. The chain of virtuous men from the beginning of

---

144. For Augustus' program of peace, see Suet. *Aug.* 21; Dio, 54.9.1; *Res Gestae* 13.

145. Cf. Vell. 2.126.

146. All attested also in *SCPP*. Cf. Cooley, "Moralizing Message of the *Senatus Consultum de Cn. Pisone Patre*," 199–212; and Potter, "Political Theory in the *Senatus Consultum Pisonianum*," 65–88.

147. Cf. Gowing, *Empire and Memory*, 43: "[Rome] has moved not from Republic to Empire, but from Republic to a better Republic."

Rome has not been broken; on the contrary, it seems to have reached its peak with the emperor Tiberius. Very much like the statues of the *viri illustres* in the forum of Augustus,[148] Velleius' republican heroes display both types of *virtus* in his narrative in order to give continuity to Roman history and to lend more luster to the culminating figure, the emperor Tiberius.

Velleius is consistent in his analysis of and approach to history. He repeats the same idea throughout his work. For him, writing history during the principate implied both change and continuity. Change, because historiography now tended to be more biographical, more personal: the rule of one man required him to take this perspective, hence the importance of personal *virtus*. Change, also, because the greatness of the Roman Empire made it necessary to deal with universal themes. And continuity, because the treatment of the past had not been altered. *Virtus* remained the same and had to be emphasized more and more, and this for two reasons: it was a feature of the past, and it was the main attribute of the present emperor. *Virtutes* in Tiberius are exceptional, in that he had them all,[149] but not in the sense of a novelty. Velleius is aware that he is presenting the emperor as a type of the traditional "true Roman," as part of an overall scheme. Thus he achieves a certain consistency for his line of argument within the totality of the work.

The author of the *Historiae* is an optimist, and he has his reasons. Prosperity has grown for him in every possible aspect. He does not see the end of the republic as the end of the most glorious times for Rome. Rather, he presents Roman history as a continuum where the advent of the principate was the natural result of the civil wars, not in a nostalgic or bitter tone, but introducing the reader to the idea that Rome is definitely marching forward, in an endless progression which, despite all vicissitudes, is leading the Roman people to the culminating *felicitas* of Tiberius' reign.[150] He has witnessed the end of turbulent and violent times; he has experienced the restoration—*revocata* again—of laws, order, and peace.

The concept of *pax*—and particularly *pax augusta*—is also part of Velleius' historiographical program. The idea of peace as something positive

---

148. For this, see Luce, "Livy, Augustus, and the Forum Augustum," 123–38. On this continuity, see Kuntze, *Zur Darstellung des Kaisers Tiberius*, 155–68; Schmitzer, *Velleius Paterculus*, 291–92 (who also points out that the statues in Augustus' Forum Romanum were likewise emblematic of an unbroken tradition and may have influenced Velleius); Gowing, *Empire and Memory*, 34–48, 106, 122, 157 (who notes that such a view disappears in the generations after Velleius).

149. Cf. Gowing, "Imperial Republic of Velleius Paterculus," 414.

150. Cf. Vell. 2.89.2 and 2.126.3.

had appeared with real strength only with Augustus.[151] It came to represent one of the most important factors that made the principate both strong and popular: calm and tranquility at home and abroad.[152] Without doubt peace had been one of the most powerful messages in the *Res Gestae*: "It was the will of our ancestors that the gateway of Janus Quirinus should be shut when the victories had secured peace by land and sea throughout the whole empire of the Roman people."[153] Velleius reinforces this idea by telling us that this peace was continued by Tiberius and spread even further and more strongly: "the *pax augusta*, which has spread to the regions of the east and of the west and to the bounds of the north and of the south, preserves every corner of the world safe from fear and brigandage."[154] For Velleius the pacification of the world was absolutely essential, and it was the result of something deeper: this peace was not obtained only by those who had most power, but by the nation that had individuals with most personal *virtus*. Hence his prayer at the end of his work: *custodite, servate, protegite hunc statum, hanc pacem, hunc principem*.[155]

To a certain extent Velleius' conception of history is different from that of other Roman historians. His perception is teleological. Everything is moving toward an end, which appears to him as the summit that started with Augustus and was continued by Tiberius. The history of Rome is seen as an indefinite progression, as something that flows continually and finds its culmination in the new regime, and particularly in its *optimus princeps*: Tiberius. His *virtus* and *virtutes* are at the center and perform several roles. On the one hand, they serve to propagate the political idea of the triumph of the principate, as the morality of the head was intimately linked with success in politics. On the other hand, they are the facts through which the narrative is developed, and they manifest a particular teleological program within the historical writing. Throughout the account of the *virtus*—both *virilis* and *humana*—of the emperor Tiberius, Velleius' version of historical reality seems to blend smoothly with his political ideology and interpretation of history.

THE RECORD OF *VIRTUS* in Velleius' *Historiae* could be seen as an answer to that of previous historians. For Sallust and, to a certain extent, Livy, *virtus* in

---

151. Peace had previously been seen by the Romans as a negative concept: the absence of war implied no expansion, no wealth, and less power.
152. The dedication of the *Ara Pacis* in 13 B.C. was an important landmark.
153. *Res Gestae*, 13. See also 25; 26; 34.
154. Vell. 2.126.3.
155. Vell. 2.131.1.

Rome had had its day. Sallust seemed keener to denounce the lack of *virtus* toward the end of the republic and registered only a few examples of men of *virtus*. Livy, on the other hand, presented a long chain of deeds of *virtus*, but placed them far back in time. It was in the glorious past of the republic where they saw *virtus* realized. *Virtus* for them was inseparably associated with the republic: the decline of this latter had inevitably implied the decline of *virtus*. Velleius' interpretation is more positive. The period of decline had been left behind, and Rome had passed the test successfully: the Roman state, identified with its ruler the emperor, was again a stage for *virtus*. The example of its head promoted and encouraged *virtus* in the whole of the Roman people.

Virtus—with its double meaning of courage and virtue, and also in the plural, *virtutes*—is for Velleius the unifying link in the development of this succession. It is absolutely necessary to reinforce this concept after the vicissitudes of the previous age. *Virtus* was somehow hidden during the late republic, only shining out every now and then in individual cases. Now, when peace is spread throughout the empire and its head is a model of *virtus*, Romans—aristocrats and *homines novi*—can practice it openly and without fear. Even though the term was used from one century to the next, and the meaning was somehow altered by different generations, *virtus* was not worn out: the concept had an emotional power that went beyond transient aspects. If Velleius emphasized the coming of a new and better era, his writings show us that it was better precisely because people could live according to the *mores maiorum*. Hence his stress on the recovery: *revocata in forum fides*... Restitution and novelty: Velleius restores the belief of the empire as a place where *virtus* could reign, and at the same time he helps to consolidate the ways in which autocracy was going to be seen and shaped henceforward. Rome has recovered her essence, and history can continue advancing to perfection.

CHAPTER FIVE

Virtus in Tacitus

Amissa virtute pariter ac libertate

They lost *virtus* at the same time as liberty

—Tac. *Agr*, 11.4

I have been arguing throughout the previous chapters that *virtus* was a key concept for the understanding of Roman history. Regardless of the period, the style, or the author, *virtus* occupied a central role in the development of Roman historiography. The historians present different perspectives and viewpoints that respond to a double stimulus: on the one hand, they write *about* a period of history in which *virtus* appears to be especially important (by its presence or its absence), but on the other hand, these same historians are necessarily writing *within* a precise moment of history, and therefore their approaches or responses to *virtus* are conditioned by the circumstances of their own times. Historians of the late republic and the early centuries of the principate became particularly insistent and repetitive about *virtus*. The political transitional period they were living through made them aware that Rome was unconsciously redefining her values in the fight for survival. Was Rome going to give in, and forget precisely what had made her great: the *virtus* of her people? Was it possible for a Roman in the imperial times to behave as he had done in the times of the republic?

The historians tried to answer these questions. Sallust showed the decline of *virtus* and predicted that if Romans continued to behave with *saevitia, superbia et ambitio*, it would be the end of the empire. Livy, more hopeful in outlook, decided that the solution was to look at the past and take lessons from it for the present situation. Livy encouraged his readers to be heroes, whereas Sallust scared them with the prospect of a dark future if they did not change. For Velleius Paterculus, who thought he was experiencing the climax of history, the way to progress was to look at and follow the model of the most virtuous prince: Tiberius. Velleius stressed the continuity from the republic to the empire, this being a time in which conditions were still more favorable for exercising *virtus*. In all cases, *virtus* appears to play not only a central role but also one that was very dear to the authors themselves; the concept of *virtus* helped to show the values in which they believed—or at least said that they believed—most deeply, and the ideal for which it was worthwhile writing a new interpretation of the history of Rome.

The depth of Tacitus' insight and analysis gives the concept of *virtus*, together with that of *libertas* and Roman history in general, a new perspective. If Tacitus has often been considered superior to other Roman historians, this is not just because of his style, or his psychological insight in describing people, or his genius in the art of innuendo, but because he enlarges his audience's expectations and sensibilities. He shows the reader that behind the dark panorama he paints of Rome under the Julio-Claudian emperors, during the year of the four emperors, or under Domitian, there were also some good Romans who deserved praise and became models of conduct. Tacitus' approach to history not only searches for causes and explanations of the events that occurred, but implicitly proposes a redefinition of Roman values in an original and demanding way. These values will also be delineated by means of a contrast with those of the barbarians with whom Rome came in contact.

For Tacitus, the fundamental change from republic to empire had, in a sense, diminished Romans' opportunities for showing courage or moral excellence, but had not completely destroyed them. And as history's function was still to provide *exempla*, he would supply his readers with new models to imitate in the new regime inaugurated by Augustus.[1] These examples would fulfill the double purpose of promoting the old values in a new guise adapted to the principate, and of maintaining the Roman core in relation to their own past and the new imperial power in an original way.

The historical narratives of previous Roman historians showed that the functioning of the republican system in Rome had allowed the creation of a political culture where *virtus* could especially shine forth. In certain periods or under particular circumstances, it had been more difficult to find *virtus* playing an active role, but on the whole, deeds of courage were performed and the prize had been glory and honor. When these deeds were done to preserve freedom (*libertas*), that is to say, to save the republic from an external peril or to defend her from a domineering faction within, *virtus* had been publicly acknowledged and rewarded, if not in real life, at least in historical records. During the principate, however, as we shall see, the competition for *virtus* had to be exercised in a slightly different way, as it was somewhat thwarted by the presence of a jealous *princeps* who claimed *virtus* as his personal attribute and saw it as a threat to his own person when other men possessed and dis-

---

1. Cf. Alston, "History and Memory," 153–54.

played *virtus*. Personal courage was still the criterion for measuring deeds done for the *res publica*, but now courage when defending freedom—especially civil freedom—was not always recognized and did not receive the reward it deserved.

Investigation of Tacitus' concept of *virtus* throughout his works does not show either that the author radically changed his perception of this key Roman concept from the *Agricola* to the *Annales* or that he kept its meaning frozen and intact throughout the first century A.D. On the contrary, occurrences of these new aspects of *virtus* appear to escalate from the *Annals* to the *Agricola*, in inverse order to that in which Tacitus wrote the works. Political situations and people's reactions, which appeared only timidly at the beginning of the principate, became glaringly visible by the end of the second dynasty. In the world of Tacitus' father-in-law, in Rome and in the provinces, men and deeds appeared bolder and in some respects more blatant than in the world of, say, Tiberius, and quite rightly: in Tacitus' view, tyranny had also been escalating within the empire from Tiberius to Domitian, with some brief intervals.

As my main purpose is to throw some light on Tacitus' concept of *virtus* and his novel approach to *libertas*, I will not analyze his style in detail.[2] I do not claim that style has primacy over content, or that Tacitus is mainly a literary artist. He is first and foremost a historian, who thinks deeply about men and change, and who happens to write these thoughts in an extraordinarily powerful way.[3] Recognizing that Tacitus was a literary artist or even a poet should not weaken his reputation as a bona fide historian. Tacitus' rhetoric does not impugn his integrity in any sense: allusions, *sententiae*, innuendos are there to lead us to look deeper, because beneath this surface something else is happening. His narrative technique is not something that could be stripped away from the story to leave the bare facts. On the contrary, it is an essential feature of the period itself, not only of his perception of it. Tacitus'

---

2. The amount of bibliography on Tacitus' style is far too large to give here; for some good and telling examples, see Goodyear, "Development of Language and Style," 22–31; Hellegouarc'h, "Le style de Tacite, bilan et perspectives," 2385–2453; Tanner, "Development of Thought and Style in Tacitus," 2689–2751.

3. I am reluctant to wholly agree with statements like "Dealing with Tacitus we are dealing first and foremost with a literary artist and [. . .], for him, in any conflict between style and content, style will inevitably prevail: in other words, actual historical facts will be altered or rearranged in the interests of a smoother narrative flow, a striking antithesis or even a sardonic epigram," in Murison, "Historical Value of Tacitus' *Histories*," 1711; or "The *Annals* is an artistic creation to be judged as one judges the *Aeneid*," in Walker, *Annals of Tacitus*, 257.

style is part of his task as a historian in matching words and deeds, and it will appear as part of the historian's prowess to be at the same time truthful and illuminating. If we stay on the surface, it is our problem, not Tacitus'. As Sinclair has rightly said, "the contradiction between Tacitus the literary artist and Tacitus the historian is a problem in modern thought, rather than a problem in Tacitean historiography."[4]

The *Agricola* and the *Germania*: Roman *Virtus* beyond the Boundaries?

The *Agricola* and the *Germania* have usually been considered, among other things, as useful examples of the contrast between barbaric societies on the northern frontier of the empire—Britons and Germans—on the one hand, and Roman society on the other. This contrast is mainly drawn from the comparisons, whether explicit or less so, that Tacitus provides throughout his narrative. But these works have also served to illustrate that between barbarians and Romans there was something more than a simple spatial boundary or a geographical *limes*; there was a "temporal frontier" too, especially related to the political system the societies lived in, and another border, perhaps less visible but deeply imbedded and having to do with cultural self-definition: that of identity. It is on this double frontier—political and cultural—that I would like to center the analysis of *virtus* in Tacitus' shorter works.[5] Some of the questions to be dealt with in this section are the way in which Roman *virtus* is challenged or even threatened when peoples outside the border of the Roman Empire can be also defined and identified for their *virtus*; and in what respect *virtus Romana* differs—if at all—from the *virtus* of these Britons and Germans.

Even though the *Agricola* and the *Germania* play different roles in the definition and interpretation of Roman *virtus* under the principate, and represent different literary genres, their central preoccupation and goals have some common ground. Their message—somewhat hidden under the surface of biographical or ethnographical elements—emphasizes the same idea: it is still possible for the Romans to exercise *virtus* and to live with *libertas* under the

---

4. Sinclair, "Rhetorical Generalizations in *Annales* 1–6," 2828. See also Martin, *Tacitus*, 243.

5. As my analysis of *virtus* is mainly through the historical works, I have left out the *Dialogus de Oratoribus*, where *virtus* is used only twice (both in chapter 31) in the plural meaning "good qualities" in general. For the *Dialogus*, see, for example, Mayer, *Tacitus*; and lately, van den Berg, *World of Tacitus' Dialogus de Oratoribus* (with bibliography).

rule of one man. In the same way as the Romans had adapted—with varying success—to the political changes of the last century, they would have to adapt their system of values too by integrating new qualities, while remaining Roman to the core.

There are some common elements that I have identified in Tacitus' *Agricola* and *Germania*. In the first place, the importance of the idea of an active type of *virtus* and an active man of *virtus* appears prominently in both works. Tacitus was especially concerned with political *virtus*, and so, for him, political action was the real field where *virtus* could be proven. For a Roman this meant primarily serving the *res publica* actively, as will be shown especially in the case of Agricola. The second overarching element in Tacitus' redefinition of *virtus* is its very individual and personal relation to freedom or *libertas*, no matter which society or activity—Roman or not—he was talking about. The third aspect common to these works seems harder to pin down, but is perhaps the one that gives coherence and unity to the other two: the need for flexibility. For Roman values to survive, they had to be adjusted to the new times and the new political game; it was important to realize that there was not only one rigid, static way of being Roman. When Tacitus gave a detailed account of the peoples in Britannia or Germania, or when he compared Roman society in the past and in the present, he did it with a purpose. Illustrating other possible behaviors would show the Romans that there were various ways of being a true Roman. The typically Roman claim to the *mores maiorum* would be in vain if the *maiores* were invoked merely as a reason for maintaining something unchanged. In that case, they would be unable to provide real role models, and definitely incapable of being the foundation of values for a society in which exemplarity played such an important role.

Virtus Romana *under Domitian*

The life of his father-in-law was for Tacitus a source of inspiration for how men should behave under a *princeps*. Tacitus' first work, the *Agricola*, was at the same time a record of the deeds and ways of eminent men (*clarorum virorum facta moresque*),[6] and a detailed description of a particular province of the empire and its inhabitants during a given period.[7] The historian chooses

---

6. Tac. *Agr*, 1.1.

7. For the complex identification of an exact genre for the *Agricola*, see Marincola, "Genre, Convention and Innovation in Greco-Roman Historiography," 281–324, esp. 318. See also Ogilvie and Richmond, *Tacitus: Agricola*, 11; and Dorey, "Agricola and Germania," 1–4; and more recently, Sailor, *Writing and Empire in Tacitus*, 116–18; Woodman (with Kraus), *Tacitus: Agricola*.

this topic to refer to the complex account of *virtus* and *libertas* not only under bad rulers but also in a non-Roman society. He is going to weave together the biography of an outstanding Roman with the description of a society on the borders of the empire that little by little becomes Roman.

For the description of Roman *virtus* under Domitian, Agricola seems the obvious place to start. Tacitus presents Agricola as an honest, virtuous Roman, particularly admired for his *moderatio*.[8] Moderation appeared as a sort of prerequisite for Romans to maintain a certain amount of *libertas* and independence from the emperors, and Agricola certainly represents its champion under Domitian's regime. The principate had rearranged the republican values, and *moderatio* had come to be very near the top of the list.[9] Apart from setting moderation as a more appropriate and low-profile way of showing *virtus* under the principate, Tacitus qualifies this *modestia* as something industrious and vigorous, of which Agricola's life offers a very clear model.[10] The *Agricola* illustrates, on the one hand, the importance of a moderate man and the practice of *modestia* under a tyrant, and on the other, the need to be always active in service of the state.

Tacitus starts his description of Agricola by going back to his family so as to show that young Agricola had not been lacking *exempla virtutis*: his father had been courageous in refusing to do wrong by following Caligula's wishes, and his mother had had a woman's most valued virtue: chastity.[11] To this was added a life lived with refinement and simplicity in Massilia, which was a good basis for enabling the virtues of their son to flourish too.

Agricola found an opportunity to show his *moderatio* from his early youth when, being inclined to devote too much time and energy to the study of philosophy, he followed his mother's prudent advice (*prudentia matris*) and soon managed to be knowledgeable, while still keeping a sense of proportion (*ex sapientia modum*).[12] It is this *modus* or measure that, according to Tacitus, would become proverbial in Agricola's life. We can see that his craving for philosophy was restrained with moderation, but not totally obliterated. He controlled his passion with temperance, but did not give up his occupation:

---

8. Scholars have duly noted Agricola's *moderatio*; see, for example, Liebeschuetz, "Theme of Liberty," esp. 134; Ogilvie and Richmond, *Tacitus: Agricola*, esp. 17; Martin, *Tacitus*, esp. 25, and "Tacitus on Agricola," 9–12; Classen, "Tacitus—Historian between Republic and Principate," esp. 115–16; Clarke, "Island Nation," esp. 112.

9. For *moderatio*, see chapter 4 in this book.

10. Tac. *Agr*, 42.4: *modestia, si industria ac vigor adsint, eo laudis excedere*.

11. Cf. Tac. *Agr*, 4.1 and 4.2, respectively.

12. Cf. Tac. *Agr*, 4.3.

he remained active and sensible. It is possible to observe this same pattern in his military training as well.[13]

Agricola's martial merits are given in the first place: he was brave; he kept strict discipline without falling into the self-indulgence typical of young soldiers; he made himself known to the army, learned from experts, and followed the best examples.[14] In this respect, Tacitus follows a traditional Roman approach, attributing military *virtus*, the highest and foremost Roman quality, to Agricola.[15] Furthermore, he describes his father-in-law as the perfect balance of conduct between caution and eagerness, "aspiring to nothing in bravado, yet shrinking from nothing in fear [*nihil adpetere in iactationem, nihil ob formidine recusare*]."[16] Once again, prudence and action are apparent. Thus, the desire for military distinction grew in young Agricola's heart, despite the unwelcoming attitude of the age toward any kind of eminence. According to Tacitus, the struggle to achieve this *gloria* by serving the state was one of Agricola's old-fashioned—or perhaps "republican"—and very characteristic Roman traits.

Tacitus also tells us about Agricola's offices, portraying an energetic *cursus honorum*: he was military tribune in Britannia under Suetonius Paulinus from 58 to 62, quaestor in the province of Asia in 64; back in Rome he was tribune of the plebs in 66 and praetor in 68. Agricola is presented as a successful young man—he was only twenty-eight when Nero died—who devoted himself to actively serving the state following the traditional *cursus honorum*, even though the real honors of this career were much diminished in the principate. Tacitus' references to *otium* (ease) and *quies* (tranquility) in 6.3 seem to refer here more to the quiet and unassuming way in which Agricola held his posts rather than to actual passivity,[17] because he did hold games and performed the proper activities of a person in office, but he managed to keep a "mean between thrift and lavishness [*medio rationis atque abundantiae duxit*]."[18] After Nero's death, Agricola passed to Vespasian's side and obeyed Mucianus' orders honestly and vigorously (*integreque ac strenue*).[19] He was given the difficult task of quieting the Twentieth Legion and making it loyal to Vespasian, a task that could have been carried out with punishments and harshness but

---

13. Tac. *Agr*, 5.1: *neque licenter ... neque segniter*.
14. Cf. Tac. *Agr*, 5.1: *sed noscere provinciam, nosci exercitui, discere a peritis, sequi optimos*.
15. For young Agricola's *virtus*, see 8.3 and 9.4.
16. Tac. *Agr*, 5.1.
17. Tac. *Agr*, 6.3: *tribunatus annum quiete et otio transiit*.
18. Tac. *Agr*, 6.5.
19. Tac. *Agr*, 7.3; note the active sense of the adverb *strenue*.

that was achieved by Agricola with *rarissima moderatio*.²⁰ Chapters 7 to 9 of the work are devoted to the different virtues that Agricola possessed: he tempered his energy, checked his excessive enthusiasm, and respectfully obeyed his superior; he combined duty, work, and danger with success and personal distinction, escaping envy without missing glory.²¹ These good qualities were all his own personal achievements: he could not have found either encouragement or models under Domitian, and this made him all the more admirable. Besides, Agricola also possessed the rare quality of being amiable without impairing his authority; affectionate, yet strict (*nec illi . . . aut facilitas auctoritatem aut severitas amorem deminuit*).²²

According to Tacitus, once in Britain, Agricola stood out as a general for his resourcefulness (*ratio*) in planning, and his firmness (*constantia*) in choosing hard work and peril.²³ Like a good general of old, he restored discipline in the army, and was the first in the march, praising the energetic and rebuking the indolent along the way.²⁴ In governing his province, he conducted public business with justice and discipline, yet leniently.²⁵ As a result, he was regarded as a brilliant and great man (*clarus ac magnus*), and his glory increased.²⁶ Agricola seemed to have carried out the conquest and "Romanization" of Britain successfully, and Tacitus adds that his attitude toward the vanquished went beyond simple *clementia*, as he began to train the sons of the chieftains in a liberal education (*liberalibus artibus*) and to prefer the native talents of the Britons over those of the Gauls.²⁷

There were lots of things that Agricola "could have done" with the excuse that "everybody did them" but chose not to. He did not corrupt his office by choosing his staff on the basis of personal likings or private recommendation;²⁸ he could have punished the soldiers harshly, and boasted of his military exploits, or even his virtues. All this is part of Agricola's *moderatio* which, for Tacitus, would play a particularly important role in his career. But still more important than the things that Agricola refrained from doing were the

---

20. Cf. Tac. *Agr*, 7.3.
21. Agricola's virtues: *pietas* (7.2); *moderatio* (7.3); *temperantia* (8.1); *modestia* (8.3); *verecundia* (8.3); *prudentia* (9.2); *iustitia, gravitas, severitas, misericordia* (9.3); *integritas, abstinentia* (9.4).
22. Tac. *Agr*, 9.4.
23. Cf. Tac. *Agr*, 18.4–6.
24. Cf. Tac. *Agr*, 20–21. See also 36–37 for his role in the battle of Mons Graupius.
25. Cf. Tac. *Agr*, 19.
26. Cf. Tac. *Agr*, 18.4–6.
27. Tac. *Agr*, 21.2.
28. Cf. Tac. *Agr*, 19.2. See also 6.2 regarding his term of office in Asia.

things that he did achieve. Many of these achievements are told to us by Tacitus through Agricola himself in the speech delivered before the battle of Mons Graupius in A.D. 84: campaigns, battles, conquered lands, perils, and successes.[29]

But according to Tacitus, Agricola's feats were greeted by the emperor with unease.[30] The times were cruel and cynical toward virtues (*tam saeva et infesta virtutibus tempora*),[31] and Domitian could not but contrast his own recent faked triumph over the Germans—where he had in fact purchased people who could look like prisoners—with Agricola's real and decisive victory with enemies slain in the thousands. Everything else was to no avail if someone could rob the prince of his military distinction (*militarem gloriam*). Glory won in the battlefield was still the main source of honor by Roman standards, or at least the most valued one, and Domitian was defeated in this. Moreover, Tacitus emphasizes Agricola's active performance by narrating his indisputable feats and contrasting them not with Domitian's actions but with his ambiguous thoughts and feelings.

For Tacitus, Agricola possessed the rare combination of truly behaving like the *maiores* and, at the same time, adapting to the times in which he was living. Agricola's flexibility in the cloudy waters of politics during the principate is manifested above all in that precisely when everything seemed triumph and victory for him, he retired from the limelight and went back to the obscurity of a *privatus*, contenting himself with a simple life.[32] Tacitus shows that Agricola was shrewd enough to realize that "qualities of other kinds could be more easily overlooked, but good generalship was the emperor's *virtus*."[33] Domitian could not bear a successful general to have the quality that was proper to an emperor.[34] The fear of being outdone by anyone in any aspect, but especially in *virtus*, became almost an obsession to the emperors; and we shall see later on how the *principes* kept a keen eye on good men and consequently the mere existence of anyone who excelled in *virtus* became dangerous.

---

29. Cf. Tac. *Agr*, 33–34.
30. Tac. *Agr*, 39.1.
31. Tac. *Agr*, 1.4.
32. Liebeschuetz, "Theme of Liberty," 134, calls this the "realistic attitude" to empire.
33. *Ducis boni imperatoriam virtutem esse*: Tac. *Agr* 39.3, my translation. See Woodman (with Kraus), *Tacitus: Agricola*, ad loc. The Loeb ed. (1914, transl. Hutton, rev. Ogilvie, 1970) has *virtus* translated into the plural "qualities," which alters the meaning.
34. For the special relationship between Domitian and *virtus*, see Mattingly, *Coins of the Roman Empire in the British Museum, Volume 2: Vespasian to Domitian*, xci; and Tuck, "Origins of Roman Imperial Hunting Imagery," 221–45.

Agricola's retirement and *otium* came to an end when he was asked by the people to take command of the army and counteract the Romans' heavy losses in Moesia, Dacia, Germany, and Pannonia. His energy together with his firmness and experience in war (*vigorem, constantiam et expertum bellis animum*) were required once again, and his active qualities shone all the more in opposition to the sloth (*ignavia*), idleness (*inertia*), and panic (*formidine*) of the previous generals in charge.[35]

Agricola did not hold any other office or command afterward. If we follow Tacitus, it was Domitian who denied him the opportunity, but the narrative is so full of innuendo and *rumores* that alternative explanations may also have existed.[36] A striking fact for Tacitus is that Domitian's jealousy was after all somewhat diminished by Agricola's moderation and prudence (*moderatione tamen prudentiaque Agricolae leniebatur*).[37] And it is here, therefore, that Tacitus chooses to give us his conclusion with rare clarity: "that there can be great men even under bad emperors, and that duty and discretion, if coupled with energy and a career of action, will bring a man to no less glorious summits than are attained by perilous paths and ostentatious deaths that do not benefit the Commonwealth [*posse etiam sub malis principibus magnos viros esse, obsequiumque ac modestiam, si industria ac vigor adsint, eo laudis excedere, quo plerique per abrupta sed in nullum rei publicae usum ambitiosa morte inclaruerunt*]."[38] Agricola's life, not only by his wisdom and common sense but also by his active hard work, lies in between the two poles that Tacitus would describe later on in the *Annals* as repellent servility (*deforme obsequium*) and violent obstinacy (*abrupta contumacia*).[39] The moderation that Tacitus attributes to his father-in-law is not of a passive kind; it sits perfectly in the midpoint between rash courage and apathy or inaction. It was expedient for Tacitus to leave the question of Agricola's death open.[40] If Agricola had died by the emperor's hand, Tacitus' picture of Domitian as a tyrant would certainly have been complete; but on the other hand, he would not then have been able to say that great men could "live" under bad emperors. In some way Tacitus needed Agricola to have died a natural death in order to make it clear that glory in the principate was not restricted only to the moment of death,[41] but that a life of

---

35. Cf. Tac. *Agr*, 41.3–4.
36. Cf. Ogilvie and Richmond, *Tacitus: Agricola*, 283–84; 294.
37. Tac. *Agr*, 42.3.
38. Tac. *Agr*, 42.4. Birley's trans., 1999.
39. Cf. Tac. *Ann*, 4.20.
40. For the rumors about Agricola's death, see Shatzman, "Tacitean Rumours," 549–78.
41. Cf. Sailor, *Writing and Empire in Tacitus*, 114.

renown was also available to men who were willing to work hard rather than make an ostentatious display of independence (*inani iactatione libertatis*).[42]

In Tacitus' prayer for his dead father-in-law—a beautiful piece, eloquent of filial piety—he encourages his audience not only to contemplate Agricola's virtues but also to imitate them as a way of paying the ultimate tribute.[43] But this prayer, however final it may seem, is not the last homage that Tacitus gave to Agricola. He did something that would never end: he recorded his life for posterity; the *memoria virtutis* would live an independent life from its author and outlive him. This is his definitive tribute; this is what history is all about for Tacitus, *ne virtutes sileantur* (that virtues shall not lack their record):[44] "All that we have loved and admired in Agricola [his virtues] abides and shall abide in the hearts of men through the endless procession of ages, by the fame of his achievements [actions]."[45]

Up to now we have followed the *Agricola* as if it were a straightforward biography of Tacitus' father-in-law. The main message, that good men could live under bad rulers, was declared and proved clearly enough, but there were also a fair number of secondary messages that make the *Agricola* a less obvious work than is at first apparent. Agricola's moderation helped to redefine the virtue of *moderatio* and its role not only in the principate but also under tyranny; the "republican" and Roman stress on activity and achievement was still the main feature of men of *virtus*, even under an authoritarian political system, and *libertas* was no longer something you could only boast about or show off through flamboyant deeds—particularly in death—but something to exercise responsibly, sometimes submitting to power, but always retaining a core personal freedom. These topics will be looked at in greater detail when dealing with the *Annals* and *virtus* in the city of Rome.

But what are we to make of the detailed description of the Britons with reference to Agricola and Domitian's Rome? Did Tacitus need to give such a thorough account of the people of Britain, their battles, and their leaders? In

---

42. Tac. *Agr*, 42.3.

43. Cf. Tac. *Agr*, 46. It has, however, been argued by Luce, "Tacitus on History's Highest Function," 2904–27, that Tacitus is more interested in commemoration and he is not, by praising characters in his works, necessarily setting them as models for emulation.

44. Tac. *Ann*, 3.65.

45. Tac. *Agr*, 46.4. I am aware that there is a less rosy view of Agricola; see, for example, Batomsky, "Not-so-Perfect Man," 388–93; Hanson, *Agricola and the Conquest of the North*, and "Tacitus' *Agricola*," 1741–84. But while one can admit that some laudatory generalizations are scattered throughout the narrative (cf. Martin, "Tacitus on Agricola," 9–12), it is difficult to deny his factual achievements in Britain.

theory, perhaps they should either have acted as a foil to Agricola in order to emphasize his qualities more, or have represented the opposite of Agricola's values. But another explanation of Tacitus' careful account of the province of Britannia seems to show that the historian was looking for or intended to stress some of the same ideas he had also highlighted in Agricola's life, namely, *virtus*, freedom, and a life of action.

Tacitus was not only concerned with Roman *virtus* and *libertas*; he also cared for the nature of virtue and freedom themselves, even if their purest form was found outside Rome. In fact, what appeared to him as the noblest quality of the inhabitants of Britain was their spirited determination to maintain their freedom. Tacitus presents the Britons as subjects who have found the middle way of accepting an outsider as master, but without completely surrendering their freedom: "their submission, complete enough to involve obedience, does not involve slavery [*iam domiti ut pareant, nondum ut serviant*]."[46] The ability to preserve *libertas* is, therefore, given as the foremost quality of these peoples.

Britain had many geographical advantages: the location of the island, its wealth, even its weather had worked in its favor on different occasions.[47] The warriors were brave and wild—*feroces*—and they gave the Romans a tough time.[48] Tacitus compares the Britons with other barbarians, especially to point out the way in which they should maintain their pristine energy and not be debased or weakened by long years of peace: "The Gauls also according to history, once shone in war: afterward indolence [*segnitia*] made its appearance hand in hand with tranquility [*otio*], and courage and liberty have been lost together [*amissa virtute pariter ac libertate*]."[49] This had not happened yet to the Britons, but one can detect a note of warning in the comparison. One can see *libertas* and *virtus* again working together: freedom was a prerequisite for real bravery, and at the same time, courage was necessary for maintaining one's freedom. The Britons encouraged themselves to keep on fighting against the Romans through recalling the actions and bravery of their *maiores*—a very Roman thing to do: "the invaders would withdraw, as the late Julius had withdrawn, if Britons would but emulate the valor of their fathers [*virtutem maiorum suorum aemularentur*]."[50] Boudicca's revolt in the past was

46. Tac. *Agr*, 13.1.
47. Cf. Tac. *Agr*, 22.1–2. For the topic of Britannia being an island, with its political and ideological consequences, see Clarke, "Island Nation," 94–112.
48. Cf. Tac. *Agr*, 11.4.
49. Tac. *Agr*, 11.4.
50. Tac. *Agr*, 15.4.

an attempt to put this wish into practice, and though successful at first, the final results had been unfortunate for the Britons.[51] Tacitus also recalls other governors, such as Petronius Turpilianus, and Trebellius Maximus, who, though milder (*mitior*) and less energetic (*segnior*), kept the province quiet and inactive.[52] According to Tacitus, this dormant situation brought to the province more evil than good, because the barbarians learned to indulge the vices of *otium* and became idle. Tacitus seems to point out that the move toward inaction necessarily implied a move against freedom; the liberty and high spirit of previous generations of Britons had been the result of their energy and vigor in confronting adversity. Courage to preserve one's *libertas* necessarily meant an active, dynamic, and sometimes risky response to the circumstances.

Remaining free was also related to keeping one's own traditions alive and safe, and not falling in with somebody else's way of life. With time and ceaseless conquests, Britons, who "used to reject the Latin language, began to aspire to rhetoric: further, the wearing of our dress became a distinction, and the toga came into fashion, and little by little the Britons went astray into alluring vices: to the promenade, the bath, the well-appointed dinner table."[53] The effects of "Romanization" were not always presented as positive; blind imitation was seen here as a kind of enslavement, and Tacitus seemed keen to illustrate the stages and phases of the loss of liberty in Britain. Firstly, peace in the conquered land had brought *otium*, and with it came inaction. This inaction had fostered vices and sloth: the promenades, the baths, and the luxurious banquets. The inexperienced and simple natives called these ways of indulging idleness by the name of *humanitas*, whereas for Tacitus they were just *servitus*.[54] The historian insists on showing a strong link between inaction and slavery on the one hand, and energy and liberty on the other.

Even if the Britons' strong desire to maintain their freedom was diluted to a certain extent by the incorporation of Roman customs, freedom would still be the central idea and battle cry in the speech given by the British chief, Calgacus, before the final engagement against the Romans.[55] The speech—a

---

51. Cf. the Boudicca revolt (A.D. 61) in *Ann*, 14.31, clearly set off by the abuses of the Romans and focused around the *arx aeternae dominationis*. For Boudicca's revolt, see Webster, *Boudicca, the British Revolt against Rome*; and Mattingly, *Imperial Possession*, 107–113.

52. Cf. Tac. *Agr*, 16.3.

53. Tac. *Agr*, 21.2.

54. Cf. Tac. *Agr*, 21.2: *Idque apud imperitos humanitas vocabatur, cum pars servitutis esset*.

55. Cf. Ogilvie and Richmond, *Tacitus:Agricola*, comm. ad loc., who place this type of speech within a historiographical tradition. For the rhetorical elements of the speech, see Clarke, "Island Nation," 105; and Woodman (with Kraus), *Tacitus: Agricola*, comm. ad loc.

wonderful piece of Tacitean rhetoric and not at all what one could expect from a barbarian leader[56]—showed "the other side of the coin" regarding Roman conquest and domination:

> These deadly Romans, whose arrogance you cannot escape by obedience and self-restraint. Robbers of the world, now that earth fails their all-devastating hands, they probe even the sea: if their enemy have wealth, they have greed; if he be poor, they are ambitious; East nor West has glutted them; alone of mankind they covet with the same passion want as much as wealth. To plunder, butcher, steal, these things they misname empire: they make a desolation and call it peace.[57]

> *Et infestiores Romani, quorum superbiam frustra per obsequium ac modestiam effugias, raptores orbis, postquam cuncta vastantibus defuere terrae, iam mare scrutantur: si locuples hostis est, avari, si pauper ambitiosi, quos non Oriens, non Occidens satiaverit: soli omnium opes atque inopiam pari adfectu concupiscunt. Auferre trucidare rapere falsis nominibus imperium, atque ubi solitudinem faciunt, pacem appellant.*

This speech, like others that have been written by Roman historians from the point of view of the enemy, reveals Tacitus' flexibility and broadmindedness to be able to "think" and to "feel" as the enemy would have done toward Rome, but it does not necessarily mean that the author endorsed the feelings and views conveyed in it. On the other hand, the speech may reflect the author's opinion in another matter, namely, how the conquests were carried out in his own times. Ambiguity starts to appear: the times of the "Virgilian euphoria" of the *imperium sine fine* had passed,[58] and it seems that Tacitus was not sure whether they could transmit to other peoples the values that had made Rome great any more. The three Sallustian vices, which had magisterially described the republican crisis—*superbia*, *avaritia*, and *ambitio*—and which Tacitus assigns to the speech on Roman imperialism, give a definite negative tone to the process of conquest and show a change of values about the expansion of Rome. Her mission—neatly expressed in *tu regere imperio populos, Romane, memento* (you, Roman, be sure to rule the nations)[59]—has nothing to

---

56. For Walser, *Rom, das Reich und die Fremdem Völker in der Geschichtsschreibung der frühen Kaiserzeit*, 155–60, Calgacus was totally a Tacitean construction. Cf. also Fick, "Calgacus, héros breton," 235–48.
57. Tac. *Agr*, 30.3–5.
58. Virg. *Aen*, 1.279, although the end of the *Aeneid* brings a rather different idea to light.
59. Virg. *Aen*, 6.851.

do with the plundering, butchery, and stealing (*auferre, trucidare, rapere*) that we see in Tacitus through Calgacus' words.[60]

The speech as a whole is a hymn to *libertas*, and it is Calgacus' only appeal to stir up the Britons to fight. Freedom calls for action. Their *animus*, their *virtus*, their *ferocitas* even are summoned to the fore, and they are reminded that it was their own inactivity (*socordia*) that had prevented them from throwing off the yoke of their masters.[61] Calgacus urges them to "fight as men uncorrupted and unconquered, men who have been trained for freedom not for regrets."[62] The adjectives *integri* and *indomiti* are given here to emphasize once again the contrast between the Britons and the Romans. To disparage the enemy's valor, Calgacus ponders upon the actual greatness of the so-called Roman *virtus*, and the outcome is not very flattering to the Romans: "it is our dissensions and feuds that bring them fame: their enemy's mistake becomes their army's glory."[63] The chieftain reminds his soldiers that the Roman army they are fighting is not the same as that which had conquered Carthage: the amount of courage (*virtus*) they show in battle does not match the wantonness (*lascivia*) they have in peace.[64]

Calgacus' appeal to *virtus* and *libertas* somehow expressed what being a Roman was all about, and it has been argued that Britain in the *Agricola* appeared as a "republican space."[65] Britons are at present what Romans had been in the past. There is a temporal frontier between the two. Tacitus illustrated to the Romans where the true values were maintained in those times, and how little it took for them to disappear under new vices of idleness that became new values. For how long would Britain be able to live in this "republican space," resisting the Roman temptation of idle submission? How soon, by succumbing to it, would she lose her *virtus* and *libertas* as the Gauls had done?[66]

When Tacitus introduced these Britons as barbarians who were still brave and free, and contrasted their attitudes with the *virtus* of Agricola, he presented Romans with the idea that *virtus* was not something rigid or univocal.

---

60. Cf. Tac. *Agr*, 30.5. For historians' critique of Roman imperialism, see Griffin, "Iure plectimur," 85–111.
61. Cf. Tac. *Agr*, 31.3–4.
62. Tac. *Agr*, 31.4.
63. Tac. *Agr*, 32.1: *nostris illi dissensionibus ac discordiis clari vitia hostium in gloriam exercitus sui vertunt*.
64. Tac. *Agr*, 32.1: *An eandem Romanis in bello virtutis quam in pace lasciviam adesse creditis?*
65. Cf. Sailor, *Writing and Empire in Tacitus*, 92. See also Rutledge, "Tacitus in Tartan," 75–95; Clarke, "Island Nation," 94–112.
66. Cf. Tac. *Agr*, 11.4.

There were multiple ways of showing *virtus*, manifesting multiple ways of exercising *libertas*. First, there was a political freedom: the freedom that senators in the republic used to exercise, namely, the right to express one's own opinion freely on political matters. For Tacitus, this *libertas* seemed now lost, and it had been *olim dissociabilis* (for a long time irreconcilable) with the principate. Second, there was also the liberty of the *indomiti*, the peoples who had not been yet conquered by the Romans. Third and very near second, there was the liberty that subjected nations, like the Britons, were still able to preserve by avoiding servility in their behavior toward their masters. Another type of freedom was the personal kind mainly portrayed in Agricola, the man who remains free before a tyrant, not feeling forced to act in a particular way by the circumstances. This was a difficult and demanding type of freedom, which required more inner strength than the other kinds and whose rewards were immaterial. This fortitude was manifested particularly in the virtue of *constantia* which belonged to the sort of man whom no adversity would prevent from accomplishing his purpose or resolution.[67] To be able to exercise one or many of these "freedoms," one needed the essential *virtus* or courage to put up with the consequences. Freedom was available to all, but paradoxically could not be obtained for free.

With the excuse of writing a biography of his father-in-law, Tacitus gives a complex account of freedom and *virtus*, not only under bad rulers but also in a non-Roman society. His conclusion is that these terms are not completely outdated; they are still in force but are manifested differently on either side of the frontier. In Britannia they mainly represented republican values; in Rome, although they could still be found, it was necessary to look for them from the new and more restricted angle of the principate. What Tacitus really condemned in Rome and in Britain was being carried away by *desidia* (sloth) and *inertia* (inactivity). Hence the stress on *industria* and *vigor* in Tacitus' conclusion: *virtus* had to be performed with perseverance and energy. On this side of the *limes*, under the rule of one, the emphasis was more on *constantia* and *moderatio*; on the other side, in the "republican space," the stress was more on vigor and competitive spirit.

Beyond the Rhine: Virtus *in the* Germania

Even though at first sight the *Germania* looks totally different from the *Agricola*, on a second reading one can observe similar aims: the same insistence on

---

67. For Agricola's *constantia*, see 18.3; 41.3.

the freshness of the barbarians' courage and their indomitable independence of spirit.

Right from the beginning of the *Germania*—which in some way recalls the opening of Caesar's *Gallic Wars*—Tacitus places the reader at a frontier: in space, in time, and in character, the Germans will be very different from the Romans. The geographical and spatial description is powerful and precise; by trying to illustrate and explain *de origine et situ Germanorum* the author is somehow aiming to achieve a certain control of the land and its people. It has been argued that in some way Tacitus "conquered" Germania through his writing—as Caesar had done with Gaul through his wars and commentaries—by incorporating it into the Roman literary world.[68] With this work of ethnography,[69] Tacitus is expressing something more than just curiosity to understand German culture or a desire to make Romans aware of this powerful barbarian nation. To say that the author intended no moral or political teaching, except to warn the Romans of the German menace, may be somewhat overhasty.[70] One can argue that the *Germania* was not a historical work "proper,"[71] but it certainly aimed at identification and self-definition, and these categories in Roman writing were indeed moral and political.

On the other hand, the view that Tacitus idealized the German tribes and held them up as a mirror of morals for the corrupted Romans of his time, though true in some respects, has by now lost some of its force, and could be an oversimplification in the reading of the *Germania*.[72] As will become clear in this section, Tacitus' *Germania*, read together with the *Agricola*, shows that essential *libertas*, meaning freedom from a master, and *prisca virtus*, or the courage displayed in wars to preserve this freedom, were present in Tacitus' time in more primitive societies, and they acted as a contrast to Rome not only in the moral sphere—showing barbarians' virtues as against Romans' vices—but also in the political one, contrasting the ways in which political cultures functioned: the republican competitiveness found among the barbarians beyond the frontiers, with the submissiveness to the emperor evident in Rome.

---

68. Cf. Rives, *Tacitus: Germania*, 56. Cf. Nicolet, *Space, Geography, and Politics*.

69. Cf. Marincola, "Genre, Convention and Innovation," 296.

70. Cf. Warmington's introduction to the *Germania* in the Loeb rev. ed. of 1970, 120. For the purpose of the *Germania*, see, for example, Lund, "Zur Gesamtinterpretation der '*Germania*' des Tacitus," 1857–1988; Perl, "Interpretationen der *Germania* des Tacitus mit Hilfe romischer Denkmäler," 99–116; and Rives, *Tacitus: Germania*, esp. 48–56.

71. For the specific characteristics of the ethnographic tradition, see Rives, *Tacitus: Germania*, 11–21.

72. Cf. Dorey, "*Agricola* and *Germania*," 12–13.

The new virtues needed in Rome at that time derived from the new political system. *Moderatio, constantia,* and the like could develop more naturally in the people under an autocratic regime, as we will see in the *Histories* and the *Annals*.[73] By contrast, these same virtues were nowhere to be seen in the fierce society of the German tribes: one man's bravery against another's could not foster *moderatio*, but only rivalry; *virtus* against *virtus* shown in war achieved *gloria*, the opposite of moderation, and their tireless fight for freedom brought the Germans only disorder and internal quarrels, not *constantia*, which meant mainly steadiness and dependability.

The second part of the work is dedicated to a description of individual tribes, and we see many ethnic groups with similarities and differences among them. However, Tacitus does not only give an exhaustive account of the German peoples with encyclopedic precision; he also opens and widens the Roman imagination. On the one hand, he is concerned with the "otherness" of German tribes as opposed to the Romans, and on the other, he is adamant in transmitting a message. If the Romans could grasp his idea, this would be advantageous not only for their political understanding of the future threat that Germania could pose to Rome but also for the present situation: learning about the ways and customs of the people who lived beyond the *limes* would help the Romans to identify, assess, and check their own more effectively.

Tacitus emphasizes primarily the ethnic and spatial differences between the Romans and the Germans, but he also emphasizes a politico-temporal one. In some respects, the Germans—like the Britons—appeared to behave as the Romans had done in earlier times,[74] and although they were contemporary societies, they seemed to be practicing a different code of values. In redefining what it meant to be Roman under the new circumstances of autocracy—and even under tyranny—Tacitus' *Germania* challenges the Romans to look around them, not necessarily to imitate others or to revert to their previous modes of conduct, but to strengthen the foundations of the real motives of their behavior under a *princeps*. Thus, the *Germania*, like the rest of Tacitus' works, needed an alert Roman reader to be able to draw out the moral and political lessons, especially the political ones.

The author approaches his topic with implicit praise for the Germans: marriage and chastity were taken seriously, and that was probably the highest

---

73. This did not mean, however, that it was easy to cultivate them.
74. Cf. O'Gorman, "No Place like Rome," 146.

point in their character;[75] good habits carried more force than good laws elsewhere;[76] and the Germanic concept of *virtus* is given by Tacitus a prominent place in his description: "when the battlefield is reached it is a reproach for a chief to be surpassed in courage [*virtus*]; a reproach for his retinue not to equal the courage [*virtus*] of its chief: but to have left the field and survived one's chief, this means lifelong infamy and shame."[77] It is clear that for Tacitus these practices were highly commendable; so too was the election of kings and generals for their nobility and bravery: *reges ex nobilitate, duces ex virtute sumunt*.[78] Germanic tribes seemed to have pinned their hopes for war upon firm and trustworthy foundations; they relied above all on courage and did not count too much on luck: *fortunam inter dubia, virtutem inter certa numerare*.[79]

In the individual description of the tribes in the second part of the *Germania*,[80] the key word is again *virtus*. The valor of the Germans received the highest praise. The Batavi are *virtute praecipui*,[81] the Chatti have their name linked with *virtus* on at least three occasions,[82] the Chauci are also *praecipui virtute*,[83] and the Cimbri have proved their *virtus* against the Roman army since the end of the second century B.C.[84] All the peoples described by Tacitus excel in *virtus* in one way or another. The Romans had experienced this firsthand, and Tacitus recalls, "Neither the Samnites, nor the Carthaginians, neither Spain nor Gaul, not even the Parthians have taught us more lessons. The German fighting for liberty has been a keener enemy than the absolutism of Arsaces."[85] They had become more dangerous than any other nation because they defended their freedom more vigorously. The German *virtus* could be practiced everywhere because they were free, and at the same time, with their *virtus* they fought for and preserved their *libertas*.

But courage was not the only virtue to be praised in the Germans. Even though the traditional view that defined *Germania* as the land of the "noble savage" has changed, there are certainly enough elements for Tacitus to show the high moral standards of the German tribes. They were not ambitious for

---

75. Tac. *Germ*, 18.1 and 19.1.
76. Tac. *Germ*, 19.5: *plusque ibi boni mores valent quam alibi bonae leges*.
77. Tac. *Germ*, 14.1.
78. Tac. *Germ*, 7.1.
79. Tac. *Germ*, 30.2.
80. From chap. 28 to 37.
81. Tac. *Germ*, 29.1.
82. Cf. Tac. *Germ*, 30.2; 31.1; 31.3.
83. Tac. *Germ*, 35.4.
84. Cf. Tac. *Germ*, 37.2.
85. Tac. *Germ*, 37.3: *quippe regno Arsacis acrior est Germanorum libertus*.

gold or silver, and what was more, they were not affected by the possession of those things;[86] good example was of more value to the general in controlling his people than commands;[87] they had a simple diet;[88] and in their burials there was no ostentation.[89]

Sometimes Tacitus described the Germanic customs in a way that made them more relevant to his own times, and although he did not make explicit references to Rome, it was evident that the comparison should arise in the reader's mind: "there is no arena with its seductions, no dinner-tables with their provocations to corrupt them. Of the exchange of secret letters men and women alike are innocent; adulteries are very few for the number of people.... For prostituted chastity there is no pardon (...). No one laughs at vice there; no one calls seduction, suffered or wrought, the spirit of the age."[90] The allusions could not be clearer.

But were the Germans simply the same as the Romans had been in past times? One side of the *Germania* has, of course, a tone of reproach regarding the abandonment of Roman native qualities, namely, *virtus* and *libertas*. But the other side of the work can lead us to infer that precisely these two qualities, present in the Germans, were tainted with a touch of unruliness or *indisciplina* which was particularly manifested in a general unconcern toward the well-being of the commonwealth. This German flaw is illustrated especially in the description of their times of peace. When in war, the Germans fought for freedom courageously, and that was certainly commendable, but when peace came, they spent all their time eating, drinking, and sleeping.[91] Drunkenness and revelry were the main occupations of these barbarians when they were not engaged in battle.[92] Tacitus gives no evidence of moderation in the Germans, who let themselves be carried away equally by their desires to fight and by their compulsion to satisfy their basic needs. Furthermore, they were not accustomed to hard work, for which they had no patience or constancy.[93] In peacetime, the best and bravest did nothing (*nihil agens*) to secure their homes

---

86. Cf. Tac. *Germ*, 5.4.
87. Cf. Tac. *Germ*, 7.2.
88. Cf. Tac. *Germ*, 23.
89. Cf. Tac. *Germ*, 27.
90. Tac. *Germ*, 19: (...) *nullis spectaculorum inlecebris, nullis conviviorum inritationibus corruptae. Litterarum secreta viri pariter ac feminae ignorant. Paucissima in tam numerosa gente adulteria* (...) *publicatae enim pudicitiae nulla venia* (...) . *Nemo enim illic vitia ridet, nec corrumpere et corrumpi saeculum vocatur.*
91. Cf. Tac. *Germ*, 15.1.
92. Cf. Tac. *Germ*, 23–24.
93. Cf. Tac. *Germ*, 4.3: *laboris atque operum non eadem patientia.*

or serve the state or even toward establishing one; on the contrary, they left everything to women and old men.[94] This inaction regarding the *res publica*—something alien, at least in their discourse, to republican Romans—was silently censured by Tacitus and could be seen as an admonition to the Romans of his own times. By alerting Romans against idleness and inertia,[95] to which it seemed so easy to fall under the emperors, Tacitus appears to be spurring them on to active collaboration in the perpetuation of the state: he reminds his audience that for the Romans—unlike the barbarian Germans—the *res publica* was always everybody's concern and responsibility. The wild *virtus* of the Germans was admirable, and through it they had been able to preserve a certain amount of political *libertas* from a foreign master, but the Romans under a *princeps* were in a different situation. They needed to "domesticate" their ancestral valor in their desires to excel in glory through the temperance of self-control (*moderatio*), and to "tame" their aspirations of unlimited freedom by remaining firm and steady in their purpose (*constantia*), not being overcome by the temptation to indolence which could accompany obedience. Taming and domesticating republican political competitiveness implied some adaptability on the one hand, but the same energy and hard work to achieve the goal on the other.

Tacitus' Germans could not be simply compared to or put on a par with the old Romans. Both peoples had courage and freedom as their supreme values, but the *virtus* and *libertas* in the Romans—as well as their novel manifestations under the principate—were permeated with an *industria* toward the *res publica* that was not to be seen in the Germans, who had a tendency toward inaction in peacetime, according to the historian. Perhaps it was precisely this *industria* that enabled the Romans to adapt their *virtus* and display *moderatio* and *constantia* later on. Their traditional *labor, patientia,* and *gravitas* had trained them toward the acquisition of these more sophisticated virtues. In Tacitus' categories it was difficult for a barbarian to be moderate or constant. These qualities appeared as virtues for "civilized" people; people who having experienced the dramatic fall from freedom to slavery were now finding out how to recover their liberty. And yet, there were some Romans who still preferred to move within the comfortable boundaries of the old *virtus* and the old *libertas*, as the Germans did. They seemed to have forgotten that together with the splendor of bravery, *virtus* in Rome always meant active work in the

---

94. Cf. Tac. *Germ,* 15.1.
95. For references to *inertia* and *otium* meaning inaction, see Tac. *Germ,* 15.1–2; 28.4; 36.2; 37.6; 44.3; 45.4.

service of the state, service that sometimes could require more effort and bring less glory. We will come back to this point in our analysis of the *Annals* later in this chapter.

In the *Germania* we are confronted with more "basic" types of courage and freedom. In a warrior society, courage is shown in war, and liberty means the freedom of not being subjected to anybody's power. This *prisca virtus* and *libertas*, together with responsibility toward the community and being actively concerned for the welfare of the state, had once been the privileges of the Romans. Now, however, they needed to move with more care and caution in the uncertain waters of the principate, so that these values required redefinition. The *Germania* shows that other societies with simpler versions of politics could keep their native versions of *virtus Romana* to a certain extent. It was only in Rome, with the changes in her political system, that people had to readjust, and transform this *virtus* by learning how to put it into practice with moderation and firmness of purpose when fighting bravely for personal liberty under an autocrat.

In the *Agricola* and the *Germania*, Tacitus presents a concept of *virtus* that, although at first sight it might seem similar to the primitive Roman concept—indeed, Tacitus himself also encourages Romans to imitate this barbarian *virtus*—is in truth deeply different. Subtly, the historian reveals an identity boundary, a cultural frontier between Romans and barbarians. To understand Roman *virtus*, one needs to consider one of its essential components: active service for the *res publica*. This is perfectly exemplified in Agricola's political career, which does not leave any room for barbarian *desidia*. Roman *virtus*, then, has an eminently political connotation: it must be shown and proved in political action. This *virtus* also manifests itself in the flexibility necessary to find an adequate answer to whichever political situation the Romans may find themselves dealing with: the proper characteristics of *virtus* during the republic are not exactly the same as those of the principate, as one can see specifically in the moderation and constancy of Agricola under a despot. The redefinition and reevaluation of important political concepts made by Tacitus may have helped the Romans to be more aware of the changes they were undergoing, and to some extent, the historian's *exempla* may also have influenced the manner in which they would react to these changes.

The northern frontier of the empire inhabited by Britons and Germans, instead, meant for Tacitus a place where the essentials of freedom and courage could perhaps be found more easily or more abundantly than in Rome itself, but at the same time, this *virtus* and *libertas* were more primitive and basic and expressed a more natural and less sophisticated phenomenon. The courageous struggle to maintain freedom—personal or community—can be seen as something proper to any society, and it plays an important role in the historian's view of the more general panorama of the history of any people.

It could be argued that beyond what Tacitus actually said in his *Agricola* and *Germania*, the definition of a key concept such as *virtus*—essential to an understanding of what it meant to be Roman—was irremediably linked with the political system. To practice *virtus* in a barbarian space was not the same as practicing *virtus* in Rome; and practicing *virtus* in a republic was not the same as practicing it in an imperial and autocratic regime such as Rome in the first century A.D. When one's identity is partly bound up with the political system, to change it can involve a fracture in the foundations of one's very self. The way in which this identity breakdown was experienced in Rome is what Tacitus would show in a masterly way in his two great subsequent works: the *Histories* and the *Annals*.

The *Histories*: Roman *Virtus* in Imperial Civil War

The number of occurrences of the word *virtus* falls dramatically from the *Agricola* to the *Histories*. This can be explained partly by the different levels of military activity under the emperors of that time.[96] Under Domitian, the time of the *Agricola*, there were many active wars: in Gaul with the Chatti, across the Danube with the Suebi, the conquest of Britannia, and wars against the Dacians and Sarmatians, so that *virtus Romana* had plenty of opportunities to shine forth. Under Nero, however, the Parthian war was the only really serious one, and that had been concluded in A.D. 63. In A.D. 69, then, when the civil wars started, the generals encountered idle and undisciplined soldiers, and their main objective should have been to train them again as befitted the Roman army. But this was not possible because of the presence of factions and groups following this or that commander, and thus there could be no agreement on a united imperial strategy toward allies or enemies.

However, this is not the only possible explanation for the decrease in references to *virtus* in the *Histories*. The civil wars produced by the violent struggles and competition of the would-be emperors in A.D. 69 promoted—besides

---

96. *Virtus* and its plural appear twenty-seven times in the *Agricola*, and fifty-two times in the *Histories*. Given the length of the extant works, the *Histories* being eight times longer than the *Agricola*, this means an occurrence of 0.62 per page of *virtus* in the *Agricola* and 0.15 per page in the *Histories*.

military disorder and political chaos—very individualistic goals that prevented action for the good of the *res publica* as a whole. Therefore it interfered with one of the central aims of the practice of real *virtus*. Tacitus announces the subject matter of his *Historiae* in general terms: not only civil wars, but civil wars under the rule of one, and he somehow prepares the reader to face new and really terrible things: "The history on which I am entering is that of a period rich in disasters, terrible with battles, torn by civil struggles, horrible even in peace. Four emperors fell by the sword; there were three civil wars, still more against foreigners, and often both at the same time [*Opus adgredior opimum casibus, atrox proeliis, discors seditionibus, ipsa etiam pace saevum. Quattuor principes ferro interempti: trina bella civilia, plura externa ac plerumque permixta*]."[97]

It is difficult to imagine the actual effect that these facts had on the people of those times. Without realizing it perhaps, throughout the centuries, Tacitus' audiences have become somewhat impervious to the real situation of Rome in A.D. 68–69, and have taken the historian's version with a pinch of detachment. Tacitus' panorama of the Roman Empire—cruel wars and endless conquests in the provinces, and in the city, disorder and murder—is certainly fixed in his readers' minds, but in a sort of "matter-of-fact way" that by now may not touch us very deeply. Perhaps we are not wholly shocked when we read that four emperors were savagely assassinated; we may think that almost all of them died like that anyway. Tacitus' narrative and style have been in some sense "counterproductive"; we have read about and studied these events so much that now they appear overfamiliar and we have got used to them. It seems necessary, then, to visualize the actual panorama that the historian is describing if we are to be able to weigh the interactions and dynamics of the actors in the *Histories* and the consequences of civil war.

Rome had undergone other serious crises in her political history: the one in A.D. 68–69 was not the first and would not be the last. Roman history had seen bad generals, selfish consuls, self-centered senators, and rebellious people before. But what seemed novel and worthy of recording for posterity was that all this happened simultaneously; there was a generalized state of confusion and distrust at all levels of society. For the historian, the days were so turbulent that not even heaven missed the opportunity of darkening the

---

97. Tac. *Hist*, 1.2. Thus, Damon, *Tacitus, Histories: Book 1*, 6, says of Woodman's comment, "To say that 'his interest in the disasters centers primarily on their capacity to furnish gripping narrative material' (Woodman, *Rhetoric in Classical Historiography*, 167) is to ignore the note of moral seriousness first sounded in *cura posteritatis* and heard on every page of T.'s historical work."

scene.⁹⁸ The vicissitudes of human affairs were matched by strange signs and portents in nature, and never was it so powerfully demonstrated that the gods intended to punish men.⁹⁹ Tacitus claims that there was a generalized weakness in the people that brought out the worst in them: "the leading men of the Senate were weak from old age [*aetate invalidi*] and had grown inactive [*desides*] through a long peace; the nobility was indolent and had forgotten the art of war [*segnis et oblita bellorum*]; the knights were ignorant [*ignari*] of military service; the more all tried to conceal their fear, the more evident they made their terror [*manifestius pavidi*]."¹⁰⁰ He clearly portrays the sense of insecurity, messiness, and chaos that was probably what people were feeling at that time with a particular choice of strong words:

> The cities on the rich fertile shores of Campania were swallowed up or overwhelmed; Rome was devastated by conflagrations, in which her most ancient shrines were consumed and the very Capitol fired by citizens' hands. Sacred rites were defiled; there were adulteries in high places. The sea was filled with exiles, its cliffs made foul with the bodies of the dead. (...) Slaves were corrupted against their masters, freedmen against their patrons; and those who had no enemy were crushed by their friends.¹⁰¹

> Haustae *aut* obrutae *urbes, fecundissima Campaniae ora; et urbs incendiis vastata, comsumptis* antiquissimis delubris, ipso Capitolio civium manibus incenso. Pollutae *caerimoniae, magna* adulteria*: Plenum* exiliis *mare,* infecti caedibus *scopuli.* (...) *Corrupti in dominos servi, in patronus liberti: et quibus deerat inimicus per amicos* oppressi.

The *Histories* of Tacitus not only shows the commotion that the aftermath of Nero's death brought to the city and the provinces, and the changes with which the Romans interacted and participated in politics under an autocratic government, but also manifests the ways in which the people of Rome related to each other and reacted under difficult circumstances. Complex portraits of

---

98. Tac. *Hist*, 1.3: *caelo terraque prodigia et fulminum monitum et futurorum praesagia.* See also 1.12; 1.37.
99. Tac. *Hist*, 1.3: *non esse curae deis securitatem nostram, esse ultionem.*
100. Tac. *Hist*, 1.88.
101. Tac. *Hist*, 1.2 (my highlighting). This is very strongly reminiscent of another silver Latin author, Lucan, also dealing with civil war; see, e.g., *BC* 2.148–51: "The servant drove the accursed sword to the hilt through his master's body; sons were sprinkled with their father's blood and strove with each other for the privilege of beheading a parent; and brother slew brother to earn rewards." Cf. Masters, *Poetry and Civil War*. For more on this, see Keitel, "Principate and Civil War," esp. 309–10 and 314–15.

emperors, generals, armies, and masses will develop as the narrative progresses and the intricate relationships among them will be powerfully described. Civil war under a *princeps* brought rapid changes for those in power who held loyalty cheap; for the people of Rome, civil war meant that fear and flattery became general practice, and the more endemic they became, the greater was the danger.[102]

The chaotic situation of Rome in the year of the four emperors was seriously aggravated by this omnipresence of fear. Fear itself is not necessarily bad; it depends on how one deals with it. Fear and courage or *virtus* are not always direct opposites; on the contrary, if a person feels fear, but manages to overcome it and acts in spite of it, he or she is on the whole more courageous than the person who performs a brave action but did not dread it in the first place.[103] However, fear can, of course, undermine courage and therefore *virtus* can be under threat. In the *Histories*, Tacitus records that there was fear in the people and fear in the armies; senators, generals, and even the emperors themselves felt fear, but the worst was that their decisions and actions were sometimes the result of giving in to this fear. This meant that *virtus* was not just under threat but was being actually destabilized.

Fear works in the *Histories* in two ways simultaneously.[104] On the one hand, fear seems to have been very important in the principate not only because of its connection with adulation—fear of the powerful led to unrestrained flattery—but also because of its more profound relationship with *servitus* and the lack of *libertas*. Above all, fear became a serious political feature that not only transformed Romans' relationships to one another but also conditioned the development of events in the political, military, and social spheres. Fear in Tacitus' *Histories* became a means—and an important one—of communication between the emperor and his people, the generals and their armies, the leaders and the mob. Extreme fear not only implied changes to the definition of Roman *virtus* but also complicated the dynamics of the political

---

102. Fear and flattery appear also at the beginning of the *Annals* when Tacitus identifies the problems of historical writing under the principate: *temporibusque Augusti dicendis non defuere decora ingenia, donec gliscente adulatione deterrerentur. Tiberii Gaique et Claudii ac Neronis res florentibus ipsis ob metum falsae* (1.1) (my highlighting).

103. Cf. Arist. *EN* 3.7.1115b17–18. See chapter 1 in this book.

104. For the topic of fear in the works of Tacitus, see, for example, Heinz, *Die Furcht als politisches Phänomen bei Tacitus*; Cardauns, "Mechanismen, der Angst. Das Verhältnis von Macht und Schrecken in der Geschichtsdarstellung des Tacitus," 52–69; Mastellone, *Paura e Angoscia in Tacito*; and Levene, "Pity, Fear and the Historical Audience," 128–49. For fear in historiography in general, see Marincola, "Beyond Pity and Fear," 285–315; and Kapust, "On the Ancient Uses of Political Fear," 353–73.

system. On the one hand, fear could trigger and motivate actions—fear as *causa*—and on the other, fear could also be the result or outcome of some actions, decisions, or behaviors—fear as *finis*. An example of fear as *causa* is the case of Galba's assassins, who, moved by fear (*metu*), promoted mutiny and disorder in the city so that they could pass unnoticed.[105] Fear as a result of actions can be seen, for instance, in the people and the masses at the spectacle of the city's massacre and the emperor Galba being caught by Otho's forces.[106]

Although instances of fear in the *Histories* are frequent and significant, it will not be the main focus of this section. Instead it will be on how Tacitus shows the great instability after Nero's death and the consequent civil wars resulting in fewer men being prepared to serve the state in the way that Agricola had done under Domitian or in the way that Marcus Lepidus was going to serve it under Tiberius in Tacitus' *Annals*. The number of individuals who might be considered as *capax imperii* had not diminished; indeed, there were more men who could be made emperors, but perhaps the disposition of these men appeared to have weakened and, consequently, *virtus* waned. As will become apparent, their participation in power for the welfare of the *res publica* is definitely more ambiguous. Unsteady government had helped to change the behavior of those who could have behaved as true Romans. The times in which a Roman could maintain a certain degree of independence by refusing to join the emperor's flatterers and behaving with courage and freedom were past, for the government was changing quickly and it was difficult to comply with the new head of state and adapt to his ways. The disclosure of the secret of empire, namely, that an emperor could be made elsewhere than at Rome (*evulgato imperii arcano posse principem alibi quam Romae fieri*),[107] had in fact had alarming consequences: if a man could be made and hailed as an emperor in any part of the empire, how was Rome going to know who was the legitimate one? Part of the resistance of the Roman people to accepting Galba, Otho, Vitellius, and even Vespasian as emperors of Rome was due to the idea that they had not been legitimately acknowledged and that the Senate had had nothing to do with their accession to the throne, but had only bestowed upon them the corresponding honors and titles *a posteriori*.[108] This state of uncertainty, fostered and increased by rumors coming from the armies in the provinces, did not help to create an atmosphere in which true

---

105. Cf. Tac. *Hist*, 2.23.
106. Cf. Tac. *Hist*, 1.40.
107. Tac. *Hist*, 1.4.
108. Cf. Tac. *Hist*, 1.47 (Otho); 2.55 (Vitellius); 4.3 (Vespasian).

virtus could arise. *Virtus* needed freedom, and freedom was somewhat restricted by the overwhelming presence of fear, which inhibited people from always behaving as consistently and firmly as they would have been expected to.

As will be seen, there are not many real heroes in Tacitus' *Histories*. The ones who had displayed virtues at the beginning of their careers were then corrupted by the fear of being destroyed by the new emperor or by their own ambition to get a position in power by betraying their old loyalties. On the other hand, those who had at first appeared most corrupt showed signs of real courage or fidelity in their last moments. In this section, I will not follow Tacitus' account of the civil wars strictly, but will approach the study of *virtus* in the *Histories* by grouping people neither chronologically nor by social status, but by the role—political or military—we see them playing in Tacitus' narrative. In this way, I think, it will be easier to draw more significant and effective comparisons, providing the necessary backdrop for understanding the different functions and expressions that *virtus* fulfilled in this work.

The Emperors

In his historical account of the civil wars, Tacitus stresses the enormous influence that the emperor had over his empire: citizens, armies, provincials, even enemies. His character and behavior affected everybody's conduct. Analyzing the *mores* of the actors was a distinctive feature of Roman historiography, a method of finding the explanations—*rationes et causae*[109]—for political changes, but it was particularly relevant under the principate, when the morals of the prince could alter and condition so much. Thus, a succession of bad emperors had profoundly weakened the Romans: "the world has been shaken to its foundations."[110] For Tacitus, it is the psychological impact that in some way conditions events. For him, the loss of fortune, dignity, or even life appears to be less sad than the loss of character experienced by the Romans who survived these events: very few seemed to have had the courage to continue to believe in *virtus* and freedom.

In the case of the emperors who succeeded Nero, as will be seen, some good qualities and important shortcomings appear quite openly in the text. It is in comparing the four men that the real complexity arises. Was it better to be stingy like Galba, or extravagant like Vitellius? Was Vespasian's courage greater than Otho's? It would be a complex task to establish a "ranking" of

---

109. Cf. Tac. *Hist*, 1.4.
110. Tac. *Hist*, 1.16.

emperors and their virtues and vices from Tacitus' *Histories*, because the traditional canon is tainted not only by the fact of being ruled by failing emperors but by the additional pollution of civil war.

Here I will not provide a full description of the four emperors who held power in A.D. 69, but will examine some of their virtues and vices, especially those more closely related to traditional *virtus Romana* in the sense in which I have been analyzing it up to now. It is important to note that Galba, Otho, Vitellius, and Vespasian were generals who commanded armies, and as such one would have expected that *virtus* as courage should have been present throughout their careers, but it was not. In fact, *virtus* was only once attributed to Vespasian, and not directly by Tacitus the historian, but on the lips of Caecina, Vitellius' general.[111] By contrast, Tacitus gives his audience other characteristics of the emperors, and the choice of these particular qualities is quite telling in itself but reveals that he will not be dealing with the glorious men and battles of old. In the *Histories*, all the emperors fall short of their duty and mission, and it is in this "disappointing" factor that the failure to practice *virtus* would lie.

Galba, for example, in spite of being probably the most illustrious Roman with regard to the nobility of his family and in military achievement,[112] displayed a mixture of good and bad qualities which, in the end, made Tacitus come to the tepid conclusion that he was "rather free from faults than possessing virtues [*magis extra vitia quam cum virtutibus*]."[113] According to Tacitus, Galba's position in Rome, once he had finally reached the city after a long and bloody march, was not strong enough to be able to place himself at the center of affairs of state with the *auctoritas* of an emperor. Unfavorable comments regarding his old age and avarice started to spread and the massacre of unarmed soldiers inspired fear in the population, undermining his reputation.[114] At first sight, it seemed that his excessive strictness (*nimia severitas*) in maintaining military discipline together with his old-fashioned rigor (*antiquus rigor*) and parsimony (*parcitas*) might be virtues from the traditional republican catalogue, and that perhaps these virtues could have helped to restore morale in the Roman army.[115] Besides, Galba also sometimes showed a

---

111. Cf. Tac. *Hist*, 3.13.

112. Cf. Murison, *Galba, Otho and Vitellius*, 31.

113. Tac. *Hist*, 1.49. Galba's characterization in Tacitus does not come out as negative as that of Catiline in Sallust, but they share important things: both are nobles with military achievements, and both become a disappointment to their own class by not displaying the right and expected *virtus*. Cf. Sall. *BC* 5.

114. Cf. Tac. *Hist*, 1.5.

115. Cf. Tac. *Hist*, 1.18; 1.49.

remarkable spirit (*insigne animo*), was not cowed by threats (*intrepidus*), and was incorruptible (*incorruptus*) by flattery.[116] But Galba proved inadequate: he had no prudence in the exercise of these qualities, and failed to adjust to the times. He was not a man of *virtus* in Tacitus, although Galba has his person linked to *virtus* in a coin (see figure 3). The lack of *moderatio* in the application of *disciplina* became something very near to cruelty (*saevitia*), and his *avaritia* in not giving the customary donative to the soldiers certainly did not help to improve his reputation, to which problems were added his weakness and old age (*invalidum senem*).[117]

For Tacitus, Galba also showed a natural indecisiveness (*mobilitate ingenium*), which resulted in great harm for Rome and the emperor himself: the rise of powerful freedmen, greedy slaves, discreditable nominations for office, and a city for sale.[118] What Galba did not have was determination (*constantia*); in fact, according to Tacitus, he displayed *foeda inconstantia* (hideous fickleness),[119] which entailed a certain lack of courage, an incapacity to stand firm against tribulation.

There was a spark of hope, however, as Galba had demonstrated some common sense in the adoption of Piso. Galba, acting freely, considered the candidate's high patriotic character and did not seem to be led by ambition or fear. For Tacitus, it seems to have been Otho's similarity to Nero that prevented Galba from adopting him as heir to the throne, and therefore he demonstrated some *curam rei publicae* (care for the state).[120] The fact that the emperors could now choose their successors not only from among their relatives was presented by Galba as a sort of liberty because adoption meant, at least in theory, that only the best would be chosen.[121] He set a precedent of looking for a successor outside the imperial house.[122] The emperor showed signs of being *capax imperii*: he had plans for the empire, and he thought he was giving back some of the political freedom that had been seriously undermined under the principate: after nearly one century of autocracy, the Romans regretted their lack of freedom, but were sadly getting used to servitude.

---

116. Tac. *Hist*, 1.35.
117. Tac. *Hist*, 1.6. For other references on Galba's old age, see 1.5; 1.7; 1.12; 1.49.
118. Cf. Tac. *Hist*, 1.7; 1.19.
119. Tac. *Hist*, 1.19.
120. Tac. *Hist*, 1.13. See also Sochat, "Tacitus' Attitude to Galba," 199–204.
121. Cf. Tac. *Hist*, 1.16.
122. Tac. *Hist*, 1.15: *Sed Augustus in domo successorem quaesivit, ego in re publica.*

Galba's display of amiability (*facilitas*) toward his friends,[123] his moderation (*moderatio*) in governing Africa and uprightness (*iustitia*) as a proconsul of Hither Spain, and his *eloquentia* in communicating Roman values to his people[124] certainly made him able to become *princeps*, but the result—and Tacitus says that there was consensus in the opinion—was that he was an incompetent emperor: *capax imperii nisi imperasset*.[125] It was disappointing for the historian to acknowledge that Galba had first been great as a private citizen, and then a failure as *princeps*. It is interesting to note the cause of this failure for Tacitus. Galba's relationship with the army, his lack of tact, and stinginess made him unpopular, and he was not quick enough to realize that precisely his supposed "virtues"—*severitas* and *rigor*—were going to bring about his fall. His severity and strictness seemed like virtues, but in reality were performed with no moderation, which was becoming, by that time, one of the most important aspects of *virtus* to be exercised during the principate. Galba did not manage to keep up, as emperor, the moderation he had shown as governor. He took the power of the soldiers too lightly, while in fact "the soldiers' will was henceforth supreme [*omnia deinde arbitrio militum acta*]";[126] and he did not realize that generosity (*liberalitas*) was no longer an optional virtue for the head of state, but a duty, as Velleius had shown with Tiberius.[127] His stubbornness regarding these points so undermined his authority that it left the soldiers prepared to abandon him and give their loyalty to someone from whom it could reap more advantageous fruits: Otho.[128] The good qualities that Tacitus was able to recognize in Galba seemed to be of the wrong type or performed in an unsatisfactory manner.[129]

Otho's characterization in Tacitus' *Histories* is perhaps one of the most complex of the work.[130] His early days were spent in heedlessness and under no restraint; he even imitated Nero in his extravagance,[131] and his body was

---

123. Cf. Tac. *Hist*, 1.12. Cf. Syme, "Partisans of Galba," 460–83.
124. Cf. Tac. *Hist*, 1.15–18. But see Keitel, "*Sententia* and Structure in Tacitus' *Histories* 1.12–49," 237.
125. Tac. *Hist*, 1.49.
126. Tac. *Hist*, 1.46. For Murison, *Galba, Otho and Vitellius*, 60, Galba's behavior, especially toward the praetorians, was "utterly foolish."
127. Cf. Vell, 2.126–130. See chapter 4 in this book.
128. Cf. Tac. *Hist*, 1.36; 1.46.
129. Again, very much like Catiline.
130. Even the main sources do not agree; apart from Tacitus, see Suetonius and Plutarch, *Life of Otho*. For Otho, see, for example, Murison, *Galba, Otho and Vitellius*, 75–143; Morgan, 69 A.D., 74–138.
131. Tac. *Hist*, 1.13: *Otho pueritiam incuriose, adulescentiam petulanter egerat, gratus Neroni aemulatione luxus.*

effeminate (*mollis*).¹³² His profligacy (*luxuria*) had made him poor, and as a result, he could only place his hopes in disorder (*turbido*).¹³³ His anger (*ira*) and jealousy (*invidia*) appeared still more strongly after Galba's adoption of Piso, and later on, his fiery passions (*flagrantissimae libidines*) were certainly a cause of fear in Rome.¹³⁴ For Tacitus, Otho's corruption was also manifested in the way he corrupted others, sometimes by offering bribes, sometimes by his unmanly flattery (*muliebribus blandimentis*).¹³⁵ He acted at times out of fear (*metus*),¹³⁶ and did not always behave according to the dignity of his imperial position, bringing shame on the state.¹³⁷ All these character traits could have led the reader to judge Otho as a worthless emperor, but he also seemed to have displayed some good qualities that Tacitus could not deny.¹³⁸ Tacitus acknowledges that Otho had administered the province of Lusitania pleasantly (*comiter*),¹³⁹ and had been an active (*nec segnis*) and brilliant (*splendidissimus*) supporter of Galba's cause at the beginning.¹⁴⁰ He did not let luxury and ease prevail over the serious matters he had in hand when he was head of state, and he ordered his life as befitted an emperor.¹⁴¹ Besides, he behaved as a good general in war, setting an example by marching first and forgetting about his own needs.¹⁴²

From the way Tacitus acknowledged Otho's display of these good character traits, it looks as if these latter were, to some extent, wholly unexpected. Companion of the excesses of Nero, it seemed difficult for Otho's reputation to take a positive turn, and this is perhaps what surprised Tacitus: that, *contra spem omnium*, Otho behaved well,¹⁴³ or rather, did not do anything bad. There was something unpredictable in Otho, something that people did not expect from him, precisely because according to his reputation it was difficult to foresee.¹⁴⁴ In the midst of civil war, Otho performed his duties as emperor

---

132. Tac. *Hist*, 1.22.
133. Cf. Tac. *Hist*, 1.21.
134. Tac. *Hist*, 2.31.
135. Cf. Tac. *Hist*, 1.24; 1.74.
136. Cf. Tac. *Hist*, 1.27; 1.81; 2.23.
137. Tac. *Hist*, 1.82: *contra decus imperii*.
138. Contra: Stolte, "Tacitus on Nero and Otho," 177–90, for whom Tacitus was too biased to acknowledge anything good in Otho. See also Sochat, "Tacitus' Attitude to Otho," 365–77.
139. In *Annals* 13.46 Tacitus even enthusiastically describes him as governing *integre sancteque*.
140. Tac. *Hist*, 1.13.
141. Tac. *Hist*, 1.71: *non deliciis neque desidia torpescere ... et cuncta ad decorem imperii composita*.
142. Cf. Tac. *Hist*, 2.11.
143. Tac. *Hist*, 1.71.
144. Tac. *Hist*, 1. 50. Cf. also Perkins, "Tacitus on Otho," 855.

as in profound peace (*ut in multa pace*), and some things he did in accordance with the dignity of the state (*dignitate rei publicae*).¹⁴⁵ It looks as if Otho surprised Tacitus when, in the middle of all the fear and confusion of the time, "he showed himself the better man [*inter adversa melior*]."¹⁴⁶ Here there was somebody who, because of his conduct, had previously been seen as *incapax imperii* but who had become *magis capax* precisely by governing.

Another remarkable feature of Tacitus' Otho is the accusation Tacitus makes of the corruption of language under Galba: "For what other men call crimes he [Galba] calls 'remedies,' falsely naming cruelty 'strictness,' avarice 'frugality'; the punishment and insults you suffer, 'discipline.' "¹⁴⁷ In some aspects of this speech, Otho, who could by no means be said to have been one of Tacitus' favorites, appears to share some of Tacitus' previous judgments of Galba. Tacitus' statement of *nimia severitatis* and *antiquus rigor* in applying discipline to the armies can be compared to that of Otho assigning Galba *saevitia* and *supplicia*,¹⁴⁸ and both—Tacitus the author and Tacitus through Otho's words—refer to Galba's main fault: *avaritia*.¹⁴⁹

Otho's suicide before Vitellius took supreme power was, ironically, the highest point of his popularity, and it was preceded by a speech delivered with dignity and gravity where the ruling emperor explained the motives for killing himself and tried to persuade his men not to oppose but to accept his death. He addressed his men with courtesy (*comiter*) and exercised his authority (*auctoritas*) for the last time. Although Tacitus himself does not call Otho "brave" as such, his description of the whole situation implies to his readership that the emperor behaved courageously when he gave up his life so that civil war may come to an end: "others may hold the power longer than I; none shall give it up more bravely [*alii diutius imperium teneruint, nemo tam fortiter reliquerit*]."¹⁵⁰ Otho had many defects, but he was also capable of great things; he did not lack determination and firmness of purpose to carry out either the most outrageous (*flagitiosissimo*) deed, such as Galba's assassination, or a glorious (*egregio*) one, like his sacrifice on behalf of his country.¹⁵¹ This was a

---

145. Cf. Tac. *Hist*, 1.77.
146. Tac. *Hist*, 2.23.
147. Tac. *Hist*, 1.37: *Nam qui alii scelera, hic remedia vocat, dum falsis nominibus severitatem pro saevitia, parsimoniam pro avaritia, supplicia et contumelias vestras disciplinam appellat.* For the significance of the corruption of language, see chapter 2 in this book, and cf. Sall. *BC* 52.11.
148. Cf. Tac. *Hist*, 1.18.
149. Cf. Tac. *Hist*, 1.5.
150. Tac. *Hist*, 2.47.
151. Tac. *Hist*, 2.50. Cf. also Syme, *Tacitus*, 205.

singular difference from Galba, who was rather free from faults than the possessor of virtues. Compared to Galba, Otho appears to have possessed the tenacity and resolution that could sometimes count as *constantia*, which Galba lacked, and he also seems to have exercised his authority with the armies in a more effective way. The soldiers ended up hating Galba and plotting against him.[152] On the contrary, toward the closing stages of his career, Otho's soldiers loved him, were faithful to him, and even wanted to imitate his example of death.[153] However, it cannot be said that for Tacitus Otho was a good *princeps*. He was more popular than Galba, but not a better man. His suicide, committed to save the state and stop the bloodshed, was in the end disappointing in that it raised a worse general to be the first man of Rome: Vitellius.

For this emperor Tacitus has a much harsher judgment than for the two previous ones.[154] According to his friends, Vitellius displayed some affability and kindness (*comitas bonitatemque*), but this was only because he gave away his property and was generous (*largiretur*) with what belonged to others, a fact that for Tacitus deserved ample criticism since it was done without limit and without judgment (*sine modo, sine iudicio*).[155] His extravagant life (*prodiga vita*) made him lazy and not suited for dealing with serious matters.[156] When he heard that armies from different parts of the empire had sworn allegiance to him, he displayed pride and negligence (*superbiae socordiaeque*),[157] and did not possess the necessary *auctoritas* to rule the empire.[158] While Otho was feared because his faults could be politically dangerous to the state, Vitellius' indolent pleasures (*ignavae voluptates*), mainly sensuality and gluttony, were seen as harmless, though more disgraceful and mean.[159]

Among the differences between Otho and Vitellius was that, although both had displayed *luxuria*, Otho was active and was not ruled by his pleasures when action was needed, whereas Vitellius was ruined by his idleness. The adjectives that accompany the description of Vitellius are passive and lethargic: "Vitellius, however, was sunk in sloth [*torpebat*] and was already

---

152. Cf. Tac. *Hist*, 1.7; 1.41.
153. Cf. Tac. *Hist*, 2.49.
154. Cf. Engel, "Das Charakterbild des Kaisers A. Vitellius bei Tacitus und sein Historischer Kern," 345–68; Keitel, "Feast Your Eyes on This," 441–46.
155. Tac. *Hist*, 1.52.
156. See, for example, 2.59: *impar curis gravioribus*; 2.67: *numquam ita ad curas intento Vitellio ut voluptatum obliviceretur*.
157. Tac. *Hist*, 2.73.
158. Tac. *Hist*, 2. 92: *Vitellio nihil auctoritas*. See also 1.67.
159. Cf. Tac. *Hist*, 2.31 and 2.71.

enjoying a foretaste of his imperial fortune by indolent luxury [*inerti luxu*] and extravagant dinners; at midday he was tipsy and gorged with food."[160] There is a lack of dignity in these faults; they might be less significant than Otho's, but they were uglier and more shameful.[161]

Another difference between these two emperors is Tacitus' description of their ability as generals. Despite Otho's vices, he could still guide an army and lead it to victory.[162] Vitellius, on the contrary, not only was unskilled in war and without any military foresight but also, after questioning others with visible anxiety, would drink heavily and abandon his concern for the war for some time.[163] Moreover, his revisiting Bedriacum, the site of the battle where his troops had defeated Otho's, only forty days after his great triumph, was considered by Tacitus as a *foedum atque atrox spectaculum* (hideous and dreadful spectacle) as the place was still filled with corpses and disgusting remains of the encounter of the two armies.[164] But what Tacitus seemed to find most striking about Vitellius as leader was his capacity for corrupting and damaging his troops, which in the end was very detrimental to his own position. Vitellius' army was subject to a steady degradation: "his soldiers began to lose their diligence and courage [*laborem ac virtutem*], as they became accustomed to pleasures [*adsuetidines voluptatum*] and learned to despise their leader [*contempti ducis*]."[165]

The deaths of Otho and Vitellius can also be a way of comparing Tacitus' opinion regarding these two short-lived emperors. According to the historian, Otho won a glorious reputation (*egregiam famam*) by his voluntary end, while Vitellius, on the contrary, earned infamy by the performance, once again, of a *foedum spectaculum*.[166] Otho deserved praise not for the action itself—suicide—but for the promptness with which he carried it out and the reason that moved him to action: *rei publicae causa*. With Vitellius instead, the whole situation was hideous and dishonorable. He also claimed to be giving up power *pacis et rei publicae causa*, yet the difference was that he did not actually do it. He appeared to have gone back to his palace several times in

---

160. Tac. *Hist*, 1.62: *Torpebat Vitellius et fortunam principatus inerti luxu ac prodigis epulis praesumebat, medio diei temulentus et sagina gravis.*
161. Cf. Scott, "Religion and Philosophy," 92.
162. See esp. 2.11–14.
163. Cf. Tac. *Hist*, 3.56.
164. Cf. Tac. *Hist*, 2.70. For the revisiting of Bedriacum by Vitellius, see Morgan, "Smell of Victory," 14–29; and Manolaraki, "Picture Worth a Thousand Words," 243–67.
165. Cf. Tac, *Hist*, 2.62. For more on this topic, see Ash, *Ordering Anarchy*, 37–54, 105–25.
166. Cf. Tac. *Hist*, 2.32 and 3.84.

search of refuge and was finally caught by surprise by a tribune while hiding shamefully. Tacitus comments that the very ugliness (*deformitas exitus*) of the sight and the cowardly escape prevented people from feeling pity for the emperor.[167]

Although Vitellius looks a straightforwardly black character in Tacitus, there were some sparks of light. His proconsulate had been judged as honest and popular (*integrum ac favorabilem*),[168] and in his obituary the historian attributed to Vitellius the qualities of simplicity and liberality (*simplicitas ac liberalitas*).[169] These were very much needed by an emperor. Being simple and open implied sincerity and a lack of elaboration, which were as highly appreciated in Tacitus as their opposites—simulation and obscurity—were rebuked. This can be seen especially when the author deals with the emperor Tiberius in the first hexad of his *Annals*. But the acknowledgment of this simplicity probably referred to an earlier period of Vitellius' life, as it does not tie up well with the emperor plotting Blaesus' poisoning, for example, or his disgraceful last scene. On the other hand, his generosity and magnanimity (*liberalitas*) were surely popular imperial virtues, and to be deficient in them could precipitate an emperor's fall, as we saw with Galba. But above all Tacitus also censured Vitellius' lack of steadfastness and constancy (*non constantia morum*).[170] *Constantia* or firmness, and particularly *constantia morum*, was a way of showing valor and determination in maintaining one's resolution in pursuit of one's aims in life. Vitellius' indecision together with his fickle nature (*mobilitate ingenii*),[171] however, seem not only to have precipitated his own fall but also to have predisposed the mobs to inconsistency.[172] He was further from *virtus* than the other two.

With Vespasian we finally come to an emperor who, in Tacitus' account, was changed for the better while in power. However, he was not to be presented as a straightforward character in the narrative. At the beginning he had an uncertain reputation (*ambigua fama*),[173] perhaps because as a proconsul in Judea his rule was notorious and hated (*famosum invisumque*),[174] and prob-

---

167. Tac. *Hist*, 3.84. See Keitel, "*Foedum Spectaculum* and Related Motifs," 342–51. For a different position, see Levene, "Pity, Fear and the Historical Audience," 128–49.
168. Tac. *Hist*, 2.97.
169. Tac. *Hist*, 3.86.
170. Tac. *Hist*, 3.86.
171. Tac. *Hist*, 2.57 and 3.84.
172. Cf. Yavetz, "Vitellius and the Fickleness of the Mob," 557–69.
173. Cf. Tac. *Hist*, 1.50.
174. Tac. *Hist*, 2.97.

ably because he also displayed avarice (*avaritia*) on several occasions.[175] His connection with omens and miracles made him suspect of superstition and credulity,[176] but on the whole, his good qualities did positively prevail over his defects. He was energetic (*acer*) in war, and Tacitus attributes to Vespasian the typical characteristics of the good general of old.[177] Vespasian appears as *antiquis ducibus par*: marching first, thinking prudently, sharing luck and peril with the rest, being an equal among his soldiers. He showed no arrogance or pride in his speeches and did not alter his behavior in his new position.[178] This moderation was well received and restored some hope to the Senate, because he was able to speak of himself with humility, refraining from exaggerations and grandiloquent words, and to speak magnificently and with decorum about the state.[179] This gave Tacitus the opportunity of praising Vespasian, who acted as an emperor (*ut princeps*),[180] and the comparisons with previous *principes* were undoubtedly to Vespasian's advantage.[181]

Tacitus also records that Vespasian had deserved praise and admiration from his own people as well, as can be seen in the speeches of Caecina and Montanus. Both his courage (*virtus*) and moderation (*moderatio*) are pointed out by these generals in such a way that they signify not just the qualities of the good Romans of old, but particularly the qualities that were needed in those specific times of turmoil.[182]

But even though Vespasian changed for the better when he was *princeps* of Rome, he also disappointed Tacitus, and is not presented as a model emperor. He seemed to possess some of the indispensable virtues for one who wanted to achieve success under the principate, but his final victory was not, for Tacitus, a direct consequence of Vespasian's own *virtus*. The shrewdness

---

175. Tac. *Hist*, 2.5. For Vespasian's early career, see Levick, *Vespasian*, 14–42; for his parsimony, ibid., 202.

176. For Syme, *Tacitus*, 206, Vespasian's tendency toward superstition is treated ironically by Tacitus. Ash, *Ordering Anarchy*, 129–36, instead assigns the narrative of portents and omens the role of describing Vespasian's relationship with his subordinates.

177. Tac. *Hist*, 2.5: *Vespasianus acer militiae anteire agmen, locum castris capere, noctu diuque consilio ac, si res posceret, manu hostibus obniti, cibo fortuito, veste habituque vix a gregario milite discrepans*. See also 2.82.

178. Tac. *Hist*, 2.80: *in ipso nihil tumidum, adrogans aut in rebus novis novum fuit*.

179. Tac. *Hist*, 4.3: *at Romae senatus (. . .) laetus et spei certus*.

180. Tac. *Hist*, 4.3.

181. For Damon, "*Potior Utroque Vespasianus*," 245–80, Tacitus included certain passages in the narrative mainly to provide a broader context for the comparison of Otho's, Vitellius', and Vespasian's early careers and to present the latter in a better light.

182. Cf. Tac. *Hist*, 3.13 and 4.42, respectively.

and determination of his subordinates, together with the mistakes made by the Vitellians, plus a great amount of *fortuna* had brought the war to an end, and therefore, also enabled Vespasian to attain the throne. Vespasian's qualities were undisputed; his energy and good generalship, his decorous speech, and the fact that he did not show arrogance or pride over his newly acquired position made the fundamental virtue of *moderatio* shine forth, and this was duly acknowledged by Tacitus. His old-fashioned lifestyle appeared as exemplary in a world governed by excess. But it also seems that although the historian recognized Vespasian's success, he attributed some kind of responsibility to the emperor for the bloody events that happened simultaneously throughout the empire on his march toward the capital and during the consolidation of his position as emperor.[183] Furthermore, the burning of the capitol in December A.D. 69 by an army loyal to Vespasian was seen as a real sacrilege,[184] and to the barbarians meant a sign that Rome's end was at hand.[185] All these things may have given Tacitus the reason for saying that when civil war had ended, this time was horrible even in peace: *ipsa etiam pace saevum*.[186]

None of the emperors could count as men of real *virtus* in Tacitus' *Histories*. Although there were differences among them—Galba was not as bad as Vitellius, and Vespasian was better than Otho—they all possessed intermittent good qualities, but these were not strong enough to count as *virtus* and counteract their vices. None of them was a coward, and they did show a certain amount of courage, especially on the battlefield. However, the appearances of the word *virtus* were related to the Roman army as a whole when fighting barbarians, and not to the emperors in their ascent toward supremacy. Active courage for the welfare of the state could not be found in internal conflict when a faction of Romans fought other Romans for power. The sensation of chaos and instability during civil war, aggravated by the personal shortcomings of the emperors, either prevented the exercise of *virtus* at all or made it too wavering and unsteady to be counted as such. The emperors of Tacitus' *Histories* did not even possess the fragmented *virtus* we saw previously in Sallust's monographs.

The Generals

The figure that more traditionally embodied *virtus* in Rome was, in fact, the general or commander of the armies. In the *Histories*, one can see the pres-

---

183. The endless battles with Gallic and Germanic tribes are mainly narrated in Books 3 and 4.
184. Cf. Tac. *Hist*, 3.72: *id facinus ... luctuosissimum foedissimumque*.
185. Cf. Tac. *Hist*, 4.54.
186. Tac. *Hist*, 1.2.

ence of relevant generals who had a significant amount of political or military power and, in a certain way, conditioned the behavior of the people—soldiers and civilians—as well as the reactions of the emperors. Here I would like to consider briefly four figures who were going to play a decisive role in the progression of their superiors' careers: Mucianus, Valens, Caecina, and Antonius Primus. These generals helped the emperors of A.D. 69 along their way toward power and are presented by Tacitus as typical products of their times of turmoil. No true *virtus* was acknowledged of any of them; it could be said in a sense that they followed their emperors' ways: some good qualities, many vices. They all showed a serious weakness that was going to prevent the development of *virtus* either as courage proper or as moral excellence: uncontrolled rivalry and sheer self-interest. The descriptions of them and their actions given by Tacitus portray both the complexity of the fight for the throne by the aspirants and the actual power of armies and their commanders.

Vitellius' aides, Alienus Caecina and Fabius Valens, appear in the narrative as active and vigorous men but possessed of boundless greed and extraordinary recklessness (*profusa cupidine et insigni temeritate*):[187] Valens showed himself to be immoderate in his desires (*cupidines immoderatus*);[188] Caecina, on the other hand, was eager for war (*belli avidus*) and displayed signs of cruelty.[189] The two generals appear to have shown a little more moderation in their military actions later on, though Tacitus hints that this was a result of the experience gained when dealing with the mutinous behavior of the troops. Both jealous of their reputation, Valens and Caecina each thought they could safeguard their own good names by belittling and ridiculing their opponent.[190] This was not the struggle for personal glory seen during republican times: then, aristocratic rivalry had been shown—at least in theory—in acts of *virtus* for the benefit of the *res publica*; the competition had been about who had more *virtus* and therefore attained more glory. Now, instead, the generals competed not in acts of courage, but in cunning words to destroy their rival.

However brief and partial the description of the contrasted generals given here might be, one can draw some general ideas from their personalities and careers. Even though both had some virtues and contributed to Vitellius' success, their personal faults appeared greater in Tacitus' account. Good military men, not always by their own abilities but also by the imprudence of their

---

187. Tac. *Hist*, 1.52.
188. Tac. *Hist*, 1.66. Cf. Morgan, "Rogues' March," 103–25.
189. Tac. *Hist*, 1.67. For Caecina's behavior, see Morgan, "Caecina's Assault on Placentia," 338–61.
190. Tac. *Hist*, 2.30: *Caecina ut foedum ac maculosum; ille ut tumidum ac vanum inridebat*.

enemies, they come out in the narrative as having taken advantage of every possible situation, but then, when a testing moment came, both worked toward their own personal benefit instead of the good of the *res publica*. It was perhaps this aspect that, above all others, did in fact prevent them from finally achieving some glory in Tacitus: although it was difficult to establish what it meant to fight *rei publicae causa* in civil war, working for individual aims and fostering one's own advancement was certainly not the way.

The second pair of rivals that I would like to consider is Mucianus and Antonius Primus, who both worked for the consolidation of the Flavian dynasty. Licinius Mucianus is first mentioned by Tacitus quite early in the narrative, at the beginning of Book 1. He had been consul under Nero and in A.D. 67 had been appointed governor of Syria. He is described by Tacitus as having shown ambition in the pursuit of friends among the nobility when he was young and to have "displayed a mixture of luxury and industry, of affability and insolence, of good and wicked arts. His pleasures were extravagant if he was at leisure; whenever he took the field, he showed great virtues. You would have praised his public life, but his private life bore ill repute [*luxuria industria, comitate adrogantia, malis bonisque artibus mixtus: nimiae voluptates, cum vacaret; quotiens expedierat, magnae virtutes: palam laudares, secreta male audiebant*]."[191] In Tacitus' description, Mucianus' *magnae virtutes* appear to be related to military matters, but not exclusively, as he was also experienced in civil affairs (*civilium rerum peritus*).[192] Mucianus' conduct, particularly at the beginning of the long march toward achieving the supreme power for Vespasian, was in fact quite good: he did not promise the soldiers a large donative, but a moderate one;[193] he contributed generously to the war from his own fortune;[194] and he displayed some prudence and foresight in battles.[195] But when Antonius Primus also started to shine because of his triumphs in the fight for Vespasian, jealousy prevailed.[196] The moderation that Mucianus appeared to display at the start of his career with Vespasian seemed to vanish when he started fearing that the glory of victory could be shared with others. For Tacitus, it was fear, especially of Primus, that made Mucianus fall into flat-

---

191. Tac. *Hist*, 1.10. For Mucianus' role in A.D. 69, see, for example, Syme, *Tacitus*, 166–67, 264, 598; and Syme, "March of Mucianus," 78–92; Williamson, "Mucianus and a Touch of the Miraculous," 223–25; Morgan, *69 A.D.*, 174–89.

192. Cf. Tac. *Hist*, 2.5.

193. Tac. *Hist*, 2.82: *donativum militi neque Mucianus prima contione nisi modice ostenderat*.

194. Tac. *Hist*, 2.84: *propriis quoque opibus Mucianus bellum iuvit, largus privatim*.

195. Cf. Tac. *Hist*, 3.46.

196. Cf. Tac. *Hist*, 3.52–53; 3.78.

tery and deceit. Although real power was in his hands, he felt anxious and fretful of losing his own position because of others' successes.[197] *Invidia* led to *metus* and *metus* to excesses, and Mucianus ended up betraying his promising beginning.

Antonius Primus, on the other hand, seemed less concerned with others' achievements, and swiftly accomplished what he had to do, thus becoming very useful to the Flavian cause.[198] Tacitus describes him as being "vigorous in action, ready of speech, skillful in sowing differences among his enemies, powerful in stirring up discord and strife, ever ready to rob or to bribe—in short he was the worst of mortals in peace [*pace pessimus*], in war a man not to be despised [*bello non spernandus*]."[199] In fact Tacitus shows Antonius as much more than *non spernandus* in military matters. Not only did he seem to have conducted battles successfully, but his strategic decisions and his energy throughout the campaign were also remarkable. Primus' *auctoritas* was definitely above the rest.[200] Tacitus also states that Antonius performed the duties of a determined general (*constantis ducis*) and a brave soldier (*fortis militis*).[201] Unfortunately we cannot be sure of what made him *pessimus in pace*, because we do not know very much about Antonius' deeds before he joined Vespasian, but Tacitus himself tells us in the *Annals* that he had *audacia* and had been involved in the forgery of a will, charges for which he had been condemned together with other members of the Senate.[202] This *pessimus*, however, may have also referred to Antonius' later career after the war was brought to an end, when he seemed unable to make himself useful to Vespasian's reign and had to retire.[203]

Whatever Tacitus may have implied by the word *pessimus* in Book 2, he showed Antonius in a very different light in his third book. He appeared to be the main character in the narrative, not only because he was leading the war but also because he was doing it very well. Tacitus attributed to him the good

---

197. Tac. *Hist*, 4.39. Mainly the triumphs of Antonius Primus but also of Arrius Varus, cf. 4.11; 4.68; 4.80.

198. On Primus, see Dorey, "Tacitus' Treatment of Antonius Primus," 244; Shotter, "Tacitus and Antonius Primus," 23–27; Ash, *Ordering Anarchy*, 147–65.

199. Tac. *Hist*, 2.86: *strenuus manu, sermone promptus, serendae in alios invidiae artifex, discordiis et seditionibus potens, raptor, largitor, pace pessimus, bello non spernandus*.

200. Cf. Tac. *Hist*, 3.4; 3.10; 3.20; 3.80.

201. Tac. *Hist*, 3.17.

202. Cf. Tac. *Ann*, 14.40.

203. Ash, *Ordering Anarchy*, 164–65, compares Antonius with Augustus' general, M. Agrippa, who could also have become dangerous to the new emperor but who in the end integrated and contributed to the *princeps*' reign.

qualities of the generals of old, especially in the battles just before the destruction of the Italian city of Cremona. These qualities are illustrated throughout eight detailed chapters in which Tacitus narrates Antonius' victory over the Danubian armies, how he led the invasion of Italy, captured Aquileia, and won the second battle of Bedriacum.[204] Despite these merits, Antonius would later be blamed by Tacitus for not having prevented the cruel devastation of Cremona, a fact that Antonius himself seems to have been ashamed of.[205]

Antonius and Mucianus are both shown to be good generals in the *Histories*, but their lack of *moderatio* prevented them from attaining the glory proper to virtue. Mucianus did not have sufficient temperance to rest content with his already very high position in the state but, on the contrary, aimed to dispose of rivals by underhand procedures. Antonius, on the other hand, although by Tacitus' account a far better leader in war than Mucianus, was unable to bear any equal or superior who was not the emperor himself, and he lost popularity because of his conceit and arrogance.[206] He could not bear his merits to be belittled, and lost control. Both characters emerge as ambitious in Tacitus: Antonius more for his own glory, Mucianus for power. Again, two powerful generals were shown to be overcome by their flaws and to act out of individualism, with an unconcern for the *res publica* that stained all their achievements.

There are, however, other military men in the *Histories* that deserve Tacitus' *virtus* praise. On the one hand, there is the bravery displayed by the barbarians in their battles for freedom from servitude to the Roman Empire, and the relationship between *virtus* and *libertas*—omnipresent in Tacitus' works—becomes even more evident in these episodes: the valor of the different Germanic tribes such as the Batavians, the Canninefates, and others when fighting for liberty against Rome is always duly acknowledged by the historian.[207] On the other hand, and related to this type of *virilis-virtus*, is the bravery exhibited by the Roman army, which Tacitus ascribes to the soldiers when fighting a foreign enemy. This is the case of Otho's men attacking the

---

204. Cf. Tac. *Hist*, 3.24–32.
205. Cf. Tac. *Hist*, 3.34. Shotter, "Tacitus and Antonius Primus," 26, seems to find in Tacitus some justification for Antonius' conduct because Antonius was being provoked; but see Scott, "Religion and Philosophy in the *Histories* of Tacitus," 97. Antonius ended his career and retired quietly to a private life in his birthplace, Tolosa, and lived at least till A.D. 95. Cf. Mart. 9.99; 10.23.
206. Cf. Tac. *Hist*, 4.80.
207. For *virtus* in barbarians, see *virtus Sarmatarum*: 1.79; *virtus Germanici*: 3.9 and 3.38; *virtus Batavi*: 4.23; 4.29; 4.34; 5.17; 5.25; *virtus Canninefati*: 4.15.

Batavians,[208] or the Romans fighting under Cerialis against the Treviri.[209] The majority of occurrences of the word *virtus* applying to the Roman army, though, came from the Romans themselves; that is, Tacitus did not commit himself to confirming such *virtus*, even less so when this was displayed against other Romans during civil war. It was the emperor Otho who acknowledged and encouraged his soldiers' *virtus* several times and counted on it to defeat the Germans and the Vitellians,[210] and Vitellius, on the other hand, did something very similar with his own troops.[211] The times that Tacitus did use his authorial voice to recognize the *virtus* of Roman soldiers were when he compared the present warriors with those of the past, to the advantage of the latter, naturally: "Their strength [of Vitellius' soldiers] also was corrupted by luxury in contrast to the ancient discipline and maxims of our forefathers [*veterem disciplinam et instituta maiorum*], in whose day *virtus* formed a better foundation for the Roman state than money [*apud quos virtute quam pecunia res Romana melius stetit*]."[212] Tacitus' use of *virilis-virtus* is similar to that of Livy in his *Ab Urbe Condita* when dealing with external wars. To be counted as proper *virtus*, bravery had to be exercised against a foreign enemy and for the good of the whole of the *res publica*, not just party spirit. *Virtus* as courage in this particular type of military matters, then, seems to remain quite stable in Tacitus from the *Agricola* to the *Histories*.

Exemplary Men without Virtus?

If the main actors of the civil wars of A.D. 69—emperors and generals—could not be counted as true examples of *virtus* in the *Histories*, was there anybody who could? Where were those Romans who, following the logic of the statements in the *Agricola* and the *Annals*,[213] were prepared to behave courageously and yet with moderation, with firmness though not obstinately?

Tacitus says at the beginning of his work that in the midst of all this chaos there still seemed to be some room for virtues—*non tamen adeo virtutum sterile saeculum ut non et bona exempla prodiderit*—good mothers and wives supporting or accompanying their sons and husbands; men showing courage,

208. Cf. Tac. *Hist*, 2.19.
209. Cf. Tac. *Hist*, 4.71.
210. Cf. Tac. *Hist*, 1.38; 1.83; 1.84; 2.47.
211. Cf. Tac. *Hist*, 2.57. And Vitellians about themselves: 3.66; 4.2.
212. Tac. *Hist*, 2.69. See also 3.11: "While once the soldiers had vied with one another in bravery and good discipline, they now strove to excel in insolence and audacity [*ut olim virtutis modestiaeque, tunc procacitatis et petulantiae certamen erat*]."
213. Cf. Tac. *Agr*, 42.4; *Ann*, 4.20.

firmness, or loyalty.[214] In the *Histories* Tacitus will give *exempla* of good men but in a different way from those he had given in the *Agricola*. In this latter work one could see in the main character an exhibition of all virtues, including *virtus*. *Virtus* in Agricola meant *virilis-virtus* as much as *humana-virtus*; the first was more present in the extraordinary feats performed by Agricola in Britannia, and the second was shown by him in the city of Rome under the orders of Domitian. In the *Histories*, instead, the good men who are acknowledged as such by Tacitus do not have the word *virtus* in their description, but they are presented as possessing different good qualities or virtues, which sometimes—though not always—are very closely related to *virtus* in the way we have been looking at it throughout this study. There seems to be an expansion in the "virtuous vocabulary" which can be explained partly by the increase of the possible circumstances in which a Roman could find himself, especially during civil wars in the principate. It is striking, then, that they do not seem to deserve the word *virtus* in Tacitus' view.

There are several individuals who are praised for their merits, but not with the word *virtus*, in Tacitus' account. Petilius Cerialis, for example, certainly stands out as an exceptional Roman general. He was brave (*intrepidus*), ready and quick (*promptus*),[215] and he possessed a healthy moderation (*salubris temperamento*).[216] Vocula, another good general, restored the discipline of the armies with admirable firmness (*mira constantia*) and encouraged them to perform deeds that fired their bravery.[217] Other military men praised in Tacitus are Julius Agrestis, for his outstanding determination (*notabili constantia*) and loyalty (*fides*),[218] and the centurion Sempronius Densus, *insignis vir*, who was wounded while saving Piso's life.[219] Vipstanus Messalla is admired by Tacitus not only for his military deeds—"he was the only one who had brought with him to the war some honorable pursuits"[220]—but also for his *pietas* toward his brother and the *eloquentia* by which he made his appeal.[221] Galba's heir, Piso, also seemed to have possessed, in Tacitus' account, some of the qualities that could make him *capax imperii*: he was a young man of great

---

214. Tac. *Hist*, 1.3: *Comitatae profugos liberos matres, secutae maritos in exilia coniuges: propinqui audentes, constantes generi, contumax etiam adversus tormenta servorum fides.*
215. Tac. *Hist*, 4.77.
216. Tac. *Hist*, 4.86.
217. Tac. *Hist*, 4.26.
218. Tac. *Hist*, 3.54.
219. Cf. Tac. *Hist*, 1.43.
220. Tac. *Hist*, 3.9.
221. Cf. Tac. *Hist*, 4.42.

name,[222] who showed *moderatio*[223] and *comitas* in his speech,[224] and who practiced the old *mores*.[225]

But perhaps more interesting than giving an exhaustive account of good men in Tacitus' *Histories* is to see some of the particular instances where Tacitus illustrates how these men showed that virtue in general posed different challenges in an imperial system stricken with internal turmoil. I will concentrate on three specific cases in which Tacitus shows three different ways of behaving in an exemplary way in these turbulent years, although the results of their conduct and attitudes were very different for all three of them.

Marius Celsus, for example, could be counted as one of these good men.[226] Celsus had led the Fifteenth Legion into war against the Parthians in A.D. 63, and later was called by Galba as an adviser. Celsus, who remained loyal to Galba throughout, was protected from the anger of the soldiers by the new emperor Otho, for whom he also worked faithfully. Tacitus' characterization is, without any doubt, highly positive, and he attributes to Celsus a series of merits that make Celsus an exemplary man. Celsus' character is first illustrated as having the qualities of a "proper" Roman within the traditional standard: he is said to have displayed his energy (*industria*) and blameless character (*innocentia*) in carrying out his duties, especially the military ones,[227] and was renowned for his *vigor*.[228] In this respect, the description of Celsus very much resembled that of a republican hero; these merits look like those of Marius given by Sallust in the *BJ*, and imply active performance. But Tacitus also attributes qualities of a different type to Celsus, such as *constantia* and *prudentia*, which started to appear more frequently under the principate.[229] His prudence, in fact, prevented him from stubbornly opposing Otho's plans concerning the war.

For Tacitus, Celsus seemed to have cooperated with the regime using all the means he had: he achieved brilliant successes (*res egregiae gestae*),[230] but never allowed his uprightness (*innocentia*) to be compromised.[231] Even though he

---

222. Cf. Tac. *Hist*, 1.34.
223. Tac. *Hist*, 1.17.
224. Tac. *Hist*, 1.19.
225. Tac. *Hist*, 1.14.
226. On Celsus, see Shotter, "Tacitus and Marius Celsus," 197–200.
227. Cf. Tac. *Hist*, 1.45.
228. Cf. Tac. *Hist*, 1.87.
229. Cf. Tac. *Hist*, 1.71 and 2.25, respectively.
230. Tac. *Hist*, 2.24.
231. Cf. Tac. *Hist*, 1.45.

was in real danger several times, Celsus never defended himself at the cost of his honesty or principles as, according to Tacitus, Suetonius Paulinus, his partner in generalship, seemed to have done.[232] It was certainly his prudence (*prudentia*), although it was not always acknowledged,[233] together with his constant fidelity, that permitted him to keep his consulship even after Otho's downfall, a remarkable recognition of his good reputation considering that he had fought on the "wrong" side of the war. Celsus' loyalty could be seen working as a virtue and a fault at the same time. A virtue, because by being loyal and by keeping one's word, Roman *fides* was exercised and honored.[234] But this *fides* could also be seen as a defect when it was given to the wrong men or cause. Celsus, however, makes his *fides* to Galba,[235] which was definitely considered a mistake under Otho's reign, appear as his strongest virtue and relies on it for recommending himself to the new emperor.[236] It appears in Tacitus that Marius Celsus is moderate in his desires, industrious in his work as a general, a good leader to his soldiers, and above all, firm in his loyalty, to whoever represented the head of the *res publica*. He might have been one of the great men under bad emperors (*viri magni sub malis principibus*) to whom Tacitus referred in the *Agricola*:[237] he did what he could to contribute to the welfare of the state, even under civil war.

Iunius Blaesus was another character worthy of praise in the *Histories*. Tacitus tells us that in A.D. 69 he was in charge of the province of Gallia Lugdunensis, together with the Italian legion and the Taurian squadron of horse.[238] He is described as a man of distinguished family who displayed *liberalitas*, *magnificentia*, and *comitas*, virtues through which he earned Vitellius' hatred,[239] and even the emperor's brother who plotted against Blaesus' life. Blaesus appeared dangerously popular for Vitellius, as he never missed an opportunity of showing himself as courteous and magnificent (*comem ac magnificum*) toward the soldiers.[240] *Magnificentia* and *comitas* were certainly fitting virtues for a

232. Cf. Tac. *Hist*, 2.60: *donec auditi necessariis magis defensionibus quam honestius uterentur.*
233. Cf. Tac. *Hist*, 2.39. See also 2.25.
234. For *fides* in republican and imperial context, see Říhová, "Vir bonus chez Tacite," 7–30, esp. 9–13.
235. Tac. *Hist*, 1.45: *[Marium Celsum] Galbae usque in extremas res amicum fidumque.*
236. Cf. Tac. *Hist*, 1.71: *Celsus constanter servatae erga Galbam fidei crimen confessus, exemplum ultro imputavit.*
237. Tac. *Agr*, 42.5.
238. Tac. *Hist*, 1.59.
239. Tac. *Hist*, 2.59: *genere inlustri, largus animo et par opibus, circumdaret principi ministeria, comitaretur liberaliter, eo ipso ingratus, quamvis odium Vitellius vernilibus blanditiis velaret.*
240. Cf. Tac. *Hist*, 3.38.

princeps or an emperor, and so Vitellius decided to eliminate Bleasus by poisoning him.[241] Tacitus seems urged to repeat once more that Blaesus had respected the customs of the ancestors with *elegantia* and displayed *fides* till the end. His obituary describes Blaesus as not only *capax imperii* but also *vir sanctus*, which is higher praise than any the author had bestowed upon any other good character in the *Histories*.[242] Blaesus, in fact, had opposed revolution, and was not moved by any desire for sudden honors and least of all for the principate, but was nevertheless regarded worthy of it. Again we can see *moderatio* playing a key role in good men under the principate, though in this case—as in others elsewhere in Tacitus—the moderate man was unable to prosper because of the *immoderatio* of others and had to die. His glory, however, was not lessened by his end.

In this same line we find Helvidius Priscus, who is also praised by Tacitus for some of his virtues.[243] He had been tribune of the plebs in A.D. 56 and had been banished after the condemnation of his father-in-law Thrasea Paetus in A.D. 66, but in A.D. 70 he again entered public life and was elected praetor. From the start, Helvidius showed a critical attitude toward the Flavian dynasty.[244] After the Senate had conferred on Vespasian all the honors and privileges common to emperors, Helvidius delivered a speech, whose whole content we cannot know because of a lacuna. However, from Tacitus' remarks together with the reactions it provoked in the Senate, we can infer that Helvidius spoke his mind very bluntly. It is interesting to note that this speech marked his career henceforward both for disfavor and for glory (*isque praecipuus illi dies magnae offensae initium et magnae gloriae fuit*),[245] but Tacitus does not tell us who felt one way and who the other.[246] In any case, Tacitus' tone seems to imply that either "great displeasure" or "great glory" under the rule of a *princeps* would equally bring trouble and disgrace.

---

241. Cf. Tac. *Hist*, 3.39. For Blaesus' death in Tacitus, see Miller and Jones, "Critical Appreciations III," 70–80.

242. Tac. *Hist*, 3.39. Tacitus gives this same epithet to Arruntius in *Annals*, 6.7.

243. He comes out in a very different light in Cassius Dio, 65.12.2. Cf. Wirszubski, *Libertas as a Political Idea at Rome during the Late Republic and Early Principate*, 147–50.

244. For Helvidius' opposition especially to Vespasian, see Malitz, "Helvidius Priscus und Vespasian. Zur Geschichte der 'stoischen' Senatsopposition," 231–46.

245. Cf. Tac. *Hist*, 4.4.

246. Another example of the outspoken speeches of Helvidius was the one regarding the restoration of the capitol (4.9), where he assigns the task to the Senate and only a secondary role to the emperor Vespasian. For more on this, see Wardle, "Vespasian, Helvidius Priscus," 208–22, who suggests that the responsibility for the restoration of the capitol implied important issues of government and ideology. Cf. also Sailor, *Writing and Empire in Tacitus*, 183–250.

Tacitus says that Helvidius seemed to have dedicated his extraordinary talents to pursuing an education that could help him to be prepared to face reversals of fortune with fortitude when serving the *res publica*.[247] The historian then gives a neat summary of the Stoic doctrine learned by Helvidius, which appears to have been fostered and encouraged by the example of his father-in-law.[248] Thrasea's independence would be shown later on in the *Annals* with potent language and undisguised admiration by Tacitus, which certainly helped Thrasea to attain the epithet of *virtutem ipsam*.[249] It looks as if Helvidius was eager to imitate his father-in-law's character and independence (*libertas*), and, according to Tacitus, he did achieve a high level of conduct, behaving as a steady citizen, senator, husband, son-in-law, and friend. In the *Histories*, Helvidius is described as not being materially ambitious and despising riches (*opum contemptor*), but especially as having *constantia* in a double way: firstly being determined to work with rectitude (*recti pervicax*), and secondly, being unmoved by fear (*constans adversus metus*).[250]

However, in his description of Helvidius, Tacitus gives a more complex portrayal, also taking into account the different opinions that existed among the senators, which were not always positive. Tacitus does not even commit himself to any definite judgment on Helvidius, and he presents, for example, Helvidius' revengeful attitude toward Thrasea's informer and accuser, Marcellus, as difficult to define and ambivalent.[251] When Helvidius finally gave up the prosecution, senators were divided: one group praised him for his moderation, while the other blamed him for his lack of firmness: *sermonibus moderationem laudantium aut constantiam requirentium*.[252] It is striking that *moderatio* and *constantia*, a pair of virtues that often work together in good men under the principate, are here presented in opposition, as if too much moderation were incompatible with the necessary courage to be steadfast. The antagonism, though, is only apparent, and each side of the Senate is reinforcing the importance of the particular virtue they want to present as the one most needed. Real *moderatio* cannot be opposed to *constantia* because moderation is related to self-control and the restraint of not being overcome by any pas-

---

247. Tac. *Hist*, 4.5: *ingenium inlustre altioribus studiis iuvenis admodum dedit, non, ut plerique, ut nomine magnifico segne otium velaret, sed quo firmior adversus fortuita rem publicam capesseret*.
248. Cf. Tac. *Hist*, 4.5. For more on Tacitus' view of Stoicism and philosophy in general, see André, "Tacite et la Philosophie," 3101–54.
249. Cf. Tac. *Ann*, 14.49 and 16.21. Although not Tacitus' perfect hero, see later in this chapter.
250. Tac. *Hist*, 4.5.
251. Cf. Tac. *Hist*, 4.6: *ea ultio, incertum maior an iustior*.
252. Tac. *Hist*, 4.6.

sion or emotion that could make one yield through weakness. To be really moderate—which was not the same as vacillating or uncommitted—one needed to be constant and firm. Rather than being in opposition, therefore, *moderatio* and *constantia* appear as the two sides of the same coin of fortitude. We will come back to this point in the *Annals*.

The continuous and hostile discussions between Helvidius and Marcellus, present in Tacitus' account through extensive speeches delivered in the Senate, revealed not only Helvidius' vigorous temperament but also the violent eloquence with which the two rivals confronted one another. They may well have reminded the reader about that republican oratory characterized by freedom of speech that Tacitus himself had described and illustrated in the *Dialogus*.[253] Helvidius reproached Marcellus harshly for his previous crimes;[254] Marcellus, on the other hand, displayed bitter irony and scorned Helvidius' alleged "determination [*constantia*] and courage [*fortitudo*], equal to that of the Catos and the Brutuses of old times, while he, Marcellus, was only a member of a servile Senate."[255] Besides his sarcasm in equating Helvidius to Cato's famous resolution or *constantia* and Brutus' well-known fortitude, Marcellus also acknowledged two other things that may be revealing of Tacitus' own opinions about the nature of the principate, especially bearing in mind what the historian had said in other places.[256] Marcellus affirms that his attitude toward the emperors is "to pray for good ones, but endure any sort [*bonos imperatores votos expetere, qualiscumque tolerare*]."[257] This could seem a reasonable stance to adopt if one is to be ruled by a *princeps*, and it is perhaps what Tacitus had advised in the *Agricola* and would repeat later on in the *Annals*.[258] It was a cruel irony to say this to Helvidius, for it was precisely his lack of moderation and tolerance that would lead him to be finally exiled and executed in A.D. 75.

---

253. Cf. Tac. *Dial*, 40.4; 41.4. For the role of oratory in Roman politics, see lately, van der Blom, *Oratory and Political Career*, esp. 25–45.

254. Mainly, of course, having been Thrasea Paetus' accuser and having allowed his death.

255. Cf. Tac. *Hist*, 4.8: *Denique constantia fortitudine Catonibus et Brutis aequeretur Helvidius: se unum esse ex illo senatu, qui simul servierit*. The plurals of the *exempla* seem to express still stronger disdain, as if Marcellus were laughing at Helvidius for belonging to "the same old lot" of heroes of Rome.

256. The fact that Tacitus may express his own opinions through a character with whom he cannot identify himself may reveal partly the sound distance needed between the author and his narrative. But see Pigoń, "Helvidius Priscus, Eprius Marcellus, and *iudicium senatus*," esp. 235 and 246. See also Pelling, "Tacitus' Personal Voice," 159.

257. Tac. *Hist*, 4.8.

258. Cf. Tac. *Agr*, 42.4; *Ann*, 4.20.

The second point is related to *libertas*: "Just as the worst emperors wish for absolute tyrannical power, even the best emperors wish some limit to the freedom of their subjects [*quo modo pessimis imperatoribus sine fine dominationem, ita quamvis egregiis modum libertatis placere*]."[259] It looks as if, through Marcellus' words, Tacitus was referring to that senatorial *libertas* that was tightly associated with freedom of speech and political action, which was in fact the *libertas* that Helvidius, at least in Tacitus' narrative, appears to be displaying most openly and caused his ruin. Helvidius in Tacitus appears as if his personal freedom of being true to himself could not be kept under control and had to come out almost aggressively through speaking and confrontation. Helvidius is undoubtedly a highly regarded man in Tacitus' account, but perhaps a little too vehement for comfort. Like his father-in-law in the *Annals*, he is praised and admired by the historian but is not presented as a straightforward model to be followed by all. Despite Helvidius' bold and even courageous speech, something like *abrupta contumacia* is seen in his conduct, and he would not be linked to the word *virtus* as Thrasea would be.

As may be seen from these examples, other keywords related to *virtus* started appearing in the description of good men. The exercise of *constantia*, for instance, was another way of practicing *virtus* in the *Histories*. *Constantia* appeared as a special facet of both *virilis-virtus* and *humana-virtus*, which consisted mainly in keeping one's freedom of thought and not being overcome by fear, being determined to hold on to one's principles. This was perhaps subtler and less tangible courage, but very appropriate for times of internal struggle.[260] *Constantia* in the *Histories* presented also a new shade that evidenced the more troubled times the Romans were facing in A.D. 69; it was necessary to maintain one's *fides* to the emperor to whom one had sworn allegiance: *fides* became a serious concern in times of civil war. Tacitus gives us great examples of *fides militaris*.[261] *Fides* inspired brave actions, and there was also a touch of magnanimity in this *fides* in the sense that the loyal subordinate was able to put his own benefit in second place for the sake of a larger cause, namely, the state. Tacitus' praise of Celsus' *constantia* in showing *fides* to Galba first and then, after his death, to Otho, together with the *fides* of Blaesus to Vitellius, shows that he saw *fides* as a virtue that required courage for a subordinate to be loyal to his commander even if the latter was not totally worthy of this loyalty. *Constantia* is praised by the historian in military

---

259. Tac. *Hist*, 4.8. Cf. Oakley, "Res olim dissociabiles," 187.
260. See, for example, Tac. *Hist*, 1.3.
261. Cf. Tac. *Hist*, 1.51; 1.75; 2.11; 4.21.

situations, but it also appears in internal affairs of the city because *constantia*, being more a mental attitude than a proper act, could be exercised in any circumstance.

The other side of this novel aspect of *virtus* under civil war was, not surprisingly, *moderatio*. If the *Agricola* had been mainly concerned with the moderation of politicians and generals toward the emperor, particularly in contenting themselves with their own positions, the *Histories* would show the same need for restraint not only in adulation toward the volatile emperor but also in self-control toward rivals and competitors. The chaos of civil war had created new and more possibilities for Romans of becoming emperor and had allowed more candidates to hope for the throne. Moderation in the *princeps'* collaborators meant that they had to consent to be "only" collaborators and obey. Tacitus' Piso seemed to have had this *moderatio*;[262] Mucianus at the beginning of his career as Vespasian's *socius* had it too, but when the competition with Primus started, he lost it and failed. There was also the moderation of the *princeps* himself. There were more successful men, in fact, several of whom could aspire to command the empire, and in some way this implied a certain debasement of the imperial dignity.[263] Romans knew that those men in power were essentially equal to them—they had seen them in action—and so an emperor who boasted or showed off too much could be seen as ridiculous. In Tacitus' account Galba and Vespasian seemed to understand this, whereas Otho and Vitellius, displaying *luxuria*, *superbia*, and immoderate *largitio*, did not.

But *moderatio* in Tacitus' *Histories* was relevant for more reasons than these. Moderation was a virtue that could be practiced under bad emperors (*sub malis principibus*). Moderation allowed the Romans to live an honest life, not too exposed to the dangers of a regime of absolute power. *Moderatio* was important too regarding the liberty with which they expressed their ideas and performed their actions. A moderate attitude toward the emperor and toward one's equals was of capital importance because it became an indispensable condition to work *rei publicae causa* and for the good functioning of the state. This may have seemed a less alluring way to acquire *gloria* compared with the glory achieved through the glittering battles of republican times, but these "less heroic" struggles still had to be fought, even more in times of civil war where both sides claimed to be fighting for the common good of Rome.

262. Cf. Tac. *Hist*, 1.17.
263. One could not compare the *dignitas* and *auctoritas* of an Augustus with those of an Otho or a Vitellius, not even with a Vespasian.

The examination of the different types and forms in which *virtus* can be manifested or expressed in the historical period that Tacitus is writing about leads the reader—through a very Roman approach, centered on conduct or "*virtus* in action"—both to unfold the narrative of events and to discover the virtues—real and affected, private and public—that appear in the behavior of the historical characters. Tacitus, as an acute Roman thinker and historian, did not write his *Histories* as a philosopher, giving an exhaustive catalogue of the virtues needed to overcome the disruption of any civil war in any given state. Instead, by means of his historical narrative, he showed these virtues in action in real Romans during the year of the four emperors, blending thought and achievement magisterially. For Tacitus it was essential to convey the message clearly: there was still a need to fight for *libertas* in the principate, and the *virtus* of republican times was still necessary to maintain it, but in a more subdued way. The historian shows the tensions and ambiguities of the period he is recounting; he is occupied not only in illustrating the bad examples but also in finding new role models and orienting the reader between rash action on the one hand and servile passivity on the other. For this purpose, he portrayed good, active Romans who did not confuse *moderatio* with weakness and softness, and for whom *constantia* was not the same as inertia and apathy.

Although for Tacitus the civil wars that followed Nero's death made political behavior—or at least the consequences of this behavior—more radical, the representation of the idea of *humana-virtus* was still his main purpose when writing history. He seems to be consciously giving these descriptions not only to provide the readers with enough material to be able to judge the real decadence of good *mores* but also, and perhaps more importantly, to suggest a new prototype of good behavior under the principate. If the writing of history in antiquity looks for an edifying purpose at all, it is by the characterization of these good Romans that Tacitus is interested in achieving it.

The *Annals: Virtus* and *Princeps*

The *Annals* were written after the *Agricola* and the *Histories*, but if one reads Tacitus' works chronologically, that is, according to the order of real historical events, one could probably note a sort of evolution in the manifestations of *virtus* from the newly established system around 27 B.C. to the end of the first century A.D. The specific qualities that the historian linked to *humana-virtus* and *virilis-virtus* under Domitian or in the year of the four emperors had already started appearing, timidly and diffidently under Tiberius and the other Julio-Claudians.

Although the rule of one saw crime, slavery, cruelty, and fear under bad emperors, Tacitus' view that no matter what the circumstances, one had the personal capacity to decide how to behave made his conclusion very clear at the end of his first work: "that great men can live even under bad rulers [*posse etiam sub malis principibus magnos viros esse*]."[264] However tempting he may have found it to transfer responsibility for men's conduct to the political system, he demonstrated that true *libertas* did not depend only on constitutions, or on favorable exterior circumstances that made its exercise easy, but also on the inner strength to feel free even in the most difficult conditions, as Agricola had shown.[265] The challenge under autocracy, then, was to discover that there was a way out: demanding, arduous and difficult, but possible. *Virtus* seemed dangerous, because it attracted the anger of the powerful, who became jealous of it—because of the glory it carried—but it was still worth practicing. The bad emperors, the trying circumstances, the lack of freedom to express one's ideas and opinions, together with the fear of injustice and the indolence of the good, did not determine one's conduct, although they made it more difficult and challenging. Standing firm in the face of tribulation and showing unyielding endurance and courage in serving the *res publica* had always been the characteristics of a true Roman, and, throughout the *Annals*, Tacitus hints that they still were, even if one did not find *virtus* very often or if the circumstances for *libertas* had changed for the worse.[266]

Furthermore, Tacitus invites the reader to look beneath the surface of events: *introspicere illa primo aspectu levia*.[267] Tacitus' expansion of *libertas* from the narrow sense of active political participation to broader fields of expression—mainly personal behavior and attitude toward circumstances—means an extension of the manifestations of *virtus* as well. I will show here that, since for Tacitus some kind of *libertas* is still alive, he not only cites

---

264. Tac. *Agr*, 42.4.

265. Cf. Wirszubski, *Libertas as a Political Idea at Rome during the late Republic and early Principate*, 165–67; Percival, "Tacitus and the Principate," 125–26; Kraus, "From Exempla to Exemplar?," 181–200; Kapust, "Between Contumacy and Obsequiousness," 293–311, and "Tacitus and Political Thought," 504–28.

266. For the idea of *libertas* in Tacitus and the principate, see, for example, Syme, *Roman Revolution*, esp. 155–56, 513; Wirszubski, *Libertas as a Political Idea at Rome*, 160–67, with Momigliano's review in *JRS* 41 (1951): 146–53;. Hammond, "Res olim dissociabiles," 93–113; Liebeschuetz, "Theme of Liberty in the *Agricola* of Tacitus," 126–39; Ducos, "La liberté chez Tacite: Droits de l'individu ou conduite individuelle?," 194–217; Roberts, "Revolt of Boudicca," 118–32; Brunt, "*Libertas* in the Republic," esp. 283–33; Morford, "How Tacitus Defined Liberty," 3420–50; Oakley, "*Res olim dissociabiles*," 184–94.

267. Tac. *Ann*, 4.32.

210 Chapter Five

manifestations of *virtus* under the new sociopolitical order but also shows how they were expressed in more varied and multifaceted ways and could, in some cases, be more admirable than previously. For Tacitus, virtuous conduct in the principate will involve the courage and determination to preserve one's own personal *libertas*, not so much the freedom of the community, but the inner freedom of an individual or the internal decision to remain free, at least in thought. Expressions of *virtus* in the *Annals*, then, will be related more to moral courage than to physical courage. Moral courage implies standing up for what men think is right; it involves constancy and endurance, especially when the struggle is not against a conventional enemy, but against the very power under which they live.[268]

In the analysis of *virtus* in the *Annals*, I will refer separately to *virtus* exercised (or not) within a military context and *virtus* in the political activities of the city of Rome. Although this distinction of *domi militiaeque* will help us to delineate the different features of the type of *virtus* we are dealing with, it is important to bear in mind that Tacitus' narrative not only blends the two scenarios but also mixes good and evil examples within both; therefore the instances that I have chosen to examine appear more blurred in the broader picture of the work.

Virtus *and War in the* Annals

Though Tacitus is mainly concerned with showing expressions of the new *virtus* that will be more appropriate to the principate, this does not mean that he will not also record examples of the more traditional military *virtus*, meaning the exercise of courage when facing the enemy in battle. One can find some examples of this type of *virtus* in the *Annals*, and its presence in a general or an army certainly adds an ironic contrast to the gloomy situation in the city of Rome.

Especially ironic is the fact that the ones who appear to be portrayed with more *virtus* are the barbarians, not the Roman soldiers. In this sense, Tacitus is consistent with what he has shown in his previous writings, namely, that less sophisticated societies are able to perform deeds of courage, and manifest their valor in battle fighting for their freedom and independence from Roman domination, much more frequently than the Romans themselves trying to conquer them.

In the German war, for example, the first war against a foreign foe in Tacitus' *Annals*, the Germans fought courageously to preserve their pristine liberty, as

---

268. For moral courage, see Miller, *Mystery of Courage*, passim, but esp. 65 and 118.

they questioned even such a light bond as friendship with the Romans, and saw it as servitude. This contempt is shown particularly in Arminius' speeches and actions, where he demonstrated—once again after A.D. 9 and Varus' disaster—his strength, determination, and valor in fighting the Romans.[269] The German leader, as the acclaimed champion of liberty,[270] even scorned his brother Flavus for being a Roman ally, and asserted the sacred call of their country, their ancestral liberty, and the German gods. Flavus, on the other hand, argued in favor of Roman greatness, the power of the Caesar, and the mercy always accorded to the antagonist who surrendered.[271] The two brothers seemed to defend opposing views, but it was Arminius, with his loyalty to the gods and his fight to preserve freedom, who was praised for his *virtus*.[272]

Apart from the brave Arminius, other German leaders are praised for their *virtus* too, such as Maroboduus and Inguiomerus.[273] Courage, together with their cunning strategies, made them and their people formidable enemies for the Roman army, especially because according to Tacitus they placed all their hopes in *virtus* (*spes in virtute*),[274] rather than in *fortuna*. If the barbarians were in the end defeated by the Romans, it was more because luck had deserted them, not *virtus*.[275] Despite Rome's resounding triumph, German prowess was not belittled. On the contrary, the Roman army's success would not have been so great had the enemy's bravery not shone as it did. The striking difference between Romans and barbarians here is that while Tacitus acknowledges the Germans' *virtus*, he does not link the Romans with this word explicitly, and never attributes *virtus* to a Roman general in his own authorial voice. The Roman army is said to be brave only by the Germans in a battle exhortation where allusion to the enemy's courage is almost to be taken for granted as a *topos*.[276]

Later in the *Annals*, *Britannica virtus* also has an opportunity to shine forth. Their chieftain Caratacus recalled the *virtus* of their ancestors with such strength that it moved his people to fight fiercely.[277] The attitude of the barbarian leader appears very Roman both in content and in form: evoking

269. For Arminius' feats in this war, see Tac. *Ann*, 1.57; 1.63; 1.65; 1.68; 2.17.
270. Tac. *Ann*, 2.44: *Arminium pro libertate bellantem favor habebat*.
271. Cf. Tac. *Ann*, 2.9–10.
272. Cf. Tac. *Ann*, 2.44.
273. Cf. Tac. *Ann*, 2.44 and 2.21, respectively.
274. Tac. *Ann*, 2.20.
275. Tac. *Ann*, 2.21: *fortuna magis quam virtus deserebat*.
276. Cf. Tac. *Ann*, 2.25.
277. Cf. Tac. *Ann*, 12.34.

their forefathers, he uses the power of example to elicit the same behavior from his own soldiers.

More non-Roman *virtus* appears in Tacitus' *Annals* in the war with Parthia in Armenia under Nero. The author bestows it on particular leaders such as the Parthian king Vologeses (*virtutis regis*),[278] and even on a foreign woman, queen Zenobia.[279] This latter case is particularly interesting since it is striking that Tacitus should devote an entire chapter to narrating this episode which does not provide any relevant information regarding the war with Parthia, but only a touch of heroism and romance. After the internal revolt in Armenia, King Rhadamistus fled with his pregnant wife, Zenobia. Exhausted with the long flight, she asked her own husband to kill her to avoid the possibility of violence if her enemies found her. Her courage won the admiration of Rhadamistus (*virtutem admirans*), who stabbed her and threw her into the river to conceal the corpse. With this act, Zenobia certainly gave example of her *pudicitia* and faithfulness toward her husband, but it was her *virtus* that won admiration because to a certain extent, she—like Cloelia in Livy—had performed an act of manly *virtus*.[280] It did not actually matter whether these stories were part of the historian's *inventio*; what was more important was the effect he sought to produce on his audience. The Romans would be reminded of a time long past when their own ancestors had also fought with *virtus* to defend their freedom from external enemies, as these foreigners—men and women—were doing now.

It is important to note the wars and the peoples that did have *virtus* attached to them, because Tacitus will not do the same with every single military achievement. On the contrary, there are Roman generals who win Tacitus' admiration for their strength, skilled management of battles, and even valor, but to whom he will not attribute *virtus*.[281] This is the case of Publius Dolabella, for example, who is commended for having put an end to the troubles in Numidia. He was a good commander who showed his *scientia rei militaris* in the battlefield toward an elusive enemy. Through a combination of prudence and daring he managed to get rid of Tacfarinas and brought the war to a successful conclusion. Even though the emperor Tiberius denied triumphal honors to Dolabella, his reputation increased when the Romans learnt of his achieve-

---

278. Tac. *Ann*, 15.11.

279. Tac. *Ann*, 12.51. For the topic of women, see, for example, Baldwin, "Women in Tacitus," 83–101.

280. Cf. Livy, 2.13.

281. See Kajanto, "Tacitus' Attitude towards War and the Soldier," 699–718; Meulder, "Bons et mauvais généraux chez Tacite," 75–89.

ments in North Africa.²⁸² Tacitus also pays tribute to two other Romans who had been brave in commanding armies: Gnaeus Lentulus, on the one hand, is admired by Tacitus not only for his military success against the Getae, which won him triumphal distinctions, but also for his dignity in poverty (*bene tolerata paupertas*) and, after his success, for his moderation (*modestia*) in wealth. His partner in the obituary, Lucius Domitius, managed to cross the river Elbe, penetrating deep into Germany, and also won the *insignia triumphi* for his exploits.²⁸³ Soon after this in Book 4, Tacitus devotes some chapters to the narrative of the Thracian insurrection, which was crushed by Poppaeus Sabinus. His orders were precise and well planned; with *auctoritas* he urged his soldiers to follow his directions, encouraged them to be brave, and finally secured victory.²⁸⁴ Later on, during the rebellion in Britannia, Publius Ostorius also proved to be a brave and efficient chief officer leading the Roman legions, and facing battle on very difficult terrain;²⁸⁵ and his son, Marcus, showed his courage too by saving a Roman life and earned the *corona civica*.²⁸⁶

Success in these military men is accompanied by some good qualities which merit them Tacitus' approval and mention in his work, but even though they certainly provide fine instances of good generalship, he does not attribute *virtus* to them. Contrary to what one would have expected, *virtus* should not be taken for granted when Tacitus deals with good commanders fighting external wars for imperial Rome. He denies them *virtus* but confers something else. Tacitus seems to engage in a process of conscious selection with regard to the merits that he chooses to underline, and his reluctance to acknowledge *virtus* in his own authorial voice makes this central quality seem, if not completely unattainable, at least very difficult to achieve. By acknowledging *virtus* in the barbarians and withholding it from the Romans, Tacitus seems to be warning his contemporaries of the impossibility of achieving *virtus* in the traditional way.

That said, there are two Roman generals who are said to have *virtus* in the *Annals*, namely, Germanicus and Corbulo. These two leaders, as will be seen, are presented by the historian as having more than one thing in common, but perhaps the most striking characteristic shared by both is the rare combination

---

282. Cf. Tac. *Ann*, 4.25–26.
283. Cf. Tac. *Ann*, 4.44.
284. Cf. Tac. *Ann*, 4.46–51. The same Sabinus sometime later dealt deftly with the incident of the appearance of the false Drusus (Germanicus' son) in the eastern provinces.
285. Cf. Tac. *Ann*, 12.35.
286. Cf. Tac. *Ann*, 12.31.

of on the one hand being to some degree out of their times, appearing somewhat nostalgic for the old republican generals' ways, and on the other, possessing some of the new features and shades that *virtus* required under the Julio-Claudian principate.

Tacitus' presentation of Germanicus has been the center of many discussions. His personal virtues and family connections place him at the heart of speculations about Rome's future, but he also appears in Tacitus' work as by no means a straightforward character. Modern judgments about him range from that of being a good, noble, old-time general, to his being a failed caricature of that figure.[287] Whichever he was, there is no doubt that Tiberius' adopted son represents an important contrast to the reigning emperor in the earlier books of Tacitus' *Annals*.

Since the wars fought in Germania occurred before the period covered by the *Annals*, we only get Tacitus' narrative of Germanicus handling the mutinies.[288] The soldiers' uprising gave him a tough time, and his performance, full of impulsiveness and theatricality, showed that his *auctoritas* was not yet mature enough.[289] Like Drusus before him, he had the opportunity to show his loyalty to his political father, Tiberius, and even though his imprudence was censured, the mutiny was finally brought to an end.[290] Germanicus has sometimes been seen as a case of "unjustified popularity";[291] the enthusiasm that he provoked among the soldiers and the people of Rome seems disproportionate compared with his actual achievements, at least in Tacitus' account. However, his popularity is not totally unjustified. It is true that Germanicus carried with him the unrealized hopes of being the future *princeps*, but he also carried real qualities that Romans appreciated in a general: fame and personal virtues. Tacitus tells us that his father, Drusus, was popular and esteemed by the people because they believed that, had he succeeded, he

---

287. For a positive view on Germanicus, see, for example, Walker, *Annals*, 9: "Tacitus' political hero," 232: "true Roman ideal of *prisca virtus*"; also Wankenne, "Germanicus idéal du prince selon Tacite," 270–79. For the opposite view, see Ross, "Tacitean Germanicus," 227: "a figure of failure and futility." For a more nuanced description of Germanicus, see Pelling, "Tacitus and Germanicus," 59–85; and O'Gorman, *Irony and Misreading*, 46–77; and more recently Woodman, "Tacitus and Germanicus."

288. For more on Germanicus and the mutinies, see Borszák, "Das Germanicusbild des Tacitus," 588–600; Rutland, "Tacitean Germanicus," 53–64; Williams, "Four Mutinies," 44–74; Fulkerson, "Staging a Mutiny," 169–92; Woodman, "Mutiny and Madness," 303–29.

289. For Germanicus' theatricality, see Shotter, "Tacitus, Tiberius and Germanicus," 198–99; Pelling, "Tacitus and Germanicus," passim.

290. Cf. Tac. *Ann*, 1.34–44.

291. Cf. Pelling, "Tacitus and Germanicus," 67.

would have restored the age of liberty, and Germanicus' own merits were no less attractive: he had an unassuming disposition (*civile ingenium*) and remarkable courtesy (*mira comitas*).[292] Even Tiberius praises Germanicus before the Senate after he ended the soldiers' revolt, and spoke above all about his courage (*virtus*): *multaque de virtute eius memoravit*; but as Tacitus observes, the language and tone sounded too florid to be an expression of the emperor's true feelings.[293]

The other two mentions of Germanicus' *virtus* appear in connection with his funeral. Even though Tacitus clearly seeks to emphasize the contrast between Tiberius the taciturn emperor and Germanicus the cherished heir, he will only acknowledge the latter's virtues as expressed in the people's opinion of him, or even as described by foreign nations, but not as Tacitus' own authorial judgment. Besides, the plural *virtutes* here plays an important role, because in fact, it is not Germanicus' martial *virtus* that is praised at his funeral, but his other good qualities: "his consideration for allies [*comitas in socios*], his humanity to enemies [*mansuetudo in hostis*]: in aspect and address alike venerable [*venerabilis*], while he maintained the magnificence and dignity [*gravitatem*] of exalted fortune, he had escaped envy and avoided arrogance [*invidia et adrogantiam effugerat*]."[294] His *clementia, moderatio, temperantia*, and other good qualities were also praised.[295] But it is a recognition of his *militaris virtus* that the Roman people miss at Germanicus' funeral and that will be thrown in Tiberius' face: "where were (...) the set poems to the memory of the departed valor? [*ubi illa ... meditata ad memoriam virtutis carmina?*]."[296] *Virtus* here could not mean anything but courage, because all other virtues had already been duly praised. To commend or applaud a general's *virtus* could be risky, as it could be seen to diminish the emperor's *virtus*. Tacitus had recorded something similar in the *Agricola*, with Domitian being jealous of Agricola's bravery.[297] At such an early stage of the principate, being outdone in what Rome had always considered one of its highest-identity values for holding power and magistracies could destabilize the legitimacy of the ruler, and therefore with touchy and prickly emperors, it was safer to celebrate other virtues, not bravery.

---

292. Cf. Tac. *Ann*, 1.33.
293. Cf. Tac. *Ann*, 1.52.
294. Tac. *Ann*, 2.72.
295. Tac. *Ann*, 2.73: *quantum clementia, temperantia, ceteris bonis artibus praestitisset*.
296. Tac. *Ann*, 3.5.
297. Cf. Tac. *Agr*, 39.3. See earlier in this chapter.

Within this context of praising (or not) *virtus* as martial bravery, it may seem appropriate to refer briefly to the evolution of the institution of the Roman triumph and other military distinctions.[298] Tacitus' account enables us to track the way in which the glory of winning a triumph and the glamour it carried for the victor started to fade under the principate. Titles and insignia were sometimes conferred by the emperor even before the wars were finished, to forestall the more spectacular scene of the successful general being hailed spontaneously by the legions: Tiberius, for example, chose to treat the war that Blaesus was commanding as finished before it had actually ended;[299] Claudius ordered Corbulo to retreat when, according to the general, victory was at hand;[300] and Nero recalled Suetonius Paulinus to Rome from his activities in Germania.[301] Military awards seemed to have lost even more of their meaning when the emperor Claudius started to give the honors of a triumph—traditionally awarded for winning a major victory with at least 5,000 enemies killed—to actions not directly related to success in war against Rome's adversaries. The example of Curtius Rufus recorded by Tacitus is very significant. He received the distinction for having opened a silver mine, at the cost of great losses for the legionaries, so much so that the soldiers—with great common sense—wrote a letter to the emperor begging him, when "he thought of entrusting an army to a general, to assign triumphal honors in advance."[302] Tacitus' picture of military distinctions under the principate did not seem to fit with the traditional republican pattern of martial honors, and it definitely affected the attribution of *virtus* to military men.[303]

A striking feature of Tacitus' references to Germanicus' *virtus* is that the word is always juxtaposed to *memoria*; that is, it refers to the memory of *virtus*, as if it belonged to the past, and not the present times. Germanicus' *virtus* was remembered by the emperor Tiberius, but in an overelaborate way that made people suspicious of his sincerity (*multaque de virtute eius memoravit, magis in speciem verbis adornata quam ut penitus sentire crederetur*), and later

---

298. On the triumph, see Beard, *Roman Triumph*; and Lange and Vervaet, *Roman Republican Triumph*. For the *dona militaria* in general and their significance, see Maxfield, *Military Decorations of the Roman Army*.

299. Cf. Tac. *Ann*, 3.74.

300. Cf. Tac. *Ann*, 11.19–20.

301. Cf. Tac. *Ann*, 13.9. Cf. Griffin, "Nero's Recall of Suetonius Paulinus," 138–52. Suetonius Paulinus was another of Tacitus' *capax imperii* according to Benario, "*Imperium* and *Capaces Imperii* in Tacitus," 14–26. For Paulinus, see also Tac. *Ann*, 14.29 and *Hist*. 2.32.

302. Tac. *Ann*, 11.20.

303. For more on faked or frustrated triumphs, see Beard, *Roman Triumph*, 109–10, 167, 185, 271–72, and 274; and Roller, *Constructing Autocracy*, 100–101.

on, his *virtus* was not recalled in the usual laudatory poems for the dead (*ubi... meditata ad* memoriam *virtutis carmina*...?) although all his other virtues were duly recorded in his funeral oration (*Funus... per laudes ac* memoriam *virtutum eius celebre fuit*).[304] The fact that Germanicus' *virtus* appears only as something to be included in or omitted from memory—Tacitus does not actually give us any act of *virtus* related to Germanicus—helps to build him up as a general nostalgic for bygone times, and one who was not fully adapted to the present ways of the current political system. Roman military *virtus* in Tacitus' writings appears as a Roman trait more to be reminisced or evoked than actually possessed by someone in the present.

The other character with whom martial *virtus* is connected in the *Annals* is the general Corbulo. The emergence of Gnaeus Domitius Corbulo as the commander in charge of dealing with the troubles arising in Germany under Claudius is one of the rare instances of military *virtus* being ascribed to Romans in Tacitus' military narrative of the *Annals*.[305] Although Tacitus' praise for Corbulo is not always unrestrained,[306] the general usually acted like the great commanders of old times, and his *magna cura* in dealings with the German affairs soon won him *gloria*.[307] He, "lightly dressed and bareheaded, was continually among his troops, on the march or at their toils, offering his praise to the stalwart, his comfort to the weak, his example to all."[308] Like some old Roman generals, Corbulo had the qualities that made him successful: he exercised *severitas* toward traitors, and *disciplina* reigned

---

304. Tac. *Ann*, 1.52; 3.5; 2.73, respectively (my highlighting).

305. For Corbulo, see Syme, "Domitius Corbulo," 27–39; Benario, "*Imperium* and *Capaces Imperii* in Tacitus," 14–26; Gilmartin, "Corbulo's Campaigns in the East," 583–626; Gallota, "Cneo Domizio Corbulone," 305–17; Allison, "Corbulo's Socratic Shadow," 19–25; Vervaet, "Tacitus, Domitius Corbulo and Traianus' Bellum Parthicum," 289–97; "*CIL* IX 3426," 574–99; "Domitius Corbulo and the Senatorial Opposition," 135–93; and "Domitius Corbulo and the Rise of the Flavian Dynasty," 436–64; Malloch, "Date of Corbulo's Campaigns in Lower Germany," 76–83.

306. Cf. Tac. *Ann*, 15.10.

307. Cf. Tac. *Ann*, 11.18. For a cautious view of Tacitus' portrait of Corbulo, see Ash, "Following the Footsteps of Lucullus?," 355–75.

308. Tac. *Ann*, 13.35. Corbulo's attention to the troops matched that of Metellus: "on the march too he was now with those in the van, now in the rear, often in the middle of the line (...) he made sure that the soldiers carried food and arms," Sall, *BJ* 45.2; and that of Marius: "he went from place to place, now succoring those of his men who were in difficulty, now charging the enemy where they were pressing in great number," Sall, *BJ* 98.1; and even that of Catiline: "Meanwhile Catiline, with his light-armed troops, was busy in the van, aided those who were hard pressed, summoned fresh troops to replace the wounded, had an eye to everything, and at the same time fought hard himself," Sall, *BC* 60.4.

everywhere.³⁰⁹ He was first in the field on the appointed day, avoided a protracted and fruitless campaign, made suitable provisions for the assault, urged on the troops, was not surprised by the enemy's attack, but was prepared for battle.³¹⁰ He was also an example of *patientia* to his soldiers, bearing the shortage of water and the same privations as the common legionaries.³¹¹ In this case, Tacitus' presentation of Corbulo's actions would perhaps have reminded the reader of the old republican generals, sharing the toils of war with his soldiers and encouraging them along the way by his example.³¹²

Even though Tacitus never says explicitly that Corbulo had *virtus*, he is said to have inspired it. His examples of *severitas* had a double effect: they produced terror in the enemy,³¹³ while to the Romans they meant an increase in courage: *nos virtutem auximus*.³¹⁴ Paradoxically, it seems as if Corbulo was playing, in the present, the role of an ancestor to his own men: he stirred them to act with *virtus* as the *maiores* did for the younger generations.³¹⁵ However, as in the case of Germanicus, Corbulo's own firm and energetic action against the Germans contrasted too much with the principate's negotiations and military passivity; it roused suspicion as a possible threat to peace. In the end, the emperor Claudius thought it more prudent to order the army to retreat. Corbulo obeyed with the *prisca disciplina* of the generals who had conquered the empire, but, denied the glory of war, he said with a touch of nostalgia, "Happy the Roman generals before my time."³¹⁶ The emperor, as a sort of "consolation prize," conceded him ensigns of a triumph for constructing a canal between the Meuse and the Rhine. As we have seen, military exploits were being exchanged for nonmilitary ones, and this suggests on the one hand that sometimes daring and bravery in war against enemies were not always the appropriate qualities to exercise under the principate, when many things were accomplished by diplomacy. On the other hand, the figure of the successful general posed a threat to the reputation of the ever-jealous emperors: as Agricola had been to Domitian and Germanicus to Tiberius, Corbulo

---

309. Cf. Tac. *Ann*, 13.35; 14.23. Ash, "Following the Footsteps of Lucullus?," 374, maintains, however, that this *disciplina* declined into cruelty.

310. Cf. Tac. *Ann*, 13.38–41.

311. Cf. Tac. *Ann*, 14.24.

312. Cf. Livy's description of general Valerius Corvinus: "there was never a commander who more endeared himself by his men by cheerfully sharing all the duties with the meanest of the soldiers," 7.33.1.

313. Cf. Tac. *Ann*, 11.18.3; 11.19.1; 13.35.4.

314. Tac. *Ann*, 11.19.

315. Cf. Sall. *BJ* 4.6.

316. Tac. *Ann*, 11.20.

would be efficient and useful to Claudius, and later to Nero, only if he kept within limits.

Corbulo reappears in the narrative when he was appointed to save Armenia from the Parthians. This appointment, which caused great joy in the city, was seen by the Romans as "a measure that seemed to have opened a career to the virtues [*locus virtutibus patefactus*]."[317] Again, Corbulo represented the possibility of exercising virtues, but once more the opportunity was thwarted. This time it was not so much due to the emperor's jealousy, but to the unrestrained rivalry among commanders. Ummidius Quadratus, for example, the governor of the province of Armenia, resented Corbulo's intervention in his territory.[318] Later on, Caesennius Paetus, Corbulo's helper, was not content to rank second after such a leader and started acting thoughtlessly, showing no *moderatio*.[319] Toward the end of the campaign, Paetus' haste and imprudence brought nothing but humiliation to the Roman army, and what could have worked as a healthy *aemulatio* between commanders slid toward failure and despair: "all rivalry in valor [*certamen virtute*] and all ambition for glory [*ambitio gloriae*], emotions confined to the fortunate, had taken their leave; pity alone held sway."[320] Tacitus' words recall those of Livy in Book 10—*quod certamen virtutis viros in hac civitate tenet*—when the matrons of the city set up a competition in modesty (*pudicitia*) in similar terms to that of men regarding bravery.[321] It was a feature of past times to be able to have contests in *virtus*. Sallust had also said it when referring to the period before the fall of Carthage: *cives cum civibus de virtute certabant*.[322] This may be idealization on the part of the historians, but it is nonetheless very telling that the three of them choose to describe the past in the same way and with the same words, as if Rome had been, at some point in her history, a wonderful place where everybody fought against one another to excel in *virtus*. This competition in *virtus* that Sallust and Livy had described as belonging to times of the early republic was gradually transformed into a competition solely for glory. In Tacitus' words one can perceive an added tone of disappointment and disillusion as the hope for *virtus* and *virtutes* that Corbulo had represented for the Roman army and also to the people at Rome had been annulled not only by the

---

317. Tac. *Ann*, 13.8.
318. Cf. Tac. *Ann*, 13.9.
319. Cf. Tac. *Ann*, 15.8.
320. Tac. *Ann*, 15.16.
321. Livy, 10.23.7.
322. Sall. *BC* 9.2.

external circumstances but also because there was something in Corbulo's own conduct that prevented the display of *virtus*. His ambition to prevail over others led him to delay the help that Caesennius desperately needed, placing his own glory above the safety of the *res publica*, and *virtus* was left floating in the air as an unfulfilled promise.[323]

Corbulo appears one last time in the *Annals*, in charge of the legions when king Vologeses started hostilities again.[324] According to Tacitus, the emperor raised Corbulo's powers nearly to the level of Pompey's in 67 B.C. when commanding the war against the pirates.[325] The comparison is significant, for both situations implied grave dangers to Rome and special commands were given to both generals. It may have been simply the geographical area in which Corbulo was fighting that reminded Tacitus of Pompey, but more probably, perhaps, the author was drawing the reader's attention to the similarities (and differences) of a war waged during the republic, just over a century before.[326] After being granted special powers for the war against the pirates, Pompey received yet another exceptional command to fight Mithridates, and he became the most successful and popular general of the time, paving his way to supremacy. Corbulo was successful too, but the reputation that he won throughout his brilliant career put him in a risky position not only regarding the emperor but also regarding the imperial system itself, and he was compelled by Nero to commit suicide in A.D. 66. In just one century, the consequences of being a successful Roman general had changed completely.

Under the principate, wars against external enemies seemed to have the same value as they had had during the republic, and they should have provided the chance of displaying *virtus* at its best. But Tacitus shows that this opportunity was seldom taken by Romans. It is not that the Romans lacked *virtus* altogether or that their commanders were men of vice; in fact one may have the impression that they would have shown *virtus* in another context. But what was revealed in reality was that it was difficult to exercise *virtus* because of the circumstances. This was not only because of the dominating presence of the emperor but also because imperial Rome's external policy required the display of both diplomatic talents and persuasive political

---

323. Cf. Tac. *Ann*, 15.10.

324. Cf. Syme, "Domitius Corbulo," 39; Gilmartin, "Corbulo's Campaigns in the East," passim; Ash, "Following the Footsteps of Lucullus?," 357.

325. Cf. Tac. *Ann*, 15.25.

326. Pompey, however, appeared elsewhere in the *Annals* in a less favorable light, cf. 1.1: *Pompei Crassique potentia cito in Caesarem*. For more on this comparison, see Ash, "Following the Footsteps of Lucullus?," 373–74.

negotiations which in some sense prevented military superiority from being exercised in the traditional way. The spectacle of military *virtus* is not completely absent from the *Annals*, but it is perceived as through a somewhat opaque looking-glass.

Apart from this cloudy view of martial Roman *virtus* in the *Annals*, it is also possible to discover some new shades that qualify this bravery under the rule of the *princeps*, namely, *moderatio* and, to a lesser extent, *comitas*. These qualities seemed to become more important to a Roman general during the principate. *Comitas* was that touch of civility and politeness in military matters that attracted Roman soldiers and enemies alike. Good manners added a new type of splendor to the glory of the generals, because it made them appear more humane.[327] It is not that *comitas* now became a prerequisite or condition for *virtus*, but it certainly added to the military man something more than just a useful attribute in politics and a valuable tool for courting popularity. *Comitas* was not just an inborn talent for making oneself agreeable, but more an attitude or a mental disposition.[328] Consideration and affability were a way of recognizing the other's dignity. Although Germanicus is not presented as Tacitus' unconditional hero, the historian does acknowledge that part of Germanicus' popularity was based on his exceptional kindness (*mira comitas*) which, together with his unassuming disposition (*civile ingenium*), made him the center of affection and hopes after Augustus' death.[329] Tacitus contrasts Germanicus' *mira comitas* to Tiberius' inscrutable arrogance of word and look. Courtesy brought a feeling of safety, security, and proximity; arrogance, on the contrary, inspired distance, uncertainty, and anxiety. Germanicus' closeness, not only to people in general but especially to soldiers, was demonstrated above all after the battles: "To soften by kindness also their recollections of the late havoc, he made a round of the wounded, praised their individual exploits (. . .) and confirmed their enthusiasm for himself and battle, here by the stimulus of hope, there by that of glory, and everywhere by his consolation and solicitude."[330] This same courtesy made

---

327. Compare with Velleius' attribution of *humanitas* to Tiberius in 2.114; see chapter 4 in this book.

328. Cf. Hellegouarc'h, *Le vocabulaire Latin*, 215–16.

329. Cf. Tac. *Ann*, 1.33.

330. Tac. *Ann*, 1.71: *Utque cladis memoriam etiam comitate leniret, circumire saucios, facta singulorum extollere, vulnera intuens, alium spe, alium gloria, cunctos adloquio et cura sibique et proelio firmabat.* However, it is possible to argue that Germanicus also put the army's loyalty to the state at risk, not merely by helping the soldiers with his private means: *propria pecunia militem iuvit*, but especially by intensifying their loyalty to himself: *sibique et proelio firmabat.*

kings and foreign nations feel the pain after Germanicus' departure: "so great had been his courtesy to allies [*comitas in socios*], his humanity to enemies [*mansuetudo in hostis*]: in aspect and address alike venerable, while he maintained the magnificence and dignity of exalted fortune, he had escaped envy and avoided arrogance."[331]

Another example of *comitas* in Tacitus' *Annals*, even when dealing with the opponent, was that of Corbulo. His name was also respected by enemies, who bore no bitterness or rancor toward the Roman commander.[332] After he put an end to the war in Armenia, he showed signs of civility with king Tiridates by swiftly dismounting from his horse and shaking hands with the king on foot, and later "to his glories [he] added kindness and banquets [*addidit gloriae comitatem epulasque*]."[333] Being a courteous and considerate general was more congruent with the rule of one, as it demanded not only polished manners in dealing with people but also forgoing the normal arrogance of a victorious individual leader who might cast a shadow over the emperor's glory.

Apart from other qualities that are illustrated in the narrative, good generals also appear to have displayed *moderatio* in or after the wars they fought. Their legitimate desires to acquire glory did not distract them from fulfilling their duty by obeying the emperor's orders, even when they seemed to hinder Rome's progress by limiting its conquest and expansion. Germanicus, for example, was recalled by Tiberius to Rome: according to Tacitus he was told to refrain from any more fighting in Germany and to leave Drusus some material for winning repute.[334] Corbulo, on the other hand, was ordered by Claudius to withdraw his garrison to the west side of the Rhine and told that no aggression should be committed against the Germans.[335] Even Helvidius Priscus, who in the *Histories* appears as a bolder and more rebellious character, is also praised for his moderation, by which he in fact accomplished more than others had done with force: *moderatione plura quam vi composuerat*.[336] He, however, in spite of his achievements—or precisely because of them—was ordered back to Syria, lest by his brave exploits he should give occasion for a Parthian war. Other cases of *moderatio* are not shown in the battlefield, but in the way the

---

331. Tac. *Ann*, 2.72.
332. Cf. Tac. *Ann*, 15.28. See also 13.9.
333. Cf. Tac. *Ann*, 15.30.
334. Cf. Tac. *Ann*, 2.26.
335. Cf. Tac. *Ann*, 11.19.
336. Cf. Tac. *Ann*, 12.49.

victors dealt with their successes after the wars. This is the case Cn. Lentulus, who is admired by Tacitus not only for his military success against the Getae but also for his *modestia* in displaying his wealth after his victory.[337]

For Tacitus, military *virtus* under the principate showed at the same time some traditional and some novel aspects that are clearly illustrated in the *Annals*. On the one hand, the same customary "republican" courage was needed to fight the enemy, but it had to be exercised toward an external enemy: there was no real bravery or *virtus* in mutinies among the troops. This courage or *virilis-virtus* was often displayed by the foreign nations defending their freedom against Rome. But on the other hand, courage for Romans had to be moderated by the recognition that too much glory could awaken the *princeps'* jealousy and therefore one had to be content not with the highest triumph one could win, but with a "sensible" level. It is not that *virtus* as bravery had to be moderate, for it needed to be as great as ever, but the glory attained by it had to stay under control. Under the rule of one the whole point of being triumphant and playing the *triumphator* too much was questioned and subject to revision.[338] The ones who, by showing their courage, triumphed over the enemy later had to be satisfied with perhaps a more modest reward, but the challenge of fighting and displaying *virtus* was still worthwhile and taken up by some. Freedom, then, was manifested in this less spectacular way: the free acceptance of not attaining all the glory one could win in war (perhaps an unthinkable attitude during republican times), but nevertheless giving everything as if fighting for the highest honors.

Martial *virtus* in the *Annals* of Tacitus is not as straightforward as it might seem at first sight. Reckoning according to the number of wars that appear in the work, *virtus* should have been much more present throughout the narrative than it is. Tacitus acknowledged barbarians' *virtus*—especially that of their commanders—much more openly than he did the *virtus* of Romans. This is partly explained because the barbarians were united in fighting to maintain their original independence, whereas the Romans showed rivalry, jealousy, and mixed motivations that tainted their struggle. Part of the explanation is also Tacitus' view that military values were changing rapidly and the character of the *princeps* made a difference to those values. The change of values and the emperor's influence are seen even more strongly in the case of civic *virtus*.

---

337. Cf. Tac. *Ann*, 4.44.

338. As Beard states in *Roman Triumph*, 297, "the extraordinary prominence that a triumph gave to the successful general was too much for the canny emperor to risk sharing widely."

Virtus *in the City of Rome under a* Princeps

At first sight, it looks as if for Tacitus there was something inevitably tragic about political and civil *virtus* under the principate. All too often, choosing to behave courageously had a high price: life. We find many examples in the *Annals* of Romans who decided to be consistent with their principles and ended up accepting death on the emperor's orders, or taking their lives by their own hand. The ending was not completely bad—they actually achieved *gloria*—but it was almost always a sad one: many virtuous men had to die.[339]

Nevertheless, although death in the name of *libertas* or to preserve freedom was a glorious end, and Tacitus admired it, it was not the only way out in the principate, not even under the worst emperors. Tacitus' complaint that his work was *in arto et inglorius labor* applies not only to his task of recording the petty intrigues of the principate compared with the great republican wars but also to recording the lives of people who did not die like heroes, but rather who simply carried on living heroically in bad circumstances. Under the rule of one man, serving the state meant taking a rather novel approach: collaborating with the regime but without becoming contaminated. Even though the imperial political system did not promote *virtus* in the same way as the republic had done, individual *virtus* was still important. Each and every one could make a difference; one's presence in the government still mattered.[340] In short, serving the state meant actually being a hero, without playing the hero. Presumably, this is the idea behind Tacitus' words in the *Agricola* when he says that "submission and moderation, if animation and energy go with them, reach the same pinnacle of fame, whither more often men have climbed by perilous courses, but with no profit to the state, and have earned their glory by an ostentatious death [*obsequiumque ac modestiam, si industria ac vigor adsint, eo laudis excedere, quo plerique per abrupta sed in nullum rei publicae usum ambitiosa morte inclaruerunt*]."[341] Paradoxically, these unheroic lives achieved great glory and Tacitus' *inglorius labor* turned out to be most glorious after all.[342] The principate had changed the meanings of old concepts and perhaps of values, but the core of being Roman remained. It only had to be exercised in a different way.

---

339. For political suicide in imperial Rome, see, for example, Edwards, *Death in Ancient Rome*, esp. chaps. 3, 4, and 5; Griffin, "Philosophy, Cato and Roman Suicide," 64–77 and 192–202.
340. As shown by Agricola in Domitian's reign.
341. Tac. *Agr*, 42.
342. Cf. Clarke, "In arto et inglorius labor," 98.

In this section I will illustrate how these unheroic heroes lived and by what means they attracted praise from Tacitus and won glory in history. It is through their lives that Tacitus shows that some kind of *virtus* is still present under the principate. He does not idealize the past while overlooking present reality; on the contrary, he can also find good things in these terrible times: "Nor, indeed, were all things better in the old time before us; but our own age too has produced much in the sphere of true nobility and much in that of art which posterity well may imitate. In any case, may the honorable competition of our present with our past long remain! [*verum haec nobis in maiores certamina ex honesto maneant*]."[343] This *certamen* between past and present is very similar to that which we have seen in the other Roman historians. Tacitus is well aware that emulation and sound rivalry work as a trigger to improvement, and this is why he expresses his disappointment when he sees his own class mired in the mediocrity of adulation and inactivity caused by fear.

If the *Annals* are concerned with the loss of freedom of the senatorial class after Augustus' reign, and describe everybody rushing headlong into slavery,[344] it seemed all the more necessary for Tacitus to bring to light those noteworthy people who overcame fear and did not fall into servitude, but persevered in quietly fulfilling their duties. Admittedly there are not as many of these examples in Tacitus as of baseness and corruption, but there are quite a few, and very remarkable ones. The generalized conduct of the weak is recorded in his work to highlight the free decisions of those few who resisted bravely.

All of Tacitus' "heroes" in the *Annals* have in common their opposition to flattery and their refusal to act out of fear. Tacitus shows quite clearly in the *Annals* that under Tiberius fear [*metus*] was leading to flattery [*adulatio*];[345] in fact, in some cases to extreme adulation.[346] It was difficult to navigate safely under this *princeps* because everybody feared something: whether they spoke the truth or lied, they ran great risks;[347] and some senators even feared that they might seem to comprehend him.[348] The lack of expression of Tiberius' face was also a cause for dread: "But nothing daunted him [Piso] more than the sight of Tiberius, pitiless and angerless, barred and bolted against the

---

343. Tac. *Ann*, 3.55. See further Ginsburg, "*In Maiores Certamina*," 86–103.
344. Tac. *Ann*, 1.7: *At Romae ruere in servitium consules, patres, eques*.
345. Tac. *Ann*, 4.74: *pavor internus occupaverat animos, cui remedium adulatione quaerebatur*.
346. Cf. Tac. *Ann*, 2.32; 3.57; 3.69; 15.73–74. For an explanation on how flattery worked differently during the republic and the principate, see Roller, *Constructing Autocracy*, 108–24.
347. Cf. Tac. *Ann*, 1.6.
348. Cf. Tac. *Ann*, 1.11.

ingress of any human emotion."[349] The expressions *pavor internus*,[350] *priores metus*,[351] and *vi metus*[352] illustrate the extent to which fear and uncertainty became a regular feature of political decisions under Tiberius and his successors. Tacitus is disappointed at the circumstances, but even more so at the ignoble response of his own class. The whole matter was made sadder for him not so much by the way the tyrannical behavior of the *princeps* destroyed their freedom, but by the way their base conduct made the *princeps* behave like a tyrant. This is particularly clear with the emperor Tiberius, whose reign would perhaps have been different had the senators been more honest in their opinions, or had they taken up their responsibility for participating politically in the *res publica*, with more courage and less fear and flattery. This may be one of the reasons why Tacitus is so intrigued with Tiberius' personality. The good intentions of Augustus' successor were patent, but the atmosphere of *adulatio* and *metus* in which he moved made him resentful and devious, almost forcing him to behave in an autocratic way.

I intend to show that these two deep-rooted weaknesses of the new regime, flattery and fear, allowed different manifestations of *virtus*—which were less active during the republic—to flourish and prosper in the new heroes of the principate. These new expressions, which appear to be directly related, by opposition, to *adulatio* and *metus*, are moderation (*moderatio*) and firmness (*constantia*).[353] On the one hand, adulation and flattery toward the emperor were produced by excess and intemperance. Those who complimented the *princeps*—whoever of the Julio-Claudians he was—knew perfectly well that they were exaggerating his merits, and sycophancy advanced in widening spirals until it became generalized. Only personal *moderatio* could counteract the excesses of *adulatio*. Moderation in the principate meant having sufficient restraint and self-control not to fall into amplification and overstatement concerning the emperor and his decisions. The moderate person was temperate and avoided extremes, was content with his lot, and did not covet higher political posts or seek the emperor's favor at any cost. Moderation was the opposite of "senators rushing into slavery."[354] It was not governed by the actions

---

349. Tac. *Ann*, 3.15. See also 3.22.
350. Tac. *Ann*, 4.74.
351. Tac. *Ann*, 6.18.
352. Tac. *Ann*, 6.19.
353. For their role in politics, though in republican times, see Hellegouarc'h, *Vocabulaire Latin*, 264–65 and 283–85, respectively. For *constantia*, see also Schofield, "Republican Virtues," esp. 201–3.
354. Tac. *Ann*, 1.7.

of the *princeps* or by the system itself, owing more to each individual's mental attitudes and personal reactions. On the other hand, the pervading *metus* which had contaminated everything resulted in trepidation, doubt, and, in some cases, inertia, inaction, or even flight. This *metus* was contrasted with *constantia*, which was the firmness, resolution, and fearlessness that enabled men to accept or resist difficulties bravely and without complaints. *Constantia* implied an ability to remain steady in one's own judgment, steadfastness in being true to one's conscience.

A quick reading of the *Annals* may surprise us by showing that, to a certain extent, the examples of *constantia* and *moderatio* seem to replace the examples of *virtus* in the other historical narratives. However, rather than actually replacing *virtus*, what these examples do is qualify the "mode" and even the "mood" of traditional *virtus*. *Constantia* and *moderatio* opposed *metus* and *adulatio*, and as such they were closely related to *virtus*, the customary courage and valor that had always been essential in Roman political life. Courage and fortitude implied two primary actions: attack and resistance. The republic had brought out the attacking side of *virtus*, demonstrated by brave deeds in defense of *libertas*. The principate brought out, instead, the resisting side of *virtus*, demonstrated by bravely standing firm against evil through *constantia* and *moderatio*. The problem was that the way of practicing *virtus* in the principate did not appeal to all, since the Romans were traditionally competitive, seeking glory through the performance of spectacular feats, whereas this new mode of *virtus* involved resisting wrong through the unspectacular qualities of patience, self-control, resolution, and endurance. In the *Annals*, Tacitus continuously denounces the generalized unwillingness to serve the *res publica*—now under a *princeps*—in this new, quieter way which, in fact, implied no less courage and demonstrated no less inner freedom; but he also highlights the few men who did so.

The most conspicuous and popular case of *moderatio* in the *Annals* is, of course, Marcus Lepidus.[355] He first appears at the very beginning of the

355. This Marcus Lepidus has been the object of a long-standing discussion concerning his *praenomen* [M.], which appears to be sometimes confused in the *Annals* with that of Manius Lepidus [M'.]. In some cases it is, indeed, very difficult to say for certain to whom Tacitus is referring, and even the manuscripts had to be emended to maintain consistency throughout the narrative (the OCT [Fisher, 1906], for example, records the eight [!] emendations made by Lipsius to the Mediceus codex changing M. to M'). Syme has argued, quite persuasively, for a definitive distinction between the two, and this is what we follow here. See Syme, "Marcus Lepidus, *capax imperii*," 22–33, and "Marcus Lepidus" in *Augustan Aristocracy*, 128–40; followed by Benario, "*Imperium* and *Capaces Imperii* in Tacitus," 14–26; and "Marcus Lepidus, Galba and Thrasea," 45–51. Hayne, "Last of the Aemilii Lepidi," 497–506, does not agree with either author and proposes his own differentiation.

narrative when Tacitus records Augustus' discussion about the possible holders of the principate. The words "capable but disdainful [*capax sed aspernans*]" reveal a possible candidate in terms of talent and skill, but one who wanted to stay aloof from the vicissitudes of governing the empire.[356] With the word *capax*, Tacitus is ascribing to Marcus Lepidus not only the qualities that he displayed when Augustus was alive and having that conversation, which were mainly his military exploits,[357] but also all the good things he was going to carry out under Tiberius' reign. *Aspernans*, however, works as a more complex adjective and is related in some way to *moderatio*. Someone who does not show interest in becoming *princeps* is probably someone who does not intend to ascend higher than is convenient or prudent, but is content with the political offices he has achieved. Lepidus' authentic prudence regarding posts was also shown when he declined the offer of the proconsulate of Africa and let Blaesus, Sejanus' uncle, take it.[358] Marcus Lepidus appeared moderate in his aspirations, and this is perhaps one of the reasons why Tiberius thought highly of him.[359] He seemed reluctant to accept very high positions or privileges—he even declined to choose his own legate *per modestiam*[360]—but did not hesitate to burden himself with difficult tasks, and demonstrated this by accepting the defense of Cn. Piso after others had declined on various pretexts.[361] Here Lepidus showed not only his self-control but also his disposition to serve the state in what was required. It was evidently not easy to find somebody willing to defend such a delicate case as the death of Germanicus, especially because in some way it involved the emperor himself.

However, Lepidus was praised not only by the *princeps*[362] but also by the Senate as a whole. When Sextus Pompeius attacked Lepidus as spiritless (*socordis*) and poverty-stricken (*inops*), the senators protested and declared that he was "gentle rather than cowardly [*mitis magis quam ignavus*]," giving proof of his temperance again.[363] His gentleness was displayed once again at the trial of Clutorius Priscus for a *maiestas* case. In his speech, given in full by Tacitus, he appealed to Tiberius' own moderation (*principis moderatio*) and

---

356. Cf. Tac. *Ann*, 1.13.
357. See, for example, Vell. 2.114.5; 2.115.2; 2.125.5; and Dio, 56.12.2.
358. Cf. Tac. *Ann*, 3.35.
359. Tac. *Ann*, 4.20.2: *cum aequabili auctoritate et gratia apud Tiberium viguerit*.
360. Tac. *Ann*, 4.56.
361. Cf. Tac. *Ann*, 3.11.
362. Cf. Tac. *Ann*, 3.51.
363. Cf. Tac. *Ann*, 3.32. "Gentle" or "mild" can act here as a synonym of "temperate" or "moderate."

proposed having Clutorius exiled instead of executed. Lepidus' proposal revealed much common sense—not evident in the rest of the senators, who finally decided in favor of capital punishment—because he argued that evil-speaking was different from evildoing, so that sparing Clutorius' life could involve no threat to the public, and a death sentence would not work as a deterrent. Tacitus shows how Lepidus' suggestion accords with the *mores maiorum*, where only "deeds were challenged, words went immune."[364] Tiberius' ambiguous response in this case—praising Lepidus and not blaming Agrippa, the accuser—would become paradigmatic for other trials, where the emperor on the one hand regretted the quick executions, but on the other hand did nothing to prevent the Senate from taking decisions out of fear.[365]

Marcus Lepidus showed his moderation not only in trials and punishments but also in his knowledge of the law and how to apply it properly. After Silius' suicide, his wife Sosia, who had incurred the emperor's hatred through her friendship with Agrippina, was condemned to exile by a proposal of Asinius Gallus. Lepidus presented a countermotion that was more lenient to Sosia and more in accordance with the law.[366] At this point in the narrative, Tacitus draws attention to Lepidus' prudence and discretion under Tiberius. The unequivocal praise—in his own authorial voice—is precise and sober, and for this very reason, all the more powerful: "This Lepidus, I gather, was for his period, a serious and wise man [*gravem et sapientem*]: for the number of motions that he steered away from savage adulations of others for the better is very considerable."[367] One can see not only moderation shining out here in his avoidance of flattery but also constancy: it seems probable that, if Tacitus says that the number of cases in which Lepidus intervened was "very considerable [*pleraque*]," he must have shown temperance and discretion

---

364. Tac. *Ann*, 1.72.2: *Facta arguebantur, dicta impune erant*. According to Tacitus, Augustus was the first to introduce punishments for words; cf. Severus' case at *Ann*, 1.72.3 and 4.21.3.

365. On the politics of how the emperors handled treason trials, see, for example, Plass, *Game of Death in Ancient Rome*, 81–134.

366. Cf. Tac. *Ann*, 4.20.

367. Tac. *Ann*, 4.20: *hunc ego Lepidum temporibus illis gravem et sapientem virum fuisse comperior: nam pleraque ab saevis adulationibus aliorum in melius flexit*. The phrase *gravem et sapientem virum fuisse comperior* reminds us of Sallust's commendation of Metellus in *BJ*, 45: *magnum et sapientem virum fuisse conperior* ("I find that Metellus showed himself a great and prudent man"). A significant comparison. For more on this, see Martin and Woodman, *Tacitus*, ad loc.

continuously, and it was for this motive that "he stood uniformly high in Tiberius' influence and favor."[368]

This positive remark on Marcus Lepidus led Tacitus to a broader and more significant observation on the causes of human actions: "a circumstance that compels me to doubt whether sympathies and antipathies of princes are governed in their incidence by fate and the star of our nativity, or whether our purposes count and we are free, between the extremes of bluff contumacy and repellent servility, to walk a straight road, clear of intrigues and perils."[369] *Dubitare cogor* is clearly ironic; otherwise Tacitus would not have said in the *Agricola* "that good men could live under bad princes." For the author of the *Annals* it was personal conduct and free decisions that counted, rather than fate and one's stars, in preventing one from falling into the extremes of haughty obstinacy or shameful servility (*abruptam contumaciam et deforme obsequium*), as the uprightness of Lepidus had shown. This middle course was not inertia or inaction, but the fortitude of being brave in acting according to one's principles regardless of the consequences, and overcoming fear. Lepidus is the true virtuous man in the way newly developed under the principate: he still shows courage in the fight for personal freedom—one still needed *virtus* to protect *libertas*—but exhibited it in a different way, through constancy and moderation. It is on Lepidus' example that Tacitus can model ideal conduct henceforward. For Tacitus, the influence that men like him can have on the emperor is essential.[370] The final mention of Lepidus is his obituary, where Tacitus recalls once again his moderation and wisdom (*moderationem atque sapientiam*).[371] From the *Agricola* to the fourth book of the *Annals*, it has taken the author some time to develop his theory of good men under the rule of one man; but he has finally made it clear what it meant to be brave in civil life under the principate.

Marcus Terentius in Book 6 appears as another example of *constantia*. Though a more modest case than Lepidus, he showed no less personal freedom and independence of speech. Marcus Terentius was a Roman knight at a

---

368. Tac. *Ann*, 4.20. So great was Tiberius' esteem for Lepidus that Cotta Messalinus complained of his influence over the emperor, cf. 6.5.

369. Tac. *Ann*, 4.20: *Unde dubitare cogor, fato et sorte nascendi, ut cetera, ita principium inclinatio in hos, offensio in illos, an sit aliquid in nostris consiliis liqueatque inter abruptam contumaciam et deforme obsequium pergere iter ambitione ac periculis vacuum.* Luce, "Tacitus' Conception of Historical Change," 143–57, is still useful; and more recently also Griffin, "Tacitus as a Historian," 168–72.

370. Cf. Ducos, "La liberté chez Tacite," 207.

371. Tac. *Ann*, 6.27.

time when all others had falsely disclaimed the friendship of Sejanus, and he, accused on that score, dared to embrace the accusation. He said that not only was he Sejanus' friend, but he also sought that friendship and intimacy on the grounds that he could thus have a stronger claim to the emperor's friendship, "for we courted not Sejanus of Vulsinii, but the member of those Claudian and Julian houses into which his alliances had won him entry: your son-in-law, Caesar; the partner of your consulate, the agent who discharged your functions in the state. It is not ours to ask whom you exalt above his fellows, or why: you the gods have made the sovereign arbiter of things; to us has been left the glory of obedience [*nobis obsequii gloria relicta est*]."[372] These words can be interpreted as somewhat sarcastic and, therefore, unlikely to work as an appeal in the trial, but even the sarcasm displayed shows courage in speaking to the emperor. Terentius' own defense was perhaps his last act of courage, and it was worth trying. Tacitus tells us that he dared to say what he really thought—that is, to acknowledge with frankness his own *obsequium*—and, appealing to Tiberius, he asked the Senate to draw a true dividing line: "let treason against the realm, projected assassination of the sovereign, meet their punishment; but, when friendship and its duties are in question, if we terminate them at the same moment as you, we are vindicated, Caesar, along with yourself."[373] The firmness of his speech (*constantia orationis*) and "the fact that a man had been discovered to utter what the world was thinking [*quia repertus erat qui efferret quae omnes animo agitabant*]" was this time successful: Terentius was acquitted and his accusers penalized with exile or death.[374] *Constantia*, not only in action but also in words, would come to have a preponderant role in the principate, as firmness of speech was one of the few ways in which one could show courage in political life under the rule of one.

Other characters in the *Annals* also displayed *moderatio* and were admired by Tacitus. Gnaeus Lentulus, for example, spent his great fortune temperately (*modeste*);[375] Quintus Servaeus and Minucius Thermus "had refrained from abusing their friendship with Sejanus [*modeste habita Seiani amicitia*]: a fact that gained them peculiar sympathy."[376] Lucius Piso, the pontiff, appeared as "never the willing author of any slavish proposal; if ever necessity pressed too

---

372. Tac. *Ann*, 6.8.
373. Tac. *Ann*, 6.8.
374. Tac. *Ann*, 6.9.
375. Cf. Tac. *Ann*, 4.44.
376. Tac. *Ann*, 6.7.

hard, he was still a discreet and restraining influence [*sapienter moderans*],"[377] and Helvidius Priscus was a good diplomat in Armenia who "settled more points by moderation than by force [*moderatione plura quam vi*],"[378] although he may have lacked this same moderation as a politician in Rome.

Lucius Arruntius' name does not appear explicitly connected with the virtue of moderation, but the fact that he was kept in Rome for ten successive years when he should have been appointed a province[379] leads us to conclude that this *capax imperii*[380] must have been one of those men who did not oppose the wishes of the emperor and contented himself with having no glorious magistracy even when he had done everything to deserve one. Arruntius defended the *mores maiorum*,[381] and his influence on Tiberius was paired with that of Lepidus.[382] The unjust accusation that associated him with the reprobate Cotta Messalinus made Tacitus defend Arruntius as *vir sanctissimus*.[383] His suicide, narrated with some detail, was a proof of his misery: he was always hated by one of the emperor's prefects, Sejanus or Macro; he could not bear more crimes; and he foresaw that things would get worse under Caligula.[384]

The case of Rubellius Plautus, this time under Nero's reign, is presented as another *capax imperii* who had to withdraw from the scene not on account of his own deeds, but because of the emperor's jealousy of Plautus' high repute and popularity.[385] He is introduced as a possible candidate for the throne announced by the apparition of a comet, and his name starts appearing on everybody's lips.[386] This Plautus "cherished the views of an older generation: his bearing was austere [*severo*], his domestic life being pure and secluded; and the retirement that his fears led him to seek had only brought him an accession of fame."[387] After hearing the *rumores* about Plautus, Nero decided to

---

377. Tac. *Ann*, 6.10.
378. Tac. *Ann*, 12.49.
379. Cf. Tac. *Ann*, 6.27.
380. Cf. Tac. *Ann*, 1.13.
381. Cf. Tac. *Ann*, 3.31.
382. Tac. *Ann*, 6.5: *de potentia M. Lepidi ac L. Arruntii*.
383. Cf. Tac. *Ann*, 6.7.
384. Cf. Tac. *Ann*, 6.48.
385. For Plautus as a possible "candidate" for the throne, see Tac. *Ann*, 13.20–21. Plautus and Nero stood in the same relationship to Augustus by direct descent on their mother's side.
386. Tac. *Ann*, 14.22: *Et omnium ore Rubellius Plautus celebratur*.
387. Tac. *Ann*, 14.22: *Ipse placita maiorum colebat, habitu severo, casta et secreta domo, quantoque metu occultior, tanto plus famae adeptus*.

write a letter advising him to retire to Asia where he had family estates. Plautus did as the emperor suggested: he had not sought popularity, and therefore his moderate life was not interrupted, and he remained firm: *sed Plautum ea non movere*.[388] A remarkable note of this episode is that, in spite of the corruption of the times, Tacitus records that the people of Rome thought of a good and austere man to succeed Nero; at least some upright men, then, must have been alive and were willing to acclaim a virtuous man as emperor. But Plautus' end was a sad one: Nero continued to be alarmed at his rival's ascension in popularity and plotted his death. Plautus, though innocent, was advised by some Stoic friends to show his *constantia* by facing death instead of living an uncertain and harassed life.[389]

A luckier *capax imperii* under Nero was Memmius Regulus, "whose authority, firmness, and character [*auctoritate, constantia, fama*] had earned him the maximum glory possible in the shadows cast by imperial greatness."[390] Regulus, consul in A.D. 31, had been loyal to Tiberius and had helped in Sejanus' downfall. Under the subsequent governments, he never provoked the emperor's jealousy and was even acknowledged as a possible candidate for the throne by Nero himself. Memmius Regulus appeared to be not so dangerous an applicant; his quietness of life, his modest fortune, and the fact that he rose from a recently ennobled family made him more innocuous than Plautus, who, like Nero, drew his nobility from the Julian house on his mother's side.[391]

More men of high rank are described by Tacitus as achieving *constantia* in death, even when the holders of this good quality had not always been an example of virtue in life. This is the case with Silius, Messalina's lover, who "set before the tribunal, attempted neither defense nor delay, and asked for an acceleration of death. His firmness [*constantia*] was imitated by a number of Roman knights of the higher ranks."[392] Caninius Rebilus, a famous and wealthy jurist, also demonstrated great resolution in opening his veins even when nobody had expected it of him: "he had been thought incapable of the firmness of committing suicide [*haud creditus sufficere ad constantiam sumendae mortis*]."[393] Fortitude and determination were also shown by some of the

---

388. Tac. *Ann*, 14.59.

389. Cf. Tac. *Ann*, 14.59: *constantiam opperiendae mortis pro incerta et trepida vita suassisse*.

390. Tac. *Ann*, 14.47. Syme described Memmius Regulus as the "exemplary *homo novus*," in "Obituaries in Tacitus," 24.

391. Cf. Tac. *Ann*, 14.22. Plautus was great-grandson of Tiberius and therefore great-great-grandson of Augustus, Tiberius' adoptive father.

392. Tac. *Ann*, 11.35.

393. Tac. *Ann*, 13.30.

conspirators against Nero after their scheme had been discovered by the emperor, and Tacitus reports their *constantis exitus*, especially those of Sulpicius Asper[394] and Lateranus.[395] It seems that showing *constantia* in one's own death achieved in Tacitus' view some sort of "redemption"—or at least some praise—from a life that might not have been lived in an exemplary way.

It is significant to note that in almost all the examples given earlier in this section, Tacitus is indirectly referring to the courage displayed by these Romans: Marcus Lepidus is brave when he accepts the brief to defend Cn. Piso after Germanicus' dubious death, and he is also brave when he constantly opposes the other senators' measures regarding *maiestas* trials. Marcus Terentius too shows courage when he speaks out the bald truth before the emperor Tiberius, and so is Rubellius Plautus, valiantly dying in Asia. Even the ones who are praised for their moderation also display their courage in a certain sense, because they are presented as showing their valor by renouncing flattery: Lentulus, Lucius Piso, Lucius Arruntius, and others. However, Tacitus does not use the term *virtus* in dealing with them; he uses *constantia* and *moderatio* instead. He does not choose to use the word *virtus* even with the more general meaning of *humana-virtus*, although the Romans he describes may have truly deserved the compliment. The historian decides instead to specify the type of *virtus* needed in the principate. Although it appeared different from the *virtus* exercised in the republic, being less showy, it had nonetheless the same main qualities: courageous behavior for the benefit of the state.

That said, there are, however, some specific cases where Tacitus did select the word *virtus* to talk about individual men. These instances are very few, and for that very reason all the more significant regarding the author's broader picture of the Julio-Claudian dynasty. The Romans who are linked with *virtus* in Tacitus' account of Roman politics are Seneca, Burrus, Thrasea Paetus, and Barea Soranus, all living under Nero's reign.

Seneca and Burrus are presented as two parallel cases of manifesting *virtus* in the new way. Both of these eminent and influential men show throughout the narrative that their mission of advising the young *princeps* Nero was not an easy task and often not entirely successful. The manner in which they came to be the emperor's mentors could have conditioned their relationship with power and in some way could have led them to extreme adulation and fear, especially under someone like Nero. Tacitus says that they were chosen

---

394. Cf. Tac. *Ann*, 15.68: *proximum constantiae exemplum Sulpicius Asper centurio praebuit*.
395. Cf. Tac. *Ann*, 15.60: *plenus constantis silentii*.

by Agrippina, on the one hand because of their well-deserved professional reputation—Seneca as a literary man and Burrus as a military one—and on the other on account of their fine characters.[396] Agrippina would certainly have wanted to ensure that her son was educated and instructed by the best tutors, and at the same time she would have presumed that they would show their gratitude toward her for this privileged appointment by complying with her wishes when required. But Nero's two guardians tried to exercise their influence on the young emperor with a certain independence from Agrippina, and they were able to express some *libertas* or freedom of judgment over what they thought good for the *princeps*, although in agreement regarding the goals, they had different methods: "Burrus with his soldierly interests and austerity [*severitate morum*], and Seneca, with his lessons in eloquence and his honorable affability [*comitate honesta*], aided each other to ensure that the sovereign's years of temptation should, if he were scornful of *virtus* [*si virtutem aspernaretur*], be restrained within the bounds of permissible indulgence."[397] The joint efforts of the tutors complemented each other, leading us to infer that the *virtus* that was in danger of being despised by the young Nero was probably quite a broad concept, including *virilis-virtus* as well as *humana-virtus*.

Burrus' and Seneca's political careers always appear at risk in Tacitus' account, not only because of the emperor's character but also on account of Agrippina's influence. Their relationship with the emperor was strained and marked by their numerous attempts to prevent scandal and crime.[398] Despite their not always succeeding in their advice and having a difficult time trying to keep the situation under control—particularly when Nero decided to get rid of his mother[399]—people did recognize publicly their experience in affairs of state.[400]

The particular circumstances of Burrus' and Seneca's deaths came to be for Tacitus great examples of what it meant to die bravely under a bad emperor without giving way to fear. Burrus stayed firm and silent till the end, and

---

396. Cf. Tac. *Ann*, 12.8 and 12.42, respectively. The specific topic of Seneca in Tacitus' writings has been generously dealt with in scholarship; see, for example, Henry and Walker, "Tacitus and Seneca," 98–110; Dyson, "Portrait of Seneca in Tacitus," 31–84; and lately, Woodman, "*Aliena Facundia*," 294–308; Ker, "Seneca in Tacitus," 305–29.

397. Tac. *Ann*, 13.2.

398. Cf. Tac. *Ann*, 13.2; 13.5; 13.11; 13.20.

399. Tacitus does not say whether Seneca and Burrus could not do anything to prevent it or did not actually want to. Cf. Tac. *Ann*, 4.7 and 14.11.

400. Cf. Tac. *Ann*, 13.6.

although Tacitus leaves the cause of his death open, Suetonius and Dio account for it by poisoning.[401] The stern general was remembered by all in Rome; his *virtus* did not pass unnoticed and "was regretted deeply and permanently by the country [*civitati grande desiderium eius mansit per memoriam virtutis*]."[402] The memory of a life lived with *virtus* stayed in the Romans' minds.

Seneca's death, narrated in greater detail, was more complex. There was between Seneca and Nero a certain kind of rivalry that did not exist with Burrus. Seneca's wealth was so large that even the emperor grew envious of his pedagogue, and his brilliant eloquence was also a cause for competition.[403] Seneca's speech asking for retirement, and especially his petition to submit the administration of his riches to the emperor himself, was a wonderfully calculated piece of imperial court rhetoric, but Nero's reply was no less shrewd and astute.[404] However, the tutor's appeal was to no avail and Seneca's end was only a matter of finding the right moment. The death itself has received much attention,[405] and in spite of its theatricality, it is difficult to deny that it was a brave death.[406] He not only bore the excruciating pain without complaints but also encouraged his friends to pass from tears to fortitude, and his wife to moderate her grief. The last words he addressed to his wife Paulina, recorded by Tacitus, were a call to keep alive her remembrance of a life lived in *virtus*: *in contemplatione vitae per virtutem actae*.[407] When he finally breathed his last, Seneca was cremated simply and without much ceremony according to his wishes, as a final testimony to his moderation.[408]

Even though, for Tacitus, Nero's counselors did not achieve as much as they would have liked to and on occasion they gave the appearance of acting out of anxiety,[409] he shows that they had taken the middle path between

---

401. Cf. Suet. *Nero*, 35.5; and Dio, 62.13.3.
402. Cf. Tac. *Ann*, 14.51.
403. Cf. Tac. *Ann*, 13.3.
404. Cf. Tac. *Ann*, 14.53–56.
405. See, among others, Griffin, *Seneca*, 367–86; Edwards, *Death in Ancient Rome*, 110–12; 152–59; and Ker, *Deaths of Seneca*.
406. Cf. Tac. *Ann*, 15.62–65. Griffin, *Seneca*, 368. For the attraction of Romans to these deaths scenes, see, for example, Pliny, *Epist.* 5.5.3; 8.12.4; Tac. *Ann*, 16.16. For more on the topic, cf. Pomeroy, *Appropriate Comment*; Hill, *Ambitiosa Mors*.
407. Cf. Tac. *Ann*, 15.63.
408. Cf. Tac. *Ann*, 15.64.
409. Especially concerning Agrippina's murder. For Tacitus' judgment on Burrus and Seneca, see, for example, Gillis, "Portrait of Afranius Burrus in Tacitus' *Annals*," 5–22; D'Anna, "Seneca,

fighting stubbornly against the authority and withdrawing from the scene by voluntary suicide on the one hand (*abrupta contumacia*) and the *deforme obsequium* of servility on the other. They navigated as well as they could the turbulent waters of a despot's rule, and in spite of their failures they showed resolution and free speech, combined with loyalty and restraint. This seemingly inglorious *via media* implied no less courage and freedom than in republican times, but it entailed a more personal response and was less showy.[410]

It is important to underline the fact that when Tacitus mentions the *virtus* of these two men, he is referring not only to the *virtus* of their deaths. Their demises were a silent example of courage and fortitude, and even though their deaths are narrated with more care and detail than their lives in the extant work, it is in fact their lives that merited Seneca and Burrus the attribution of *virtus* in Tacitus' account: it is Burrus' *virtus* during his life that is remembered by the people of Rome, and it is Seneca's life of *virtus* that should stay before Paulina's eyes. It is interesting to note that once again Tacitus has linked *virtus* to *memoria*.

The last men of *virtus* in the *Annals* are Thrasea Paetus and Barea Soranus, to whom it is attributed in a way unique in Tacitus' writings. The succinct description of both senators as *virtus ipsa* poses different questions: whether one person could actually embody *virtus Romana* at all, and if so, how this worked in practice. I will concentrate here on Thrasea's case, as it is narrated in more detail by Tacitus.[411]

Thrasea Paetus was admired by Tacitus especially for qualities that shone all the more when contrasted with his colleagues' behavior. His constancy and firmness in remaining independent of any political pressure from the emperor became most noticeable by contrast with the servility of the other senators: *libertas Thraseae servitium aliorum rupit*.[412] Nero's evident displeasure at Thrasea's performance in the Senate left the latter unmoved in his determination

---

uomo politico nel giudizio di Tacito," 193–202; Ker, "Seneca in Tacitus," 305–29.

410. For Seneca's glory, see Habinek, "Seneca's Renown," 264–303. For an entirely different opinion of Seneca, see Henry and Walker, "Tacitus and Seneca," 98–110; Dyson, "Portrait of Seneca in Tacitus," 71–83.

411. For the important figure of Thrasea, see, for example, De Vivo, "Dissenso e Astensione. Trasea Peto negli Annali di Tacito," 79–103; Heldmann, "Libertas Thraseae aliorum servitium rupit," 297–331; Devillers, "Le rôle des passages relatifs à Thrasea dans les *Annales* de Tacite," 296–311; Pigoń, "Thrasea Paetus, *Libertas Senatoria* and Tacitus' Narrative Methods," 143–53; Strunk, "Saving the Life of a Foolish Poet," 119–39.

412. Tac. *Ann*, 14.49.

to be consistent in thought and conduct: "Thrasea did not waive his proposal (...) because of his usual firmness of spirit, and lest his glory should fall out of sight [*sueta firmitudine animi et ne gloria intercideret*]."[413] For Thrasea, the glory attached to the virtue of constancy was higher and more solid than the favors that the powerful could bestow. He had spoken on several occasions before the senators on how steadiness and determination had belonged to Rome in a very special way; therefore it was natural that when the opportunity was given—in the trial of the Cretan Claudius Timarchus, a case of provincial arrogance to the detriment of Roman dignity—Thrasea should propose to take the final decision in consonance with Roman honor and firmness (*fide constantiaque Romana*).[414]

In praising strictness, steadiness, and consistency, Thrasea was approving the Romans of old times, but also justifying his own conduct: the times when he had walked out of the Senate or had not complied with Nero's whims, abstaining from political participation and not falling into the widespread sycophancy.[415] His acknowledgment that certain virtues were a ground for *odium* was in fact prophetic of his own death.[416] Tacitus' words are highly expressive: "Nero in the end conceived the ambition to extirpate *virtus* herself [*virtutem ipsam*] by killing Thrasea Paetus and Barea Soranus."[417] Apart from showing the emperor's hatred, the words hold a subtle double hint of irony, as if Nero sought to achieve something possible—when in fact nobody could actually kill *virtus*—on the one hand, or as if *virtus* could present itself wholly incarnate in one person.

Tacitus narrates Thrasea's trial and death in full detail. The charges against Thrasea presented by his enemies were varied and plentiful. The most striking one is the complaint of not fulfilling the duties proper to a senator, presented by Cossutianus and later reinforced by Eprius Marcellus.[418] To a certain extent, Thrasea's death is not described by Tacitus in unequivocal terms. On the one hand, it is presented as admirable because it displayed a degree of independence and personal *libertas* seldom found in Nero's reign. It may have been Thrasea's *libertas* from *metus* that Nero hated and, most of all, feared. It was the senator's lack of anxiety and apprehension, together with

---

413. Tac. *Ann*, 14.49. See also 14.12.
414. Tac. *Ann*, 15.20.
415. Cf. Tac. *Ann*, 14.12; 14.48–50.
416. Cf. Tac. *Ann*, 15.21.
417. Tac. *Ann*, 16.21.
418. Cf. Tac. *Ann*, 16.21–22.

his steadiness and firmness in facing risks, that offended the emperor. Being constant under Nero's unsteadiness was almost invariably a death-sentence. On the other hand, although Thrasea's *virtus* was manifested in his free speech and especially in his *constantia*,[419] in the end it lacked that touch of *moderatio* and self-control that was so important to be able to contribute to the welfare of the state under the rule of a *princeps*.

The accounts in Tacitus of Thrasea's and Seneca's deaths have in common not only the *constantia* with which both met their end but also the fact that both appear to be seeking to set an example for posterity: an *exemplum virtutis*. Both deaths were almost "performed," and their final words reproduce the Stoic doctrine at its highest.[420] Seneca's last words to his friends and wife are spoken with the conscious desire that they should be repeated to others and foster emulation. Thrasea, on the other hand, in a meaningful gesture poured a libation to Jupiter Liberator while he exclaimed to the quaestor there, "Look, young man, and—may Heaven, indeed avert the omen, but you have been born into times when it is expedient to steel the mind with instances of firmness [*firmare animum expediat constantibus exemplis*]."[421] But this tremendous awareness of dying for the public and having the mission of setting an example was not always so evident in political deaths. And although Thrasea and Seneca had no doubt trained their consciences with Stoic doctrines to face the last battle, they should not be fully identified with the abstract Stoic *sapiens* in Tacitus' narrative; on the contrary, they are presented as more balanced figures who blend Stoic readings with the Roman tradition of active experience in the service of the *res publica*. Above all they showed that the strength of exemplarity—so powerful in Roman thought—was still a motive for acting bravely. On the other hand, the fact that they did not manage to survive in tyranny does not necessarily imply that they should be included in the category of *ambitiosa mors* or *abrupta contumacia*. They did not seek death, but were forced to commit suicide, and that made all the difference.

All the examples given in this section on *virtus* in civil life demonstrate the comparatively little political liberty—in some cases none at all—that Romans were able to exercise in their actions. However, Tacitus confirms that they did have the individual freedom to choose their attitude toward the circumstances, and to show courage. By expanding the conventional meaning of

---

419. Cf. Tac. *Ann*, 16.25; 16.35.
420. For the performance of death, see Edwards, *Death in Ancient Rome*, esp. chap. 5.
421. Tac. *Ann*, 16.35.

libertas—the freedom of senators to express themselves freely and direct political affairs according to their wishes—and shifting it toward the freedom to adopt an independent attitude to power, Tacitus also challenges the traditional interpretation of *virtus*. Since it was now the emperor—that is, the state—who was trying to annihilate the individual's integrity and dignity by destroying his freedom, *virtus*, once exercised as the first and foremost service *for* the state, now had to be practiced *despite* the state. Tyrants may have been able to kill men of *virtus*, but they could not corrupt Roman *virtus* itself. *Virilis-virtus* and *humana-virtus* were now manifested through the quieter *constantia* and *moderatio*. By showing different types of *exempla virtutis* in imperial times, Tacitus presents a demanding ideal for the definition of bravery and goodness in action under the principate. Throughout the records of history, *virtus* outlives the emperor and the state.

TACITUS' CAREFUL SELECTION of words shows the transformation that Roman politics underwent in the first century A.D. This change in vocabulary well expressed the change in Roman history: autocracy needed a different terminology to be properly understood. It was not always easy to act with the right type of courage; not everybody understood that *moderatio* was not the same as being lukewarm or that *constantia* was not a passive acceptance of political events. What emerged in the *Agricola* was going to develop and bloom in the *Annals*: the more external manifestations of *virtus* belonged to the republic, where competition was allowed and was part of the game, but became less frequent under the exclusivism of an autocrat. Precisely because the word maintained its original strength and did not start to mean something more diluted, fewer Romans appeared to understand that the manifestations of the original *virtus* needed to be adapted to suit the new regime but that this had nothing to do with watering down the meaning. *Virtus* does not change in the same way as politics, but its manifestations do. *Virtus* could be shown either externally or internally; it could be offensive, as in the republic, or defensive, as in the principate.

Traditionally, Tacitus has proved to be a relevant actor in the construction of the identity of vice and corruption under the principate; he has successfully illustrated the changes that the values of the Roman Republic underwent in the new regime. I hope to have shown the extent to which he has also contributed to redefining *virtus* and the virtuous man in the imperial period. The many cases with which he exemplifies the new nuances that traditional *virtus* acquired at that time show that rather than disappearance of *virtus* under the emperors, the Romans were experiencing an internal adjustment of it. As a historian, Tacitus explains how and why *virtus* had to be reassessed when the political system changed. Not only does he reevaluate the intellectual and moral categories by which *virtus* is still to be seen as playing one of the most important roles in Roman political life, but also his *exempla virtutis* qualify and redefine the standards by which good and virtuous Romans may be judged in the principate.

Conclusion

Spes in virtute

Hope is in *virtus*
—Tac. *Ann*, 2.20

This study has stressed that the characterization of *virtus* in Roman historical writing is important not only to the understanding of a central idea in the Roman value system, or a crucial notion for political success, but also for explaining and interpreting historical reality. The analysis of *virtus* in the Roman historians of the late republic and early empire has shown the ways in which a concept is shaped and reshaped through time and according to the historico-political circumstances. The decline and fall of the Roman Republic brought about a transformation that involved many more aspects than just the change of the political system. The historians played a particularly important role in creating the framework for the reception of the full implications of these changes. Through the writing of history, they sought to generate the principles by which they could explain and make sense of both change in time and the situation in which they found themselves.

Although I have mainly adopted a chronological view through the historians analyzed, the nature of this project prevented me from following a purely temporal approach. Undoubtedly, *virtus* did develop in time, and the concept evolved and matured, but it is also true that from the beginning the idea of *virtus* was always a rich and complex term, waiting to be uncovered. Thus, the chronological approach serves to depict only one aspect of the evolution of the concept, for, as has been shown, all historians use *virtus* in its double meaning of, on the one hand, "courage" or "bravery" and on the other, "virtue" in a general moral way. It is not that for Sallust, or for the historians before him, *virtus* had the more original meaning of "courage" and later, after the influence of philosophy had spread, *virtus* meant "virtue" more broadly speaking. The meanings overlap in time. And it is precisely here that its power and strength lie. The fact that Roman *virtus* was hard to define or, more precisely, that there were many different ways of defining it made the term less concrete or specific and therefore multiplied the contexts in which it could be used. *Virtus* was not just a word that represented reality, it was also a concept that stood for ideals, principles, and even emotions, and therefore, rather than being translated, it needed to be interpreted. Searching for memory and identity, two particularly important missions of history, was a way of interpreting, and so the writing of history became a major and distinctive stage in this process of interpretation. Thus, the Roman historians became relevant actors in the construction of the identity of *virtus*. Especially in a period when political horizons had to be reconsidered, they looked for reevaluation. Historians, then, not only re-created the history of a particular period, but helped powerfully with the assimilation of changes and with political reconstruction. They were, to a greater or lesser extent, guides who showed the way and offered answers.

The Romans' insistence on explaining political life through moral standards justified the position of *virtus* both as a political slogan and as an ethical ideal for self-definition. Each author analyzed in this study assigns a particularly important place and role to *virtus* in his historical narrative. When reconstructing and remembering the past life of the *res publica*, the authors show that political systems or institutions are not enough to guarantee a healthy community; the morals of its individuals are essential, and it is here that *virtus* will be shown as a central motif in justifying and understanding the vicissitudes of the state.

Thus, Sallust—the first extant Roman historian who assigns a paramount role to the concept of *virtus* in history—proceeds to give his analysis of political decline by deploring its disappearance at a specific time, and explicitly connecting the collapse of the republic and its ideals with the failure of *virtus*. By illustrating decay and showing how widespread political corruption had become at all levels of society, he aims to appeal to a broader concept of *virtus* to remedy the unhealthy condition of the state. But he only hints at an answer to the problem, for within a declining republic even the *virtus* of the *homo novus* would not remain untarnished. When men sought personal power in the name of *dignitas*, *virtus* was forgotten or used for private pursuits which went against its true nature of serving the state. Sallust showed his contemporaries how little was needed to pass from *virtus* to *vitium*, how fragile the boundaries were, and how often they had been crossed.

Livy's history, on the other hand, focuses not on the *vitia* of the present, but on the *virtus* of the past. It is a clear-cut *virtus*, less vague or broad than that of Sallust. *Virtus* in Livy has a specific meaning and purpose: linked with patriotism, it is a guiding thread to understanding the history of the Roman people. Therefore, by illustrating deeds of *prisca virtus*, Livy seeks to give a persuasive picture of Rome that might move his contemporaries to identify themselves with past Romans and behave in the same way. Having constructed this memory, Livy presents *virtus* in this idealized past as being intimately connected with *libertas*. Freedom, especially the political freedom of the *res publica*, was preserved by acts of *virtus*.

Velleius Paterculus somehow follows Livy's train of thought by making *virtus* the key evaluative word for characters throughout Roman history. *Virtus* provides the link between republican past and imperial present, and it is represented primarily in the *virtus* of the emperor. Velleius shows the acceptance of the principate not as a dramatic change from the republic, but as a restoration of its main features. The reestablishment of peace and order had brought back the possibility of exercising and displaying *virtus* in the traditional Roman way, and the *princeps* was the primary model to imitate.

With Tacitus we come again to the more open *virtus* of Sallust, but in a more refined form. The political circumstances and the change of the system brought about a crisis in the identity of *virtus*, as well as a crisis in the identity of what was implied by the move from republic to principate. A serious reduction in the number of occurrences of *virtus* can be seen in Tacitus' historical writings compared with those of other Roman historians. It is as if *virtus* cannot be shown as it used to—mainly in courageous acts in defense of the state—but new expressions of it can be found in less public or less conspicuous manifestations, such as resistance, moderation, and constancy. Rather than reporting *virtus* in action, Tacitus chooses to narrate perceptions or impressions of *virtus* in different characters. External *virtus*—linked to action—tends to be replaced by an internal kind, related to the individual's attitude toward reality. The memory of *virtus*—*memoria virtutis*—also opened up different paths to accepting this new way of showing *virtus* under the emperor.

As a small exercise, it would be helpful perhaps to try to imagine these four historians having some sort of Ciceronian dialogue about *virtus* in Rome. This will enable us to stand back from the purely chronological view and facilitate our understanding of the question as something of constant contemporary relevance in Roman thinking. Sallust starts the conversation by complaining that *virtus* cannot be found anywhere in the present age; he chooses specific examples to describe the situation, which ends up as an escalating pathway to corruption. He is passionate in his language, and completely discouraged by the situation. Livy interrupts him before he has even attempted to draw a conclusion and, to cheer him up, gives a lengthy account of the whole history of Rome; it seems somewhat unfair, he suggests, to look just at the present situation when they have had so long and powerful a tradition of their city being a model of *virtus*. In fact, they have had other periods of political turmoil and they have overcome them, so let them remember where they came from and the great things they have achieved. At this point Velleius says that they do not need to look so far back in the past as Livy was doing, because even in the present times examples of true *virtus* could be found. The Roman state, identified with its ruler the emperor, was again a stage for *virtus*; the example of its head promoted and encouraged *virtus* in the rest of the Roman people. The period of decline has been left behind and they have passed the test successfully. Tacitus, like the good orator speaking at the end, expands and deepens their idea of *virtus* and suggests that there are other ways of living it, especially when the circumstances are adverse. Courage or *virilis-virtus*, he says, is even more necessary now than when they fought the republican expansionist wars, because a brave man in the principate has to discover and face a different kind of enemy. *Virtus* is manifested differently, mainly through moderate and constant behavior; it implies defense of one's own principles for the right reasons. The panorama is certainly dark, but there is a way out—though a demanding one.

THE HISTORIANS' LANGUAGE also played a significant part in their interpretation and analysis of the history they were writing. As seen in the Introduction on the importance of rhetoric in Roman historical writing, the selection of *verba* by which the historians unfolded their narratives was made in accordance with the subject matter they were treating, and it was certainly part of the structure or *exaedificatio* in the Ciceronian historical building. Personal choices of language and style were not completely arbitrary signifiers, but matured and evolved in a particular way through contact with the real world, in an effort to name and identify reality as the historians saw it. Throughout this study we have seen that each author developed a specific vocabulary to illustrate his theme, almost working as another form of evidence or content in their histories: Sallust's vocabulary of decline and *vitium* articulated his main idea in a different way from Livy's vocabulary of honor and virtue. Perhaps the idea was not so dissimilar in its essence, but it was expressed through different *logos*. Velleius' vocabulary of restoration not only conveyed the hope he felt with the advent of the new regime but also helped to show the main features of the republic that for him were worth restoring. Tacitus' insistence on presenting us with the inner nature, thoughts, and motives of historical characters was the way he chose to portray and interpret the inner reality of the drama of the principate and its possible solution.

But the aim of this book has been not only to explore a particularly important concept used by Romans historians and identify the role they assign to it in their works but also to help us discover their particular view on history and human nature. Thus, the study of *virtus* in Roman historiography is significant in telling us about and expanding our knowledge of the people who produced this concept and lived by it. To place *virtus* at the very center of history and make it the cause of Roman greatness is to believe that men are intrinsically political and ethical beings. This assertion, which at first sight may not seem overwhelmingly novel, had nevertheless profound and original practical consequences in Roman society. In the first place, it meant that politics and morality were necessarily intertwined and that their goals and ends could not be separated: if an action went against the moral code of the *maiores*, it would inevitably have a disastrous effect on politics too, and vice versa. To be a political being meant that politics, in a broad sense, was everything that happened to the organized community: it constituted the very life of people. Thus, the social dimension of any action was something real and omnipresent: for the Romans, anything that a man did affected others as much as himself. No private action could remain private forever. It would leave a mark on the doer and it would, sooner or later, appear in his dealings with others. The four historians analyzed prove exactly this: time after time, the decisions of generals, politicians, or rulers affected not only the actors themselves but the whole political community.

Another significant consequence of placing *virtus* at the center of the moral and political reality depicted is that it emphasized the importance of action. "The glory of *virtus* is in activity," Cicero had said.[1] As practical men, Romans had to show their values in actions, and it was by these actions that they were assessed and evaluated in life and also in history. Not being natural theorists, the Romans placed the weight of ethical education on *exempla*, but this was not an automatic process: it required the individual's decision to follow a particular course of behavior. To carry out an action of *virtus* and to imitate (or not) the example of *virtus* set by someone else, one needed to be free. As shown in chapter 1, free human action implied being accountable for one's own deeds and bearing the responsibility of dealing with the consequences. This accountability of moral action, plus the fact that every moral action bore political consequences, made political failure the result of human decisions: decline never happened by chance or as the result of a sum of blind forces. This notion went hand in hand with the thought that despite the bad circumstances, not everything was lost: the hope of return lay also with man-

---

1. Cic. *De Off*, 1.6.19: *virtutis enim laus omnis in actione consistit*.

kind. Even though Roman historians approached the history of Rome from very different angles and backgrounds, they all insisted on making the individual accountable for his actions. From Sallust's Catiline to Tacitus' Nero, history taught what men had done, hence the kind of men they were: *quae vita, qui mores fuerint, per quos viros*... The political life of the *res publica*—success or catastrophe—was a corollary to the characters and actions of the men who composed it.

Virtus was also a role-related idea, and in this sense, it helped men to fulfill their function in the social order. It referred to the particular behavior that was expected of the individuals who formed the community; it also guaranteed the commitment to society and the primacy of the common good over private good. But *virtus* in the Roman historians was depicted not only as an instrumental capacity but also as a fundamentally valuable aspect of human character. And character was a relevant actor in the development of history.

The account of Roman political history through individuals with (or without) *virtus* enabled Roman historians not only to promote the type of good person necessary for the social order to flourish but also to endorse a particular mode of political thought that made personal *virtus* the basis and source of civic *virtus*.

In a culture where personal success is sought at all costs and utility is the criterion for measuring anyone's worth, the Roman historians' approach to history from the moral agent's point of view appears somewhat alien but, to a certain extent, revitalizing. Through their politics of *virtus*, Romans were aiming to fulfill what they saw as the natural goal of human beings in society. With their historical narratives, the Roman historians both reconstructed the politics of *virtus* that Rome had had in the past and shaped the categories by which Roman politics would be measured in the present.

It is, therefore, possible, and all the more relevant, to consider the *virtus* of the historian himself. Just as a soldier ought to display *virtus* in battle, or an emperor *virtus* in his ruling, so too the historian was expected to perform his role competently and with *virtus*. The need for interpretation, organization, and selection; for matching words and deeds; and for truthful and imaginative reconstruction of the events of the past make the historian's *virtus* an essential element of his job. Roman historians were aware of this and struggled, with various degrees of success, to live up to it. Historical writing in Rome was immersed in the need for *virtus*, which had both a purpose and a plan.

Bibliography

Adams, J. N. "The Vocabulary of the Later Decades of Livy." *Antichthon* 8 (1974): 54–62.

———. *Bilingualism and the Latin Language*. Cambridge: Cambridge University Press, 2003.

Adcock, F. E. *Roman Political Ideas and Practice*. Ann Arbor: University of Michigan Press, 1959.

Adkins, A. W. H. *Merit and Responsibility*. Oxford: Clarendon Press, 1960.

———. *From the Many to the One*. Oxford: Oxford University Press, 1972.

Allen, W. "The Source of Jugurtha's Influence in the Roman Senate." *CP* 33 (1938): 90–92.

Allison, J. W. "Corbulo's Socratic Shadow." *Eranos* 95 (1997): 19–25.

Alonso-Núñez, J. M. *La Historia Universal de Pompeyo Trogo*. Madrid: Ediciones Clásicas, 1992.

Alston, R. "Arms and the Man: Soldiers, Masculinity and Power in Republican and Imperial Rome." In *When Men Were Men: Masculinity, Power, and Identity in Classical Antiquity*, edited by L. Foxhall and J. Salmon, 205–23. London: Routledge, 1998.

———. "History and Memory in the Construction of Identity in Early Second-Century Rome." In *Role Models in the Roman World: Identity and Assimilation*, edited by S. Bell and I. Hansen, 147–59. Ann Arbor: University of Michigan Press, 2008.

André, J. M. "L'otium chez Valère Maxime et Velleius Paterculus, ou la reaction morale au debut du principat." *REL* 43 (1965): 294–315.

———. *L'otium dans la vie morale et intellectuelle romaine, des origenes à l'epoque augusteenne*. Paris: Presses Universitaire de France, 1966.

———. "Tacite et la Philosophie." *ANRW* II, 33, no. 4 (1991): 3101–54.

———. "Les Res Gestae d'Auguste ou les nuances de l'egotism politique." In *L'invention de l'autobiographie d'Hésiode a Saint Augustin*, edited by M. F. Baslez, 97–114. Paris: Presses de l'école normale supérieure, 1993.

Arena, V. *Libertas and the Practice of Politics in the Late Roman Republic*. Cambridge: Cambridge University Press, 2012.

Arieti, J. A. "Rape and Livy's View of Roman History." In *Rape in Antiquity*, edited by S. Deacy and K. F. Pierce, 209–29. London: Duckworth, 1997.

Arnold, E. V. *Roman Stoicism*. Cambridge: Cambridge University Press, 1958 [1911].

Ash, R. *Ordering Anarchy: Armies and Leaders in Tacitus' Histories*. London: Duckworth, 1999.

———. "Following the Footsteps of Lucullus? Tacitus' Characterisation of Corbulo." *Arethusa* 39 (2006): 355–75.

———. "The Wonderful World of Mucianus." In *Vita Vigilia Est: Essays in Honour of Barbara Levick*, edited by E. Bisphan, G. Rowe, and E. Matthews, 1–17. London: Institute of Classical Studies, 2007.
———, ed. *Tacitus. Histories II*. Cambridge: Cambridge University Press, 2007.
Astin, A. E. *Scipio Aemilianus*. Oxford: Clarendon Press, 1967.
———. *Cato the Censor*. Oxford: Oxford University Press, 1978.
Aubert, J. J., and Z. Várhelyi, eds. *A Tall Order: Religion, Law, Society and Imperialism in the Ancient World; Essays in Honour of William Harris*. Munich: Saur Verlag, 2005.
Auerbach, E. *Mimesis. The Representations of Reality in Western Literature*. Princeton, N.J.: Princeton University Press, 1953 [1946].
Badel, C. "La noblesse equestre a-t-elle existe sous l'Empire? Reflexions sur la Vie d'Agricola." *REL* 77 (1999): 205–15.
Badian, E. "Marius and the Nobles." *Durham University Journal* 25 (1963–64): 141–54.
———. "The Early Historians." In *Latin Historians*, edited by T. A. Dorey, 1–38. London: Routledge, 1966.
———. *Roman Imperialism in the Late Republic*. Pretoria: Communications of the University of South Africa, 1967.
———. "A Phantom Marriage Law." *Philologus* 129 (1985): 82–98.
———. "Livy and Augustus." In *Livius: Aspekte seines Werkes*, edited by W. Shuller, 9–38. Konstanz: Univ. Verl., 1993.
Baldwin, B. "Women in Tacitus." *Prudentia* 4, no. 2 (1972): 83–101.
Balmaceda, C. "Tiberio, *optimus princeps* en Veleyo Patérculo." *Scripta Antiqua* 11 (2002): 309–19.
———. "*Virtus Romana* en el siglo I a.C." *Gerión* 25, no. 2 (2007): 285–303.
———. "Historia y Retórica: ¿Relaciones Peligrosas?" In *Letras en Humanidad: Escritos en honor a Francesco Borghesi*, edited by M. J. Cot and C. Rolle, 65–80. Santiago: Lom, 2008.
———. "*Virtus* en la Ciudad de Roma." In *La Ciudad Antigua: Espacios públicos y actores sociales*, edited by C. Balmaceda and N. Cruz, 159–80. Santiago: RIL Editores, 2013.
———. "The Virtues of Tiberius in Velleius' *Histories*." *Historia* 63, no. 3 (2014): 340–63.
———. "El oficio del historiador romano: Igualar las palabras con los hechos." In *¿Qué hace el historiador al historiar?*, edited by P. Corti, R. Moreno, and J. L. Widow, 223–31.Valparaíso: Ediciones Altazor, 2015.
Balmaceda, C., and N. Cruz, eds. *La Ciudad Antigua: Espacios públicos y actores sociales*. Santiago: RIL Editores, 2013.
Balot, R. "Pericles' Anatomy of Democratic Courage." *AJP* 122 (2001): 505–25.
———. *Courage in Democratic Polis*. Oxford: Oxford University Press, 2014.
Balsdon, J. P. V. D. "Sulla felix." *JRS* 41, no. 1–2 (1951): 1–10.
———. "T. Quinctius Flamininus." *Phoenix* 21 (1967): 177–90.
Barnes, J., and M. Griffin, eds. *Philosophia Togata II. Plato and Aristotle at Rome*. Oxford: Clarendon Press, 1997.

Barnes, T. D. "The Fragments of Tacitus' Histories." *CP* 72 (1977): 224–31.
———. "Tacitus and the Senatus Consultum de Cn. Pisone Patre." *Phoenix* 52 (1998): 125–48.
Barton, C. *Roman Honor: The Fire in the Bones*. Berkeley: University of California Press, 2001.
Bartsch, S. *Actors in the Audience: Theatricality and Doublespeak from Nero to Hadrian*. Cambridge, Mass.: Harvard University Press, 1994.
Batomsky, S. J. "The Not-So-Perfect Man: Some Ambiguities in Tacitus' Picture of Agricola." *Latomus* 44 (1985): 388–93.
Batstone, W. "Incerta pro certis: An Interpretation of Sallust's *Bellum Catilinae* 48.4–49.4." *Ramus* 15 (1986): 105–21.
———. "The Antithesis of Virtue: Sallust's Syncrisis and the Crisis of the Late Republic." *CA* 7 (1988): 1–29.
———. "Intellectual Conflict and Mimesis in Sallust's *Bellum Catilinae*." In *Conflict, Antithesis, and the Ancient Historian*, edited by J. Allison, 112–32. Columbus: Ohio State University Press, 1990.
———. "Catiline's Speeches in Sallust's *Bellum Catilinae*." In *Form and Function in Roman Oratory*, edited by D. H. Berry and A. Erksine, 227–46. Cambridge: Cambridge University Press, 2010.
———. "Word at War: The Prequel." In *Citizens of Discord: Rome and Its Civil Wars*, edited by B. Breed, C. Damon, and A. Rossi, 45–71. Oxford: Oxford University Press, 2010.
Beard, M. *The Roman Triumph*. Cambridge, Mass.: Harvard University Press, 2007.
Bell, S. "Introduction: Role Models in the Roman World." *MAAR Volumes* 7 (2008): 1–39.
Bell, S., and I. L. Hansen, eds. *Role Models in the Roman World: Identity and Assimilation*. Ann Arbor: University of Michigan Press, 2008.
Benario, H. W. "Tacitus and the Principate." *CJ* 60 (1964): 97–106.
———. "*Imperium* and *Capaces Imperii* in Tacitus." *AJP* 93 (1972): 14–26.
———. "Tacitus' View of the Empire and the *Pax Romana*." *ANRW* II 33.5 (1991): 3331–53.
———. "Marcus Lepidus, Galba and Thrasea." *Acta Ant. Hung.* 39 (1999): 45–51.
———, ed. *Tacitus: Germany*. Warminster: Aris and Phillips, 1999.
Béranger, J. *Principatus: Etudes de notions et d´ historie politiques dans l´Antiquité gréco-romaine*. Geneva: Université de Laussane, 1975.
Bernard, J. E. *Le portrait chez Tite-Live: Essai sur l'écriture de l'histoire romaine*. Brussels: Collection Latomus, 2000.
———. "*Historia magistra mortis*: Tite-Live, Plutarque et la fin de Marcellus." In *Hommages à Carl Deroux: II—Prose et linguistique, médecine*, edited by P. Defosse, 30–39. Brussels: Éditions Latomus, 2002.
Berthier, A., J. Juillet, and R. Charlier. *Le "Bellum Jugurthinum" de Salluste et le problème de Cirta*. Constantine: Attali, 1949.
Bieber, M. "*Honos* and *Virtus*." *AJA* 49 (1945): 25–34.

Birch, R. A. "The Settlement of 26th June AD 4 and Its Aftermath." *CQ* 31 (1972): 443–50.
Blockley, R. C. "Ammianus and Cicero on Truth in Historiography." *ABH* 15, no. 1 (2001): 14–24.
Bloomer, W. M. *Valerius Maximus and the Rhetoric of the New Nobility*. Chapel Hill: University of North Carolina Press, 1992.
Bolaffi, E. *Sallustio e la sua fortuna nei secoli*. Rome: Perelli, 1949.
Bonner, S. *Education in Ancient Rome*. London: Methuen, 1977.
Borszák, I. "Das Germanicusbild des Tacitus." *Latomus* 28 (1969): 588–600.
Bowman, A. K., H. M. Cotton, M. Goodman, and S. Price, eds. *Representations of Empire: Rome and the Mediterranean World*. Oxford: Oxford University Press, 2002.
Boyancé, P. "La connaissance du grec á Rome." *REL* 34 (1956): 111–31.
Boyd, B. "Virtus Effeminata and Sallust's Sempronia." *TAPA* 117 (1987): 183–201.
Braund, S. M. *Latin Literature*. London: Routledge, 2002.
Breed, B., C. Damon, and A. Rossi, eds. *Citizens of Discord: Rome and Its Civil Wars*. Oxford: Oxford University Press, 2010.
Brescia, G. *La Scalata del Ligure*. Bari: Edipuglia, 1997.
Brinton, A. "Cicero's Use of Historical Examples in Moral Argument." *Philosophy and Rhetoric* 21 (1988): 169–84.
Briscoe, J. "The Second Punic War." In *The Cambridge Ancient History VIII*, edited by S. A. Cook, F. E. Adcock, and M. P. Charlesworth, 44–80. Cambridge: Cambridge University Press, 1989.
———. "Livy and Polybius." In *Livius: Aspekte seines Werkes*, edited by W. Shuller, 39–52. Konstanz: Univ.Verl., 1993.
Broadie, S. "On the Idea of the *summum bonum*." In *Virtue, Norms and Objectivity*, edited by C. Gill, 41–58. Oxford: Clarendon Press, 2005.
Brouwer, R. *The Stoic Sage: The Early Stoics on Wisdom, Sagehood, and Socrates*. Cambridge: Cambridge University Press, 2014.
Brown, R. D. "Livy's Sabine Women and the Ideal of Concordia." *TAPA* 125 (1995): 291–319.
Bruno, L. "Crimen, regni e superbia in Tito Livio." *Giornale Italiano di Filologia* 19 (1966): 236–59.
———. "Libertas Plebis in Tito Livio." *Giornale Italiano di Filologia* 19 (1966): 107–30.
Brunt, P. A. *Italian Manpower 225 B.C.– A.D. 14*. Oxford: Clarendon Press, 1971.
———. "Stoicism and the Principate." *PBSR* 30 (1975): 7–35.
———. "Nobilitas et Novitas." *JRS* 72 (1982): 1–17.
———. *The Fall of the Roman Republic and Other Related Essays*. Oxford: Clarendon Press, 1988.
———. "*Libertas* in the Republic." In *The Fall of the Roman Republic and Other Related Essays*, 281–350. Oxford: Clarendon Press, 1988.
———. "Philosophy and Religion in the Late Republic." In *Philosophia Togata I: Essays on Philosophy and Roman Society*, edited by M. Griffin and J. Barnes, 174–98. Oxford: Clarendon Press, 1989.

———. "Cicero and Historiography." In *Studies in Greek History and Thought*, edited by P. A. Brunt, 181–209. Oxford: Oxford University Press, 1993.
———. *Studies in Stoicism*. Oxford: Oxford University Press, 2013.
Brunt, P. A., and J. Moore, eds. *Res Gestae Divi Augusti*. Oxford: Oxford University Press, 1967.
Bruun, C. "M. Furius Camillus: Italic Legends and Roman Historiography." In *The Roman Middle Republic: Politics, Religion, and Historiography c. 400–133 B.C.*, edited by C. Bruun, 41–68. Rome: Institutum Romanum Finlandiae, 2000.
———, ed. *The Roman Middle Republic: Politics, Religion, and Historiography c. 400–133 B.C.* Rome: Institutum Romanum Finlandiae, 2000.
Büchner, K. *Humanitas Romana*. Heidelberg: Carl Winter, 1957.
———. *Sallust*. Heidelberg: Carl Winter, 1960.
———. "Altrömische und Horazische Virtus." *Studien zur römischen Literatur* III (1962): 1–22.
Burck, E. "The Third Decade." In *Livy*, edited by T. A. Dorey, 21–46. London: Routledge & Kegan Paul, 1917.
———. *Die Erzählungskunst des T. Livius*. Berlin: Weidmannsche Buchhandlung, 1934.
———. *Wege zu Livius*. Darmstadt: Wissenschaftliche Buchgesellschaft, 1967.
———. "Livius und Augustus." *ICS* 16 (1991): 269–81.
Burckhardt, L. A. "The Political Elite of the Roman Republic: Comments on Recent Discussion of the Concepts 'Nobilitas and Homo Novus.'" *Historia* 39 (1990): 77–99.
Burian, J. Review of Eisenhut's *Virtus Romana*. *Eirene* 13 (1975): 157–59.
Burn, A. R. "Tacitus on Britain." In *Tacitus*, edited by T. A. Dorey, 35–61. London: Routledge and Kegan Paul, 1969.
Burnand, C. *Roman Representations of the Orator during the Last Century of the Republic*. D.Phil thesis, Oxford University, 2000.
Burton, P. "The Last Republican Historian, a New Date for the Composition of Livy's First Pentad." *Historia* 49 (2000): 429–46.
Calevo, I. *Il problema della tendenziosità di Sallustio*. Udine: Istituto delle Edizioni Accademiche, 1940.
Cameron, A. *History as Text: The Writing of Ancient History*. London: Duckworth, 1989.
———. "Postlude: What Next in History?" In *History as Text: The Writing of Ancient History*, edited by A. Cameron, 1–10, 206–8. London: Duckworth, 1989.
Cape, R. W. "Persuasive History: Roman Rhetoric and Historiography." In *Roman Eloquence: Rhetoric in Society and Literature*, edited by W. J. Dominik, 212–28. London: Routledge, 1997.
Carawan, M. "The Tragic History of Marcellus and Livy's Characterization." *CJ* 80 (1985): 131–41.
Cardauns, B. "Mechanismen der Angst. Das Verhältnis von Macht und Schrecken un der Geschichtsdarstellung des Tacitus." *Antike Historiographie in literaturwissenschaflicher Sicht* (1981): 52–69.

Carney, T. F. *A Biography of Caius Marius*. Assen: Royal Van Corcum, 1961.

———. "Cicero's Picture of Marius." *Wiener Studien* 73 (1960): 83–122.

———. "Once again Marius' Speech after Election in 108 B.C." *SO* 35 (1959): 63–70.

Carter, C. J. "Valerius Maximus." In *Empire and Aftermath: Silver Latin II*, edited by T. A. Dorey, 26–56. London: Routledge, 1975.

Cataudella, M. R. "Livio storico augusteo?: Una rilettura sulle tracce della praefatio." In *Scrivere la storia nel mondo antico: Atti del convegno nazionale di studi: Torino, 3–4 maggio 2004*, edited by R. Uglione, 175–95. Alessandria: Ed. dell'Orso, 2006.

Champion, C. B. *Cultural Politics in Polybius' Histories*. Berkeley: University of California Press, 2004.

Chaplin, J. *Livy's Exemplary History*. Oxford: Oxford University Press, 2000.

———. "Livy's Use of Exempla." In *A Companion to Livy*, edited by B. A. Mineo, 102–12. Malden, Mass.: Wiley-Blackwell, 2015.

Chaplin, J., and C. Kraus, eds. *Livy: Oxford Readings in Classical Studies*. Oxford: Oxford University Press, 2009.

Charlesworth, M. P. "The Virtues of a Roman Emperor: Propaganda and the Creation of Belief." *PBA* 23 (1937): 105–33.

Chilver, G. E. F. *A Historical Commentary on Tacitus' Histories I and II*. Oxford: Clarendon Press, 1979.

Chilver, G. E. F., and G. B. Townend. *A Historical Commentary on Tacitus' Histories IV and V*. Oxford: Clarendon Press, 1985.

Christ, K. "Velleius und Tiberius." *Historia* 50 (2001): 180–92.

Claassen, J. M. "Sallust's Jugurtha: Rebel or Freedom Fighter? On Crossing Crocodile-Infested Waters." *CW* 86, no. 4 (1993): 273–97.

———. "The Familiar Other: The Pivotal Role of Women in Livy's Narrative of Political Development in Early Rome." *Acta Classica* 41 (1998): 71–103.

Claridge, A. *Archaeological Guide of Rome*. Oxford: Oxford University Press, 1998.

Clark, A. J. *Divine Qualities: Cult and Community in Republican Rome*. Oxford: Oxford University Press, 2007.

Clarke, K. "Universal Perspectives in Historiography." In *The Limits of Historiography: Genre and Narrative in Ancient Historical Texts*, edited by C. S. Kraus, 251–79. Leiden: Brill, 1999.

———. "An Island Nation: Re-reading Tacitus' Agricola." *JRS* 91 (2001): 94–112.

———. "*In arto et inglorius labor*: Tacitus' Anti-history." In *Representations of Empire: Rome and the Mediterranean World*, edited by A. Bowman, H. Cotton, M. Goodman, and S. Price, 83–103. Oxford and London: Oxford University Press, 2002.

Clarke, M. L. *The Noblest Roman: Marcus Brutus and His Reputation*. London: Thames and Hudson, 1981.

Classen, C. J. "Tacitus—Historian between Republic and Principate." *Mnemosyne* 41, fasc. 1–2 (1988): 93–116.

Coarelli, F. *Il Foro Romano*. Rome: Edizioni Quasar, 1983.

———. *Roma, Guide Archeologiche*. Rome: Laterza, 2001.

Cogitore, I. *Le doux nom de liberté: Histoire d'une idée politique dans la Rome antique.* Bordeaux: Ausonius, 2011.
Collingwood, R. G. *The Idea of History.* Oxford: Oxford University Press, 1946.
Comber, M. R. "Re-reading the Roman Historians." In *Routledge Companion to Historiography*, edited by M. Bentley, 43–56. London: Routledge, 1997.
Comber, M. R., and C. Balmaceda, eds. *Sallust: The War against Jugurtha.* Oxford: Oxbow, 2009.
Conley, D. F. "The Stages of Rome's Decline in Sallust's Historical Theory." *Hermes* 109 (1981): 379–82.
Conte, G. B. *Latin Literature, a History.* Baltimore: Johns Hopkins University Press, 1994 [1987].
Cooley, A. "The Moralizing Message of the *Senatus Consultum de Cn. Pisone Patre.*" *G&R* 45 (1998): 199–212.
———. *Res Gestae Divi Augusti: Text, Translation, and Commentary.* Cambridge: Cambridge University Press, 2009.
Conte, G. B. *Latin Literature, a History.* Baltimore and London: John Hopkins University Press, 1994 [1987].
Cornell, T. J. "The Formation of the Historical Tradition of Early Rome." In *Past Perspectives Studies in Greek and Roman Historical Writing*, edited by I. S. Morton, J. D. Smart and A. J. Woodman, 67–86. Cambridge: Cambridge University Press, 1986.
———. "The Recovery of Rome." In *The Cambridge Ancient History*, 2nd ed., Vol. 7, pt. 2, edited by F. W. Walbank, A. E. Astin, M. W. Frederiksen, R. M. Ogilvie, and A. Drummond, 334–47. Cambridge: Cambridge University Press, 1989.
———. *The Beginnings of Rome. Italy and Rome from the Bronze Age to the Punic Wars.* London: Routledge, 1995.
———, ed. *Fragments of the Roman Historians.* Oxford: Oxford University Press, 2013.
Cornell, T. J., B. Rankov, and P. Sabin, eds. *The Second Punic War: A Reappraisal.* London: Institute of Classical Studies, 1996.
Coudry, M. "Camille." In *L'invention des grands hommes de la Rome Antique: Actes du Colloque du Collegium Beatus Rhenanus*, edited by M. Coudry and T. Späth, 47–81. Paris: De Boccard, 2001.
Cova, P. V. "Il ritratto del buon generale e la fortuna della versione ciceroniana." *Paideia* 54 (1999): 133–43.
Cowan, E., ed. *Velleius Paterculus: Making History.* Swansea: Classical Press of Wales, 2011.
Crawford, M. *Roman Republican Coinage.* Cambridge: Cambridge University Press, 1974.
———. "Reconstructing what Roman Republic?" *BICS* 54 (2011): 105–14.
Crawley, L. W. A. "Rome's Good Old Days." *Prudentia* 3 (1971): 24–38.
D'Anna, G. "Seneca, uomo politico nel giudizio di Tácito." In *Seneca uomo politico e l'età di Claudio e di Nerone*, edited by A. de Vivo and E. Lo Cascio, 193–202. Bari, Italy: Edipuglia, 2003.
Dagger, R. *Civic Virtues: Rights, Citizenship, and Republican Liberalism.* Oxford: Oxford University Press, 1997.

Daly, G. *Cannae: The Experience of Battle in the Second Punic War*. London: Routledge, 2002.

Damon, C. "*Potior Utroque Vespasianus*: Vespasian and His Predecessors in Tacitus' Histories." *Arethusa* 39 (2006): 245–80.

———, ed. *Tacitus, Histories: Book 1*. Cambridge: Cambridge University Press, 2003.

Davies, J. P. *Rome's Religious History: Livy, Tacitus, and Ammianus on Their Gods*. Cambridge: Cambridge University Press, 2004.

Deacy, S., and K. F. Pierce, eds. *Rape in Antiquity*. London: Duckworth, 1997.

de Bouvrie, S. "Augustus' Legislation on Morals: Which Morals and What Aims?" *SO* 59 (1984): 93–113.

Defosse, P., ed. *Hommages à Carl Deroux: II—Prose et linguistique, medicine*. Brussels: Éditions Latomus, 2002.

Deininger, J. "Livius und der Prinzipat." *Klio* 67 (1985): 265–72.

de Monte, J. "Velleius Paterculus and 'Triumphal' History." *AHB* 13, no. 4 (1999): 121–35.

Dench, E. "The Roman Historians and Twentieth-Century Approaches to Roman History." In *The Cambridge Companion to the Roman Historians*, edited by A. Feldherr, 394–406. Cambridge: Cambridge University Press, 2009.

Deroux, C., ed. "Studies in Latin Literature and Roman History." *Revue belge de philologie et d'historie*. Collection Latomus 79.1 (2001): 256–58.

Develin, R. "The Integration of the Plebeians to the Political Order after 366 B.C." In *Social Struggles in Archaic Rome: New Perspectives on the Conflict of the Orders*, edited by K. Raaflaub, 293–311. Berkeley: University of California Press, 2005.

Devillers, O. "Le rôle des passages relatifs à Thrasea dans les *Annales* de Tacite." *Neronia* 6 (2002): 296–311.

De Vivo, A. "Dissenso e Astensione. Trasea Peto negli Annali di Tácito." *Vichiana* 9 (1980): 79–103.

———. "Luxuria et mos maiorum. Indirizzi programmatici della storiografia velleiana." *Vichiana* 13 (1984): 249–64.

De Wever, J. "Recherches sur la chronologie de Velleius Paterculus pour la fin du IV siècle avant notre ère (334–302)." *Latomus* 28 (1969): 378–90.

Dix, C. V. *Virtutes und vitia: Interpretationender Charakterzeichnungen in Sallusts Bellum Iugurthinum*. Trier: Wissenschaftlicher Verl, 2006.

Dominik, W. J., J. Garthwaite, and P. A. Roche, eds. *Writing Politics in Imperial Rome*. Leiden: Brill, 2009.

Dondin-Payre, M. "*Hommo novus*, un slogan de Caton à Cesar?" *Historia* 30 (1981): 22–82.

Dorey, T. A. "Tacitus' Treatment of Antonius Primus." *CP* 53, no. 4 (1958): 244.

———. "*Agricola* and *Germania*." In *Tacitus*, edited by T. A. Dorey, 1–18. London: Routledge and Kegan Paul, 1969.

———, ed. *Cicero*. London: Routledge and Kegan Paul, 1965.

———, ed. *Tacitus*. London: Routledge and Kegan Paul, 1969.

Douglas Botha, A. D. *The Speeches of Scipio Africanus in the Third Decade of Livy's Ab Urbe Condita*. Ph.D. diss., University of Pretoria, 1975.
Dover, K. J. *Greek Popular Morality in the Time of Plato and Aristotle*. Malden, Mass.: Wiley-Blackwell, 1974.
Drummond, A. *Law, Politics and Power: Sallust and the Execution of the Catilinarian Conspirators*. Stuttgart: Steiner, 1995.
Drummond, A., F. W. Walbank, A. E. Astin, M. W. Frederiksen, and R. M. Ogilvie, eds. *The Cambridge Ancient History*, 2nd ed., Vol. 6, pt. 2: "The Rise of Rome to 220 B.C." Cambridge: Cambridge University Press, 1989.
Ducos, M. "La liberté chez Tacite: Droits de l'individu ou conduite individuelle?" *Bulletin de l'Association Guillaume Budé* (1977): 194–217.
———. "Les passions, les hommes et l'histoire dans l'oeuvre de Tite Live." *REL* 65 (1987): 132–47.
Dugan, J. *Making a New Man: Ciceronian Self-fashioning in the Rhetorical Works*. Oxford: Oxford University Press, 2005.
Dunkle, R. "The Rhetorical Tyrant in Roman Historiography: Sallust, Livy and Tacitus." *CW* 65 (1971): 12–20.
Dunsch, B. "Variationen des metus-hostilis Gedankens bei Sallust: (Cat.10; Iug.41; Hist.1, fr.11 und 12 M.)." *Grazer Beiträge* 25 (2006): 201–17.
Dyck, A. "Narrative Obfuscation, Philosophical Topoi, and Tragic Patterning in Cicero's Pro Milone." *HSCP* 98 (1998): 219–41.
Dyson, S. L. "The Portrait of Seneca in Tacitus." *Arethusa* 3 (1970): 71–83.
Earl, D. C. *The Political Thought of Sallust*. Cambridge: Cambridge University Press, 1961
———. "Sallust and the Senate's Numidian Policy." *Latomus* 24 (1965): 532–36.
———. *The Moral and Political Tradition in Rome*. London: Thames and Hudson, 1967.
———. "Prologue-Form in Ancient Historiography." *Festschrift Vogt* 1, no. 2 (1972): 842–56.
Eck, W., A. Caballos, and F. Fernández. *Das senatus consultum de Cn. Pisone patre*. Munich: C. H. Beck, 1996.
Eckstein, A. E. *The Moral Vision in the Histories of Polybius*. Berkeley: University of California Press, 1995.
Eder, W. "Augustus and the Power of Tradition: The Augustan Principate as a Binding Link between Republic and Empire." In *Between Republic and Empire: Interpretations of Augustus and His Principate*, edited by K. A. Raaflaub and M. Toher, 71–123. Berkeley: University of California Press, 1990.
Edwards, C. *The Politics of Immorality in Ancient Rome*. Cambridge: Cambridge University Press, 1993.
———. *Writing Rome: Textual Approaches to the City*. Cambridge: Cambridge University Press, 1996.
———. *Death in Ancient Rome*. New Haven, Conn.: Yale University Press, 2007.

Edwards, M. J., and S. Swain, eds. *Portraits: Biographical Representation in the Greek and Latin Literature or the Roman Empire*. Oxford: Oxford University Press, 1997.

Egerman, F. *Die Prooemien zu den Werken des Sallust*. Leipzig: Hölder-Pichler-Tempsky A.G., 1932.

Eigler, U. "Aemilius Paullus: Ein Feldherr auf Bildungsreise." In *Formen römischer Geschichtsschreibung von den Anfängen bis Livius*, edited by U. Eigler, U. Gotter, N. Luraghi, and U. Walter, 250–67. Darmstadt: Wissenschaftliche Buchgesellschaft, 2003.

Eigler, U., U. Gotter, N. Luraghi, and U. Walter, eds. *Formen römischer Geschichtsschreibung von den Anfängen bis Livius*. Darmstadt: Wissenschaftliche Buchgesellschaft, 2003.

Eisenhut, W. *Virtus Romana: Ihre Stellung im römische Wertsystem*. Munich: Wilhem Fink Verlag, 1973.

Elliot, J. *Ennius and the Architecture of the Annales*. Cambridge: Cambridge University Press, 2013.

Engel, R. "Das Charakterbild des Kaisers A. Vitellius bei Tacitus und sein Historischer Kern." *Athenaeum* 55 (1977): 345–68.

Ernout, A., and A. Meillet. *Dictionnaire étymologique de la langue latine*. Paris: Klinksieck, 1951.

Erskine, A. *Roman Imperialism: Debates and Sources*. Edinburgh: Edinburgh University Press, 2010.

Evans, R. J. *Gaius Marius: A Political Biography*. Pretoria: University of South Africa, 1994.

Eyben, E. "The Concrete Ideal in the Life of the Young Roman." *L'Antiquité Classique* 41 (1972): 200–17.

Fantham, E. "Liberty and the People in Republican Rome." *TAPA* 135 (2005): 209–29.

Farney, G. D. *Ethnic Identity and Aristocratic Competition in Republican Rome*. Cambridge: Cambridge University Press, 2007.

Fears, J. R. "The Cult of Virtues and Roman Imperial Ideology." *ANRW* II 17, no. 2 (1981): 827–948.

Feeney, D. "Beginning Sallust's *Catine*." *Prudentia* 26.1. (1994): 139–46.

Feldherr, A. "Livy's Revolution: Civic Identity and the Creation of the *res publica*." In *The Roman Cultural Revolution*, edited by T. Habinek and A. Schiesaro, 136–57. Cambridge: Cambridge University Press, 1977.

———. "The Translation of Catiline." In *A Companion to Greek and Roman Historiography*, edited by J. Marincola, 385–90. Malden, Mass.: Wiley-Blackwell, 2007.

———, ed. "Introduction." In *The Cambridge Companion to the Roman Historians*, 1–8. Cambridge: Cambridge University Press, 2009.

Ferguson, J. *Moral Values in the Ancient World*. London: Methuen, 1958.

Fick, N. "Calgacus, héros breton." In *Melanges Francois Kerlouegan*," edited by D. Conso, N. Fick, and B. Poulle, 235–48. Paris: Presses Univ. Franche-Comté, 1994.

Flower, H. I. *Ancestor Masks and Aristocratic Power in Roman Culture.* Oxford: Clarendon Press, 1996.

———. "The Tradition of the Spolia Opima: Cl. Marcellus and Augustus." *CA* 19 (2000): 34–64.

———. "Memories of Marcellus: History and Memory in Roman Republican Culture." In *Formen römischer Geschichtsschreibung von den Anfängen bis Livius*, edited by U. Eigler, U. Gotter, N. Luraghi, and U. Walter, 39–52. Darmstadt: Wissenschaftliche Buchgesellschaft, 2003.

Forbis, E. *Municipal Virtues in the Roman Empire: The Evidence of Italian Honorary Inscriptions. Beiträge zur Altertumskunde* 79. Stuttgart: Teubner, 1996.

Fornara, C. *The Nature of History in Ancient Greece and Rome.* Berkeley: University of California Press, 1983.

Forsythe, G. *Livy and Early Rome: A Study in Historical Method and Judgment.* Stuttgart: Steiner, 1999.

———. *A Critical History of Early Rome: From Prehistory to the First Punic War.* Berkeley: University of California Press, 2005.

Fowler, D. P. "Lucretius and Politics." In *Philosophia Togata I: Essays on Philosophy and Roman Society*, edited by M. Griffin and J. Barnes, 120–50. Oxford: Clarendon Press, 1989.

Fox, M. *The Roman Historical Myths: The Regal Period in Augustan Literature.* Oxford: Oxford University Press, 1996.

———. "Dionysius, Lucian and the Prejudice against Rhetoric in History." *JRS* 91 (2001): 76–93.

———. *Cicero's Philosophy of History.* Oxford: Oxford University Press, 2007.

Foxhall, L., and J. Salmon, eds. *When Men Were Men: Masculinity, Power, and Identity in Classical Antiquity.* London: Routledge, 1998.

Frank, E. "Marius and the Roman Nobility." *CJ* 50, no. 4 (1955): 149–52.

Frank, R. I. "Augustus' Legislation on Marriage and Children." *California Studies in Classical Antiquity* 8 (1975): 41–52.

———. "The Dangers of Peace." *Prudentia* 8 (1976): 1–7.

Frede, D. "Stoic Determinism." In *The Cambridge Companion to the Stoics*, edited by B. Inwood, 179–205. Cambridge: Cambridge University Press, 2003.

Fulkerson, L. "Staging a Mutiny: Competitive Role-Playing on the Rhine (*Annals* 1.31–51)." *Ramus* 35 (2006): 169–92.

Gabba, E. "Italia e Roma nella Storia di Velleio Patercolo." *Critica Storica* I (1962): 1–9.

———. "The True and False History in Classical Antiquity." *JRS* 71 (1981): 50–62.

———. "The Historians and Augustus." In *Augustus, Seven Aspects*, edited by F. Millar and E. Segal, 61–88. Oxford: Clarendon Press, 1984.

Gaertner, J. F. "Livy's Camillus and the Political Discourse of the Late Republic." *JRS* 98 (2008): 27–52.

Galinsky, K. *Augustan Culture.* Princeton, N.J.: Princeton University Press, 1996.

Gallota, B. "Cneo Domizio Corbulone." *Rendiconti dell'Istituto Lombardo* 112 (1978): 305–17.

Garbarino, G. *Roma e la filosofia greca dale origini alla fine del II secolo a.C.*, 2 vols. Turin: Paravia, 1973.
Gardner, J. *Women in Roman Law and Society*. Bloomington: Indiana University Press, 1986.
Gärtner, H. A. "Politische Moral bei Sallust, Livius und Tacitus." *Act. Ant. Hung.* 40 (2000): 101–12.
Gelzer, M. *The Roman Nobility*. Oxford: Blackwell, 1969 [1912].
Gibson, B., and Harrison, T., eds. *Polybius and His World: Essays in Memory of F. W. Walbank*. Oxford: Oxford University Press, 2013.
Gilbert, C. D. "Marius and Fortuna." *CQ* 23 (1973): 104–7.
Gildenhard, I. "*Paideia Romana*: Cicero's Tusculans Disputations." *CPS*, supplementary volume 30, 2007.
Gill, C. "Character-Development in Plutarch and Tacitus." *CQ* 33 (1983): 469–87.
——— . "The Character-Personality Distinction." In *Characterization and Individuality in Greek Literature*, edited by C. Pelling, 1–31. Oxford: Clarendon Press, 1990.
——— . *Personality in Greek Epic, Tragedy and Philosophy*. Oxford: Clarendon Press, 1996.
——— . "The School in the Roman Imperial Period." In *The Cambridge Companion to the Stoics*, edited by B. Inwood, 33–58. Cambridge: Cambridge University Press, 2003.
——— . "In What Sense Are Ancient Ethical Norms Universal?" In *Virtue, Norms, and Objectivity: Issues in Ancient and Modern Ethics*, edited by C. Gill, 15–40. Oxford: Clarendon Press, 2005.
Gill, C., and T. P. Wiseman. *Lies and Fiction in the Ancient World*. Exeter, Devon, UK: University of Exeter Press, 1993.
Gillis, D. "The Portrait of Afranius Burrus in Tacitus' *Annals*." *PP* 18 (1963): 5–22.
Gilliver, C. M. "Mons Graupius and the Role of Auxiliaries in Battle." *G&R* 43 (1996): 54–67.
——— . "The Roman Army and Morality in War." In *Battle in Antiquity*, edited by A. Lloyd, 219–38. London: Duckworth, 1996.
Gilmartin, K. "Corbulo's Campaigns in the East: An Analysis of Tacitus' Account." *Historia* 22 (1973): 583–626.
Gilmore, D. D. *Manhood in the Making*. New Haven, Conn.: Yale University Press, 1990.
Ginsburg, J. *Tradition and Theme in the Annals of Tacitus*. New York: Arno Press, 1981.
——— . "*In Maiores Certamina*: Past and Present in the Annals." In *Tacitus and the Tacitean Tradition*, edited by T. J. Luce and A. J. Woodman, 86–103. Princeton, N.J.: Princeton University Press, 1993.
Giovannini, A., and B. Grange. *La Révolution Romaine après Ronald Syme*. Vandoeuvres-Geneva: Fondation Hardt, 2000.
Gissel, J. A. P. "Germanicus as an Alexander Figure." *C&M* 52 (2001): 277–301.
Giua, M. A. "Paesaggio, Natura, Ambiente come elementi strutturale nella storiografia di Tacito." *ANRW* II 33.4 (1991): 2879–902.

Gleason, M. *Making Men: Sophists and Self-Presentation in Ancient Rome*. Princeton, N.J.: Princeton University Press, 1995.
Goar, R. J. "Horace, Velleius Paterculus and Tiberius Caesar." *Latomus* 35 (1976): 443–54.
Goldhill, S. "The Failure of Exemplarity." In *Modern Critical Theory and Classical Literature*, edited by de J. F. Jong and J. P. Sullivan, 51–74. Leiden: Brill, 1994.
———. *The Invention of Prose*. Cambridge: Cambridge University Press, 2002.
Goodyear, F. R. D. "The Development of Language and Style in the *Annals* of Tacitus." *JRS* 58 (1968): 22–31.
———. "Sallust." In *The Cambridge History of Classical Literature*, Vol. 2, pt. 2, edited by E. J. Kenney and W. V. Clausen, 268–80. Cambridge: Cambridge University Press, 1982.
Görler, W. "Zum Virtus-Fragment des Lucilius (1326–1338 Marx) und zur Geschichte der stoischen Güterlehre." *Hermes* 112, no. 4 (1984): 445–68.
Gowing A. *Empire and Memory: Representations of the Roman Republic in Imperial Culture*. Cambridge: Cambridge University Press, 2005.
———. "The Imperial Republic of Velleius Paterculus." In *A Companion to Greek and Roman Historiography*, edited by J. Marincola, 411–18. Malden, Mass.: Wiley-Blackwell, 2007.
———. "The Roman *exempla* Tradition in Imperial Greek Historiography: The Case of Camillus." In *The Cambridge Companion to the Roman Historians*, edited by A. Feldherr, 332–47. Cambridge: Cambridge University Press, 2009.
Grant, M. *Roman Anniversary Issues*. Cambridge: Cambridge University Press, 1950.
Grether, G. "Livia and the Roman Imperial Cult." *AJP* 67 (1946): 222–52.
Grethlein, J. "Nam Quid Ea Memorem: The Dialectical Relation of the Res Gestae and Memoria Rerum Gestarum in Sallust's Bellum Jugurthinum." *CQ* 56 (2006): 135–48.
———. "Unthucydidean Voice of Sallust." *TAPA* 136 (2006): 299–327.
———. *Experience and Teleology in Ancient Historiography*. Cambridge: Cambridge University Press, 2013.
Griffin, M. "Nero's Recall of Suetonius Paulinus." *SCI* 3 (1976): 138–52.
———. "Philosophy, Cato and Roman Suicide: I and II." *G&R* 33 (1986): 64–77; 192–202.
———. "Philosophy, Politics and Politicians at Rome." In *Philosophia Togata I: Essays on Philosophy and Roman Society*, edited by M. Griffin and J. Barnes, 1–37. Oxford: Oxford University Press, 1989.
———. *Seneca: A Philosopher in Politics*. Oxford: Clarendon Press, 1992 [1976].
———. "Tacitus, Tiberius and the Principate." In *Leaders and Masses in the Roman World: Studies in Honour of Zvi Yavetz*, edited by I. Malkin and Z. W. Rubinsohn, 33–57. Leiden: Brill, 1995.
———. "Cynicism and the Romans: Attraction and Repulsion." In *The Cynics: The Cynic Movement in Antiquity and Its Legacy*, edited by R. B. Branham and M. O. Goulet-Gazé, 190–204. Berkeley: University of California Press, 1996.

———. "The Composition of the *Academica*: Motives and Versions." In *Assent and Argument: Studies in Cicero's Academic Books*, edited by B. Inwood and J. Mansfield, 1–35. Leiden: Brill, 1997.
———. "The Senate's Story." *JRS* 87 (1997): 349–63.
———. "*Clementia* after Caesar." In *Caesar against Liberty? Perspectives on His Autocracy*, edited by F. Cairns and E. Fantham, 157–82. Chippenham: Francis Cairns, 2003.
———. "Iure plectimur: The Roman Critique of Roman Imperialism." In *East and West: Papers in Ancient History Presented to Glen W. Bowersock*, edited by T. C. Brennan and H. I. Flower, 85–111. Cambridge, Mass.: Harvard University Press, 2008.
———. "Tacitus as a Historian." In *The Cambridge Companion to Tacitus*, edited by A. J. Woodman, 168–72. Cambridge: Cambridge University Press, 2009.
Grillo, L. *The Art of Caesar's Bellum Civile: Literature, Ideology, and Community*. Cambridge: Cambridge University Press, 2012.
Gsell, C. *Histoire Ancienne de l'Afrique du Nord*. Paris: Librairie Hachette, 1913.
Gunderson, E. "The History of the Mind and the Philosophy of History in Sallust's *Bellum Catilinae*." *Ramus* 29 (2000): 85–126.
Haas, H. "Virtus Tacitea." *Gymnasium* 49 (1938): 163–80.
Haberman, L. "*Nefas an libidine ortum*: Sexual Morality and Politics in the Early Books of Livy." *CB* 57 (1980): 8–11.
Habinek, T. N. "Ideology for an Empire in the Prefaces to Cicero's Dialogues." *Ramus* 23 (1994): 55–67.
———. *The Politics of Latin Literature: Writing, Identity, and Empire in Ancient Rome*. Princeton, N.J.: Princeton University Press, 1998.
———. "Seneca's Renown: Gloria, Claritudo and the Replication of the Roman Elite." *CA* 19 (2000): 264–303.
Habinek, T., and A. Schiesaro, eds. *The Roman Cultural Revolution*. Cambridge: Cambridge University Press, 1977.
Hall, U. "Species libertatis: Voting Procedures in the Late Roman Republic." *BICS* 42, S71 (1998): 15–30.
Hallett, J. "Women as Same and Other in the Classical Roman Elite." *Helios* 16 (1989): 59–78.
———. "Women in Augustan Rome." In *A Companion to Women in the Ancient World*, edited by S. L. James and S. Dillon, 372–84. Malden, Mass.: Wiley-Blackwell, 2012.
Halliwell, S. "Traditional Greek Conceptions of Character." In *Characterization and Individuality in Greek Literature*, edited by C. Pelling, 32–59. Oxford: Clarendon Press, 1990.
Hamblenne, P. "Cura ut vir sis! . . . ou une (vir(tus) peu morale." *Latomus* 43 (1984): 369–88.
Hammond, M. "Res olim dissociabiles: Principatus ac libertas." *HSCP* 67 (1963): 93–113.
Händl-Sawage, U. *Der Beginn des 2. Punischen Krieges*. Munich: Editio Maris, 1995.

Hanson, W. S. *Agricola and the Conquest of the North*. London: Batsford Ltd., 1987.
———. "Tacitus' *Agricola*: An Archaeological and Historical Study." *ANRW* II 33, no. 3 (1991): 1741–84.
Harmand, J. *L'armée et le soldat à Rome de 107 à 50 avant notre ère*. Paris: Picard, 1967.
Harris, W. V. *War and Imperialism in Republican Rome, 327–70 B.C.* Oxford: Clarendon Press, 1979.
———. "Can Enemies Too Be Brave? A Question about Roman Representation of the Other." In *Il cittadino, lo straniero, il barbaro, fra integrazione ed emarginazione nell'antichità. Atti del I Incontro Internazionale di Storia antica, Genova, 22–24 maggio 2003*, edited by M. G. Angeli Bertanelli and A. Donati, 465–72. Rome: Giorgio Bretschneider Editore, 2005.
Hayne, L. "The Last of the Aemilii Lepidi." *L'Antiquité Classique* 42 (1973): 497–506.
———. "Livy and Pompey." *Latomus* 49 (1990): 435–42.
Haynes, H. "Tacitus' dangerous world." *CA* 23 (2004): 33–61.
Heinz, W. R. *Die Furcht als politisches Phänomen bei Tacitus*. Amsterdam: Gruner bv, 1975.
Heldmann, K. "Libertas Thraseae aliorum servitium rupit." *Gymnasium* 98 (1991): 297–331.
Hellegouarc'h, J. "Les buts de l'oeuvre historique de Velleius Paterculus." *Latomus* 23 (1964): 669–84.
———. "Le Principat de Camille." *REL* 48 (1970): 112–32.
———. *Le vocabulaire latin des relations et des partis politiques sous la République*. Paris: Belles Lettres, 1972.
———. "Lire et comprendre. Quelques remarques sur le texte de l'*Histoire Romaine* de Velleius Paterculus." *REL* 54 (1976): 239–56.
———. "La figure de Tibère chez Tacite et Velleius Paterculus." *Melanges P. Wuilleumier* (Paris, 1980): 167–83.
———. "L'Éloge de Séjan dans l'*Histoire Romaine* de Velleius Paterculus." *Colloques Histoire et Historiographie* (1980): 143–55.
———. "Le style de Tacite, bilan et perspectives." *ANRW* II 33, no. 3 (1991): 2385–453.
Hellegouarc'h, J., and C. Jodry. "Les Res Gestae d'Auguste et l'Historia Romana de Velleius Paterculus." *Latomus* 39 (1980): 803–16.
Henderson, J. G. W. *Tacitus/The World in Pieces in Fighting for Rome*. Cambridge: Cambridge University Press, 1998.
Henry, D., and B. Walker. "Tacitus and Seneca." *G&R* 10 (1963): 98–110.
Hessen, B. *Der Historische Infinitiv im Wandel der Darstellungstechnik Sallusts*. Frankfurt: Peter Lang, 1984.
Hild, J. A. "Virtus." In *Dictionnaire des antiquités grecques et romaines d'après les textes et les monuments*, edited by C. V. Dremberg and E. Saglio. Paris: Hachette, 1917.
Hill, T. *Ambitiosa Mors: Suicide and the Self in Roman Thought and Literature*. London: Routledge, 2004.
Hinard, F. "Sur une autre forme de l'opposition entre virtus et fortuna." *Kentron* 3 (1987): 17–20.

Hine, H. M. "Livy's Judgment on Marius." *LCM* 3 (1978): 83–87.
———. "Seneca, Stoicism and the Problem of Moral Evil." In *Ethics and Rhetoric*, edited by D. Innes, H. Hine, and C. Pelling, 93–106. Oxford: Clarendon Press, 1995.
Hock, R. J. "The Role of Fortuna in Sallust's Bellum Catilinae." *Gerión* 3 (1985): 141–50.
Hoffmann, M. "Virtus Romana bei Plautus." *ACD* 20 (1984): 11–20.
Hölkeskamp, K.-J. "Conquest, Competition and Consensus." *Historia* 42 (1993): 12–39.
———. "Images of Power: Memory, Myth and Monuments in the Roman Republic." *SCI* 24 (2005): 249–71.
Holroyd, M. "The Jugurthine War: Was Marius or Metellus the Real Victor?" *JRS* 18 (1928): 1–20.
Hopkins, K. "Rules of Evidence." *JRS* 68 (1978): 178–86.
Houston, G. W. "M. Plancius Varus and the Events of AD 69–70." *TAPA* 103 (1972): 1067–80.
Hoyos, D. *A Companion to the Punic Wars.* Malden, Mass.: Wiley-Blackwell, 2011.
Hunt, H. A. K. *The Humanism of Cicero.* Melbourne: Melbourne University Press, 1954.
Inwood, B., ed. *The Cambridge Companion to the Stoics.* Cambridge: Cambridge University Press, 2003.
Inwood, B., and J. Mansfeld, eds. *Assent and Argument: Studies in Cicero's Academic Books.* Leiden: Brill, 1997.
Jacquemin, A. "Valère Maxime et Velleius Paterculus." In *Valeurs et Mémoire à Rome: Valère Maxime ou la vertu recomposée*, edited by J. M. David, 147–56. Strasbourg: de Boccard, 1998.
Jaeger, M. K. "Custodia Fidelis Memoriae: Livy's Story of Manlius M. Capitolinus." *Latomus* 52 (1993): 350–63.
———. *Livy's Written Rome.* Ann Arbor: University of Michigan Press, 1997.
———. "Livy and the Fall of Syracuse." In *Formen römischer Geschichtsschreibung von den Anfängen bis Livius*, edited by U. Eigler, U. Gotter, N. Luraghi, and U. Walter, 213–34. Darmstadt: Wissenschaftliche Buchgesellschaft, 2003.
Jodry, C. "L'utilisation des documents militaries chez Velleius Paterculus." *REL* 29 (1951): 265–78.
Johner, A. *La Violence chez Tite-Live, mythographie et historiographie.* Strasbourg: AERC, 1996.
Joplin, P. K. "Ritual Work on Human Flesh: Livy's Lucretia and the Rape of the Body Politic." *Helios* 17 (1990): 51–70.
Joshel, S. R. "The Body Female and the Body Politic: Livy's Lucretia and Verginia." In *Pornography and Representation in Greece and Rome*, edited by A. Richlin, 112–30. New York: Oxford University Press, 1992.
Kajanto, I. *God and Fate in Livy.* Turku, Finland: Turun Yliopiston kustantama, 1957.
———. "Notes on Livy's Conception of History." *Arctos* 2 (1958): 55–63.
———. "Tacitus' Attitude towards War and the Soldier." *Latomus* 29 (1970): 697–718.

Kapust, D. "Skinner, Pettit and Livy: The Conflict of Orders and the Ambiguity of Republican Liberty." *History of Political Thought* 25 (2004): 377–401.
———. "On the Ancient Uses of Political Fear and Its Modern Implications." *Journal of the History of Ideas* 69.3 (2008): 353–73.
———. "Between Contumacy and Obsequiousness: Tacitus on Moral Freedom and the Historian's Task." *European Journal of Political Theory* 8 (2009): 293–311.
———. *Republicanism, Rhetoric, and Roman Political Thought: Sallust, Livy, and Tacitus.* Cambridge: Cambridge University Press, 2011.
———. "Tacitus and Political Thought." In *A Companion to Tacitus*, edited by V. E. Pagán, 504–28. Malden, Mass.: Wiley-Blackwell, 2012.
Kaster, R. A. "Becoming 'CICERO.'" In *Style and Tradition: Studies in Honour of Wendell Clausen*, edited by P. Knox and C. Foss, 248–64. Stuttgart/Leipzig: Teubner, 1998.
———. "The Taxonomy of Patience, or When Is Patientia Not a Virtue?" *CP* 97 (2002): 133–44.
———. *Emotion, Restraint, and Community in Ancient Rome.* Oxford: Oxford University Press, 2005.
Keaveney, A. *Sulla: The Last Republican.* London: Routledge, 2nd edition, 2005.
———. "Livy and the Theatre: Reflections on the Theory of Peter Wiseman." *Klio* 88 (2006): 510–15.
Keitel, E. "Principate and Civil War in the Annals of Tacitus." *AJP* 105 (1984): 306–25.
———. "Otho's Exhortations in Tacitus' Histories." *G&R* 34 (1987): 73–82.
———. "The Structure and Function of Speeches in Tacitus Histories 1–3." *ANRW* II 33, no. 4 (1991): 2772–94.
———. "*Foedum Spectaculum* and Related Motifs in Tacitus' Histories II and III." *RhM* 135 (1992): 342–51.
———. "Speech and Narrative in Histories 4." In *Tacitus and the Tacitean Tradition*, edited by T. J. Luce and A. J. Woodman, 39–58. Princeton, N.J.: Princeton University Press, 1993.
———. "*Sententia* and Structure in Tacitus' Histories 1.12–49." *Arethusa* 39 (2006): 219–44.
———. "Feast Your Eyes on This: Vitellius as a Stock Tyrant (Tac. Hist. 3.36–39)." In *Companion to Greek and Roman Historiography*, edited by J. Marincola, 441–46. Malden, Mass.: Wiley-Blackwell, 2007.
Keppie, L. *The Making of the Roman Army: From Republic to Empire.* London: Batsford, 1984.
Ker, J. *The Deaths of Seneca.* Oxford: Oxford University Press, 2009.
———. "Seneca in Tacitus." In *A Companion to Tacitus*, edited by V. E. Pagán, 305–29. Malden, Mass.: Wiley-Blackwell, 2012.
Klotz, A. *Livius und seine Vorgänger.* Amsterdam: Hakkert, 1964.
Konstan, D. "Clemency as a Virtue." *CP* 100 (2005): 337–46.
Koon, S. *Infantry Combat in Livy's Battle Narratives.* Oxford: Archaeopress, 2010.
Köves-Zulauf, T. H. "Virtus und Pietas." *Acta Ant. Hung.* 40 (2000): 247–62.

Kraus, C. S. *Ab Urbe Condita VI*. Cambridge: Cambridge University Press, 1994.
———. "No Second Troy: Topoi and Refoundation in Livy, Book V." *TAPA* 124 (1994): 267–89.
———. "Repetition and Empire in the Ab Urbe Condita." In *Style and Tradition: Studies in Honour of Wendell Clausen*, edited by P. Knox and C. Foss, 264–83. Stuttgart/Leipzig: Teubner, 1998.
———. "Jugurthine Disorder." In *The Limits of Historiography*, edited by C. S. Kraus, 217–48. Leiden: Brill, 1999.
———. "Forging a National Identity: Prose Literature down to the Time of Augustus." In *Literature in the Greek and Roman World*, edited by O. Taplin, 43–51. Oxford: Oxford University Press, 2000.
———. "From Exempla to Exemplar? Writing History around the Emperor in Imperial Rome." In *Flavius Josephus and Flavian Rome*, edited by J. Edmonson, S. Mason, and J. Rives, 181–200. Oxford: Oxford University Press, 2005.
Kraus, C. S., and A. J. Woodman. *Latin Historians, Greece and Rome: New Surveys in the Classics n. 27*. Oxford: Oxford University Press, 1997.
Krebs, C. "Catiline's Ravaged Mind: Vastus animus." *CQ* 58, no. 2 (2008): 682–86.
———. "Hebescere Virtus (Sall. Cat. 12.1): Metaphorical Ambiguity." *HSCP* 104 (2008): 231–36.
———. "The Imagery of 'The Way' in the Proem to Sallust's *Bellum Catilinae* (1–4)." *AJP* 129.4 (2008): 581–94.
Kukofka, D. A. *Süditalien im zweiten punischen Krieg*. Frankfurt: Peter Lang, 1990.
Kuntze, C. *Zur Darstellung des Kaisers Tiberius und seiner Zeit bei Velleius Paterculus*. Frankfurt: Peter Lang, 1985.
La Penna, A. "Il significato dei proemi Sallustiani." *Maia* 11 (1959): 23–43, 89–119.
———. *Sallustio e la 'rivoluzione' romana*. Milan: Feltrinelli Editore, 1968.
Lacks, A., and M. Schofield, eds. *Justice and Generosity*. Cambridge: Cambridge University Press, 1995.
Lacroix, J. "Fatum et Fortuna dans l'oeuvre de Tacite." *REL* 29 (1951): 247–64.
Lana, I. *Velleio Patercolo o della Propaganda*. Turin: Università di Torino Editrice, 1952.
Lange, C. H., and F. J. Vervaet, eds. *The Roman Republican Triumph: Beyond the Spectacle. Analecta Romana Instituti Danici. Supplementum, 45*. Rome: Edizioni Quasar, 2014.
Langlands, R. *Sexual Morality in Ancient Rome*. Cambridge: Cambridge University Press, 2006.
———. "Roman *exempla* and Situation Ethics: Valerius Maximus and Cicero *de Officiis*." *JRS* 101 (2011): 100–22.
Lattimore, R. *Themes in Greek and Latin Epitaphs*. Urbana: University of Illinois Press, 1942.
Lazenby, J. *Hannibal's War: A Military History of the Second Punic War*. Warminster, UK: Aris & Phillips, 1978.
Le Bohec, Y. *Histoires Militaires des Guerres Puniques*. Lonrai, France: du Rocher, 1996.

Lee, A. D. "Morale and the Roman Experience of Battle." In *Battle in Antiquity*, edited by B. Lloyd, 199–217. Swansea: Classical Press of Wales, 1996.
Leeman, A. D. "Sallusts Prologe und seine Auffassung von der Historiographie." *Mnemosyne* S. IV. 7 (1954): 323–39.
———. *Orationis Ratio*. Amsterdam: Hakkert, 1986.
Lendon, J. E. *Empire of Honour: The Art of Government in the Roman World*. Oxford: Oxford University Press, 1997.
———. "The Rhetoric of Combat: Greek Thought and Roman Culture in Julius Caesar's Battle Descriptions." *CA* 18 (1999): 273–329.
———. "Historians without History: Against Roman Historiography." In *The Cambridge Companion to the Roman Historians*, edited by A. Feldherr, 41–62. Cambridge: Cambridge University Press, 2009.
Levene, D. S. "Sallust's Jugurtha: An Historical Fragment." *JRS* 82 (1992): 53–70.
———. *Religion in Livy*. Leiden: Brill, 1993.
———. "Pity, Fear and the Historical Audience: Tacitus on the Fall of Vitellius." In *The Passions in Roman Thought and Literature*, edited by S. M. Braund and C. Gill, 128–49. Cambridge: Cambridge University Press, 1997.
———. "Sallust's 'Catiline' and Cato the Censor." *CQ* 50 (2000): 170–91.
———. "History, Metahistory, and Audience Response in Livy 45." *CA* 25 (2006): 73–108.
———. *Livy on the Hannibalic War*. Oxford: Oxford University Press, 2010.
Levene, D. S., and D. Nelis, eds. *Clio and the Poets: Augustan Poetry and the Traditions of Ancient Historiography*. Leiden: Brill, 2002.
Levick, B. "Tiberius' Retirement to Rhodes in 6 B.C." *Latomus* 31 (1972): 779–813.
———. *The Ancient Historian and His Materials*. Westmead, Farnborough, UK: Gregg International, 1975.
———. *Tiberius the Politician*. London: Routledge, 1999 [1976].
———. "L. Verginius Rufus and the Four Emperors." *RhM* 128 (1985): 318–46.
———. *Vespasian*. London: Routledge, 1999.
———. "Women, Power and Philosophy at Rome and Beyond." In *Philosophy and Power in the Greco-Roman World: Essays in Honour of Miriam Griffin*, edited by G. Clark and T. Rajak, 133–56. Oxford: Oxford University Press, 2002.
———. "Velleius Paterculus as Senator: A Dream with Footnotes." In *Velleius Paterculus*, edited by E. Cowan, 1–16. Swansea: Classical Press of Wales, 2011.
Liebers, G. *Virtus bei Cicero*. Dresden: Dittert, 1942.
Liebeschuetz, W. "The Theme of Liberty in the *Agricola* of Tacitus." *CQ* 16 (1966): 126–39.
———. "The Religious Position of Livy's History." *JRS* 57 (1967): 45–55.
Lind, L. R. "Concept, Action and Character: The Reasons for Rome's Greatness." *TAPA* 103 (1972): 235–83.
———. "Thought, Life and Literature at Rome: The Consolidation of Culture." *Studies in Latin Literature and Roman History VII*, Collection Latomus, Vol. 227 (1994): 55–68.

Linderski, J. "Roman Religion in Livy." In *Livius: Aspekte seines Werkes*, edited by W. Schuller, 53–70. Konstanz: Univ. Verl., 1993.

———. "Effete Rome: Sallust, Cat 53.5." *Mnemosyne* 52, no. 3 (1999): 257–65.

Lipovsky, J. *A Historiographical Study of Livy Books VI to X*. Salem, Mass.: Ayer Company Publishers, 1984.

Litchfield, H. W. "*National Exempla Virtutis* in Roman Literature." *HSCP* 25 (1914): 1–71.

Lloyd, A. B., ed. *Battle in Antiquity*. Swansea: Classical Press of Wales, 1996.

Lobur, J. A. *Consensus, Concordia, and the Formation of Roman Imperial Ideology*. New York: Routledge, 2008.

Long, A. A. *Hellenistic Philosophy: Stoics, Epicureans, Sceptics*. London: Duckworth, 1974.

———. "Cicero's Politics in *De Officiis*." In *Justice and Generosity*, edited by A. Lacks and M. Schofield, 213–40. Cambridge: Cambridge University Press, 1995.

———. "Greek Ethics after MacIntyre." In *Stoic Studies*, edited by A. Long, 184–99. Cambridge: Cambridge University Press, 1996.

———. "The Logical Basis of Stoic Ethics." In *Stoic Studies*, edited by A. Long, 134–55. Cambridge: Cambridge University Press, 1996.

———. "Stoic Eudaimonism." In *Stoic Studies*, edited by A. Long, 77–101. Cambridge: Cambridge University Press, 1996.

———, ed. *Stoic Studies*. Cambridge: Cambridge University Press, 1996.

Long, A., and F. Sedley, eds. *Hellenistic Philosophers*. Cambridge: Cambridge University Press, 1987.

Lovibond, S. "Virtue, Nature and Providence." In *Virtue, Norms, and Objectivity: Issues in Ancient and Modern Ethics*, edited by C. Gill, 99–112. Oxford: Clarendon Press, 2005.

Lucas, J. *Les Obsessions de Tacite*. Leiden: Brill, 1974.

Luce, T. J. "The Dating of Livy's First Decade." *TAPA* 96 (1965): 209–40.

———. "Design and Structure in Livy: 5.32–55." *TAPA* 102 (1971): 265–302.

———. "Tacitus' Conception of Historical Change." In *Past Perspectives: Studies in Greek and Roman Historical Writing*, edited by I. S. Moxon, J. D. Smart, and A. J. Woodman, 143–57. Cambridge: Cambridge University Press, 1986.

———. "Livy, Augustus, and the Forum Augustum." In *Between Republic and Empire: Interpretations of Augustus and His Principate*, edited by K. A. Raaflaub and M. Toher, 123–38. Berkeley: University of California Press, 1990.

———. "Tacitus on History's Highest Function: *praecipuum munus annalium*." *ANRW* II 33, no. 4 (1991): 2904–27.

———. *Livy: The Composition of His History*. Princeton, N.J.: Princeton University Press, 1997.

Lund, A. A. "Zur Gesamtinterpretation der ‚Germania' des Tacitus." *ANRW* II 33, no. 3 (1991): 1858–988.

MacDowell, D. "Arete and Generosity." *Mnemosyne* 16 (1963): 127–34.

MacIntyre, A. *After Virtue: A Study in Moral Theory*. London: Duckworth, 1981.

Mackie, N. "Popularis Ideology and Popular Politics at Rome in the First Century BC." *RhM* 135 (1992): 49–73.
MacMullen, R. "Legion as Society." *Historia* 33 (1984): 440–56.
Malcovati, E. *Sallustio: De Catilinae Coniuratione*. Turin: Paravia, 1971.
Malitz, J. "Helvidius Priscus und Vespasian. Zur Geschichte der 'stoischen' Senatsopposition." *Hermes* 113 (1985): 231–46.
Malloch, S. "The Date of Corbulo's Campaigns in Lower Germany." *MH* 62 (2005): 76–83.
Manolaraki, E. "A Picture Worth a Thousand Words: Revisiting Bedriacum (Tacitus Histories 2.70)." *CP* 100 (2005): 243–67.
Marincola, J. *Authority and Tradition in Ancient Historiography*. Cambridge: Cambridge University Press, 1997.
———. "Genre, Convention and Innovation in Greco-Roman Historiography." In *The Limits of Historiography: Genre and Narrative in Ancient Historical Texts*, edited by C. S. Kraus, 281–323. Leiden: Brill, 1999.
———. "Tacitus' Prefaces and Imperial Historiography." *Latomus* 58 (1999): 391–404.
———. *Greek Historians, Greece and Rome: New Surveys in the Classics* n.31. Oxford: Oxford University Press, 2001.
———. "Beyond Pity and Fear: The Emotions of History." *AncSoc* 33 (2003): 285–315.
———. "Explanation in Velleius." In *Velleius Paterculus: Making History*, edited by E. Cowan, 121–40. Swansea: Classical Press of Wales, 2011.
———, ed. "Introduction." In *A Companion to Greek and Roman Historiography*, 1–9. Malden, Mass.: Wiley-Blackwell 2007.
Marrou, H. I. *A History of Education in Antiquity*. London: Sheed and Ward, 1956.
Marsh, R. *The Reign of Tiberius*. Oxford: Oxford University Press, 1931.
Martin, R. H. "Livio storico del dissenso?" *Miscellanea di Studi in onore di Eugenio Manni* 4 (1980): 1403–23.
———. *Tacitus*. London: Batsford, 1981.
———. "Structure and Interpretation in the Annals of Tacitus." *ANRW* II 33, no. 2 (1991): 1500–81.
———. "Tacitus on Agricola: Truth and Stereotype." In *Form and Fabric: Studies in Rome's Material Past in Honour of B. R. Hartley*, edited by J. Bird, 9–12. Oxford: Oxbow, 1998.
Martin, R. H., and A. J. Woodman. *Tacitus: Annals IV*. Cambridge: Cambridge University Press, 1989.
Maslakov, G. "Valerius Maximus and Roman Historiography: A Study of the Exempla Tradition." *ANRW* II 32. 1 (1984): 437–96.
Mastellone, I. E. *Paura e Angoscia in Tacito. Studi Latini* 2. Napoli: Loffredo, 1989.
Masters, J. *Poetry and Civil War in Lucan's Bellum Civile*. Cambridge: Cambridge University Press, 1992.
Mathieu, N. "Portraits de la nobilitas dans la Conjuration de Catilina et la Guerre de Jugurtha." In *Présence de Salluste, actes du colloque, Université de Tours, 23 et 24 février*

1996, edited by R. Poignault, 27–44. Tours: Centre de recherches A. Piganiol, Institut d'études Latines, Université de Tours, 1997.

Mattingly, D. *An Imperial Possession: Britain in the Roman Empire, 54 B.C.–A.D. 409.* London: Penguin, 2006.

Mattingly, H. *Augustus to Vitellius.* Vol. 1 of *Coins of the Roman Empire in the British Museum.* London: Spink and Son, 1923.

———. *Vespasian to Domitian.* Vol. 2 of *Coins of the Roman Empire in the British Museum.* London: Spink and Son, 1930.

———. "The Roman Virtues." *Harvard Theological Review* 30 (1937): 103–17.

Maxfield, V. A. *The Military Decorations of the Roman Army.* London: Batsford, 1981.

Mayer, R. *Tacitus: Dialogus de Oratoribus.* Cambridge: Cambridge University Press, 2001.

Mazza, M. *Storia e Ideologia in Tito Livio.* Catania: Bonanno Editore, 1966.

McDonald, A. H. "The Style of Livy." *JRS* 47 (1957): 155–72.

———. "Theme and Style in Roman Historiography." *JRS* 65 (1975): 1–10.

McDonnell, M. "Roman Men and Greek Virtue." In *Andreia: Manliness and Courage in Classical Antiquity*, edited by R. Rosen and I. Sluiter, 235–62. Leiden: Brill, 2003.

———. "The *Spolia Opima* Once Again." In *A Tall Order: Religion, Law, Society and Imperialism in the Ancient World; Essays in Honour of William Harris*, edited by J. J. Aubert and Z. Várhelyi, 145–60. Munich: Saur Verlag, 2005.

———. *Roman Manliness: Virtus and the Roman Republic.* Cambridge: Cambridge University Press, 2006.

McGushin, P. *Sallust: Bellum Catilinae.* Leiden: Brill, 1977.

———. *Sallust: Catiline.* Bristol: Bristol Classical Press, 1987.

———. *Sallust: The Histories.* Vols. 1 and 2. Oxford: Clarendon Press, 1992.

Mehl, A. *Roman Historiography: An Introduction to Its Basic Aspects and Development.* Malden, Mass.: Wiley-Blackwell, 2011.

Mellor, R. *Tacitus.* London: Routledge, 1993.

Mette, H. J. "Livius und Augustus." *Gymnasium* 68 (1961): 269–85.

Meulder, M. "Bons et mauvais généraux chez Tacite." *Revue belge du Philologie et Histoire* 73, no. 1 (1995): 75–89.

Michels, A. "The Drama of the Tarquins." *Latomus* 10 (1951): 13–24.

Miles, G. B. *Livy: Reconstructing Early Rome.* Ithaca, N.Y.: Cornell University Press, 1995.

Millar, F. "Ovid and the Domus Augusta: Rome Seen from Tomoi." *JRS* 83 (1993): 1–17.

Millar, F., and E. Segal, eds. *Caesar Augustus: Seven Aspects.* Oxford: Oxford, University Press, 1984.

Miller, N. P., and P. V. Jones. "Critical Appreciations III: Tacitus, Histories 3.38–9." *G&R* 25 (1978): 70–80.

Miller, W. *The Mystery of Courage.* Cambridge, Mass.: Harvard University Press, 2000.

Milns, R. D. "The Career of M. Aponius Saturninus." *Historia* 22 (1973): 284–94.

Mineo, B. A. "Camille, dux fatalis." In *Grecs et Romains aux prises avec l'histoire: Représentations, récits et idéologie*. Colloque de Nantes et Angers 12–15 September 2001. Rennes: Presses Universitaires de Rennes, Vol.1 (2003): 159–75.
———. "Livy's Historical Philosophy." In *A Companion to Livy*, edited by B. A. Mineo, 139–52. Malden, Mass.: Wiley-Blackwell, 2015.
Mitchell, R. E. *Patricians and Plebeians: The Origin of the Roman State*. Ithaca, N.Y.: Cornell University Press, 1990.
Mitchell, S. "Requisitioned Transport in the Roman Empire: A New Inscription from Pisidia." *JRS* 66 (1976): 106–31.
Mitchell, T. N. "Cicero on the Moral Crisis of the Late Republic." *Hermathena* 136 (1984): 21–41.
Moles, J. "Livy's Preface." *PCPS* 39 (1993): 141–68.
Momigliano, A. "Livio, Plutarco e Giustino su virtù e fortuna dei Romani." *Athenaeum N.S.* 12, no. 1 (1934): 501–12.
———. Review of *Libertas as a Political Idea at Rome in the Late Republic and Early Empire*, by C. Wirszubski. *JRS* 41 (1951): 146–53.
———. "Camillus and Concord." *Secondo contributo alla storia degli studi classici* (1960): 89–104.
———. *Studies in Historiography*. London: Weidenfeld and Nicolson, 1966.
———. *Alien Wisdom: The Limits of Hellenization*. Cambridge: Cambridge University Press, 1971.
———. *Essays in Ancient and Modern Historiography*. Malden, Mass.: Wiley-Blackwell, 1977.
———. *Sui Fondamenti della Storia Antica*. Turin: Einaudi Editore, 1984.
———. *The Classical Foundations of Modern Historiography*. Berkeley: University of California Press, 1990.
Moore, T. J. *Artistry and Ideology: Livy's Vocabulary of Virtue*. Frankfurt: Athenäeum, 1989.
———. "Morality, History and Livy's Wronged Women." *Eranos* 91 (1993): 38–73.
Morello, R. "Place and Road: Neglected Aspects of Livy 9.1–19." *Studies in Latin Literature and Roman History* 11 (2003): 290–306.
Morford, M. "How Tacitus Defined Liberty." *ANRW* II 33, no. 5 (1991): 3420–50.
———. *The Roman Philosophers: From the Time of Cato the Censor to the Death of Marcus Aurelius*. London: Routledge, 2002.
Morgan, M. G. "An Heir of Tragedy: Tacitus Histories 2.59.3." *CP* 86 (1991): 138–43.
———. "The Smell of Victory: Vitellius at Bedriacum (Tac. Hist. 2.70)." *CP* 87 (1992): 14–29.
———. "The Three Minor Pretenders in Tacitus *Histories* II." *Latomus* 52 (1993): 769–96.
———. "Rogues' March: Caecina and Valens in Tacitus." *Histories* 1.61–70." *MH* 51 (1994): 103–25.
———. "Vespasian and the Omens in Tacitus' *Histories* 2.78." *Phoenix* 50 (1996): 41–55.

———. "Caecina's Assault on Placentia." *Philologus* 141 (1997): 338–61.
———. "Greed for Power? Tacitus' *Histories* 1.52." *Philologus* 146 (2002): 339–49.
———. *69 A.D.: The Year of the Four Emperors*. Oxford: Oxford University Press, 2006.
Morgan, T. *Popular Morality in the Early Roman Empire*. Cambridge: Cambridge University Press, 2007.
Morley, N. *Thucydides and the Idea of History*. New York: I. B. Tauris, 2014.
Morstein-Marx, R. "The Alleged 'Massacre' at Cirta and Its Consequences (Sallust *Bellum Iugurthinum* 26–27)." *CP* 95, no. 4 (2000): 468–76.
Moxon, I. S., J. D. Smart, and A. J. Woodman, eds. *Past Perspectives: Studies in Greek and Roman Historical Writing*. Cambridge: Cambridge University Press, 1986.
Murgia, C. "The Minor Works of Tacitus: A Study in Textual Criticism." *CP* 72 (1977): 323–43.
Murison, C. L. "The Historical Value of Tacitus' *Histories*." *ANRW* II 33, no. 3 (1991): 1686–713.
———. *Galba, Otho and Vitellius: Careers and Controversies*. Zurich: Georg Olms Verlag, 1993.
Nathan, G. S. "*Pudicitia Plebeia*: Womanly Echoes in the Struggle of the Orders." In *Studies in Latin Literature and Roman History*, Vol. 11. Edited by C. Deroux, 53–64. Brussels: Edition Latomus, 2003.
Nicolai, R. "The Place of History in the Ancient World." In *A Companion to Greek and Roman Historiography*, edited by J. Marincola, 13–26. Malden, Mass.: Wiley-Blackwell, 2007.
Nicolet, C. *Space, Geography, and Politics in the Early Roman Empire*. Ann Arbor: Michigan University Press, 1991.
Noè, E. "Il votum in Velleio Patercolo." *Athenaeum* N.S. 61 (1983): 272–75.
———. *Storiografia imperiale pretacitiana: Linee di svolgimento*. Florence: La Nuova Italia, 1984.
Noreña, C. F. "The Communication of the Emperor's Virtues." *JRS* 91 (2001): 146–68.
North, H. F. "Canons and Hierarchies of the Cardinal Virtues in Greek and Latin Literature." In *The Classical Tradition, Literary and Historical Studies in Honor of Harry Caplan*, edited by L. Wallach, 168–83. Ithaca, N.Y.: Cornell University Press, 1966.
North, J. "The Development of Roman Imperialism." *JRS* 71 (1981): 1–9.
Oakley, S. "Single Combat in the Roman Republic." *CQ* 35 (1985): 392–410.
———. *A Commentary on Livy Books 6 to 10*. Vol. 1. Oxford: Oxford University Press, 1997–2005.
———. "*Res olim dissociabiles*: Emperors, Senators and Liberty." In *The Cambridge Companion to Tacitus*, edited by A. J. Woodman, 184–94. Cambridge: Cambridge University Press, 2009.
O'Gorman, E. "No Place like Rome: Identity and Difference in the *Germania* of Tacitus." *Ramus* 22, no. 2 (1993): 135–54.
———. "Shifting Ground: Lucan, Tacitus and the Landscape of Civil War." *Hermathena* 159 (1995): 117–31.

———. *Irony and Misreading in the Annals of Tacitus*. Cambridge: Cambridge University Press, 2000.

———. "Intertextuality, Time and Historical Understanding." In *The Philosophy of History*, edited by A. Macfie, 102–17. London: Palgrave Macmillan, 2007.

———. "The Politics of Sallustian Style." In *A Companion to Greek and Roman Historiography*, edited by J. Marincola, 379–84. Malden, Mass.: Wiley-Blackwell, 2008.

Ogilvie, R. M. *A Commentary on Livy, Books 1–5*. Oxford: Clarendon Press, 1965.

———. "Livy." In *The Cambridge History of Classical Literature*, Vol. 2, part 3, edited by E. J. Kenney and W. V. Clausen, 162–70. Cambridge: Cambridge University Press, 1982.

———. "An Interim Report on Tacitus' *Agricola*." *ANRW* II 33, no. 3 (1991): 1714–40.

Ogilvie, R. M., and I. Richmond. *Tacitus: Agricola, Text, Introduction and Commentary*. Oxford: Clarendon Press, 1967.

Oniga, R. *Sallustio e l'etnografia*. Pisa: Giardini, 1995.

Oost, S. I. "The Fetial Law and the Outbreak of the Jugurthine War." *AJP* 75 (1954): 147–59.

Paananen, U. *Sallust's Politico-Social Terminology*. Helsinki: Academia Scientiarum Fennica, 1972.

Pagán, V. E. *Conspiracy Narratives in Roman History*. Austin: University of Texas Press, 2004.

———, ed. *A Companion to Tacitus*. Malden, Mass.: Wiley-Blackwell, 2011.

Paladini, M. L. "Studi su Velleio Patercolo." *ACME* 6 (1953): 447–78.

———. "Rapporti tra Velleio Patercolo e Valerio Massimo *Latomus* 16 (1957): 232–51.

Paratore, E. "Sallustio." *Quaderni della Rivista di Cultura Classica e Medievale* 12, 1973.

Parker, V. "*Romae omnia venalia esse*: Sallust's Development of a Thesis and the Prehistory of the Jugurthine War." *Historia* 53 (2004): 408–23.

Passerini, A. "Caio Mario come uomo politico." *Athenaeum* 12 (1934): 10–44.

———. "Il concetto antico di Fortuna." *Philologus* 90 (1935): 90–97.

Paul, G. M. "Sallust." In *Latin Historians*, edited by T. A. Dorey, 85–113. London: Routledge, 1966.

———. *A Historical Commentary on Sallust's Bellum Jugurthinum*. Liverpool: Arca, 1984.

Pekkanen, T. "Nomine Superioris (Tac. *Germ*, 36.1)." *Arctos* 9 (1976): 69–74.

Pelikan, P. M. *Livy's Contested Triumphs: Politics, Pageantry, and Performance in Livy's Republican Rome*. Berkeley: University of California Press, 2008.

Pelling, C. B. R. "Plutarch: Roman Heroes and Greek Culture." In *Philosophia Togata I: Essays on Philosophy and Roman Society*, edited by M. Griffin and J. Barnes, 199–232. Oxford: Clarendon Press, 1989.

———. "Childhood and Personality in Greek Biography." In *Characterization and Individuality in Greek Literature*, edited by C. Pelling, 213–44. Oxford: Clarendon Press, 1990.

---. "Tacitus and Germanicus." In *Tacitus and the Tacitean Tradition*, edited by T. J. Luce and A. J. Woodman, 59–85. Princeton, N.J.: Princeton University Press, 1993.

---. "The Moralism of Plutarch's Lives." In *Ethics and Rhetoric*, edited by D. Innes, H. Hine, and C. Pelling, 205–20. Oxford: Clarendon Press, 1995.

---. "Biographical History? Cassius Dio on the Early Principate." In *Portraits: Biographical Representation in the Greek and Latin Literature or the Roman Empire*, edited by M. J. Edwards and S. Swain, 117–44. Oxford: Clarendon Press, 1997.

---. "Epilogue." In *The Limits of Historiography*, edited by C. S. Kraus, 325–60. Leiden: Brill, 1999.

---. *Literary Texts and the Greek Historian*. London: Routledge, 2000.

---. "Tacitus' Personal Voice." In *The Cambridge Companion to Tacitus*, edited by A. J. Woodman, 147–67. Cambridge: Cambridge University Press, 2009.

---. "Velleius and Biography: The Case of Julius Caesar." In *Velleius Paterculus: Making History*, edited by E. Cowan, 157–76. Swansea: Classical Press of Wales, 2011.

Percival, J. "Tacitus and the Principate." *G&R* 27 (1980): 119–33.

Perkins, C. A. "Tacitus on Otho." *Latomus* 52 (1993): 848–55.

Perl, G. "Interpretationen der *Germania* des Tacitus mit Hilfe romischer Denkmaler." *Altertum* 39 (1993): 99–116.

Perrochat, P. *Les Modèles Grecs de Salluste*. Paris: Les Belles Lettres, 1949.

Peterson, H. "Livy and Augustus." *TAPA* 92 (1961): 440–52.

Phillips, J. E. "Current Research in Livy's First Decade." *ANRW* II 30, no. 2 (1982): 998–1057.

Pigoń, J. "Helvidius Priscus, Eprius Marcellus, and *iudicium senatus*: Observations on Tacitus' *Histories* 4.7–8." *CQ NS* 42 (1992): 235–46.

---. "Thrasea Paetus, *Libertas Senatoria* and Tacitus' Narrative Methods." In *Freedom and Its Limits in the Ancient World*, edited by D. Brodka, J. Janik, and S. Sprawski, 143–53. Proceedings of a colloquium held at the Jagiellonian University Kraków, *Electrum* 9, Kraków 2003.

Plass, P. *Wit and the Writing of History: Rhetoric of Historiography in Imperial Rome*. Madison: University of Wisconsin Press, 1988.

---. *The Game of Death in Ancient Rome: Arena Sport and Political Suicide*. Madison: University of Wisconsin Press, 1995.

Platner, S. B., and T. Ashby. *A Topographical Dictionary of Ancient Rome*. Oxford: Oxford University Press, 1929.

Pomeroy, A. *The Appropriate Comment: Death Notices in the Ancient Historians*. Frankfurt: Peter Lang, 1991.

Pöschl, V. *Grundwerte römischer Staatsgesinnung in den Geschichteswerken der Sallust*. Berlin: De Gruyter, 1940.

Potter, D. S. "Political Theory in the *Senatus Consultum Pisonianum*." *AJP* 120 (1999): 65–88.

Purcell, N. "Livia and the Womanhood of Rome." *PCPS* 32 (1986): 78–105.

———. "On the Sacking of Carthage and Corinth." In *Ethics and Rhetoric*, edited by D. Innes, H. Hine, and C. Pelling, 133–48. Oxford: Clarendon Press, 1995.
Raaflaub, K. A. "Aristocracy and Freedom of Speech." In *Free Speech in Classical Antiquity*, edited by I. Sluiter and R. Rosen, 41–62. Leiden: Brill, 2004.
———, ed. *Social Struggles in Archaic Rome: New Perspectives on the Conflict of the Orders*. Los Angeles: California University Press, 2005.
Raaflaub, K. A., and M. Toher, eds. *Between Republic and Empire: Interpretations of Augustus and His Principate*. Berkeley: University of California Press, 1990.
Raimondi, M. "I discorsi di Caio Mario nel 107 a. C. (Sall. *Jug*. 85) e di M. Valerio Corvino nel 343 v. (Liv. VII, 32)." *Aevum* 69 (1995): 95–100.
Rambaud, M. "L'idéal romain dans les livres I et V de Tite-Live." In *Mélanges offerts à Léopold Sédar Senghor: Langues, littérature, histoire anciennes*. Dakar: Nouvelles Editions Africaines (1977): 401–16.
Ramsey J. T. *Sallust's Bellum Catilinae*. New York: Oxford University Press, 2007.
Raschke, W. "The Virtue of Lucilius." *Latomus* 49 (1990): 352–69.
Rawson, E. *Intellectual Life in the Late Roman Republic*. London: Duckworth, 1983.
———. "Cassius and Brutus: The Memory of the Liberators." In *Past Perspectives: Studies in Greek and Roman Historical Writing*, edited by I. S. Moxon, J. D. Smart, and A. J. Woodman, 101–19. Cambridge: Cambridge University Press, 1986.
———. "Roman Rulers and the Philosophic Adviser." In *Philosophia Togata I*, edited by M. Griffin and J. Barnes, 233–58. Oxford: Clarendon Press, 1989.
Reinhardt, T. "Philosophy Comes to Rome." In *The Routledge Companion to Ancient Philosophy*, edited by J. Warren and F. Sheffield, 526–39. London: Routledge, 2013.
Reiter, W. *Aemilius Paullus, Conqueror of Greece*. London: Croom Helm, 1988.
Rhodes, P. "In Defence of the Greek Historian." *G&R* 41 (1980): 156–71.
Rich, J. W. "Roman Aims in the First Macedonian War." *PCPhS* 30 (1984): 126–80.
———. "Augustus and the Spolia Opima." *Chiron* 26 (1996): 85–127.
———. "Structuring Roman History: The Consular Year and the Roman Historical Tradition." *Histos* 1 (1997). www.dur.ac.uk/Classics/histos/1997/rich 1.html.
———. "Velleius' History: Genre and Purpose." In *Velleius Paterculus: Making History*, edited by E. Cowan, 73–92. Swansea: Classical Press of Wales, 2011.
Richardson, L. "Honos et Virtus and the Sacra Via." *AJA* 82 (1978): 240–46.
Richardson, L., Jr. *A New Topographical Dictionary of Ancient Rome*. Baltimore: Johns Hopkins University Press, 1992.
Richlin, A., ed. *Pornography and Representation in Greece and Rome*. New York: Oxford University Press, 1992.
Ridley, R. *The Emperor's Retrospect: Augustus Res Gestae in Epigraphy, Historiography and Commentary*. Leuven: Peeters, 2003.
Ríhová, M. "Vir bonus chez Tacite." *Acta Universitatis Carolinae. Philologica* 1 (1974): 7–30.
Rives, J. B. "Marcellus and the Syracusans." *CP* (1993): 32–35.

———. *Tacitus: Germania*. Oxford: Clarendon Press, 1999.
Roberts, M. "The Revolt of Boudicca (Tacitus *Annals* 14.29–39) and the Assertion of *Libertas* in Neronian Rome." *AJP* 109 (1988): 118–32.
Rogers, R. S. *Studies in the Reign of Tiberius*. Baltimore: Johns Hopkins University Press, 1943.
Rogo, M. "Catullus et les infortunes de la *Virtus*." *Kentron* 5 (1989): 151–60.
Roller, M. B. *Constructing Autocracy: Aristocrats and Emperors in Julio-Claudian Rome*. Princeton, N.J.: Princeton University Press, 2001.
———. "Exemplarity in Roman Culture: The Cases of Horatius Cocles and Cloelia." *CP* 99 (2004): 1–56.
———. "The Exemplary Past in Roman Historiography and Culture." In *Cambridge Companion to Roman Historians*, edited by A. Feldherr, 214–30. Cambridge: Cambridge University Press, 2009.
———. "The Politics of Aristocratic Competition: Innovation in Livy and Augustan Rome." In *Writing Politics in Imperial Rome*, edited by W. J. Dominik, J. Garthwaite, and P. A. Roche, 153–72. Leiden: Brill, 2009.
Rosenstein, N. *Imperatores Victi: Military Defeat and Aristocratic Competition in the Middle and Late Republic*. Berkeley: University of California Press, 1990.
———. "War, Failure, and Aristocratic Competition." *CP* 85 (1990): 255–65.
———. "Competition and Crisis in Mid-Republican Rome." *Phoenix* 47 (1993): 313–38.
———. "Aristocratic Values." In *A Companion to the Roman Republic*, edited by N. Rosenstein and R. Morstein-Marx, 365–82. Malden, Mass.: Wiley-Blackwell, 2006.
Roskam, G. *On the Path to Virtue: The Stoic Doctrine of Moral Progress and Its Reception in (Middle-) Platonism*. Leuven: Leuven University Press, 2005.
Ross, D. O. "The Tacitean Germanicus." *YCS* 23 (1973): 209–28.
Rossi, A. "The Tears of Marcellus: History of a Literary Motif in Livy." *G&R* 47 (2000): 56–66.
———. "Parallel Lives: Hannibal and Scipio in Livy's Third Decade." *TAPA* 134 (2004): 359–81.
Rowe, G. *Princes and Political Cultures: The New Tiberian Senatorial Decrees*. Ann Arbor: University of Michigan Press, 2002.
Rubin, Z. *Civil-War Propaganda and Historiography*. Brussels: Collection Latomus, 1980.
Russell, D. A. "Rhetoric and Criticism." *G&R* 14 (1967): 130–44.
Rutherford, R. B. "Learning from History: Categories and Case-Histories." In *Ritual, Finance, and Politics: Athenian Democratic Accounts*, edited by R. Osborne and S. Hornblower, 53–68. Oxford: Clarendon Press, 1994.
Rutland, L. W. "The Tacitean Germanicus: Suggestions for a Re-evaluation." *RhM* 130 (1987): 153–64.
Rutledge, S. H. "Tacitus in Tartan: Textual Colonization and Expansionist Discourse in the Agricola." *Helios* 27 (2000): 75–95.

Ryberg, I. S. "Clipeus Virtutis." In *The Classical Tradition: Literary and Historical Studies in Honor of Harry Caplan*, edited by L. Wallach, 232–38. Ithaca, N.Y.: Cornell University Press, 1966.
Sage, M. M. "Tacitus' Historical Works: A Survey and Appraisal." *ANRW* II 33, no. 2 (1991): 851–1030.
Sailor, D. *Writing and Empire in Tacitus*. Cambridge: Cambridge University Press, 2008.
Salvatore, A. "Il senso del male in Tacito." *Annali Della Facoltà di Lettere e Filosofía dell'Università di Napoli* 3 (1953): 21–79.
Sandbach, F. H. *The Stoics*. London: Duckworth, 1975.
Sarsila, J. "Some Aspects of the Concept of *virtus* in Roman Literature until Livy." *Studia Philologica Jyväskyläensia* (1981): 1–136.
———. *Being a Man: The Roman Virtus as a Contribution to Moral Philosophy*. Frankfurt: Peter Lang, 2006.
Saylor, C. "Amphitryon: The Play on *Virtus*." In *Studies in Latin Literature and Roman History*, Vol. 9, edited by C. Deroux, 5–22. Brussels: Collection Latomus, 1998.
Scanlon, T. F. *The Influence of Thucydides on Sallust*. Heidelberg: Carl Winter, 1980.
———. *Spes Frustrata: A Reading of Sallust*. Heidelberg: Carl Winter, 1987.
Schmid, W. T. *On Manly Courage: A Study of Plato's Laches*. Carbondale: Southern Illinois University Press, 1992.
Schmitzer, U. *Velleius Paterculus und das Interesse an der Geschichte im Zeitalter des Tiberius*. Heidelberg: Carl Winter, 2000.
———. "Roman Values in Velleius." In *Velleius Paterculus: Making History*, edited by E. Cowan, 177–202. Swansea: Classical Press of Wales, 2011.
Schofield, M. "Stoic Ethics." In *The Cambridge Companion to the Stoics*, edited by B. Inwood, 233–56. Cambridge: Cambridge University Press, 2003.
———."Republican Virtues." In *A Companion to Greek and Roman Political Thought*, edited by R. Balot, 199–213. Oxford: Wiley-Blackwell, 2009.
———, ed. *Aristotle, Plato and the Pythagoreanism in the First Century BC: New Directions for Philosophy*. Cambridge: Cambridge University Press, 2013.
Schuller, W., ed. *Livius: Aspekte seines Werkes*. Konstanz: Univ. Verl., 1993.
Scott, R. "Religion and Philosophy in the *Histories* of Tacitus." *MAAR* 22 (1968): 1–129.
Seager, R. *Tiberius*. London: Trinity Press, 1972.
Seaman, W. M. "Plautine Terms for Greek and Roman Things." *Glotta* 34 (1955): 139–52.
Sellars, J. *Stoicism*. Berkeley: University of California Press, 2006.
Shackleton Bailey, D. R. "*Nobiles* and *novi* Reconsidered." *AJP* (1987): 255–60.
Sharples, R. W. *Stoics, Epicureans and Sceptics: An Introduction to Hellenistic Philosophy*. London: Routledge, 1996.
Shatzman, I. "Tacitean Rumours." *Latomus* 33 (1974): 549–78.
Shaw, B. D. "The Divine Economy: Stoicism as Ideology." *Latomus* 44 (1985): 16–54.
Shotter, D. C. A. "Ea simulacra libertatis." *Latomus* 25 (1966): 265–71.

———. "Tacitus, Tiberius and Germanicus." *Historia* 17 (1968): 194–214.
———. "Tacitus and Antonius Primus." *LCM* 2 (1977): 23–27.
———. "Principatus ac Libertas." *AncSoc* 9 (1978): 236–55.
———. "Tacitus and Marius Celsus." *LCM* 3 (1978): 197–200.
———. "Tacitus' View of Emperors and the Principate." *ANRW* 2.33.5 (1991): 3253–331.
Siep, L. "Virtue, Values and Moral Objectivity." In *Virtue, Norms, and Objectivity: Issues in Ancient and Modern Ethics*, edited by C. Gill, 83–99. Oxford: Clarendon Press, 2005.
Sinclair, P. "Rhetorical Generalisations in *Annales* 1–6: A Review of the Problem of Innuendo and Tacitus' Integrity." *ANRW* II 33, no. 3 (1991): 2795–831.
———. *Tacitus the Sententious Historian: A Sociology of Rhetoric in Annales 1–6*. University Park: Pennsylvania State University Press, 1995.
Skaard, E. "Marius' Speech in Sallust, Jug. Chap. 85." *SO* 21 (1941): 98–102.
Skidmore, C. J. *Practical Ethics for Roman Gentlemen: The Work of Valerius Maximus*. Exeter, Devon, UK: University of Exeter Press, 1996.
Sklenár, R. "La République des Signes: Caesar, Cato, and the Language of Sallustian Morality." *TAPA* 128 (1998): 205–20.
Smith, C. *The Roman Clan: The Gens from Ancient Ideology to Modern Anthropology*. Cambridge: Cambridge University Press, 2006.
Sochat, Y. "Tacitus' Attitude to Galba." *Athenaeum* 59 (1981): 199–204.
———. "Tacitus' Attitude to Otho." *Latomus* 40 (1981): 365–77.
Sommer, M. "Scipio Aemilianus, Polybius and the Quest for Friendship in the Second Century BC." In *Polybius and His World: Essays in Memory of F. W. Walbank*, edited by B. Gibson and T. Harrison, 307–18. Oxford: Oxford University Press, 2013.
Soverini, P. "Note all'Agricola di Tácito." *Paideia* 51 (1996): 183–94.
Stanton, G. R. "*Cunctando Restituit Rem*: The Tradition about Fabius." *Antichthon* 5 (1971): 49–56.
Starr, R. J. "Velleius' Literary Techniques in the Organization of His History." *TAPA* 110 (1980): 287–301.
———. "The Scope and Genre of Velleius' History." *CQ* 31 (1981): 162–74.
Stem, S. R. "The Exemplary Lessons of Livy's Romulus." *TAPA* 137, no. 2 (2007): 435–71.
Stevenson, T. R. "*Parens Patriae* and Livy's Camillus." *Ramus* 29 (2000): 27–48.
———. "Women of Early Rome as Exempla in Livy." *CQ* 104, no. 2 (2011): 175–89.
Stolte, B. H. "Tacitus on Nero and Otho." *AncSoc* 4 (1973): 177–90.
Storoni-Mazzolani, L. *L'Impero senza fine*. Milan: Rizzoli, 1972.
Strunk, T. E. "Saving the Life of a Foolish Poet: Tacitus on Marcus Lepidus, Thrasea Paetus, and Political Action under the Principate." *Syllecta Classica* 21 (2010): 119–39.
Sumner, G. V. "The Truth about Velleius Paterculus: Prolegomena." *HSCP* 74 (1970): 265–79.

Sutherland, C. H. V. "Two Virtues of Tiberius: A Numismatic Contribution to the History of His Reign." *JRS* 28 (1938): 129–40.
———. *Coinage in Roman Imperial Policy: 31 B.C.–A.D. 68*. London: Methuen, 1951.
Swain, S. "Thucydides 1.22.1 and 3.82.4." *Mnemosyne* 46 (1993): 33–45.
Syme, R. "Marcus Vinicius. (cos. 19 B.C.)." *CQ* 27 (1933): 142–48.
———. *The Roman Revolution*. Oxford: Oxford University Press, 1939.
———. "Marcus Lepidus, *capax imperii*." *JRS* 45 (1955): 22–33.
———. "Obituaries in Tacitus." *AJP* 79 (1958): 18–31.
———. *Tacitus*. Oxford: Oxford University Press, 1958.
———. "Livy and Augustus." *HSCP* 64 (1959): 27–87.
———. "Piso Frugi and Crassus Frugi." *JRS* 50 (1960): 12–20.
———. *Sallust*. Berkeley: University of California Press, 1964.
———. "Domitius Corbulo." *JRS* 60 (1970): 27–39.
———. *Ten Studies in Tacitus*. Oxford: Clarendon Press, 1970.
———. "History or Biography: The Case of Tiberius Caesar." *Historia* 23 (1974): 481–96.
———. "Notes on Tacitus: Histories III." *Antichthon* 9 (1975): 61–67.
———. "The March of Mucianus." *Antichthon* 11 (1977): 78–92.
———. "Mendacity in Velleius." *AJP* 99 (1978): 45–63.
———. "Partisans of Galba." *Historia* 31 (1982): 460–83.
———. "History and Language at Rome." In *Roman Papers III*, edited by A. R. Birley, 953–61. Oxford: Oxford University Press, 1984.
———. *Augustan Aristocracy*. Oxford: Clarendon Press, 1986.
Takacs, L. "The Image of Camillus in Livy's Book 5 and 6: Values, History, Politics." *ACD* 44 (2008): 205–11.
Tannenbaum, R. F. "What Caesar Said: Rhetoric and History in Sallust's *Coniuratio Catilinae* 51." In *Roman Crossings: Theory and Practice in the Roman Republic*, edited by K. Welch and T. Hillard, 209–23. Swansea: Classical Press of Wales, 2005.
Tanner, R. G. "The Development of Thought and Style in Tacitus." *ANRW* II 33, no. 3 (1991): 2689–2751.
Taplin, O. *Literature in the Roman World*. Oxford: Oxford University Press, 2001.
Taylor, H. O. *Ancient Ideas: A Study of Intellectual and Spiritual Growth from Early Times to Christianity*. London: Macmillan, 1900.
Tedeschi, A. *Lo Storico in Parola, Livio, Scipione l'Africano e le tecniche dell'argumentazione*. Bari: Edipuglia, 1998.
Tiffou, E. *Essai sur la Pensée Morale de Salluste à la Lumière de ses Prologues*. Paris: Klincksieck, 1973.
Timpe, D. *Romano-Germanica. Gesammelte Studien zur Germania des Tacitus*. Stuttgart: Teubner, 1995.
Toher, M. "Augustus and the Evolution of Roman Historiography." In *Between Republic and Empire: Interpretations of Augustus and His Principate*, edited by A. Raaflaub and M. Toher, 139–54. Berkeley: University of California Press, 1990.
Townend, G. B. "Cluvius Rufus in the *Histories* of Tacitus." *AJP* 85 (1964): 337–77.

Tränkle, H. *Livius und Polybios*. Basel: Scwabe, 1977.

———. "Gebet und Schimmeltriumph des Camillus. Einige Überlegungen zum fünften Buch des Livius." *Wiener Studien* 111 (1998): 145–65.

Treggiari, S. *Roman Marriage*. Oxford: Clarendon Press, 1991.

———. "Ancestral Virtues and Vices: Cicero on Nature, Nurture and Presentation." In *Myth, History and Culture in Republican Rome: Studies in Honour of T. P. Wiseman*, edited by D. Braund and C. Gill, 139–64. Exeter, Devon, UK: University of Exeter Press, 2003.

———. "Women in the Time of Augustus." In *The Cambridge Companion to the Age of Augustus*, edited by K. Galinsky, 130–48. Cambridge: Cambridge University Press, 2005.

Tuck, S. L. "The Origins of Roman Imperial Hunting Imagery: Domitian and the Redefinition of *Virtus* under the Principate." *G&R* 52, no. 2 (2005): 221–45.

Turner, A. J. "Approaches to Tacitus' *Agricola*." *Latomus* 56 (1997): 582–93.

Turner, E. G. "Tiberius Iulius Alexander." *JRS* 44 (1954): 54–64.

Ullmann, R. *La technique des discours dans Salluste, Tite-Live et Tacite*. Oslo: J. Dybwad, 1927.

Urban, R. "Aufbau und Gedankengang der *Germania* des Tacitus." In *Beiträge zum Verständnis der Germania des Tacitus I*, edited by H. Jankuhn and D. Timpe, 80–105. Gottingen: Vandenhoeck & Ruprecht, 1989.

Usher, S. *Historians of Greece and Rome*. London: Methuen, 1969.

van der Blom, H. *Cicero's Role Models: The Political Strategy of a Newcomer*. Oxford: Oxford University Press, 2010.

———. *Oratory and Political Career in the Late Roman Republic*. Cambridge: Cambridge University Press, 2016.

van den Berg, C. *The World of Tacitus' Dialogus de Oratoribus: Aesthetics and Empire in Ancient Rome*. Cambridge: Cambridge University Press, 2014.

Vanderbroek, P. J. J. "Homo novus Again." *Chiron* 16 (1986): 239–42.

van Omme, A. N. *Virtus, semantiese Studie*. Utrecht: Kemink en Zoon, 1946.

Várhelyi, Z. "A Sense of Change and the Historiography of the Turn from Republic to Empire." In *A Tall Order: Religion, Law, Society and Imperialism in the Ancient World; Essays in Honour of William Harris*, edited by J. J. Aubert and Z. Várhelyi, 357–75. Munich: Saur Verlag, 2005.

Vasaly, A. "Livy's First Pentad and the Augustan Poetry Book." In *Clio and the Poets: Augustan Poetry and the Traditions of Ancient Historiography*, edited by D. Levene and D. Nelis, 275–90. Leiden: Brill, 2002.

———. "Characterization and Complexity." In *Cambridge Companion to the Roman Historians*, edited by A. Feldherr, 245–60. Cambridge: Cambridge University Press, 2009.

———. *Livy's Political Philosophy: Power and Personality in Early Rome*. Cambridge: Cambridge University Press, 2015.

Vervaet, F. J. "*CIL* IX 3426: A New Light on Corbulo's Career." *Latomus* 58 (1999): 574–99.

———. "Domitius Corbulo and the Rise of the Flavian Dynasty." *Historia* 52 (2003): 436–64.
Vielberg, M. "Untertanentopik zur Darstellung der Führungsschichten in der kaiserzeitlichen Geschichtsschreibung." *Zetemata* 95 (1996): 7–172.
———. "Tacitus, Domitius Corbulo and Traianus' Bellum Parthicum." *L' antiquité Classique* 68 (1999): 289–97.
———. "Domitius Corbulo and the Senatorial Opposition to the Reign of Nero." *AncSoc* 32 (2002): 135–93.
Viparelli Santangelo, V. "A proposito dell'uso del termine *moderatio* nelle storie di Livio." *Bollettino di Studi Classici* 6 (1976): 71–78.
von Albrecht, M. *Masters of Roman Prose*. Leeds: Francis Cairns, 1989 [1979].
———. *A History of Roman Literature*. Leiden: Brill, 1997.
von Carolsfeld, S. *Über die Reden und Briefe bei Sallust*. Leipzig: Teubner, 1888.
von Fritz, K. "Sallust and the Attitude of the Roman Nobility." *TAPA* 74 (1943): 134–68.
Vretska, K. *Studien zu Sallust Bellum Iugurthinum*. Vienna: M. Rohrer, 1955.
Walbank, F. W. "History and Tragedy." *Historia* 9 (1960): 216–34.
———. *Polybius*. Berkeley: University of California Press, 1972.
Walker, B. *The Annals of Tacitus: A Study in the Writing of History*. Manchester: Manchester University Press, 1952.
Walker, C. *Hostages in Republican Rome*. Washington, D.C.: Center for Hellenic Studies, 2005.
Wallace Hadrill, A. "The Emperor and His Virtues." *Historia* 30 (1981): 298–323.
———. "Civilis Princeps: Between Citizen and King." *JRS* 72 (1982): 32–48.
———. *Suetonius*. London: Duckworth, 1983.
———. "The Roman Revolution and Material Culture." In *La Revolution Romaine après Ronald Syme*, edited by A. Giovannini and B. Grange, 283–321. Geneva: Entretiens sur l'Antiquité Classique, Vol. 46, 2000.
———. *Rome's Cultural Revolution*. Cambridge: Cambridge University Press, 2008.
Wallace, J. D. *Virtues and Vices*. Ithaca, N.Y.: Cornell University Press, 1978.
Walser, G. *Rom, das Reich und die Fremdem Völker in der Geschichtsschreibung der frühen Kaiserzeit*. Baden-Baden: Verlag fur Kunst und Wissenschaft, 1951.
Walsh, J. "Flamininus and the Propaganda of Liberation." *Historia* 45 (1996): 344–63.
Walsh, P. G. "Livy's Preface and the Distortion of History." *AJP* 76 (1955): 369–83.
———. *Livy: His Historical Aims and Methods*. Cambridge: Cambridge University Press, 1961.
———. "Livy." In *Latin Historians*, edited by T. A. Dorey, 115–42. London: Routledge, 1966.
———. "Livy and the Aims of *Historia*." *ANRW* II 30, no. 2 (1982): 1058–74.
Walter, U. *Memoria und res publica: Zur Geschichtskultur im Republikanischen Zeit*. Augsburg: Verlag Antike, 2004.
Wankenne, A. "Germanicus idéal du prince selon Tacite." *Etudes Classiques* 43 (1975): 270–79.

Ward, A. M. "How Democratic Was the Roman Republic?" *New England Classical Journal* 31, no. 2 (2004): 101–19.
Wardle, D. "Vespasian, Helvidius Priscus and the Restoration of the Capitol." *Historia* 45 (1996): 208–22.
———. *Valerius Maximus, Memorabilia, Book 1*. Oxford: Oxford University Press, 1998.
Warren, J. and F. Sheffield, eds. *The Routledge Companion to Ancient Philosophy*. London: Routledge, 2013.
Waters, K. H. "Cicero, Sallust and Catiline." *Historia* 19 (1970): 195–215.
Watkiss, L. *Sallust: Bellum Iugurthinum*. Bristol: Bristol Classical Press, 1984.
Webster, G. *Boudicca, the British Revolt against Rome*. London: Routledge, 2000.
Weinstock, S. *Divus Julius*. Oxford: Oxford University Press, 1971.
Wellesley, K. "A Major Crux in Tacitus: Histories 2.40." *JRS* 61 (1971): 28–51.
———. *Cornelius Tacitus: The Histories, Book III*. Sydney: Sydney University Press, 1972.
———. "Tacitus, Histories 2.28." *CR* 87 (1973): 6–7.
———. *The Year of the Four Emperors*. London: Routledge, 2000.
West, D. *Horace Odes III. Dulce Periculum*. Oxford: Oxford University Press, 2002.
West, D., and A. J. Woodman, *Creative Imitation and Latin Literature*. Cambridge: Cambridge University Press, 1979.
Westermack, E. *The Origin and Development of the Moral Ideas in Two Volumes*. London: Macmillan, 1906.
Wheeldon, M. J. "True Stories: The Reception of Historiography in Antiquity." In *History as Text*, edited by A. Cameron, 33–63. London: Duckworth, 1989.
Whitmarsh, T. *Greek Literature and the Roman Empire: The Politics of Imitation*. Oxford: Oxford University Press, 2001.
Wiedemann, T. "Sallust's Jugurtha: Concord, Discord, and the Digressions." *G&R* 40 (1993): 48–57.
———. "Reflections of Roman Political Thought in Latin Historical Writing." In *The Cambridge History of Greek and Roman Political Thought*, edited by C. Rowe and M. Schofield, 517–31. Cambridge: Cambridge University Press, 2000.
Wilkerson, K. E. "Carneades at Rome." *Philosophy and Rhetoric* 21 (1988): 131–44.
Wilkins, A. T. *Villain or Hero: Sallust's Portrayal of Catiline*. New York: Lang Publishing, 1994.
Williams, M. F. "Four Mutinies: Tacitus *Annals* 1.16–30, 31–49, and Ammianus Marcellinus *Res Gestae* 20.4.9–5.7; 24.3.1–8." *Phoenix* 51 (1997): 44–74.
Williamson, G. "Mucianus and a Touch of the Miraculous: Pilgrimage and Tourism in Roman Asia Minor." In *Pilgrimage in Graeco-Roman and Early Christian Antiquity: Seeing the Gods*, edited by J. Elsner and I. Rutherford, 219–51. Oxford: Oxford University Press, 2005.
Wilson, J. "The Customary Meanings of Words Were Changed—or Were They? A Note on Thucydides 3.82.4." *CQ* N.S. 32 (1982): 18–20.

Wirszubski, C. *Libertas as a Political Idea at Rome during the Late Republic and Early Principate*. Cambridge: Cambridge University Press, 1950.
Wiseman, T. P. *New Men in the Roman Senate, 139 B.C.–A.D. 14*. Oxford: Oxford University Press, 1971.
———. *Clio's Cosmetics: Three Studies in Greco-Roman Literature*. Leicester: Leicester University Press, 1979.
———. "Monuments and the Roman Annalists." In *Past Perspectives: Studies in Greek and Roman Historical Writing*, edited by I. S. Moxon, J. D. Smart, and A. J. Woodman, 87–100. Cambridge: Cambridge University Press, 1986.
———. "Lying Historians: Seven Types of Mendacity." In *Lies and Fiction in the Ancient World*, edited by C. Gill and T. P. Wiseman, 122–46. Exeter, Devon, UK: University of Exeter Press, 1993.
———. *Historiography and Imagination: Eight Essays on Roman Culture*. Exeter, Devon, UK: University of Exeter Press, 1994.
———. *Remus: A Roman Myth*. Cambridge: Cambridge University Press, 1995.
———. *Roman Drama and Roman History*. Exeter, Devon, UK: University of Exeter Press, 1998.
———. "History, Poetry and *Annales*." In *Clio and the Poets: Augustan Poetry and the Traditions of Ancient Historiography*, edited by D. S. Levene and D. P. Nelis, 331–62. Leiden: Brill, 2002.
———. "The Prehistory of Roman Historiography." In *A Companion to Greek and Roman Historiography*, edited by J. Marincola, 67–75. Malden, Mass.: Wiley-Blackwell, 2007.
Wistrand, E. *Sallust on Judicial Murders in Rome*. Göteborg: Elander, 1968.
Woodman, A. J. "Sallustian Influence on Velleius Paterculus." *Collection Latomus*, Vol. 101, *Hommages à Marcel Renard* I (1969): 785–99.
———. "Questions of Date, Genre and Style in Velleius: Some Literary Answers." *CQ* 25 (1975): 272–305.
———. "Velleius Paterculus." In *Empire and Aftermath: Silver Latin II*, edited by T. A. Dorey, 1–25. London: Routledge, 1975.
———. *Velleius Paterculus: The Tiberian Narrative*. Cambridge: Cambridge University Press, 1977.
———. *Rhetoric in Classical Historiography*. London: Croom Helm, 1988.
———. "*Praecipuum Munus Annalium*: The Construction, Convention, and Context of Tacitus, *Annals* 3.65.1." *MH* 52 (1995): 111–26.
———. *Tacitus Reviewed*. Oxford: Oxford University Press, 1998.
———. "Mutiny and Madness: Tacitus' *Annals* 1.16–49." *Arethusa* 39 (2006): 303–29.
———. "*Aliena Facundia*: Seneca in Tacitus." In *Form and Function in Roman Oratory*, edited by D. H. Berry and A. Erskine, 294–308. Cambridge: Cambridge University Press, 2010.
———. (with C. Kraus). *Tacitus: Agricola*. Cambridge: Cambridge University Press, 2014.

———. "Tacitus and Germanicus: Monuments and Models." In *Fame and Infamy: Essays for Christopher Pelling on Characterization in Greek and Roman Biography and Historiography*, edited by R. Ash, J. Mossman, and F. B. Titchener, 116–43. Oxford: Oxford University Press, 2015.

Woodman, A. J., and R. H. Martin. *The Annals of Tacitus, Book 3*. Cambridge: Cambridge University Press, 2004.

Wright, H. *The Recovery of a Lost Roman Tragedy*. New Haven, Conn.: Yale University Press, 1910.

Yavetz, Z. "The Failure of Catiline's Conspiracy." *Historia* 12 (1963): 485–99.

———. "Vitellius and the Fickleness of the Mob." *Historia* 18 (1969): 557–69.

Zanker, P. *The Power of Images in the Age of Augustus*. Ann Arbor: University of Michigan Press, 1988.

Zecchini, G. "Sylla selon Salluste." *Cahiers du Centre Gustave Glotz* 13.1 (2002): 45–55.

Zetzel, J. *Cicero: On the Commonwealth and on the Laws*. Cambridge: Cambridge University Press, 1999.

———. "Plato with Pillows: Cicero on the Uses of Greek Culture." In *Myth, History and Culture in Republican Rome: Studies in Honour of T. P. Wiseman*, edited by D. Braund and C. Gill, 119–38. Exeter, Devon, UK: University of Exeter Press, 2003.

Index

Abstinentia, 164n21
Academy (philosophical school), 23
Acer, 64, 139n64, 193
Actium, battle of, 89–90, 109n170
Adulatio, 182n102, 225–26, 229n367
Aelius Sejanus, L., 57n35, 137–39, 142, 145, 231–33
Aemilius Lepidus, M. (cos. AD 11), 133, 183, 227–30, 232, 234. *See also* Tacitus on
Aemilius Paullus, L. (cos. 182, 168 BC), 96, 104–105, 139
Aemulatio, 21, 22, 219
Aeneid, 159n3, 170n58
Aequitas, 142–43
Afranius Burrus, S., 234–37
Africa, 23, 187, 213, 228
Agricola. *See* Julius Agricola, Gn.
Agrippa. *See* Vipsanius Agrippa, M.
Agrippina, the Elder, 229
Agrippina, the Younger, 235, 236n409
Albans, 93, 95
Albinus, 20
Ambigatus (king), 106
Ambitio, 55, 58, 62, 68, 71–72, 74–76, 140, 142, 157, 170, 219, 230n369
Ancestor(s), 7, 22, 37–39, 42, 44, 53, 70–71, 211–12, 218
Andreia, 11, 14–15, 17, 22, 24–25, 39. *See also* Virtus: as *andreia*
Animus, 17, 50, 57, 66, 70n104, 103, 138n53, 140, 166, 171
Annaeus Lucanus, M. (poet), 33, 46n154, 180n101
Annaeus Seneca, L., 50, 234–239. *See also* Tacitus on
Annius Milo, T., 35

Antiochus (king), 103
Antonius, M., (triumvir), 91, 117
Antonius Primus, M., 195–98, 207
Appius Claudius. *See* Claudius Crassus, A. (decemvir)
Aquileia, 198
Archimedes, 100
Arete, 11, 14, 19, 22, 24–25, 34, 41, 47, 92n40. *See also Virtus*: as *arete*
Aristocracy: Roman, 21, 39, 41–43, 47, 58, 68–69, 136; competition of, 39, 118, 195, 219, 227
Aristotle, 27n64, 29, 51
Armenia, 212, 219, 222, 232
Arminius, 211
Arpinum, 71
Arrius Varus, 197n197
Arruntius, L., 203n242, 232, 234
Arsaces, 175
Asia, 163–64, 233–34
Asinius Gallus, 150, 229
Asinius Pollio, 137
Athenian, 16, 23
Attalus, 107
Auctoritas, 21n, 99, 142–44, 153, 185, 189–90, 197, 207n, 213–14
Augustan, 84, 88–90, 109n170, 118n222, 121, 134
Augustus, 33, 87, 89–91, 97–98, 106n155, 116, 118, 129, 132, 136–37, 142–44, 147–48, 150, 153–55, 158, 197n203, 207n263, 221, 225, 228, 229n364, 232, 233n391; and *virtus*, 12, 91; moral legislation, 87, 88n18, 121
Aurelius Cotta Messalinus, M., 230n368, 232

Avaritia, 55, 58, 62, 72, 75–77, 80, 96, 105, 170, 186, 189, 193
Aventine hill, 110, 114

Batavi, 175, 198
Bedriacum, 191, 198
Beneficium, 45, 59–60, 102, 149n116
Benignitas, 86, 102
Bocchus, 63, 65, 80
Boni (good men in the Republic), 44, 74
Boudicca, 168, 169n51
Bravery, 17, 31, 33–35, 57, 62, 75, 91, 93, 95, 98, 104, 107, 117, 125, 135, 140, 146, 168, 174–75, 177, 198–200, 215–16, 218–19, 221, 223, 239, 242. *See also* Courage; Valor; *Virtus*: as
Brennus, 106
Brevitas, 133
Britain, 164, 167–69, 171–72
Britannia, 161, 163, 168, 172, 179, 200, 213
Britons, 160, 164, 167–69, 171–72, 174, 178
Brutus. *See* Junius Brutus, M.

Caecilius Metellus Macedonicus, Q. (cos. 143 BC), 139
Caecilius Metellus Numidicus, Q. (cos. 109 BC), 44, 50, 61, 63–67, 70–71, 217n308, 229n367. *See also* Sallust on
Caecina Alienus, A., 85, 193
Caelian hill, 152
Caesarian, 134, 140
Caesennius Paetus, L., 219–20
Calgacus, 169–71
Caligula (emperor), 162, 232
Calpurnius Piso, Cn., 225, 228, 234. *See also Senatus Consultum de Pisone Patre*
Calpurnius Piso Caesoninus, L. (pontiff), 231, 234
Calpurnius Piso Frugi Licinianus, L. (adopted by Galba), 186, 188, 200, 207
Camillus. *See* Furius Camillus, M.
Campania, 180

Canninefates, 198
Caninius Rebilus, G., 233
Canuleius, 115
Capitol, 180, 194, 203n246
Capri, 142
Captatio benevolentiae, 86n7
Caratacus, 211
Carneades, 23
Carthage, 38, 44, 54–55, 60–61, 72, 75, 81, 88, 132, 171, 219
Carthaginians, 96, 99, 107, 175
Carvilius, Sp., 137
Cassius Dio (historian), 130, 149n116, 150, 203n243, 235
Castitas, 118, 120–21, 125
Catilinarian conspiracy, 48. *See also* Sergius Catilina
Catiline. *See* Sergius Catilina, L.
Cato. *See* Porcius Cato, M. (the Elder or the Censor), Porcius Cato, M. (the Younger or Uticensis)
Catulus. *See* Lutatius Catulus, Q.
Celeritas, 140, 152
Cerialis. *See* Petilius Cerialis, Q.
Cethegus. *See* Cornelius Cethegus, P.
Character (as personality), 9, 20, 30n76, 43n139, 56, 61–62, 65–66, 70, 93, 107, 117, 125, 130–31, 134, 147, 173, 175, 184, 186, 188, 192, 201, 204, 214, 222–23, 233, 235, 244, 247
Chastity, 75, 79, 117–18, 120–21, 125, 162, 174, 176
Chatti, 175, 179
Chauci, 175
Cicero. *See* Tullius Cicero, M.
Ciceronian, 2, 3, 89, 134, 244–45
Cimbri, 69, 175
Cincinnatus. *See* Quinctius Cincinnatus, L.
Clastidium, battle of, 99–100
Claudius Crassus, A. (decemvir), 112n191, 113, 114, 120
Claudius (emperor), 216–19, 222

Claudius Marcellus, M. (cos. 222, 215, 214, 210, 208 BC), 44, 67, 96, 99–101, 104, 107, 133; temple of *Honos et Virtus*, 100; *spolia opima*, 99; Syracuse and, 99–100. *See also* Livius on
Claudius Marcellus, M. (nephew of Augustus, died 23 BC), 148
Claudius Quadrigarius, Q. (historian), 16
Claudius Timarchus, 238
Clementia, 1, 33, 59, 91, 102, 105, 106n155, 117, 164, 215
Cleopatra, 91
Clodius Eprius Marcellus, T., 204–205, 238
Clodius Pulcher, P., 139, 140n65
Clodius Thrasea Paetus, P., 203–206, 234, 237–39
Cloelia, 124, 212
Clutorius Priscus, 228–29
Clypeus aureus/Golden shield, 33, 91, 106n155, 147n103
Coins, 38, 61, 91n33, 151, 152n137, 186; *Honos et Virtus*, 127; *Virtus* and, 127–28
Collingwood, R., 86
Comitas, 103, 190, 196, 201–202, 215, 221–22, 235
Concordia, 54, 72, 112, 117
Consilium, 102
Constantia, 61, 93, 99, 135n38, 164, 166, 172, 174, 177, 186, 190, 192, 200–201, 204–208, 226–27, 230–31, 233–34, 238–40
Corbulo. *See* Domitius Corbulo, Gn.
Corcyra, 74, 77n
Coriolanus. *See* Marcius Coriolanus, G.
Cornelius Cethegus, P., 135
Cornelius Dolabella, P., 212
Cornelius Lentulus, G., (died in AD 25), 213, 223, 231, 234
Cornelius Lentulus, P. (*cos.* 71 BC), 135
Cornelius Nepos, 56, 94
Cornelius Scipio Aemilianus, P., 23, 26, 69, 133; Scipionic circle, 27n60

Cornelius Scipio Africanus, P., 96, 101–102, 104, 107, 137; virtues of, 102–103; and *virtus*, 103–104; exile and death, 103–104. *See also* Livius on
Cornelius Scipio Nasica, P., 55, 133, 139
Cornelius Sulla Felix, L., 49–50, 61, 63, 65–66, 70, 76, 80. *See also* Sallust on
Cornelius Tacitus, P., 3, 7, 11–12, 30n75–76, 34, 39n124, 46n155, 57n35, 103, 130–31, 138, 144, 148, 150–51, 153, 157–241 passim, 244–45, 247; and fear, 165, 181–86, 188–90, 204, 206, 209, 225–27, 229–30, 234–35; and *libertas*, 158–62, 167–69, 171–73, 175–78, 182, 184, 198, 204, 206, 208–11, 224, 227, 230, 235, 237–38, 240; on Galba, 185–90, 192, 194, 200, 206–207; on Germanicus, 213–18, 221–22, 228, 234; on Marcus Aemilius Lepidus, 227–30, 232, 234; on Nero, 181, 183, 186, 188, 208, 212, 216, 218–20, 233–39; on Otho, 186–191, 193n, 194, 199, 201–203, 206–207; on Seneca, 234–239; on Thrasea Paetus, 203–206, 237–39; on Tiberius, 159, 192, 208, 215–16, 218, 222, 225–26, 228–30, 232–33; on Vespasian, 194, 197, 207; on Vitellius, 190–192, 194, 202–203, 207; style, 158–60, 170, 180; works: *Agricola*, 159–73 passim, 178–79, 183, 199–200, 202, 205, 207–208, 215, 224, 230, 240; *Annals*, 159, 166–67, 174, 178–79, 183, 192, 197, 199, 204–206, 208–241 passim: *Dialogus*, 160n5, 205; *Germania*, 160, 172–179 passim; *Histories*, 174, 179–208 passim, 222
Corona civica, 213
Coruncarius, Ti., 137
Cossutianus, 238
Courage, 16–18, 32–37, 41–42, 53, 56, 66–67, 69, 75, 91–98, 100–104, 107, 112–19, 121, 124–25, 130, 133–35, 137, 140, 145, 151, 153, 156–59, 168–69, 171–73, 175, 177–79, 182–86, 189–91, 193–95, 199, 204–206, 209–13, 215, 218, 223, 226–27,

288 Index

Courage (cont.)
  230–31, 234, 237, 239–40, 242, 245;
  admiration of, 17, 57, 63, 93; moral, 210.
  See also Bravery; Valor; Virtus: as
Cremona, 198
Crisis, 10, 46, 48–49, 134, 136, 170, 244
Critolaus, 23
Crudelitas, 55, 96, 105
Curia, 142, 151; Julia, 33, 91
Curio. See Scribonius Curio, C.
Curtius Rufus, 216
Cynoscephalae, 104

Dacia, 166; Dacian, 179
Dalmatia, 142; Dalmatian, 134, 145
Danube, 179
Decemvir, 111, 113–14, 120
Decius, P., 116
Desidia, 172, 178, 188n141
Determinism, 28n65, 29, 84
Dignitas, 18, 74, 100, 207n263, 243
Digression, 72n111
Dillius Vocula, G., 200
Diogenes of Babylon, 23
Disciplina, 22n35, 34n94, 54, 87, 105, 186,
  189n147, 199, 217–18
Domitian (emperor), 158–59, 161–62,
  164–67, 179, 183, 200, 208, 215, 218,
  224n340
Domitius Ahenobarbus, L. (died AD 25),
  213
Domitius Corbulo, Gn., 213, 216–20, 222
Drusus the Elder (brother of the
  emperor Tiberius, died 9 BC), 133, 214
Drusus Julius Caesar (son of Tiberius,
  died AD 23), 222
Drusus Julius Caesar Germanicus (son
  of Germanicus and Agrippina, died
  AD 33), 213n284
Drusus Libo, 152

Elbe (river), 213
Elogia Scipionum, 25, 52n112

Emotions, 76, 131, 205, 219, 226, 243; and
  historical writing, 5
Ennius, Q., 9, 19, 20n23, 25, 33, 40
Epicharis, 32n82
Epicureanism, 26
Eprius Marcellus. See Clodius Eprius
  Marcellus, T.
Ethics, 7n, 24, 26, 29–30
Etruscans, 95
Eudaimonia, 27–28. See also Happiness
Excellence, 20, 24–26, 31–32, 36n, 40, 47,
  104, 158, 195. See also Virtus: as
Exemplarity, 6, 10, 83n2, 88, 91, 145n87,
  161, 239
Exemplum/exempla, 6, 59, 60, 83–85, 88,
  95, 99–100, 119, 121, 125, 133, 153, 158, 178,
  200, 205n255, 239, 246; *virtutis*, 126, 141,
  162, 239–41

Fabii Maximi, 98
Fabius Maximus Verrucosus Cunctator,
  Q. (cos. 233, 228, 215, 214, 209 BC), 44,
  67, 69, 96, 98–101, 104, 107, 147. See also
  Livius on
Fabius Valens, 195
Facilitas, 164, 187
Factio, 72, 113
Faliscans, 94
Fear, 18, 55, 61, 119, 138, 144n85, 155–56,
  163, 165, 181–86, 188–89, 196, 204, 206,
  209, 225–26, 229–30, 232, 234–35
Felicitas, 35–36, 154
Fides, 1, 56, 100, 102, 140, 142–44, 156, 200,
  202–203, 206, 238
Flamininus. See Quinctius Flamininus, T.
Flattery, 144n84, 150–51, 182, 186, 188,
  225–26, 229, 234
Flavus, 211
Fortitudo, 16, 31, 34, 36, 39–40, 66, 93, 205
Fortuna, 16, 36n110, 51, 66, 133n26, 140, 175,
  191n160, 194, 211; together with *virtus*,
  16, 107, 129, 145–6
Forum, 114, 142, 144, 154, 156

Freedom, 39, 45n152, 54, 60, 84, 95, 106–107, 109–10, 113, 117, 142, 151, 158, 168–69, 171, 173–78, 183–84, 198, 210–12, 223, 225–27, 235, 237; personal, 12, 29, 43, 161, 167, 172, 179, 206, 210, 230, 239; political, 12, 37, 39, 108–12, 114–15, 159, 172, 186, 225, 240, 244; of speech, 129, 144n84, 151, 205–206, 209, 240. See also *Libertas*; *virtus* and *libertas*
Fulvia, 118
Furius Camillus, M., 67, 94n53, 96–98, 107

Gaius Caesar (grandson of Augustus, died AD 4), 147–48
Galba (emperor), 128, 183–90, 192, 194, 200–202, 206–207. See also Tacitus on
Gallia, 35; Lugdunensis, 202
Gaul (province), 35, 73, 152, 173, 175, 179; (inhabitants), 16, 97, 99, 107, 164, 168, 171
Generosity, 59, 75, 102, 117, 123, 150, 187, 192
Germania (province), 129, 145n90, 146, 161, 173–74, 214, 216; Germans, 146, 160, 165, 173–78, 199, 210–11, 218, 222; Germany, 129, 142, 146, 166, 213, 217, 222
Germanicus Julius Caesar (Tiberius' adopted son), 34, 134–35, 145, 148, 213–18, 221–22, 228, 234. See also Tacitus on
Getae, 213, 223
Gloria, 1, 38–39, 42–43, 48, 50–54, 66, 69, 73, 75, 77, 81, 100, 103, 123, 133n25, 134, 137n47, 146, 163, 165, 171n63, 174, 203, 207, 217, 219, 221n330, 222, 224, 231, 238
Gods, 16, 28n66, 43, 51, 55, 93, 123–24, 142, 181, 211, 231; deities, 9, 93, 100
Gracchi, 49
Graupius, 164n24, 165
Gravitas, 142–43, 152, 164n21, 177, 215
Greece, 21–23, 105; culture, 1, 15, 21; Roman attitude towards, 21–23; philosophy, 11, 23, 25–26, 29–30, 41

Hannibal, 57n35, 98, 100–103, 107, 138. See also *Virtus*: of enemies/foreigners
Happiness, 28–29, 38. See also *Eudaimonia*
Hasdrubal, 103n135
Helvidius Priscus, 203–206, 222, 232
Hercules, 38
Hiempsal, 62
Hispania, 102, 140
Historiography/historical writing: aims, 6–7, 37; didactic purposes, 3, 6, 84, 88, 90, 92, 158, 208; explanation, 3, 5, 7–10, 84n, 184, 243; political, 6, 37; moral judgement, 7, 138, 208; Causation, 9, 49; Cicero and, 3–5, 7n18, 55, 245; literary construct, 4; *magistra vitae*, 7, 10; objectivity, 7; partiality/bias, 3–5, 130; *res et verba*, 3, 245; Rhetoric and, 3, 4–7, 119, 245; *delectatio*, 5–6; *inventio*, 5, 212; Truth, 3–5, 56, 89; versus fiction, 4–5, 53. See also *virtus* and historical writing
Homeric, 24
Homo novus. See New man
Honor, 17, 20, 34–35, 38, 42–43, 45, 48, 55, 71, 74–76, 95, 99, 105, 115–16, 123–24, 137n47, 144n84, 150–51, 158, 163, 165, 183, 203, 212, 216, 223, 238, 245
Honos, 38n; Coin with *Virtus* and, 127; Temple with *Virtus* and, 69, 100
Horace. See Horatius Flaccus, Q.
Horatius, P. (kills his sister), 32
Horatius Cocles, 97, 124
Horatius Flaccus, Q. (poet), 21
Hostilius Tullus (king), 93
Humanitas, 32, 146, 148, 151, 169, 221n327

Icilius, L., 113, 120
Identity, 2, 6, 92, 126, 160, 178–79, 215, 240, 243–44; Roman, 2, 8, 10, 83–85, 87, 90, 125
Illyrians, 106
Imagines (of the ancestors), 45, 53, 71

Imitatio, 21–22, 43
Imperialism, 27n60, 107, 170–171n60
Imperium, 9, 48, 55, 81, 116n214, 121, 143, 170, 189
Indibilis, 103n135
Industria, 44–45, 53, 56, 66, 69, 82, 133n27, 137n46, 140, 142–43, 162, 166, 172, 177, 196, 201, 224. See also *virtus* and *industria*
Inertia, 166, 172, 177
Ingenium, 22, 42–43, 50, 52, 58, 61, 67, 71, 79, 103, 116n214, 133n26, 135n38, 137n47, 182n102, 192, 204n247, 215, 221
Inguiomerus, 211
Innocentia, 67, 75, 137n48, 201
Integritas, 100, 164n21
Intellectual history, 2, 13–14
Invidia, 22, 100n110, 188, 197, 215
Italy, 22, 38, 198; Italian, 115, 198, 202
Ius Gentium, 108
Iustitia, 33, 91, 142–43, 164n21, 187

Janus Quirinus, 155
Judea, 192
Jugurtha, 48, 50, 61–66, 73, 75n126, 79–80. See also Sallust on; *Virtus*: of enemies/foreigners
Julia the Elder (daughter of Augustus), 118, 121, 147
Julia the Younger (granddaughter of Augustus), 121
Julius Agrestis, 200
Julius Agricola, Gn., 46n155, 161–172 passim, 178, 183, 200, 209, 218, 224n340. See also Tacitus on
Julius Caesar, G., 35, 56, 59–60, 67n90, 70, 82, 91, 99, 135, 140, 168, 173
Julius Caesar Octavianus. See Augustus
Julius Florus, 146, 152
Junius Blaesus, Q. (grandson of Sejanus' uncle, died in AD 69), 202–203, 206
Junius Blaesus, Q. (Sejanus' uncle, died in AD 31), 192, 216, 228

Junius Brutus, L. (cos. 509 BC), 120, 205
Junius Brutus, M. (pr. 44 BC), 205
Jupiter, 93, 239

Labor, 33, 53, 68, 78, 89, 176n93, 177, 191, 224
Laelius, G., 137
Largitio, 80, 207
Laudatio funebris, 103
Lavinia, 117
Lentulus. See Cornelius Lentulus, P.
Lepidus. See Aemilius Lepidus, M.
Liberalitas, 150, 152, 187, 192, 202
Libertas, 1, 54, 60, 74, 88, 93, 108–117 passim, 121, 158–62, 167–69, 171–73, 175–78, 182, 198, 204, 206, 208–10, 224, 227, 230, 235, 237–38, 240, 244; Acquisition of, 12, 84, 108, 111, 115; Patrician, 108–109, 113; Plebeian, 108–14; Senatorial, 172, 206. See also Livius and; Tacitus and; *virtus* and *libertas*
Liberty, 39, 84, 93, 108–15, 117, 120, 121, 157, 168–69, 172, 175, 177–78, 186, 198, 207, 209–11, 215, 239. See also Freedom; Libertas
Licentia, 96, 100, 105n151
Licinius, G. (laws of), 114
Licinius Lucullus, L., 36–37
Licinius Mucianus, G., 163, 195–98, 207
Licinius Murena, L. (cos. 62 BC), 35
Limes, 160, 172, 174
Liternum, 103
Livia (wife of Augustus), 118, 150
Livian, 84n, 86, 87n12
Livius, T., 1–3, 6, 8–12, 32n82, 57n35, 83–126 passim, 130, 134, 138, 147, 152, 155–57, 199, 212, 218n312, 219, 243–45; Augustus and, 84, 87–90, 97–98, 109n170; *exempla* and, 83–85, 88, 91; language, 91, 94, 105–106, 115, 245; *libertas* and, 108–117 passim, 121; no political experience, 86; on Aemilius

Paullus, 104–105; on Camillus, 96–98, 107; on Claudius Marcellus, 99–101, 104, 107, 133, 147; on Cornelius Scipio Africanus, 96, 101–104, 107; on Fabius Maximus, 98–101, 104, 107, 147; on Flamininus, 104–105; on Lucretia, 113, 117, 119, 120; preface, 12, 83, 85–92 passim, 125; Sallust and, 83–84, 88–89, 99, 105, 113; struggle of orders and, 110–16; style, 89–90, 106; women and, 117–125 passim, 212
Livius Andronicus, 1
Livius Drusus Libo, M. (cos. 15 BC), 152
Livy. *See* Livius, T.
Lollius, M., 139–40
Lucan. *See* Annaeus Lucanus, M.
Lucceius, L., 55n30
Lucian, 133n17
Lucilius, C., 20–21, 25, 33; definition of *virtus*, 20; Greek influence, 21
Lucius Caesar (grandson of Augustus, died AD 2), 147–48
Lucretia, 113, 117, 119–20
Lucretius Carus, T., (philosopher), 26
Lucullus. *See* Licinius Lucullus, L.
Ludi Saeculare, 90n30
Lusitania, 188
Lutatius Catulus, Q. (cos. 102 BC), 133
Luxuria, 33, 58, 65, 72, 75–76, 79, 105n152, 140, 188, 190, 196, 207

Macedonia, 23, 104, 142; Macedonian, 96, 104–106
Macro. *See* Naevius Sutorius Macro, Q.
Maelius, 113–14
Magnificentia, 202
Magnitudo animi, 40n, 93, 98n, 102
Maiestas, 142, 144n85, 150, 228, 234
Maiores, 1, 22, 34n94, 39, 43, 45, 52, 60, 70, 116n214, 161, 165, 168, 199, 218, 225, 246. See also *mos/mores*

Manliness, 1–2, 14–15, 17, 19, 20n25, 24, 32–34, 45, 66. See also *Virtus*: as manliness
Manlius Capitolinus, M. (cos. 392 BC), 97n80
Marcellus. *See* Claudius Marcellus, M.
Marcius Barea Soranus, Q., 234, 237–38
Marcius Coriolanus, G., 123
Marius, G. (cos. 107, 103–100, 86 BC), 45n150, 49, 55, 217n308; as new man, 42, 50, 62, 64, 68, 116, 137; civil wars, 49, 65, 72; Sallust on, 44n142, 61–73 passim, 82, 140n70; personality, 68; speech, 42, 55, 68, 70–71, 116, 137; *virtus* and, 35, 45n150, 63, 66–67, 69, 140n70; temple of, 69, 100n108
Marius Celsus, A., 201–202, 206
Mark Antony. *See* Antonius, M.
Maroboduus, 211
Mars, 93
Massilia, 162
Massinissa, 103, 107
McDonnell, M., 2, 15n, 25n, 66–67
Memmius Regulus, P., 233
Memoria, 34, 53, 167, 215–17, 221n, 236–37, 244. See also *Virtus*: memory of
Merit, 24, 45, 53, 67, 113, 115–16, 136–37, 139, 143–45, 147–48, 163, 198, 200–201, 213, 215, 226
Messalina, 233
Metellus. *See* Caecilius Metellus Macedonicus and Caecilius Metellus Numidicus
Metus, 7n19, 76n135, 132n14, 182n102, 188, 197, 204, 225–27, 232, 238; *hostilis*, 54, 74, 133
Meuse (river), 218
Micipsa, 61
Minucius, M., 98
Minucius Thermus, M., 231
Misericordia, 164n
Mithridates, 135n, 220. See also *Virtus*: of enemies/foreigners

Moderatio, 93, 112, 150–52, 162, 164, 166–67, 172, 174, 177, 186–87, 193–94, 198, 201, 203–205, 207–208, 215, 219, 221–22, 226–28, 230–32, 239, 240. See also *Modestia*
Modestia, 162, 164n21, 166, 170, 199n212, 213, 223–24, 228
Modesty, 66, 75, 79, 86n7, 118, 119, 120n228, 122, 125, 151, 219
Moesia, 166
Montanus Alpinus, 193
Moral, 1, 7–14, 18–21, 24–29, 33, 35, 37–38, 42, 49, 63, 70, 81–82, 87–90, 104, 121, 138, 141, 153, 158, 173–75, 180, 195, 210, 241–43, 246–47; Morality, 7n20, 8, 9, 15, 19, 21–22, 27, 29–30, 39n122, 40, 42, 46, 49, 155; and politics, 27, 30, 40, 51, 155, 246
Mos/mores, 9, 12, 19, 22n35, 40, 43, 49, 66, 70, 86–87, 91, 125, 175n76, 184, 201, 208, 247; *mores maiorum*, 6, 45, 64, 67, 70, 139, 153, 156, 161, 229, 232; *partium et factionum*, 72, 113
Mucianus. See Licinius Mucianus, G.
Mucius Scaevola, 97, 124
Mummius, L., 137
Munda, battle of, 140
Munificentia, 60, 80, 123, 140, 149–51

Naevius Sutorius Macro, Q., 232
Nature: human, 28, 30, 32, 49–50, 52, 56, 58–59, 61, 68, 119, 246; Stoic concept, 27–29
Nepos. See Cornelius Nepos
Nero (emperor), 163, 179, 181–84, 186–88, 196, 208, 212, 216, 219–20, 232–39, 247
New men, 42–45, 49, 55, 66–72, 82, 115n211, 116, 117, 135–39, 233n390, 243; Cato as, 42, 136; Cicero as, 42, 45, 50, 71, 135, 137; Marius as, 42, 50, 62, 64, 66–71, 116, 137; Velleius as, 130, 132, 136, 152. See also *virtus*: and new man
Nicias, 17n11, 21

Nobilis/es, 38, 42–44, 50, 52, 68–70, 72, 81, 136, 139–40
Nobilitas, 42–44, 49, 55, 68–71, 81, 115, 139, 175
Nobility, 24, 39, 42–43, 55, 58, 62, 65, 68–72, 82, 100, 115, 137, 139, 175, 181, 185, 196, 225, 233
Noble (man), 38, 42–44, 48, 52–53, 55, 58, 61–62, 64–65, 67–68, 71, 82, 108, 110–12, 115–16, 119, 136, 141, 185n113; savage, 175
Novitas, 64, 69, 115, 136. See also New men
Novus homo. See New men
Numantia, 38, 39n120, 61
Numidia, 64, 68, 212; Numidian, 61, 63–64

Octavia (Augustus' sister), 118
Octavian, 91. See also Augustus
Orator, 5, 21n34, 96, 245
Oratory, 50, 205
Ostorius Scapula, M. (son of P. Ostorius Scapula), 213
Ostorius Scapula, P. (governor of Britain), 213
Otho (emperor), 183–91, 193–94, 198–99, 201–202, 206–207
Otium, 65, 74, 92n38, 163, 166, 168–69, 177n95, 204

Paduan, 89
Panaetius, 23, 26–27
Pandateria, 121n240
Pannonia, 142, 166
Parthia, 212; Parthian, 175, 179, 201, 212, 219
Pater patriae, 97
Patientia, 33, 140, 176–77, 218
Pauci, 70; *Potentia paucorum*, 70, 78
Paulina (Seneca's wife), 236–37
Pax/pacis, 88–89, 142–43, 170, 191, 194; Augusta, 149, 154–55; *deorum*, 123
Pericles, 16

Peripatetics, 23, 25
Perpenna, M., 139
Perseus (king), 105, 107
Pertinacia, 96
Petilius Cerialis, Q., 199–200
Petronius Turpilianus, P., 169
Philaeni brothers, 72n111
Philip V (king), 104, 107
Pietas, 33, 91, 93, 103, 147–48, 151, 164n21, 200
Piso (adopted by Galba). *See* Calpurnius Piso Frugi Licinianus, L.
Plato, 17, 29, 50n7, 51; *Laches* dialogue, 17–18, 21; Platonic, 17, 41, 52
Plautius Lateranus, 234
Plautus (comedian), 20, 23n44, 25
Plutarch, 23, 64, 68, 99, 122
Political: change, 3, 10–12, 48, 120–21, 161, 184; culture, 13, 143, 158, 173; thought, 13, 40, 108n, 247
Politicians, 14, 17, 45, 86, 92, 96, 133, 137, 149, 207, 232, 246
Polybius, 7n, 23, 27, 94, 101n115
Pompeius Magnus, Gn., 134, 140, 220; *virtus* of, 35–36, 134
Pompeius Magnus Pius, S. (son of Pompey), 140, 228
Pompey. *See* Pompeius Magnus, Gn.
Pontifex Maximus, 100, 133
Pontus, 134
Poppaeus Sabinus, Q. (*cos.* AD 9), 213
Populus, 34, 67–68, 91, 94, 97n82, 115, 120
Porcius Cato, M. (the Elder or the Censor), 23, 59, 60, 137, 205; as new man, 42, 136; attack on the nobility, 42; Cicero on, 44, 136; Sallust and, 54, 60; *virtus* and, 25, 44, 66
Porcius Cato, M. (the Younger or Uticensis) (pr. 54 BC), 67n90, 74, 80, 205; Caesar and, 59–60, 99; Sallust on, 59–60, 99; speech, 59–60, 75; Velleius on, 135; *virtus* of, 59–61, 82
Porsenna, 97, 106, 124

Posidonius, 51, 54, 99
Princeps, 40, 89, 132, 141, 143–45, 147–49, 152–53, 155, 158, 161, 174, 177, 182, 187, 190, 193, 197n203, 203, 205, 207–41 passim, 244; *virtus* of, 158, 165
Principate, 10, 12–13, 40n129, 129–241 passim, 244–45. *See also Virtus*: under the Principate
Probitas, 55–56, 66
Proscriptions, 72
Providence, 26, 28, 149, 153
Providentia, 149, 151
Prudentia, 99, 149, 152, 162, 164n21, 166, 201–202
Pudicitia, 1, 79, 118–21, 125, 176, 212, 219. *See also* Women
Pythagorean, 22

Quality/ies, 8–9, 17–19, 24, 42–44, 46, 54, 58–59, 62, 65–66, 69–70, 81, 103, 117, 119–20, 123, 125, 130, 138, 140–41, 143–45, 147–48, 150, 153, 161, 163–66, 168, 176–77, 185–86, 192–94, 198, 201, 208, 213–14, 217–18, 221–22, 228, 234, 237; Good/moral, 31, 35–36, 40, 47, 52, 55–56, 68, 79, 81, 118, 133, 138n55, 139, 143, 160n5, 164, 184, 187–88, 193–95, 198, 200, 213, 215, 218, 222, 233
Quies, 163
Quinctilius Varus, P., 211
Quinctius Cincinnatus, L., 97, 114
Quinctius Flamininus, T., 104–105
Quintilian, 50, 54

Regnum, 43, 108, 109n174, 116, 175
Remus, 93, 110
Res Gestae, 155; and *virtus*, 33, 91
Responsibility, 10, 29–30, 72, 81–82, 177–78, 194, 203n246, 209, 226, 246
Res publica, 6, 9, 37, 60, 74, 76–77, 85, 109, 132, 136, 143–44, 149n116, 159, 166, 189, 198, 202, 220, 243, 247; liberty and, 91, 93, 108, 112, 114, 117, 120–21, 224, 226,

Res publica (cont.)
244; service to, 16, 35, 42, 54, 73, 81–82, 101, 112, 117, 123, 125, 147, 161, 177–78, 180, 183, 186, 191, 195–96, 199, 204, 207, 209, 226–27, 239

Rhadamistus, 212

Rhascupolis, 149, 152

Rhetoric, 4–7, 21n34, 23, 116, 131, 159, 169–70, 236, 245. *See also* Historiography/historical writing and

Rhine, 142, 172, 218, 222

Rhodes, 147–48; Rhodian, 105

Rigor, 185, 187, 189

Roman: historians, 1–14, 47–48, 67, 85–86, 88, 131, 155, 158, 170, 225, 242–44, 247; as constructors of society, 2, 6, 11, 243, 247; political experience, 2, 86; People, 14, 33–34, 39n121, 43n139, 45, 62, 84, 86, 91, 93–94, 100–102, 106–107, 109, 114, 119–20, 124, 132, 134, 136, 139, 144, 152–56, 183, 243, 245

Romanization, 164, 169

Romanness, 120

Romulus, 93, 97, 110, 116n214, 122

Rubellius Plautus, G., 232–34

Sabines, 93, 116, 122

Sacrosanctitas, 111

Sacrovir, 146, 152

Saevitia, 100, 157, 186, 189

Sallust. *See* Sallustius Crispus, C.

Sallustian, 62, 66, 69, 105, 133, 170

Sallustius Crispus, C., 3, 9–12, 46n154, 48–84 passim, 88–89, 99, 113, 116, 130, 133, 140, 152, 155–57, 219, 247; and *virtus*, 33, 48–82 passim, 136, 157, 242–44; always in singular, 56–57, 132; contrasted, 48, 59, 61; fragmented, 60–61, 194; in writing history, 52–53, 82; wider meaning, 52, 56, 71, 81, 244; Language, 11–12, 49, 50, 63, 73–82 passim, 105, 244–45; disease imagery, 58, 63, 76–77; New man and, 44n144, 49–50, 55, 68–70, 72, 115, 136, 243; on Catiline, 33, 57–59, 62, 64, 138, 185n113, 217n308; his courage, 57, 63; on Caesar, 59–60, 82, 140; on M. Porcius Cato Uticensis, 59–61, 74–75, 82; on Jugurtha, 61–64, 79–80; on G. Marius, 44n142, 62–64, 66–72, 82, 140n70, 201, 217n308; speech of, 68, 70–71, 116, 137; on Q. Caecilius Metellus, 63–65, 67, 80, 217n308, 229n367; on Sulla, 63, 65–66, 80; prologues, 32n, 48–54 passim, 68, 73, 80–81

Samnites, 116, 175

Sarmatians, 179

Scipio. *See* Cornelius Scipio Aemilianus, P. and Cornelius Scipio Africanus, P.

Scribonius Curio, C., 140

Sejanus. *See* Aelius Sejanus, L.

Sempronia, 78–79

Sempronius Densus, 200

Senatus Consultum de Pisone Patre (SCPP), 145n78, 147n103, 149n116, 152n137, 153n146, 225

Seneca. *See* Annaeus Seneca, L.

Sergius Catilina, L., 33, 43, 48, 50, 57–64 passim, 73, 76–78, 80, 135, 138, 185n113, 187n129, 217n308, 247. *See also* Sallust on

Servaeus, Q., 231

Servilius Ahala, 93, 114

Servitium, 74, 225n344, 237

Servitus, 113n195, 151, 169, 182

Severitas, 60, 137n52, 164n, 185, 187, 189, 217–18, 235

Sex, 14, 32; sexist comments, 118n223; sexual morality, 120n233

Sextius, L. (laws of), 115

Sicily, 100

Silius, G., 229, 233

Simplicitas, 192

Skeptical, 30

Slavery, 74, 106, 109–10, 168–69, 177, 209, 225–26

Slaves, 23, 32, 151, 181, 186

Socrates, 18, 24
Sophist, 24
Sophonisba, 103n133
Sosia (Silius' wife), 229
Spain, 23, 101–102, 140, 175, 187
Speeches, 24–25, 34, 37, 41n134, 42, 43, 44, 45, 116, 139, 193, 194; in historical writing, 4; in Sallust, 49, 55, 59–60, 65, 68, 70–71, 75, 78, 137; in Livy, 96–97, 101–102, 105–106, 115–16, 118–19, 122; in Tacitus, 165, 169–71, 189, 193, 203n246, 205–206, 211, 228, 231, 236; in Velleius, 129; *Oratio recta*, 102n120, 118; *Oratio obliqua*, 122
Spolia opima, 99
Statilius Taurus, T., 117, 137
Stoa, 23; Stoicism, 11, 15, 21–34 passim, 51, 204n248, 233, 239; Stoic sage, 27, 29; virtue and, 27–30, 82
Strabo Libuscidianus, 144n86
Struggle of orders, 110–115
Suebi, 179
Suetonius Paulinus, G., 163, 202, 216
Suetonius Tranquillus, G. (author), 130, 150–51, 187n130, 236
Sulla. *See* Cornelius Sulla Felix, L.
Sulpicius Asper, 234
Superbia, 55, 64–65, 70n104, 76–77, 96, 105n149, 157, 170, 190, 207
Syme, R., 2, 49–50, 86n7, 89, 129n1, 144n, 227n85, 233n390
Syracuse, 99–100
Syria, 134, 196, 222

Tacfarinas, 212
Tacitean, 160, 170
Tacitus. *See* Cornelius Tacitus, P.
Tanaquil, 115, 117
Tarquinius Priscus, L., 115–16
Tarquinius Superbus, L, 119–20
Tatius, T., 116
Telos, 28–29, 41, 46–47
Temperantia, 103, 164n21, 215

Temple: *Honos et Virtus*, 69, 100; Plebeian modesty, 118–19
Terence, 25
Terentius, M., 230–31, 234
Terentius Varro, M. (author), 56
Teutones, 69, 100n108
Thracia, 142, 213
Thrasea Paetus. *See* Clodius Thrasea Paetus, P.
Thucydides, 16, 73–74, 77n136
Tiberius (emperor), 9, 12, 46n155, 129–32, 136–55 passim, 157, 159, 183, 187, 192, 208, 212, 214–16, 218, 221–22, 225–26, 228–34; *optimus princeps*, 143–45, 147, 152, 155; Tiberian narrative, 129, 134, 141, 143, 145, 149, 152, 155; *virtus* and, 145, 147, 152–53, 155. *See also* Tacitus on; Velleius Paterculus on
Ticinus, 101
Tiridates (king), 222
Tolosa, 198n
Trebellius Maximus, M., 169
Treviri, 199
Trimerus, 121
Triumph, 16, 63, 71, 100, 105, 191, 196–97, 211, 213, 218, 223; ceremony of, 73, 106n155, 151, 165, 216
Triumvirate, 72
Triumvirs, 73, 144
Troy, 132, 153
Tullia (daugther of Servius Tullius), 117
Tullius Cicero, M. (cos. 63 BC): and Greek culture/philosophy, 21–22, 25–26, 30, 41; and historical writing, 3, 5, 7n18, 55n30, 131; as new man, 42, 45, 50, 71, 135, 137; Catiline's conspiracy and, 135; Works: *Academica*, 41n136; *De Amicitia*, 41n134; *De Imp. Cn. Pomp*, 35–37; *De Officiis*, 39–40; *De Oratore*, 21; *De provinciis consularibus*, 35; *De Republica*, 26, 40, 41n133, 44; *Pro Milone*, 35–36; *Pro Murena*, 34–36; *Pro Sestio*, 42, 137;

Tullius Cicero (cont.)
Tusculan Disputations, 15, 21, 31, 40n128; on *virtus*, 15, 18, 35, 40, 41, 42; and *industria*, 44, 56; definition of, 11, 15–18, 25, 31, 34, 40, 56; and new man, 43–45, 68, 70–71, 115–16, 136–37; rewards for, 37–38; usage in speeches, 34, 37, 44–45
Tullius Servius (king), 116
Tullus. *See* Hostilius Tullus (king)
Twelve Tables, 36n109

Ummidius Quadratus, G., 219
Unhistorical, 4, 13
Utica, 61

Valens. *See* Fabius Valens
Valerius Corvinus, M., 116, 218n312
Valerius Maximus, M., (author), 33–34, 144n86
Valor, 16–18, 22, 25, 32–33, 35–37, 44, 56–57, 61, 66–67, 91–95, 98–99, 118, 124, 134–35, 145, 168, 171, 175, 177, 192, 198, 210–12, 215, 219, 227, 234. *See also* Bravery; Courage; *Virtus:* as
Value, 1–2, 6, 8–9, 13–15, 18–25, 27, 30, 53, 81, 90–91, 97n, 125, 139, 157–58, 161, 168, 170–72, 177–78, 187, 215, 223–24, 240, 242, 246
Veii, 97
Velleius Paterculus, M., 3, 9, 11–12, 22, 46n, 129–156 passim, 244; Augustus and, 129, 132, 136, 143, 144, 147–48, 153; Biography, 130–31, 141–42; as new man, 130, 132, 136, 152; Change in historical writing, 130–31, 134, 141; positive interpretation of history, 12, 131, 152–57, 245; language, 133–34, 245; Livy and, 130, 134, 152, 155; new men and, 132, 136–37; on Caesar, 140; on Cato the Elder, 136–37; on Cato the Younger, 135; on Cicero, 135–37; on Sejanus, 137–39; on Tiberius, 129, 131–32, 136, 141–152 passim, 155, 157, 187, 221n; Sallust and, 130, 132–33, 140, 152, 155; style, 129, 131, 133; *Virtus* and, 12, 135, 145, 153, 155, 245; in plural and singular, 132–34, 155; new men and, 135–37, 155
Verecundia, 164n21
Verginia, 120
Vespasian (emperor), 163, 183–85, 192–194, 196–97, 203, 207. *See also* Tacitus on
Vestal virgins, 121
Veturia, 123
Vice, 7, 9–10, 33, 44n144, 51, 57, 60–62, 64–65, 68, 70, 75, 78–80, 87–88, 96, 129, 152, 169–71, 173, 176, 185, 191, 194–95, 220, 240
Vipsania (first wife of Tiberius), 147
Vipsanius Agrippa, M., 117, 137, 146–47, 197n203
Vipsanius Agrippa Postumus, M. (son of Agrippa), 148
Vipstanus Messalla, L., 200
Vir, 15–16, 19, 24, 31, 37, 40, 78, 123, 125, 176n, 200, 202–203, 232; *illustri*, 90, 154
Virgilian, 170
Viridomarus, 99
Virilitas, 32
Virility, 17
Virtue, 31–5, 37, 75, 79, 91, 102, 104; and Stoicism, 27–29
Virtus: active, 18, 39–42, 52, 65, 73, 125, 161, 167, 177–78, 237, 244, 246; as praise, 1, 8, 31, 92–93, 95, 101, 135, 139, 198; as courage/bravery/valor, 1, 8, 11–12, 15–20, 24–25, 31–34, 36–37, 57, 67, 91–93, 95, 98, 104, 112–14, 118, 121, 124–25, 133–35, 137, 145–46, 151, 155, 158, 171, 173, 175, 185, 193, 195, 199, 215, 223, 241; as *andreia*, 11, 14, 24, 39; as *arete*, 11, 14, 19–25, 34, 41, 47, 92n40; as excellence, 20, 24–25, 31–32, 47, 104, 195; as manliness, 1–2, 14, 19, 20n25,

32–33, 45; as a moral and ethical idea/concept, 1, 8–9, 13, 15, 25, 33, 35, 46, 49, 66–67, 81, 141, 242–43, 246; as a political idea/concept, 2, 9, 13, 15, 45–46, 49, 81, 246; political slogan, 37, 44, 243; as virtue, 11, 16, 37–38, 40, 134–35, 155, 242; Cicero and, 11, 15–18, 21, 25, 31, 34–42, 68; etymology, 11, 15–16, 18, 125; expansion of, 32, 42–47, 49, 81, 209–10, 245; glory and, 17, 19, 38–40, 42, 44n147, 51–52, 54, 61, 76, 81, 134, 158, 174, 195; Greek influence, 15, 21–22, 24–25, 66–67, 82; historical writing and, 8–10, 48, 52–53, 82, 132, 141, 157, 242, 247; *Honos* and, 38n115, 69, 100, 127; *humana-*, 11, 20, 32, 41, 46, 56, 104, 108, 134–35, 153, 155, 200, 206, 208, 234–35, 240; *industria* and, 44, 53, 82, 172, 177; *libertas* and, 12, 84, 93, 106, 108–117 passim, 156, 158–59, 161, 168–69, 172–73, 175–78, 184, 198, 209–10, 227, 230, 244; memory of, 34, 53, 167, 215–17, 236–37, 244; military/martial, 12, 16, 24, 35–36, 38, 44, 66–67, 92–108, 135, 141, 163, 194, 199, 210, 215, 217, 220–23; new man and, 42–45, 49, 55, 67–71, 82, 100n108, 115–16, 132, 136–37, 141, 155, 243; *nobilitas* and, 38, 42–44, 49, 52, 58, 67–71, 81–82, 100, 115, 141, 155; of enemies/foreigners, 94–95, 106–107, 160, 223; barbarians, 32, 160, 175, 177, 178, 198n207, 210–13, 223; Hannibal, 107; Jugurtha, 61; Mithridates, 135n; *prisca*, 58, 84, 173, 178, 214n287, 243; rewards for, 37–38, 42, 124–25, 158; *Romana*, 37, 38n120, 46, 94, 113, 160–61, 178–79, 185, 237; service for the state and, 38–39, 41–42, 44, 47, 52, 54, 73, 93, 98, 101, 109, 113, 115, 125, 155, 159, 161, 178, 180, 195, 199; Stoicism and, 11, 15, 21, 26–34; translation of, 32–34, 36, 45, 92n40; under the Principate, 12, 103, 155, 160, 162, 177–79, 187, 197, 200, 208–10, 214, 220, 223–25, 227, 240, 244; *virilis-*, 11, 17, 19–20, 31, 33–34, 39, 41, 46, 56, 93, 104, 134–35, 145, 147, 153, 155, 198–200, 206, 208, 223, 235, 240, 245; wide meaning, 14–15, 19–20, 22, 25, 31, 33, 56, 137

Virtutes, 7n19, 16, 31, 35, 56–57, 86, 98n85, 102, 132–34, 139, 141, 144–45, 153–56, 165, 167, 185, 196, 199, 215, 217, 219

Vitellius (emperor), 183–85, 189–95, 199, 202–203, 206–207. *See also* Tacitus on

Vitium, 33, 49, 50, 64, 74, 76–78, 80, 86–88, 96, 98n85, 132n14, 140, 171n63, 176n90, 185, 243, 245

Vocula. *See* Dillius Vocula, G.

Vologeses, 212, 220

Volsci, 95, 97, 123

Volumnia, 123

Vulsinii, 231

War, 8–9, 11–12, 16, 22–24, 32, 42, 44, 48–49, 52, 54, 59, 61–66, 72, 74, 92–112 passim, 124–25, 134–35, 142, 145, 147, 152, 155n151, 166, 168, 173–76, 178, 188, 191, 193, 197–98, 201, 210–14, 216, 218, 220, 222–24, 245; Civil war, 74, 88, 110, 144, 179–85, 189, 195–96, 199–200, 206; (Marius and Sulla), 65, 72; (Pompey and Caesar), 140, 181n101; (Octavian and Mark Antony), 72, 149, 154; (AD 69), 179, 183, 194, 197, 202, 207–208; Macedonian, 96, 104–106; Punic, 95–96, 99, 101, 103–105

Women, 32n, 34, 78, 102, 176–7; courage and, 18, 19n, 212; imperial, 118, 121; matrons, 117–18, 123; service for the state, 117, 122–25; *virtus* and, 32, 117–25 passim

Woodman, A., 4, 85, 90, 129–30, 138n56, 180n

Zenobia (queen), 212

www.ingramcontent.com/pod-product-compliance
Lightning Source LLC
Chambersburg PA
CBHW022010300426
44117CB00005B/110